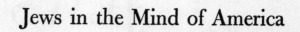

Jews in the Mind of America

PROJECT DIRECTOR

Marshall Sklare

CONTRIBUTORS

Robert Gutman

Ben Halpern

John Higham

Morton Keller

Thomas F. O'Dea

Thomas F. Pettigrew

Benjamin B. Ringer

Theodore Solotaroff

Charles Herbert Stember

Robin M. Williams, Jr.

Dennis H. Wrong

PREFACE BY

John Slawson

EDITOR

George Salomon

JEWS IN THE

PUBLISHED IN COLLABORATION WITH

Institute of Human Relations Press

MIND OF AMERICA

By Charles Herbert Stember

and Others

BASIC BOOKS, INC. · New York · London

Second Printing

© 1966 by the American Jewish Committee

Library of Congress Catalog Card Number: 66–26219

Manufactured in the United States of America

Designed by Sophie Adler

May the Children of the Stock of Abraham, who dwell in this land, continue to merit and enjoy the good will of the other Inhabitants, while every one shall sit in safety under his own vine and fig tree, and there shall be none to make him afraid. May the father of all mercies scatter light and not darkness in our paths, and make us all in our several vocations useful here, and in his own due time and way everlastingly happy.

GEORGE WASHINGTON

to the HEBREW CONGREGATION IN NEWPORT, RHODE ISLAND · 1790

Biographical Notes

ROBERT GUTMAN, Ph.D., a demographer and urban sociologist, is Professor of Sociology at Rutgers University. He has been active in the Urban Studies Center at Rutgers since its inception in 1959, and has published *Urban Sociology: A Bibliography,* as well as many monographs in the field.

BEN HALPERN, Ph.D., a specialist in Jewish history and historical sociology, is Associate Professor of Near Eastern and Judaic Studies at Brandeis University. He has written *The American Jew: A Zionist Analysis* and *The Idea of the Jewish State,* and has served for many years on the editorial board of *Jewish Frontier.*

JOHN HIGHAM, Ph.D., is Professor of History at the University of Michigan. A student of the intellectual and social history of the United States, he is the author of *Strangers in the Land: Patterns of American Nativism, 1860–1925,* and editor of *The Reconstruction of American History.*

MORTON KELLER, Ph.D., Professor of History at Brandeis University, is chiefly interested in America's political, institutional and economic development. He has written *In Defense of Yesterday: James M. Beck and the Politics of Conservatism* as well as *The Life Insurance Enterprise, 1885–1910,* and edited *The New Deal: What Was It?*

THOMAS F. O'DEA, Ph.D., is Professor of Sociology in the Department of Religion at Columbia University. He has also worked on problems of social change as related to technology. His writings include *The Mormons* and *American Catholic Dilemma: An Inquiry into the Intellectual Life,* plus many articles in scholarly and religious journals.

THOMAS F. PETTIGREW, Ph.D., Associate Professor of Social Psychology at Harvard University, has done research on race relations, public-opinion measurement and social perception. He is the author of *A Profile of the Negro American* and co-author (with Ernest Q. Campbell) of *Christians in Racial Crisis: A Study of Little Rock's Ministry.*

BENJAMIN B. RINGER, Ph.D., is Associate Professor of Sociology at Hunter College, after nearly a decade with the American Jewish Committee's Scientific Research Division. He has published a number of papers on religious sociology and collaborated with Marshall Sklare in a forthcoming study of Jews in a Midwestern suburb.

GEORGE SALOMON is an editor on the staff of the American Jewish Committee. He has contributed studies and essays to such varied publications as *The Kenyon Review,* the *American Jewish Year Book,* and *Niagara Frontier.*

MARSHALL SKLARE, Ph.D., now Professor of Sociology at Yeshiva University, was until recently Director of the American Jewish Committee's Scientific Research Division. His interests lie in the study of religious, ethnic and racial groups. He is the author of *Conservative Judaism: An American Religious Movement* and editor of *The Jews: Social Patterns of an American Group.*

JOHN SLAWSON, Ph.D., has for many years been Executive Vice President of the American Jewish Committee. A social psychologist and intergroup-relations specialist, he has also worked on youth problems, serving as consultant to numerous government panels. His writings include *The Delinquent Boy,* as well as many pamphlets and articles.

THEODORE SOLOTAROFF, formerly Associate Editor of *Commentary,* is now Editor of *Book Week,* the literary supplement of the New York *World Journal Tribune.*

CHARLES HERBERT STEMBER, Ph.D., Professor of Sociology at Rutgers University, specializes in the social psychology of prejudice and discrimination. From 1947 to 1952, he was Study Director of the National Opinion Research Center. He has published *Education and Attitude Change,* and is co-author (with Herbert H. Hyman and others) of *Interviewing in Social Research.*

ROBIN M. WILLIAMS, JR., Ph.D., is Professor of Sociology at Cornell University. His areas of study encompass values, intergroup relations and military organization; his writings include *The Reduction of Intergroup Tensions; American Society;* and *Strangers Next Door: Ethnic Relations in American Communities.*

DENNIS H. WRONG, Ph.D., is Professor of Sociology at New York University. Among his fields of interest are sociological theory, political sociology, the history of social thought, and psychoanalysis in relation to society. He has written *American and Canadian Viewpoints* and *Population and Society.*

Preface

THE MATERIALS WITH WHICH this book deals reflect a long-standing pursuit of the American Jewish Committee—a pursuit dating back to the period when Hitlerism was at its height. During the late 1930s, with Nazi influence beginning to be felt even in the United States and making disturbances in the streets of New York a commonplace occurrence, the Committee first recognized the need to utilize the tools of social science in both gauging and combatting the spread of anti-Semitism. One of the tools in this pioneering venture was public-opinion polling, which had never before been employed by an intergroup-relations agency.

The polling procedure was chosen in full awareness of its limitations. It was known, of course, that survey replies would not necessarily reveal the respondents' underlying motivations. Yet there were sufficient indications that overt responses, if accurately and authentically obtained, would reflect inner attitudes with reasonable fidelity.

Meanwhile, the advantages of opinion polling were plain. Poll findings could be compared from year to year, indicating whether hostility toward Jews was going up or down. Poll results could be sorted out according to the respondents' age, sex, religion, education, economic status, area of residence or other factors and thus help locate the focuses of prejudice within the society. And finally, poll questions could be devised to explore anti-Semitism at various levels of overtness: in public expression ("Have you heard any criticism or talk against the Jews in the last six months?"), personal relationships ("If you were moving to a new house and found that your next-door neighbor was Jewish, would it make any difference to you?"), and intimate feelings ("If a friend of yours wanted to marry a Jewish boy or girl and came to you for advice, what would you say?").

For all these reasons, opinion polling quickly became invaluable both as a measure of the fluctuations of prejudice in the United States and as a basis for programs of counteraction. Surveys were continued for more than a quarter of a century—largely on behalf of the American Jewish Committee's Scientific Research Division, which was headed successively by Max Horkheimer, the late Samuel H. Flowerman, Marc Vosk and Marshall

Sklare. The findings were periodically analyzed and at times supplemented by other techniques, such as depth interviews and historical studies. The depth-interview technique, in particular, reached a high level of sophistication during the 1940s; the most notable achievement of this research was the classic volume, *The Authoritarian Personality* (1950) by Adorno and others, originally published as one of five "Studies in Prejudice" that were sponsored by the American Jewish Committee and edited by Max Horkheimer and Samuel H. Flowerman.

In recent years, under Marshall Sklare's direction, the Committee has begun a comprehensive reanalysis of the accumulated survey data—both those obtained under its own sponsorship and others. The first subject thus explored was the correlation between people's level of schooling and their prejudices. This analysis was undertaken by Charles Herbert Stember and published under the title *Education and Attitude Change* (1961). An important by-product of the long-continued polling effort, the volume cast a clear and, in certain respects, disconcerting light on accepted notions about the effectiveness of formal education in reducing prejudice.

With overt anti-Semitism steadily and unmistakably declining, the 1960s seemed an appropriate time to reexamine the entire body of survey findings in depth—to interpret, in the broadest sense, exactly how the Jews had appeared in the mind of America during the quarter-century just past. At the Committee's request, Mr. Stember again undertook to compile and analyze the data. His study, which constitutes Part One of this volume, incorporates several analyses of individual polls, prepared at the time by members of the Committee's staff, particularly Benjamin B. Ringer.

To extract the full meaning from the material, Mr. Stember's work was submitted, in September 1964, to a conference of distinguished social scientists specializing in various relevant fields such as sociology, social psychology, demography, and Jewish and American history, each of whom considered the findings from the vantage point of his discipline. Their deliberations served to place the short-term trend of anti-Semitic manifestations into historic perspective and perhaps suggested something about the possible direction of future developments.

The 1964 symposium focused not only on the decline of overt anti-Semitism as shown by poll responses, but also on the problem of latent hostility. For, as centuries of Jewish experience inform us, anti-Semitism often resembles an iceberg: only one-eighth of it is visible, while seven-eighths are hidden below the surface. The members of the conference dealt seriously with the question of what conditions—for example, frustrations resulting from economic, political or social deprivations or anxieties—might once more transform latent anti-Semitism into hostile action.

Eight papers formally presented at the conference form Part Two of the present book. The authors are Robert Gutman, Ben Halpern, John Higham, Morton Keller, Thomas F. O'Dea, Thomas F. Pettigrew, Robin M. Williams, Jr., and Dennis H. Wrong. The discussions at the meeting are summarized in the Introduction, written by Theodore Solotaroff together with Marshall Sklare, the director of the project since its inception.

There remains the pleasant task of thanking the organizations and individuals who helped bring the present work into being. On this long list, the authors already named naturally lead all the rest. But their work could not have been done if they had not been preceded and assisted by many others.

The poll data assembled and interpreted in Part One were originally gathered by six agencies: The Gallup Organization, Inc., with its affiliate, the American Institute of Public Opinion (AIPO); the National Opinion Research Center of the University of Chicago (NORC); the Office of Public Opinion Research (OPOR), now defunct; the Opinion Research Corporation (ORC); the Psychological Corporation; and Elmo Roper and Associates. Many of the findings were obtained through the Roper Public Opinion Research Center at Williams College. Data not originally gathered for the American Jewish Committee are here reused by the generous permission of the polling agencies.

Paul B. Sheatsley of NORC proved unfailingly helpful during the fact-gathering phase of the work and deserves our special thanks. For assistance of various kinds, we are indebted to Paul K. Perry and Irving Crespi, of the Gallup Organization; Charles Mack and Mike McGarry, of NORC; Harold Mendelsohn, formerly of the Psychological Corporation; and Philip K. Hastings, of the Roper Center.

Leo Srole, now of Columbia University, kindly gave permission to use, in Chapter VII, data and findings from an unpublished study conducted by him during 1950–51.

The poll findings were painstakingly assembled and processed by a former staff member of the Committee, David E. Ryan. Later, Carol Miles, then a research assistant at Rutgers University, scrupulously verified all numerical data.

In the preparation of Part One, essential guidance was provided by an advisory group consisting of four present or former members of the American Jewish Committee's staff: Joseph Greenblum, Milton Himmelfarb, Benjamin B. Ringer and Marshall Sklare—with Abraham Yeselson of Rutgers helpfully serving as a fifth advisor during the earlier phases. The group scrutinized the original drafts, supplied additional information, and often suggested interpretations that gave meaning to obscure findings.

A most valuable contribution was made by Herbert H. Hyman, of Columbia University, who reviewed the entire manuscript of Part One and offered many suggestions that were eventually reflected in the final text.

The credit for the conference whose proceedings provided the substance for Part Two belongs first and foremost to Marshall Sklare, who both conceived and conducted it. Besides the individuals represented as authors in these pages, the following (here named with their affiliations as of the time) attended, contributing much stimulating and original thought: Daniel Bell, of Columbia; Ernest Q. Campbell, of Vanderbilt University; Sigmund Diamond, of Columbia; Howard J. Ehrlich, of the National Institute of Mental Health; Simon N. Herman, of the Hebrew University of Jerusalem; Morris Janowitz, of the University of Chicago; Irving Kristol, of Basic Books, Inc.; Daniel J. Levinson, of Harvard University; Paul W. Massing, of Rutgers; Norman Podhoretz, of *Commentary* magazine; Peter H. Rossi, of NORC; and Leo Srole. Of the American Jewish Committee's staff, David Danzig, Lucy Dawidowicz, Morris Fine, Selma Hirsh, Manheim S. Shapiro and the writer took part in the conference, in addition to the advisory group members already named. Sidney Strimpel, of the Martin C. Johnson Reporting Service, Inc., recorded the proceedings.

George Salomon of the American Jewish Committee served as editor throughout the project. He collaborated in rewriting and reorganizing entire sections of Part One, edited the papers in Part Two with perceptive attention, and supervised the progress of the text and tables from the earliest drafts to the finished volume. His involvement with both the form and the substance of the work is manifest on every page.

Thanks for secretarial services are due to a number of present and former staff members of the American Jewish Committee, who patiently produced mountains of typescript: Sylvia Babsek, Patricia Carpenter, Sally Hoffman, Elizabeth Keller, Mina Warheit and especially Ruth G. Ballan. In the publication of the book, Morris Fine of the Committee played an indispensable role. The task of proofreading manuscripts and printer's proofs was ably handled by Naomi A. Grand, Martha Jelenko and Ruth Gould, the first two also being Committee staff members.

But for the help of two organizations, the present work might not have seen the light of day at all: the Rutgers Research Council, which freed Charles Herbert Stember from teaching duties for one semester through a faculty fellowship; and the Michael Tuch Foundation, whose generous aid went far toward meeting the cost of the conference.

Finally, we acknowledge with gratitude the labors of that anonymous army of interviewers who, year after year, patiently entered myriads of answers, comments and check marks on thousands of questionnaires and thereby created the foundation upon which our edifice rests.

JOHN SLAWSON
Executive Vice President
The American Jewish Committee

New York
July 1966

Contents

Jews in the Mind of America

Introduction

THEODORE SOLOTAROFF
MARSHALL SKLARE

IN JULY 1965, a riot broke out in Laconia, New Hampshire, after the annual rally of the New England motorcyclists. As the riot gained momentum, one of the wilder-looking thugs climbed up a telephone pole, hung out a swastika, and began to lead his several thousand companions in the chant of *"Sieg . . . Heil . . . Sieg Heil."*

The chant and the flag provided a fitting anthem and emblem to cap the scene—an overturned and burning automobile, several open stands that had been set on fire, three thousand black-denim and leather-booted cyclists hurling themselves with fists, knives and tirechains against the townspeople and the police. But, beyond a certain aptness of imagery, was there any particular significance to the swastika? Did it betoken merely the latest fad in the anti-social behavior of motorcycle gangs, or did it possess a genuine, if inchoate, political meaning? More specifically, for our purposes, does the aping of Nazi totems merely signify an inspired way of being as "ugly" as possible (as a recent, not unsympathetic, article in *The Saturday Evening Post* on the most notorious gang, Hell's Angels, who look like storm troopers gone to seed, explains[1]), or was there a distinct anti-democratic syndrome at work here (as the mayor of Laconia believed), one that would inevitably locate the Jews as a target?

We begin with this incident because it helps to focus the problem of thinking about anti-Semitism in America today. Except for an occasional defaced synagogue or a tale about an "incident" in the suburbs or the ravings of a George Lincoln Rockwell, anti-Semitism is no longer a particularly overt phenomenon. For most Jews today, bigotry and discrimination are felt to exist, if at all, at a far remove from the actual course of their

3

lives. It does not cause them much anxiety that a club or a corporation excludes them, that a publication exhorts its readers to hate and fear them, since neither their careers nor private lives bring them into contact with such situations. Moreover, where anti-Semitism may seem to be occurring, it is often so entangled in other motives and issues, as in the Laconia incident, that one grows uncertain in his belief that habitual prejudice against Jews is involved in any salient way. A number of communities, for example, have been fighting out the issue of Christmas observances in the public schools. Are we to regard the gentile hostility primarily as an outcropping of latent anti-Semitism or rather as the defensive reaction of a beleaguered majority? Similarly, the exclusion of Jews from the so-called "executive suite" of the major corporations is regarded as a conscious continuation of the traditions of social discrimination against Jews, but there is also some reason to believe that long-standing patterns of executive recruitment and advancement and the silent operation of the organization man ethos are also significant.

If the evidence of anti-Semitism has become increasingly scarce and ambiguous in recent years, the facts of Jewish acceptance seem to speak for themselves. Twenty years ago the appointment of an Arthur Goldberg as the American ambassador to the United Nations would have been no more than a gleam in the eye of a Jewish mother; but from the perspective of the present it seems no more than a striking example at the highest level of society, particularly within the liberal establishment, of the new suitability of Jews at many levels of society that were once virtually closed to their ambitions and talents. As Robert Gutman points out elsewhere in this book, there has been a remarkable influx of Jews into the professions, particularly in such fields as university teaching, the natural sciences and engineering, city planning and administration—some of which were formerly more or less gentile preserves. In a study of occupational patterns in Camden, New Jersey, for example, Gutman notes that an astonishing 55 per cent of Jewish males under the age of thirty-five are in the professions. No less remarkable, certainly, is the conspicuousness of Jews today in the media and the arts. Not so very long ago, perhaps fifteen years at most, books that dealt with Jewish characters and themes went begging for publishers; today there is reason to assent to the frequent observation, most recently made by Robert Lowell, that "Jewishness is the theme of our literary culture in somewhat the same fashion that Middle Western and Southern writing occupied this position in earlier decades." Nor is this merely a matter of the Bellows and Malamuds and Roths; the popularity of Harry Golden a few years ago as a native American wit, a sort of Jewish Will Rogers, the movement of Jewish theater from Second Avenue to both Broadway and Off Broadway, as well as the staggering sales of pop fiction, such as *Marjorie Morningstar* or *Exodus,* are perhaps even more decisive examples of a public acceptance that borders on courtship.

Under these circumstances it may seem not only difficult to think about anti-Semitism, but intellectually embarrassing—a perverse vestige perhaps of a ghetto mentality that may linger covertly even unto the third generation of American Jews. Perhaps, as John Higham has said, one looks harder for anti-Semitism when it is difficult to find, such as the Jew in a joke that Freud tells who fled to the woods when he saw an ordinance that all camels were to be castrated. "You're not a camel," his friend said. "I know that and you know that," he replied. "But do they?" Yet the joke also expresses its own perception of reality: an apprehensiveness and skepticism rooted bitterly in history. If one thinks for very long about anti-Semitism, he must begin to recall the Jews of medieval Granada or more recently and tragically the Jews of Berlin and Vienna and Budapest whose prominence in the intellectual and cultural life of these societies much resembles the position of American Jews today. As the fate of the Jews testifies, acceptance or even toleration is by no means an irreversible process nor does prominence necessarily mean genuine security. On the contrary: the conspicuousness of Austrian and German Jews as liberals, as representative of the urban life, as doctors, lawyers, students and scholars, journalists and publishers, as creative artists, critics, actors, and audience—in short, in professions that were objects of suspicion and distrust or else overcrowded and influential—left them that much more exposed to the "big lies" and half-truths of the demagogues.[2]

It is not surprising, then, that a renowned Jewish scholar who grew up in Berlin recently remarked on a visit to America that, far from being reassured by the cultural prosperity of the Jews here, he found their conspicuousness quite alarming. Such apprehensions are not simply a matter of dubious historical extrapolation from Europe to America. Here and there, in recent years, one has heard of a mood of resentment in the universities, particularly in the natural and social sciences, about the Jewish "operators" who are more interested in obtaining grants and consultation fees and building up a domain of their own than they are in departmental work and teaching. This criticism is more or less covert, though it appears to be growing from year to year. The point is not that there is any particular danger at present of a backlash against the large number of Jews who have entered this profession, but rather the presence in a new form of a common stereotype of the Jew as wheeling and dealing entrepreneur, that is to say, an academic version of the Jewish capitalist. Whether the image is true or not—and stereotypes must be partly true to stick—it follows the familiar process of scapegoating, by which Jews become the agents and villains of a historical change: in this case, the transformation of the ivory tower campus into what has come to be called the knowledge industry, or the "multiversity."

Somewhat less covert and perhaps even more entrenched today is the resentment toward the Jewish role in American writing which leads a life of its own beneath the philo-Semitic fanfare that attends a *Fiddler on the Roof,* a *Herzog,* or a *How to Be a Jewish Mother.* Most of this resentment involves serious writing, where the alleged domination by Jews is believed to be the evil fruit of a conspiracy between "Jewish" publishers and critics who give undue attention and praise to any writing that bears a Jewish stamp. Thus the vogue, say, of Norman Mailer is held to be the work of a few prominent Jewish critics, and the ease with which the crop of younger writers find their way to publication is attributed to the ethnocentrism of the "Jewish" publishing houses. Along with the conspiracy theory, which overlooks the fact, among others, that most of the serious criticism of Jewish writing has been done by Jewish critics—as the files of *Commentary* and *Midstream* amply demonstrate—there is the charge that the Jewish writers —or in the Aesopian language that is used, the "New York" writers—exert a pernicious influence: insensitive to art, so the claim goes, they convert literature to "ideas" or "trends" in order to monger them; ignorant of America, they inflate their own background, interests, quarrels until the New York Jewish cultural scene becomes congruent with the national boundaries and their own reactions with the intellectual pulse of America. Again, one sees the formation of a familiar stereotype from half-truths that at once simplify the issues and generalize the offense and the offenders. The Jewish influence is clearly there in American letters, and it should be no more immune from analysis and controversy than was the Southern influence, in the "new criticism" as well as in fiction, a decade ago. Instead, however, of an open examination, there is a devious complaint, coy or snide, that is reminiscent of the attacks upon "Jewish culture" in the Europe of the 1920s.

All of which can signify much or little, depending on one's view, or even mood. One can think of these outcroppings of hostility as the first inevitable, if muffled, group conflicts within an increasingly firm pluralism, or one can regard them as a new strain of the virus which has infected the bloodstream of Western culture for many centuries, now dormant and more or less under control, now virulent and spreading to epidemic proportions. Twentieth-century history encourages both views, and, between the complacencies of apparent security and the horror of the holocaust, between the statistics that show a sharp and steady decline in discrimination and the single, stark figure of 6,000,000 killed, there seems to be no middle ground of clear understanding—merely a kind of tension strung along a paradox. Perhaps twenty years is too short a time for those who have sentiently lived through it to assimilate this antinomy: to believe both in the reality of total persecution in one advanced Western nation—spurred on by the acquiescence of the others—and increasing acceptance in the West some two decades later.

Finally, there is the problem of the vastly puzzling nature of the society that is currently evolving. Trotsky once said that "twenty-five years are like a day in the life of a society," a reminder that dramatic short-run changes need not have permanent significance. On the other hand, a day in the past two decades has been like twenty-five years in terms of the content of change that it bears, so vast and rapid have been the political, economic and social developments of this period. Can we be any more certain, or even clear, about the alterations in Jewish-gentile relations than we are about those in the means of production—or destruction—or about the growth of the mass society, or the transformation of our foreign relations, or the racial revolution, to mention only a few of the more epochal changes? Thus our view of any subject with immediate social bearings is bordered by doubts and dizziness, so that even hard data and learned opinion may seem like straws read in a whirlwind.

Backgrounds of the Present Study

However, hard data are necessary if we are to go beyond isolated clues and impressions concerning the ambiguous Jewish situation in the society, and learned opinion is indispensable if we are to make our way through the maze of historical, social and psychological issues that immediately surround the subject.

For these reasons, this book is particularly important. The first part is an analysis by Charles Herbert Stember, a well-known figure in the field of survey research, of public opinion polls concerning attitudes toward Jews which date from 1937 to 1962. These polls were conducted, for the most part, under the auspices of the American Jewish Committee. As Mr. Stember points out, they represent "a larger and more varied body of information on the subject than has been assembled in any other study we know." Mr. Stember's study was prepared for the American Jewish Committee, which, following its completion, held a two-day conference in September 1964 to explore and evaluate Mr. Stember's analysis. Some twenty prominent social scientists participated in the conference as well as members of the professional staff of the American Jewish Committee. The discussion centered around a series of papers (collected in the second part, some in revised form) that were designed to place the poll data in historical perspective and to interpret them in the light of present knowledge in the social sciences. The response to these papers, in turn, provided a further range of information, speculation and controversy concerning the nature of anti-Semitism as a Western and American phenomenon and the structure of the new society as it alters the traditional grounds of Jewish-gentile relations.

The Trend of Public Opinion, 1937–1962

Though sharp differences of opinion developed along the way, the main line of inquiry through most of the conference followed in the wake of Mr. Stember's report which finds that, since the end of the Second World War, "anti-Semitism in all its forms has massively declined in the United States." The most significant reduction, according to Stember, has been in the currency of the hostile stereotypes which have formed the liturgy of Jew-hatred. In 1940, for example, 63 per cent of the respondents said that Jews as a group had "objectionable traits," whereas only 22 per cent subscribed to this belief in 1962. Stember finds a particular meaning in the decreasing assent to the "Shylock image" or the Jew as "economic man"—mercenary, cunning, dishonest—which is the cardinal one in the anti-Semitic tradition. Almost half the respondents polled in 1938 and 1939 described Jewish businessmen as less honest than others; by 1962, fewer than one-fifth did, whereas 70 per cent said they saw no differences between Jewish and gentile businessmen in point of honesty. Similarly, the other standard "Jewish" traits—pushiness, clannishness, vulgarity—no longer pervade American consciousness to anywhere near the same extent they once did. An interesting corollary of these findings is that most of the common transvaluations of these traits—ambitiousness, intelligence, thriftiness, family and group loyalty—have also declined in frequency in keeping with the general effacement of the stereotypes. No less than 43 per cent of the respondents in a recent poll appears to believe that Jews have no distinctive group traits at all. Nonetheless, philo-Semitism itself has been increasing: 32 per cent of respondents in 1962 regarded the Jews as a group in an entirely positive way, whereas only 7 per cent regarded them entirely negatively. Mr. Stember also finds that attitudes toward association with Jews have followed much the same pattern as the beliefs about them. In matters of employment, housing, education and friendship, opposition to relations with Jews is negligible; intermarriage remains a live issue, though here, too, there has been a proportionate decrease in the number of respondents—currently less than 40 per cent—who are opposed to it.

This sharp decline in prejudice against Jews is the more remarkable in the light of Stember's figures for the period from 1937 to about 1945. In 1944, 24 per cent of the respondents in one poll regarded the Jews as "a menace to America." A series of surveys carried out between 1940 and 1945 indicates that from 31 to 48 per cent of the public throughout the war years would have actively supported a hypothetical anti-Semitic campaign or at least sympathized with it; about 30 per cent would have opposed it; and the rest would have taken no stand.

Stember attributes these attitudes to the tension of the final years of the war, which also showed a marked rise in hostility to Negroes and in the levels of general prejudice against the minorities. From at least 1938 on, there had been an increasing enmity to Jews who were reputed to have used their influence to get America to fight Germany and to have shirked military service and combat and to have engaged in profiteering (war-time variants of Jewish conspiracy, cunning, self-interest and venality). In the bloody, cataclysmic days of 1944, these feelings burned more widely and fiercely.

Nor do they appear to have been affected at all by the growing realization of what was happening to the Jews of Europe, of the horrors that anti-Semitism had led to. From first to last, the plight of Hitler's favorite victims had little effect on the climate of opinion and feeling about American Jews. In March 1938, a majority of Americans believed that the persecution of German Jews was either wholly or partly their own fault; later that year, only a bare majority approved of the official American protest against the *Kristallnacht* riots. Even the ultimate atrocities of genocide had little impact at the time on the non-Jewish population, more than 3 out of 4 of whom said that their attitudes toward Jews in this country had not been altered by the mass killings in Europe; of the 19 per cent who reported a change, more than 1 out of 5 said that they had become less sympathetic to Jews than before.

It is not surprising, then, to learn that in both 1938 and 1943, about 8 out of 10 Americans were opposed to increasing immigration quotas for political refugees from Germany, Austria and other countries that had passed under Nazi rule; nor was this opposition, as has been claimed, fostered by the fear of economic competition; in 1939 more than 6 out of 10 Americans were against special quotas for refugee Jewish children. The hostility to Jewish immigrants as such, no matter how desperate their situation, is borne out by a poll in 1944 in which they were found to be the least desirable of immigrants, with the exception of citizens of the two countries, Germany and Japan, with which we were at war. The end of the war and the decline of outright anti-Semitism did not appreciably move American hearts to the survivors of the "final solution," the full evil of which was now being revealed. In 1948, 60 per cent of respondents agreed that a "special limit" should be put on the number of Jewish refugees to be admitted—slightly more than the number that wished to see such a limit applied to Germans. In the same poll, only 10 per cent of respondents favored unrestricted immigration privileges for "displaced persons in European camps," who appear to have been thought of as predominantly Jewish, although four years later, 51 per cent of the population favored open admission of "people who have escaped from Communist countries." Evidently, as Stember observes, "more sympathy and desire to help were expressed toward refugees from Communist regimes than had ever been bestowed upon those who were seeking to escape the Nazi holocaust."

Another of the more interesting survey findings, which also comes from the critical war years, serves to point up the volatility of anti-Semitic attitudes. When asked which groups or organizations had "more to say about running this country than they should," only 4 per cent of the respondents spontaneously named the Jews—fewer than those who mentioned the unions, business, or the Government. When queried directly, however, whether Jews had "too much power and influence," 67 per cent answered "yes." The latter figure, according to Stember, "shows how ready large numbers were to accept the myth of the all-powerful Jew when it was suggested to them" and how easily resentment at the management of society by labor, business, the Federal Government, as the case might be, could be refocused on the Jewish group.

Despite these vivid reminders of the recentness and latency of strong undercurrents of anti-Semitic sentiment in America, Stember's view is, on the whole, a very positive one. All of his indices for the postwar era point to a steady erosion of hostile imagery and an increasing willingness to associate with Jews. Further, Mr. Stember believes that these trends have been firmly tested by developments during the postwar period such as the involvement of American Jewry in the new state of Israel, the tensions and frustrations of the Cold War, particularly during the McCarthy period when the names of Jews figured prominently in the "Communist conspiracy"— specifically, in the trials of Soviet spies—and, more recently, by the upheavals of the Negro protest movement: all of which might have been expected to reinvigorate gentile bigotry and re-arm its out-dated arsenal of stereotypes. Similarly, the intense competition for the prestigious schools and vocations, the pressures of our status-driven public mentality, the chipping away at the old barriers of rank and privilege might have been expected to harden the restrictions against Jews, long regarded as the main threat among the immigrants to the prerogatives of upper- and middle-class America. Instead, Stember finds that discrimination as well as prejudice have dwindled to the point where they no longer reinforce each other and that "in both feeling and behavior" toward this minority, the American public has undergone such a profound change since the Second World War that it is "unlikely to be reversed by anything short of a catastrophic crisis."

From Psychological to Social Interpretations

Stember's study is designed to chart this change, however, rather than to explain and confirm it. One of the questions frequently raised at the conference was whether his poll data provide a reliable gauge for the dramatically rapid and sweeping reversal of public consciousness that he concludes has occurred. Several participants wondered, for example, where the respondents of the 1940s, who formed in Stember's words a "vast anti-Semitic potential," had gone to in the span of less than two decades. This led to the speculation that anti-Semitic or even unsympathetic responses were no longer respectable, but could very well still be harbored in private.* There was also the question of a possible gap between attitudes and behavior, just as there has been a marked discrepancy between the national polls that

* In his study, Mr. Stember himself had acknowledged that this might be the case, but only on a limited scale. In any event, he argued, even mere repression of bigotry constituted a social gain.

report a marked decline in anti-Negro sentiment and the actual behavior of the white population in matters of housing and education when these issues press close to home or begin to be whipped up by public controversy. Or again, the point was made that two decades of relative dormancy does not allow one to be blithe about the disappearance of a prejudice as protean, tenacious and volatile as anti-Semitism has been for more than 3,000 years. As Thomas F. O'Dea, a specialist in the sociology of religion, summed up the criticism: "We do not doubt that the polls accurately reflect the expressed attitudes of the moment. . . . We question, rather, whether survey responses can be accepted as evidence of deeper sentiment when they deal with a phenomenon of the psychological depth and historical longevity of anti-Semitism. To put it bluntly: Dare we trust the plain evidence of the polls?"

In confronting this question, the authors of the individual papers as well as most of the participants at the conference were less concerned with the psychological explanations of anti-Semitism than with the historical and contemporary social forces that governed the structure and tone of relations between Jews and gentiles as well as that of the society at large. Their "fierce sociological emphasis," to use sociologist Morris Janowitz's characterization, is indicative of a distinct change in the study of intergroup prejudice and hostility that has been taking place in recent years. For example, in 1944, when a similar conference on anti-Semitism was organized by the American Jewish Committee, the main theoretical orientation of the proceedings was provided by two German social scientists, Max Horkheimer and Theodor W. Adorno, who were concerned with formulating a psychodynamic explanation for the pervasiveness of the bigotry they had witnessed in Europe and sensed in America. This approach culminated in a number of influential studies, notably *The Authoritarian Personality,* by Adorno and others.

Convened during the period when, as Mr. Stember's data indicate, anti-Semitism was most visible and menacing at home as well as most deadly abroad, the 1944 conference followed Horkheimer and Adorno in emphasizing the two questions that urgently posed themselves: what made men hate Jews and what were the most effective ways of combating bigotry. The answers to these questions dovetailed into the concept of "the anti-democratic personality," which provided both insight and propaganda. Other members of the conference—psychiatrists and psychologists, officials of Jewish agencies and other specialists in group relations—reinforced this tendency to regard anti-Semitism as primarily the function of a certain type of character structure marked by strong projective, if not paranoid, tendencies, which sought a "scapegoat" for guilt and frustration. Several social scientists in attendance introduced other perspectives for viewing anti-Semitism—as a mode of stress in the social system (Talcott Parsons) or as a way of preserving status boundaries (John Dollard)—or stressed the distinctions between traditional, religious anti-Semitism and the modern, political form (Kurt Lewin); but the prevailing line of inquiry at the conference remained the Horkheimer-Adorno approach, which called for further "research into the fundamental characteristics common to all anti-Semites . . . with particular emphasis upon the role of the subconscious in anti-Semitic manifestations."

As Dennis H. Wrong observes in his paper, the psychodynamic orientation has continued to dominate much of the theory and research about prejudice and intergroup conflicts generally in the postwar years. This is partly due to the psychologizing climate of the age and partly to the use of anti-Semitism as a model of group prejudice: the recent memory of the psychopathic behavior of the Nazis, their persecution and destruction of Jews beyond all the previous limits of custom and unreason, encouraged the clinical view; so, too, did the revulsion within the social sciences against the older, racist theories of group conflict. The result, though, as Thomas O'Dea points out, was to discourage an objective examination of these conflicts which would view anti-Semitism in a reciprocal context that involves the historical experience of both groups. Indeed, according to Mr. O'Dea, the unwillingness to recognize that stereotypes "are products, however distorted, of historical experience," that feelings of distrust and hostility over the centuries have fostered in Jews an equally intense, if less varied, imagery of Christians, and instead to attribute prejudice to gentile "pathology" alone, are themselves further examples of the residue of "mutual alienation" that exists between the two faiths.

In the more benign climate of the present, however, such a study can go forward, and the 1964 conference was more or less committed to thinking about anti-Semitism in terms of social forces rather than personality structures. Moreover, the present climate requires as well as fosters this approach, for the improvements reported by Mr. Stember, whether short-term or not, can hardly be explained by a proportionate decline in the number of authoritarian personalities in the space of less than a generation, as Dennis Wrong points out, or by a sudden decrease in the mass of free-floating frustration and aggression that is in search of scapegoats. Mr. Wrong also observes that one of the effects of the Negro revolution has been to alert social scientists and the public alike to the realities of group interests and conflicts that are more to the point of our current crisis than are the projective mechanisms of intolerance.

Anti-Semitism as an Episode in American History

In dealing with the American background of anti-Semitism, for example, John Higham emphasizes the nativist reaction in the 1920s to the earlier influx of Jewish immigrants, which culminated in the discriminatory immigration laws to protect the "Nordic" majority from being invaded and overrun by the swelling numbers of Jews and other supposedly retrograde European peoples. Though Mr. Higham recognizes that an "ugly strain of anti-Jewish feeling" ran through the nativist response, he believes it stems chiefly from "the difficulties of integrating large numbers of first- and second-generation immigrants," which produced a similar dislike of the Irish, Italians, Japanese, Mexicans, and other transplanted minorities. In the case of the Jews, to be sure, the reaction was particularly intense because of the earlier efforts of the rising class of German-Jewish immigrants to enter the preserves of the Protestant elite, just at the time—from the 1880s forward—when status and social control were becoming a major issue in a rapidly industrializing society. The barriers of social discrimination that were erected and the ideology that fostered and justified them served as precedents for the more widespread resistance to the following generations of East-European immigrants. This took the form of tacit "internal" discrimination which barred them not only from prestigious clubs, resorts and colleges, but now also from middle-class housing, employment, and educational institutions, and, eventually, of explicit "external" restrictions on further immigration. (Mr. Higham relates that a group led by Henry Cabot Lodge once attempted unsuccessfully to make the immigration restrictions bear most directly and heavily upon East European Jews.) Nonetheless, Mr. Higham regards the hostility to foreigners in general as the root of the issue and the social conflicts of the 1920s as the main determinant of its form, which was that of purposeful restriction of the access routes into the society rather than the more feverish and flailing "ideological" anti-Semitism that was common in Europe.

Viewed in this perspective, as Mr. Higham brought out repeatedly in his remarks at the conference, the decline that Mr. Stember reports is the result of the cultural assimilation of the white minorities or, in popular parlance, the workings of "the melting pot." The key variable for Mr. Higham is the "visibility" of the minority: as this decreases sufficiently through the adoption of the prevailing manners and mores, the secular, libertarian spirit of American democracy slowly asserts itself and prejudice and discrimination recede. Mr. Higham, therefore, finds the dwindling of anti-Semitism since the war to be nothing very remarkable, historically considered, but rather to follow the course of American social history, which has been unique in its capacity to absorb and accept immigrant minorities. Indeed, Mr. Higham is convinced that the position of the Jews in American society is now so unexceptional that it is difficult to conceive of the possibility of its being seriously weakened. To the point raised during the conference that the recent gains in Jewish security and acceptance might be reversible, Mr. Higham retorted: "Does anyone expect realistically that there is going to be a major revival of anti-Catholicism in the United States? . . . Why, therefore, should we expect any significant revival of anti-Semitism, which has been less important in American history . . . ?"

This assessment is more or less shared by Morton Keller, a historian of American institutions, who begins his paper on the background of the years since 1930 by asking "why wasn't there more substantial, more vigorously articulated anti-Semitism in years as traumatic as these?" His subsequent analysis of the poll data tends to minimize the levels and intensity of active prejudice when weighed against the potential of the different traumas, beginning with the economic collapse of the 1930s. Mr. Keller points up the fact, for example, that despite the growth of bigotry in the 1920s, along with the efforts by Henry Ford and others to disseminate the myth of an international Jewish conspiracy, the harvest of anti-Semitism under the favoring conditions of the Depression was relatively meager even among the extremist movements such as that of Huey Long, who attacked the Eastern capitalists rather than the Jews, or of Father Coughlin, who, Mr. Keller argues, did not seriously begin his anti-Semitic campaign until he joined with the America First Committee, the German-American Bund and the Christian Front to oppose American intervention in Europe.

In both of these crises, as in those of the war-time and postwar periods, Mr. Keller finds a common pattern of public response that by-passed, for all significant purposes, the Jewish scapegoats that had been carefully prepared. Mr. Keller's explanation for this has less to do with the assimilation of the minorities during this period than with the increasing strength of the American tradition of cultural pluralism, which received a powerful new impetus from the formation of the New Deal coalition. Moreover, the legitimation of the immigrant minorities reinforced the characteristic of Americans to direct their attention and resentments at institutions and individuals rather than at groups as happened in Germany. Thus, Mr. Keller points out that the *bêtes noires* of the impoverished and embittered masses were the representatives of finance capitalism, such as Charles E. Mitchell, Samuel Insull and Herbert Hoover. During the 1930s, even the American right had begun to shift its fire from the non-Nordic immigrants to ideological and institutional targets—Communism and Socialism, big government and labor.

That this tendency continued through the next two decades is evidenced by the content of McCarthyism and later of the radical right, movements which have avoided blaming minority groups and instead have made out the Federal Government to be a nest of conspiracy and subversion. Meanwhile, the growth of the mass society since the war which redistributed the population, created the suburban life-style, and the new folkways of mass media, has culminated in what Mr. Keller finds to be a third America—neither the "old" nativist one of the hinterlands nor the "new" immigrant one of the cities—in which cultural pluralism is dissolving and group differences are being leveled to the point of irrelevancy. Taking up Stember's data on the dimming visibility of Jews as Jews, Keller concludes that the social

climate in which they live today is best described as one of "asemitism"—
an indifference to or unawareness of their identity.

Mr. Keller's paper proved to be the most thoroughgoing statement of the
position that anti-Semitism is a disappearing problem in America. Most of
the other participants were more cautious in their assessments, if only because the Higham-Keller thesis, if true, signified, in the words of Irving
Kristol, editor of *The Public Interest,* that "a whole epoch of Western history has closed" and that an entirely new set of relations has come about
between Christians and Jews. The main questions then were whether the
uniqueness of the American experience could be said to provide the historical basis for such a massive change and whether the social developments of
the past two decades were sufficient to guarantee it.

Old and New Religious Relationships

Perhaps the most cogent, if also because the most carefully qualified,
argument for this change was made by Thomas O'Dea. Approaching the
poll data from the historical perspective of Jewish-Christian relations, Mr.
O'Dea carefully relates the imagery of religious intolerance to the relationships between the different faiths in Europe and America. The American
context, he finds, has been determined, by and large, by the institutionalized
principles of secularism. He reminds us, for example, that the Bill of Rights
was the first legal document in the West to grant full emancipation to Jews,
their rights as citizens being so taken for granted that they were not even
mentioned by name. The American nativist tradition, compounded of sectarian Protestantism as well as secularism, produced its share of ideological
bigotry, but this was directed, as a rule, against Catholic immigrants rather
than Jewish ones, the reason being that the actual relations between the two
groups were more or less structurally analogous to the Catholic-Protestant
situation in the mother country, England—including the Irish background
of most Catholic immigrants—where the hostile imagery between the two
groups had originally been bred and cultivated. As Mr. O'Dea goes on to
show, the actual relations between Jews and Protestants in America were
quite different from those that prevailed in Europe, where for almost two
millennia the Jew had been figured as the subverter of basic values—particularly as doubter and deicide since New Testament times; merchant and
usurer in the sacral society of the Middle Ages; later as rootless wanderer
and international financier in an age of nationalism and, more recently, as
liberal ideologue and revolutionary agent.

Though Mr. O'Dea would have been the last man at the conference to
underestimate the subtlety and potency of this "substrate" of hostile imagery that had been formed and reinforced as part of the collective consciousness of Europe, the point of his detailed analysis is that there usually

has had to be some kind of fit between the historic situation of the Jews in European society and the invidious roles ascribed to them. In America, however, much of the historic residue has been eliminated or attenuated by the force of secularism, and in recent years this process can be seen to have received a fresh impetus, paradoxically enough, by what has come to be known as "the religious revival." Whatever the spiritual yield of this development may prove to be (noting the large percentage of church-goers in one poll who say that they are most interested in living well and comfortably in this world and who also believe they are trying to lead a good life, Mr. O'Dea wryly remarks that if genuine religion is the enemy of self-satisfaction one wonders whether there has been any revival at all), the renewed interest in religious affiliations has carried with it an increasing acceptance of religious diversity. Mr. O'Dea follows Will Herberg's theory that the three major religions are taking over the function of the ethnic groups in providing identity and community within the evolving mass society that dissolves ethnic ties. As mediators between the individual and American society, Protestantism, Catholicism and Judaism now function as agents of democratization—what Herberg calls "the triple melting pot"—which moves them toward a consensus on secular values, a common faith in "the American way of life." All of which, in turn, has legitimized the two minority faiths and altered their relations with Protestantism and the society at large. Viewed in this light, the religious revival has masked a new development of American secularism which consolidates the gains made by the Catholic and Jewish minorities in the 1930s and enables Herberg to speak of Judaism as one of "three great religions of democracy" and an accepted vehicle of Americanism.

That Judaism has become a cultural equal of Catholicism and Protestantism and an integral part of the national life and value system would signify not only a change but indeed a reversal of its historic relations with Western culture and a reclamation of the two dominant breeding grounds of anti-Semitism—Christianity and nationalism. Mr. O'Dea is properly skeptical of reading so much significance into a period as ambiguous and brief as the one since 1945, and he remains wary of the amount of hostile imagery that inevitably remains stored in Western consciousness, because of the uncanny viability and potency that religious prejudice has demonstrated in the past. Nonetheless, he finds that the American experience has provided the basis for a distinctly different set of relations between Jews and gentiles and that the structural changes in the contemporary society, which bring them together in increasing numbers and degrees of awareness and comity, argues at least for the view that "the old hostile imagery . . . is fading at last."

The Changing Structure of the Jewish Community

This change is reinforced by the evolving character of the Jewish minority. As Mr. O'Dea points out, the basic, long-term experience of the minorities in America has been that of acculturation; in the case of the Jews, this process has been particularly marked in the past three decades. Robert Gutman's study of demographic trends indicates, first of all, that during this period "Jewish immigration has become almost invisible" when compared to its conspicuousness in earlier decades and that today only an estimated 15 per cent of the Jewish population is foreign-born. One consequence of the restrictive immigration policies, along with the low birth-rate and increasing intermarriage rates, has been to reduce the relative size of the Jewish community, which has been unusually dependent on immigration for its population growth. With the marked decline of immigration, the major urban ghettos have broken up and the geographical distribution of Jews today is becoming more decentralized and suburban. The incorporation of virtually all of the Jews into the middle class is most directly borne out by occupational distribution. As we have noted earlier, Jews are entering in preponderant numbers into the salaried professions class, while also moving from "Jewish" industries and business communities into national corporations. Ironically enough, then, the restrictions on Jewish immigration enacted in the 1920s have helped to transform the later community into a model of contemporary middle-class social tendencies and placed them more and more within the "third America" that Mr. Keller speaks of. Because of their virtually complete emergence from the working class, the Jews are also involved today with a more limited segment of gentile society, and, because of their entrance into the universities, corporations and other centrally situated institutions, the imagery of Jews inevitably takes on a different content from that bred by their segregated existence on the margins and in the interstices of the social structure.

The result of this demographic transformation can best be seen, as Dennis Wrong suggests, in the professional and academic settings where a new imagery is indeed emerging to meet the new facts of Jewish acculturation and status. Instead of the standardized imagery of traditional anti-Semitism or the stereotypes that are used to justify social discrimination, Mr. Wrong finds that this new imagery "more or less accurately" reflects the subtle realities of group differences because it stems from the experience of closer contacts in work and community life between Jews and gentiles. Mr. Wrong characterizes the perception of Jews in these circles as composed of "intellectuality, political liberalism, intense parental solicitude with close bonds between mothers and sons, great concern with the extended family, a liking for food and physical comforts in general, volubility and emotional expressiveness, fear of violence and ironic humor." Such an account may seem

unduly benign and, as with all stereotypes, these traits can be valued positively or negatively, just as the erstwhile one of Jewish economic prowess
could be admired as resourcefulness, suspected as conspiracy or reviled as
venality. Nor does a new image necessarily displace a traditional one. As
Robert Gutman points out, the revival of anti-Semitism in the Soviet Union
has been marked by the subtle adaptation of the old stereotypes to the new
class of the Jewish professionals which produces "the 'conniving' . . . organization man, professor or public servant."

Changing Values in American Society

Once again, then, we are thrown back upon the need to examine the state
of contemporary American society in order to locate the normative values
that influence the gentile imagination of Jewishness. Mr. Wrong, for example, suggests that a positive evaluation of Jewish traits among the college
generation is grounded in the development of what he calls "ethnic liberalism," whose effects are seen in the support of the Negro movement and in
the increasing rate of intermarriage between Christians and Jews on the
campuses. Mr. Wrong believes that the main cause of this increasingly militant egalitarianism lies in the need of the young to identify themselves with
"distinctive values" during a period of rapid social changes that has produced a good deal of anomie in the university communities as well as in the
society at large—a view to which the 1964 Berkeley riots amply attest.
Whatever its causes, though, "ethnic liberalism" has become the dominant
tone on the campuses—a development which Mr. Wrong regards as virtually "irreversible" and that will thereby continue to provide a major ground
of democratic values to which more and more young Americans will be
exposed at just the period in their lives when they are most likely to revise
inherited prejudices and individualize their social attitudes.

Of course, Cambridge and Ann Arbor and Palo Alto are not quite the
world, and the values that are acquired there are not irreversible, as the
lives of many former student radicals bear out. To be sure, ethnic liberalism
will probably prove to be more durable than did the radical sympathies of
the 1930s, if only because it accords much better with the changing structure of student life produced by the advent of mass college education. But
what of the society at large? How do the relations there between its evolving
structure and concomitant values affect the perception and evaluation of the
minority groups?

The essay of Robin M. Williams, Jr., who specializes in this field, focuses
on the general changes in value orientations in recent years that accord with
and help to explain the nationwide decline of anti-Semitism that Mr. Stember has found. Like most of the other participants at the conference, Mr.
Williams attempts to connect present trends with past continuities in looking for more or less stable bases in American cultural experience that sup-

port the sudden, massive shifts in the range and levels of anti-Jewish feeling. Thus, he reminds us that there have always been in the United States marked similarities between "Jewish" and "American" values, as instanced by the fact that the historic stereotype of the American—individualistic, shrewd, materialistic, aggressive, etc.—is virtually interchangeable with that of the Jew. So, too, has there been a correspondence in their respective attachments to religious freedom and cultural pluralism, democracy, voluntarism and humanitarianism, partly because both American independence and Jewish emancipation were rooted in the ideology of the eighteenth-century democratic revolutions. These similarities have not, to be sure, guaranteed tolerant relations in the past; indeed, as Mr. Williams puts it, "shared standards of active achievement meant effective competition and could well cause gentiles to feel threatened by, or hostile toward, Jews." Such was the case in the early decades of the twentieth century, when Jews bore the brunt of the nativist opposition to foreigners because of their ambitiousness and adaptability. Still it is perhaps most accurate to say that these "shared standards" in the past have both fostered and contained the tensions between Jews and the core society: Thus both John Higham and Morton Keller explain that the reason the ideological anti-Semitism of the 1920s never got off the ground, except in rural areas where it could feed upon the hatred of Wall Street finance capitalism, was that the prestige placed upon the business ethic elsewhere in the society undercut the stereotype of the Jew as "economic man."

In his analysis of the contemporary situation, Mr. Williams emphasizes that "achievement values" have increasingly been permeating the whole society, that today "all the pressures are toward recognizing and respecting position based on accomplishment, regardless of person." Noting also the social changes that have made America more middle-class, urban and mobile, the increasing emphasis on education, material prosperity, social welfare and equalization of opportunity, Mr. Williams finds the society as a whole is moving toward positions and values already held by American Jews, the effect of which is to make the Jewish presence that much less salient. When, for example, "educational achievement is stressed as practically a patriotic duty," in Mr. Williams' words, it becomes "absurd to resent the Jews' high educational aspirations and attainments." Moreover, with the growing involvement of the Government in education and research, in welfare programs and civil rights causes, more of this basic value orientation has become institutionalized, which, as Mr. Williams points out, creates "new vested interests and new ideas of normality and 'taken-for-grantedness,' " that progressively decrease the possibilities for a revival of anti-Semitism.

All of which does not signify any fundamental revision of the moral norms of Americans, but rather some shift of emphasis from the values associated with freedom to those associated with equality. This shift has resulted from substantial changes in the character of the society during the past twenty-five years along the different lines we have been considering. The effect of these changes, according to Mr. Williams' analysis, has been to dim the perception of Jews as a distinguishable group and to damp down the old networks of rivalry and prejudice, though not to dismantle them. As he graphically expressed the point during his remarks at the conference, "all the elements are still present but there is not much current coming through the printed circuits." That is to say, the respondent to one of the 1944 polls who was much aware of Jews and looked with some sympathy on the possibility of suppressing them is likely to have become deconditioned to anti-Semitic appeals. The last crisis of capitalism is now a distant memory; the vast amorphous ambiguous atmosphere of the mass society has modified his formerly sharp awareness of "them" and "us" and created, in Mr. Wiliams' phrase, "a gray mass" of otherness, which he is encouraged by television programs and subway posters alike to be tolerant of and which he mostly ignores as long as it does not press too close to home. The spirit of interfaith good will enables him to entertain the possibility that men with different beliefs can still live in the same society, while the force of consensus politics either absorbs or isolates his traditional convictions. Meanwhile, the pressures of new public issues, ranging from school integration to the war in Asia, alter his sense of the world. The result is that whatever prejudice toward Jews resides in his mind is not likely to have much voltage or currency.

As for the strengthening of the values of equality, the acid test, as Thomas F. Pettigrew points out, is to be found in the relations of the society to Negroes rather than to Jews since one can explain the decline of anti-Semitism on grounds such as acculturation. American Negroes, on the other hand, have historically been the victims of anti-democratic values, to say the least, their situation quite literally being defined by institutions, laws and customs as one of subordination and exclusion. As such, they have not been a minority group in America but rather a caste, and, as several members of the conference pointed out, their long experience of servitude and alienation, their intimate relation to the issues of American history and their role as the principal object of American guilt have made their situation much more like that of European Jews than of American ones. Nor could one attribute a change in white attitudes and behavior toward Negroes to a dimming of their visibility, which if anything has become more overt in recent years, or to the process of assimilation from which they have been effectively barred.

According to Mr. Pettigrew, who draws on poll data compiled by Herbert H. Hyman and Paul B. Sheatsley, there has been a decline in hostile stereotypes and discriminatory practices toward Negroes which runs more or less parallel to the poll data for Jews. Mr. Pettigrew goes on to argue that these polls are "reasonably accurate reflections" of a general diminution of prejudice in the American public. While Mr. Pettigrew makes a number of crucial distinctions between prejudice toward Jews and Negroes—stemming from their differences as immigrants and slaves and being organized around the concerns of the superego and the id, respectively—he holds with most of the other conference members the view that the institutionalization of safeguards to protect minority rights and opportunities is producing a change in behavior and hence in attitudes toward Negroes as well as Jews.

The term that Mr. Pettigrew uses to characterize this "sharp change of public norms concerning minorities" is "transtolerance." Originally coined by Peter Viereck to denote a coercive and manipulative egalitarianism, which he believes to be merely a "sublimated Jim Crow . . . a strictly kosher anti-Semitism," "transtolerance" represents for Mr. Pettigrew an analytic term for the disreputability of prejudice. Judging by his own examples, however, "transtolerance" is, to say the least, an ambiguous phenomenon. Indeed, to read the statement attributed to William E. Miller during his 1964 Vice-Presidential campaign—"Barry [Goldwater]'s a Protestant and a Jew, and I'm a Catholic. Anybody who's against that ticket is a damn bigot"—makes one's mind begin to boggle at the possibilities for duplicity and perversion.

A Continuing Ambivalence?

All of which brings us back to the ambiguities of public surveys of prejudice. If the rhetoric of "transtolerance" has its public uses, so, too, does it have its personal ones, and one wonders how many of the respondents in the recent polls were merely subscribing to this new climate of opinion concerning minorities. Thus, as Ben Halpern points out, though Stember finds that a small number of respondents during the McCarthy period identified Jews with Communism, they also "identified" fictitious Jewish names of spies six times more often than they did fictitious gentile ones, and that their support of the state of Israel can be viewed as the obverse of their reluctance to admit Jewish D.P.'s to America.

In general, Mr. Halpern finds that the poll data reflect what the respondents thought they should feel about the hypothetical issues at hand rather than how they would react in an actual situation involving Jews. Writing from a historian's viewpoint, Mr. Halpern also argues that the Stember analysis lacks a body of comparable data from the past which could be used to test its significance; that poll questions present semantic problems that are difficult to control for, such as the shift in the meaning of key terms such as "race," "Jews," "Communists," and so forth; and that, finally, attitude studies can prove to be superficial and transitory indices of historic changes unless they are related to the historical structure of these attitudes and to the *crucial* contemporary events that relate to them.

The superficiality of poll data was remarked upon from another perspective by Daniel J. Levinson, one of the co-authors of *The Authoritarian Personality*. In his remarks at the conference, Mr. Levinson emphasized—seconded by another social psychologist, Simon Herman—that such studies leave untapped the deeper, even pre-conscious dispositions toward Jews that accumulate in the course of cultural conditioning and that explain why, for example, hostile imagery can still be found, under proper provocation, 3,000 miles from where and 200 years after one religious group had last had contact with members of another. Peter Rossi, the head of the National Opinion Research Center, cautioned that the sociologist tends to pay attention to explicit attitudes and behavior—the top of the iceberg—rather than the more obscure predispositions that lie beneath. The latter are regarded as purely "psychological" phenomena, though, as Mr. Rossi pointed out, the main thing for social science to understand is the relationship "between the bottom part and the top . . . that makes this iceberg rise." Moreover, as Lucy Dawidowicz, a staff member of the American Jewish Committee, suggested, the sociological methods of investigation need to take into account the fact that because anti-Semitism increasingly exists outside the formal institutional structure of the society, it is likely to be missed or minimized by research that proceeds along the standard lines of survey information.

Mr. Levinson, along with Mrs. Dawidowicz and John Slawson, executive vice-president of the American Jewish Committee, also urged that attitude studies need to pay attention to the symbolic as well as literal association process of prejudice and bigotry. Mr. Slawson noted, for example, that though the respectable elements of the radical right are not anti-Semitic, their hostility to the urban East, to liberalism, intellectualism, secularism and so forth all dovetail into the standard syndrome of anti-Semitism, and in the minds of the right-wingers these images have much the same "psychological quality," to use Mr. Levinson's term, as that of the ideology of thirty years ago which surrounded the word "Jew." More concretely, as Norman Podhoretz, editor of *Commentary,* pointed out, the current interdiction against expressing one's true feelings about one or another of the minorities merely creates a kind of underground mode of expression because the banned stereotypes still contain strong elements of reality and most people resent having their sense of reality manipulated by public norms. This resentment, in turn, "generates steam which is available for tapping if one knows which valve to turn." Thus, right-wing candidates, such as Barry Goldwater and William F. Buckley, Jr., have managed to tap a great deal of anti-Negro feeling while remaining within the "transtolerance" ethos.

Though a number of others at the conference also remarked on the ambiguous character of gentile attitudes toward Jews, Mr. Halpern's essay was the only one that described it in a systematic and heuristic way. Indeed Mr. Halpern, who writes from the perspective of a Zionist historian, regards the ambivalence of gentiles as the heart of the matter, expressing as it does the basic conditions of Jewish existence throughout world history, specifically the interplay of hatred and tolerance toward an ideologically deviant minority.

One of the values of Mr. Halpern's essay is that it tests the present-mindedness of most of the other contributions, along with their tendency to regard anti-Semitism as an aspect of some other phenomenon—such as the nativist reaction to immigrants, or the social tensions produced by economic depression or war, or the fading imagery of Christian sectarianism. Eschewing topical as well as moralistic explanations of anti-Semitism and trying to restore the sense of its "independent, continuing tradition," Mr. Halpern traces the historic continuity and growth of "Jew-hatred" as the universal response to the monotheistic faith of a defeated and alien people. Unable to convert other cultures to their faith and joined by a "historical fatality . . . [to] their religion in an exclusive union," the Chosen People became the recalcitrant subjects of the empires that conquered them and of the nations they were scattered among. In the words of Haman, in the Book of Esther, which anticipate the next two millennia of the Jewish people: "There is a certain people scattered abroad . . . and their laws are diverse from those of every people; neither keep they the king's laws, therefore it profiteth not the king to suffer them."

Where it did "profit the king," the Jews were suffered; otherwise, generally speaking, they were not. The structure of Jewish existence was such that it had to be tolerated by the ruling authorities if it was to exist at all and be protected against the animosity of the populace who resented their special status. Where the Jews were the only tolerated people, as during the Middle Ages, this animosity grew particularly intense and when reasons of state finally weighed against tolerance the Jews were persecuted and banished. Such has been the "hostility-tolerance syndrome" which has dictated the terms of Jewish existence through history, modified, of course, by the particular political circumstances and ideological pressures of an age and by the individual history of nations, but nonetheless forming a continuous pattern of ambivalence.

Mr. Halpern agrees that recent history has significantly altered the syndrome, though not in the ways that were generally advanced at the conference. The Nazi destruction of European Jewry exceeded the traditional boundaries of anti-Semitism and produced "definite and conscious inhibitions against it" which explain the disreputability of Jew-hatred that he finds to be the main meaning of the poll data. Secondly, the emergence of the state of Israel has shaken the former identification of the Jews as an intransigent religious minority and the perception of Jewish nationality has thus begun to modify the long-standing formula of hostility and tolerance. As for America, Mr. Halpern argues that the tolerance factor has been strengthened but not superseded by the traditions of secularism and, in recent times, by the sharp decline in discrimination, backed by law and public opinion. The stage beyond toleration would be integration, which Mr. Halpern argues has not been reached, nor is it likely to as long as Jews remain Jews, Christians remain Christians, and America maintains its cultural traditions. The relative openness of the society to Jews, Mr. Halpern reminds us, has occurred before, and it amounts to the same options to assimilate or convert that were offered to the Jews of Rome and Alexandria and to those of post-Enlightenment Europe alike, while the basic tradition of anti-Semitism remained intact.

But what of the new status of Jewish religion in America? Mr. Halpern would say that it is a special version of "transtolerance," a product of higher public relations and of a general effort to avoid religious conflict. It gives rise to cant phrases such as the "Judeo-Christian heritage," as though the historical relations between the two faiths had been mutually fruitful and identifies Judaism and Christianity as equally authentic bases of American mores and morals, a claim that an Orthodox Jew or a Protestant Fundamentalist would equally find ludicrous. As we have noted, an all-American religion appears to be emerging which combines a maximum of tolerance with a minimum of doctrine; during the conference, Manheim S. Shapiro, a staff member of the American Jewish Committee, suggested that American Jews are becoming "Protestantized," and, by way of example, told of a letter he received in which the writer suggested that "a Jewish organization should undertake the task of informing Protestants that we don't really believe all this Jewish bit and that in our denial of Judaism we are much like them in their denial of Protestantism." Short of a wholesale merging of faiths, though, on some neutral ground such as Unitarianism, Mr. Halpern believes that the hostility-tolerance syndrome will persist. As he put it, in reply to one of his critics, "a Jew who asks the Christians to give up their hostility to Judaism simply doesn't know what he is asking. . . . Why should there have been a Christianity at all if Judaism were accepted."

In sum, Mr. Halpern believes that the force of the past and the decisive differences in ideology will maintain Jewish-gentile relations within their traditional spectrum. Even the radical changes in perception and attitude produced by the Nazi holocaust and the state of Israel will inevitably be assimilated with the historic background of the Jews and become part of the total pattern, just as the Jews, no matter what strategies of acculturation they adopt, will continue to be perceived through imagery that accommodates the old and the new.

American Jews in the Political System

Indeed, as Mr. Halpern concludes, the traumatic changes produced during the past thirty years are likely to press upon conventional Jewish attitudes much more decisively than upon gentile ones. There is no full-length treatment of the former in this volume, and the discussion of trends within the Jewish community that would relate to the poll data was confined during the conference to informally developed opinions. The tendency of such discussion as there was minimized Judaism as an operative force in contemporary Jewish behavior and stressed the influence of the secularist ethos. In other words, the prevailing image of American Jewry today was that of a highly developed American minority which was organized to ensure its rights and opportunities in the society. The most clear-cut exposition of this viewpoint was made by David Danzig, then associate director of the American Jewish Committee, in the course of criticizing the Higham-Keller position that the force of assimilation is collapsing group differences and making the Jews less "visible." Along with sociologist Leo Srole, Mr. Danzig raises the point that in key respects Jews are more conspicuous in politics, economic activity and cultural matters than they have ever been in America; moreover, the blurring of distinctive ethnic traits should not obscure the significance of what Milton M. Gordon has termed "structural pluralism"—the maintenance of group associations by means of the ties of interest and power. The selection of a "balanced" ticket, the underlying organization of industries, businesses and professions along ethnic lines, the role of religious and ethnic institutions in social welfare, education and recreation activities indicate that "groupness" is still a vital force in American society, though many of its outer trappings have become less perceptible. "Voluntarism," to use Morris Janowitz's term for this phenomenon, has played a particularly significant part in checking and discrediting anti-Semitism; the Jewish agencies have effectively blocked the exploitation of prejudice in politics at the local level and, by enlisting the media in a steady campaign against intolerance, have helped to convert what was a political ideology in Europe into a pathological syndrome in America. Furthermore, the Negro issue has placed group relations squarely at the center of American life, for it has not only begun to bring the Negro community together in a potentially powerful bloc but has also served, as Mr. Danzig pointed out, to reveal the force of ethnicity in terms of the organization of white opposition, particularly at the local level. Finally, the development of the radical right by means of the structure and ideology of Protestant Fundamentalism provides further evidence for Mr. Danzig's claim that pluralism is far from vanishing in America and that "groupness" will continue to have a decisive effect on the underlying structure of the society in the future, as the formerly ascendant native Protestants become one minority among others.

Be that as it may, the Jews can no longer be expected to view themselves or function as an insecure enclave perched on the rim of the culture and fearful that the new wave of history will swamp them. Like the other groups, they believe they have an equal stake in the society and feel increasingly free to assert it. One consequence of this development is likely to be a shift from the traditional grounds of conflict formed by alienation, persecution and prejudice to more open and objective conflicts of group interests and values. Such "ideological" clashes have already been developing—not over the issues of religious faith, but rather of secularism. Morris Janowitz pointed to church-state relations as one of the major possible sources of Jewish-gentile tension. Certainly, the controversy over prayers in public schools and the increasing number of bitter incidents over the issue of Christmas observances in the schools have begun to frame a new content of group conflict which bears study. Mr. O'Dea suggested that the impact of such conflicts may be particularly exacerbated in the Catholic community which is undergoing a slower and more problematic process of secularization. Emphasizing the view that incidents such as the one in Hamden, Connecticut in 1961, where Catholic authorities led the opposition to "taking Christ out of Christmas" in the schools, represent complex group differences rather than a simple revival of religious prejudice, Mr. O'Dea called for the development of a more open and comprehensive study of such problems than has generally prevailed, one that would enlist Catholics in this research in order to understand the "dialectic" of conflict as the communities themselves experience it and to promote closer working relations between the social scientists who come from the different groups.

Such a view was very much in keeping with the general thrust of the conference and of this collection of essays, which, as we began by noting, was the analysis of the context of relations between Jews and gentiles rather than of the psychological and moral implications of prejudice. To the extent that moral considerations arose, they were typically formulated in terms of general reference: "what was good for society," in sociologist Daniel Bell's words, rather than "what was good for the Jews." The most salient example of this tendency was Morris Janowitz's discussion of what he termed "educationism"—that is, the revision of social boundaries produced by the demand for advanced or otherwise specialized training and culminating in what has come to be called a "meritocracy." As Robert Gutman's report bears out, American Jews have been benefitting enormously from "the knowledge explosion" by virtue of their drive for higher education. By the same token, according to Janowitz, they are likely to become exposed to the resentment of those Americans who trained for positions that have been eliminated or depreciated by the new technology as well as of those who find that the access routes into the society have been so narrowed by educational criteria as to exclude them. Janowitz, however, is less concerned about the growing cadres of Jewish professionals than about the dangers of "educationism" which he believes to be a "more gruesome" way of differentiating society than ethnicity and religion because of "its vast potential for exclusion." Some of the consequences of this growing emphasis upon education as the determinant of role and status in the society are the destruction of the normal progression of careers, and the alienation of more and more individuals from the work process. Moreover, the impact of these dislocations, according to Janowitz and Bell, threatens to have a profound effect upon the political mechanisms that have stabilized group relations in the face of the stresses and anxieties of the past thirty years.

For Mr. Janowitz as for Sigmund Diamond, a sociologist and historian, the critical issue of American anti-Semitism is the operation of the political system. And if there was one common conclusion that cut across the differences in position and emphasis, in analysis and evaluation concerning Jewish-gentile relations, it was the primary importance of political authority. As Mr. Halpern pointed out, tolerance of the Jews has always depended upon the support and strength of the ruling element. Mr. Janowitz, Mr. Keller, Mr. Danzig and others stressed the importance of the Roosevelt Administration in turning the tide of popular hostility to the minorities that had developed after the First World War and in legitimizing their position in the society. It was also agreed that the political system furnished the main bulwark against the growth of anti-Semitic movements during the Second World War and that, unlike the aftermath of the First World War, the government campaign against subversive influences was so hedged against the traditional imagery of Jewish subversion that Senator McCarthy was driven to "the astounding feat," in Mr. Halpern's words, "of identifying Communist anti-Americanism with old-stock, liberal, Protestant, Ivy League, striped-pants Americans." Today, the role of the Federal Government in the civil rights movement makes that much more visible the relation of political authority to minority groups and also strengthens the view, advanced by Mr. Williams, Mr. Pettigrew and others, that a political system positively oriented toward equality may not only protect their rights but also by its initiatives through law and institutions slowly but surely alter the public attitudes toward them.

Group Survival: An Open Question

While much of the diversity of opinion at the conference stemmed from whether the participants emphasized the historical continuities or changes in the present state of Jewish-gentile relations, they were all alive to the probability that future relations will occur in a markedly different social context from any of those found in the past. The chief feature of this context is that the persistence of the Jews as a distinctive minority group can no longer be taken for granted. One consequence of this fact, as Mr. Halpern emphasized, is that the changes in attitudes toward Jews which the polls chart are likely to prove less significant for the future than the attitudes *of* Jews. For while the image of the Jew may no longer be expected to possess much significance in the mind of the secularized American gentile, the image of the gentile will remain central in the mind of the Jew, however acculturated and secularized his own life may become. For to be a Jew in any meaningful sense of the term means that one must establish and respect a certain boundary between Jews and gentiles, an act of self-definition that is hardly as necessary for a Christian in America.

In other words, as the new forms of social connection press ever more decisively upon American Jews, they are confronted by the inescapable need to clarify their objectives. Do they really wish to retain their identity as a group? If so, how are they to retain it in a society which does not provide the historical ties of threat and restriction? It is still too early in the history of religious pluralism to divine what the answers to these questions will be. All we can say is that if the American Jews should find themselves without the will and the cultural content to survive as a group, then the relations between Jews and gentiles will indeed have entered a revolutionary period; that is to say, there will no longer be any such relations, and future students of the subject will have only a purely historical phenomenon to think about.

NOTES

1. William Murray, "Hell's Angels," *The Saturday Evening Post*, November 20, 1965, pp. 32–39.

2. See Peter G. J. Pulzer, *The Rise of Political Anti-Semitism in Germany and Austria* (New York: John Wiley & Sons, 1964), pp. 5–15.

PART ONE

THE RECENT HISTORY
OF PUBLIC ATTITUDES

Charles Herbert Stember

I

Anti-Semitism and the Study of Public Opinion

THE PRESENT INQUIRY reviews the attitudes of Americans toward their Jewish fellow citizens, as revealed in the findings of nationwide public-opinion surveys from 1937 to 1962. These surveys dealt with beliefs and sentiments concerning Jews in a great many contexts, against the constantly shifting background of world events in that turbulent and tragic quarter-century. Thus, the evidence assembled here constitutes an extended footnote to American and American-Jewish history, documenting the nature and trend of anti-Semitism during a crucial period. At the same time, it shows certain socio-psychological processes in action, illustrating the interplay of images, beliefs and attitudes with one another and with reality.

Few if any of the polls recorded in these pages were originally intended as historical or socio-psychological documentation. Some were initiated by the polling organizations themselves; a larger number were sponsored by human-relations agencies—chiefly the American Jewish Committee—as practical guides to policy or action. In either case, they were carried out within the ordinary periodic assessments of the public's current concerns. The coverage of topics is accordingly uneven, reflecting the momentary needs or interests of the agency more often than the theoretical concerns of the scholar. Fortunately, in our discipline, as in others, information not intended for scholarly documentation sometimes affords the most revealing insights. The lawyers and tax gatherers of past ages compiled their records for immediate use, with never a thought for the enlightenment of future savants; yet this testimony, accidentally preserved, enables the present-day historian to reconstruct long-dead civilizations in impressive detail. Similarly, the surveys utilized here, though conducted *ad hoc,* provide findings that lend themselves to long-term interpretation and permit us to discern certain large, over-all trends in the American public's attitudes toward the Jews.

The Origin of the Inquiry

Broad studies of public attitudes toward Jews were begun in the late 1930s. What initially prompted them was the shock induced by events in Germany—specifically, the realization that the world had remained blind to the menace of Nazi anti-Semitism until it was too late.

When Adolf Hitler first made his bid for power with an openly anti-Jewish program during the 1920s, few observers were able to foresee the catastrophe into which he was to plunge European Jewry. The bulk of liberal opinion, in Germany and elsewhere, discounted Nazism as merely another of the transitory outbreaks of anti-Semitism that had been recurring in various parts of Europe for centuries. That this particular movement arose where it did served only to discredit whatever warning voices were heard. Organized anti-Semitic action on a broad scale was perhaps conceivable in backward Eastern Europe, with its deeply entrenched popular hatred of Jews and its history of government-inspired pogroms. But the Germans were not poor, illiterate peasants whose prejudices could be whipped up at will by unscrupulous politicians; Germany was a modern industrial nation under a free government dedicated to liberalism and tolerance. Nor was the secure, strongly assimilated Jewish community of Germany to be compared with the downtrodden, segregated and culturally isolated Jewry of Eastern Europe.

With economic stagnation and unemployment descending upon Europe in the years after 1929, the Nazis' growing strength gave rise to some alarm. But Hitler's defeat in the 1932 presidential election caused Jews all over the world to breathe more freely, and large segments of public opinion once more dismissed Nazism as a lunatic-fringe movement. It was therefore all the more of a shock when, only a few months later (January 30, 1933), Hitler was named Chancellor and at once turned democratic Germany into a totalitarian state. As the Hitler regime proved its durability in the ensuing months and years, anti-Semitic ideas that had been shrugged off as the property of crackpots were translated into action at every level of government throughout Germany. The country's Jews, until now full of citizens seemingly accepted by the larger society, became targets of discriminatory legislation and of government-inspired persecution and violence.

The outside world was stunned by this disaster. Signs and portents of what was to come had eluded most foreign observers, as they had the enlightened segment of the German nation itself. And indeed, in the absence of accurate long-term information about the trend of attitudes toward Jews, it hardly could have been foreseen that most of the German people would join or acquiesce in a wholesale return to barbarism. Now that the unbelievable had happened, the world asked: Why?

Among the reasons cited for the terror unleashed against Germany's Jews, the economic ills of the society loomed large. The explanation most frequently advanced was that the Versailles Treaty, the runaway inflation of 1922–23 and the Depression had successively stunted the German economy until the citizenry—especially the lower middle class—reached a state of unbearable frustration and deprivation. This frustration, observers said, was vented in anger and ultimately in aggressive action against the Jewish minority.

It was an explanation that held little comfort for American Jews, for conditions in the United States were only too similar to those in Germany. Here, as there, economic depression had wrought chronic unemployment, destitution and hopelessness, as well as a marked heightening of political extremism. In view of this parallel, it appeared by no means unreasonable to consider the possibility that "it might happen here," and to ask whether America's Jewry might not be lolling in a false sense of security, as Germany's had done. Social scientists and Jewish leaders agreed that it was urgently necessary to begin and continue measuring the attitudes of Americans toward the Jews in their midst—not as an academic exercise, but as a practical safety measure.

The Emergence of a Technique

As it happened, techniques for taking the pulse of the nation at large were just emerging. For some time, much of the research carried on in the field of intergroup relations had dealt with the relations between Jews and gentiles—partly because anti-Semitism was and is virtually a prototype of group prejudice. It is so ancient and has appeared in so many settings as to be, in the words of Simpson and Yinger,

in many ways the "classic" prejudice. Through the course of centuries it has illustrated all of the intricately related forces at work. It has ranged all the way from "polite" social exclusion to vicious pogroms. . . . A careful study of anti-Semitism is a magnifying glass of great value in the examination of prejudice. . . . Most of the forces involved are also found in other cases of prejudice, which will, therefore, be better understood by the analysis of anti-Semitism.[1]

The social psychologists who began to take so intense an interest in the study of attitudes toward Jews during the 1930s modeled their inquiries, for the most part, on contemporary research in general psychology and sociology. Thus, they adopted the controlled experiment and the attitude survey as their chief tools, together with quantitative measurement. For their hypotheses and constructs, they relied heavily on the insights of their less experimental predecessors. The ideas of Karl Marx and Sigmund Freud, the insights of W. I. Thomas and Florian Znaniecki, the concepts of Robert Park and his associates at the University of Chicago, all contributed richly to the conceptualization of empirical studies.

During this time, explorations of society's attitudes toward the Jew were sharply limited by the select character of persons available as subjects. Following in the footsteps of traditional psychology, many academic researchers concentrated their efforts on the nearest, most accessible and most manipulable quarry: the ubiquitous college student. Others, more influenced by sociological practices, went beyond the campus. But they could not go far; funds for large-scale research were lacking, as were techniques and organization for studying widely separate individuals. Thus, even field studies at first covered only circumscribed, highly select populations.

Toward the end of the decade, however, nationwide polls, originally designed to predict election results, came into use to explore other issues as well. The findings of such studies, conducted by the American Institute of Public Opinion, the *Fortune* Poll and other private agencies, were syndicated in newspapers and soon began to command the attention of administrators, social scientists and the general public.

The new techniques purported to assess the state of public sentiment on a wide variety of political and other issues. There was no obvious reason why they might not be used to gauge public sentiment toward Jews, and there were compelling indications that they should be. If the nature, extent and potential of American anti-Semitism at a given moment were known, countermeasures could be systematically applied. Scientifically conducted opinion research promised to supply a body of information that might serve as a basis for such action—information far more extensive and precise than could be obtained from the mere impressions of even the most astute journalists and social scientists. It was for this purpose that nationwide surveys of attitudes toward Jews were initiated in 1937. During the years that followed, such studies rapidly became one of the principal avenues of inquiry into the fluctuating status of anti-Semitism.

Issues Surveyed

The periodic assessments begun under the mounting threat of Nazism were continued through the years of the Second World War with their manifold group tensions, through the period of the incipient Cold War, through the early 1950s with their anxieties over Korea and left-wing activity and into the present era of the Negro revolution. As we shall see, many crucial developments of this period (for example, the last stand of isolationism in 1941, the emergence of Israel in 1948 and the trials of Communist spies in 1950–51) were explicitly reflected in the survey questions asked. Other issues, though not named, were unmistakably present in the background.

To a noteworthy extent, surveys have been occupied with the public's image of the Jew—an orientation that dates back to the late 1930s. The Jews of Germany, objectively viewed, were in many ways indistinguishable from their non-Jewish fellow citizens. Yet Germans evidently had come to look upon them as subhuman or, at least, as totally alien; for how else could they have been induced to acquiesce or take part in the most revolting outrages against them? Plainly, hostile images and perceptions were a crucial element in sanctioning aggressively anti-Semitic behavior. Moreover, such perceptions offered some of the most promising opportunities for counteraction (for example, policing the mass media for themes or representations likely to generate prejudice). At the same time, the study of images was of interest to social psychologists in that it afforded opportunities to test certain developing theories, notably the idea that cognition was the central factor in the forming of attitudes.[2]

A second line of inquiry, closely related to the study of perceptions, was the assessment of beliefs concerning the position and treatment of the Jews in American society. Measures of such beliefs, it was expected, would help account for certain widely held unfavorable images, as well as illuminate the public's seeming apathy and unconcern about the problems of minority groups. The subject has commanded continuing attention in the polls, though on a much smaller scale than image studies.

The possibility of violence against American Jewry figured prominently in the early surveys. While the Hitler regime lasted, about a fourth of all poll questions were designed to measure the potential of anti-Semitic violence or approval of Nazi policies among the American public. After the war, such questioning was almost entirely discontinued, presumably because a general falling off in measured anti-Semitism made violence appear unlikely.

From the late 1940s on, attention was concentrated on issues which until then had been only lightly explored. As the European disaster receded in time, the sense of threat lifted from American Jewry. At the same time, Jews were encountering less and less rejection in the larger society, and for the first time in many decades general public acceptance seemed a realistic possibility. The task was no longer to prevent a surge of aggressive, Nazi-style anti-Semitism in America, but to wipe out altogether the discrimination against minority groups that still tainted American life. Accordingly, discrimination and acceptance, both in public life and in personal relationships, came to rank with hostile stereotypes as leading topics of research—a development illustrative of the shift from defensive to offensive concerns that has characterized the conduct of minority-group affairs since the early postwar years.

Two other topics have been pursued concurrently with those just named. First, the prevalence of anti-Semitic talk in normal social life has been frequently estimated throughout the period, as a rough indicator of anti-Jewish feeling and of preoccupation with the Jews. Second, potential support for non-discriminatory practices in general has been measured from time to time, with the thought that the security of any one minority derives in part from popular willingness to play fair with all groups in the society.

The Relevance of Attitudes

We must now spell out the working assumptions on which this study rests. Chief among them is our conviction that attitudes play a key role in reactions to Jews. In the early years of research on prejudice, this assumption was not questioned; indeed, it was believed that anti-Semitism was altogether determined by attitudes, and could best be combated by direct methods designed to change them. Since then, social scientists have arrived at a more sophisticated view of the problem. It has been recognized that the attitudes of groups toward one another are themselves the natural outcome of social and historical forces, particularly of actual intergroup relations, and thus will often resist change unless the underlying social structure is also altered. In consequence of this sociological bias, as it might be called, the study of attitudes during recent years has been dismissed by some as relatively unimportant.

We believe this approach to prejudice to be dangerously one-sided. Its proponents often assume that relevant changes in the social structure will automatically modify attitudes;[3] but they overlook that attitudes, once formed, may exercise a force of their own—specifically, that they may become obstacles to the restructuring of actual relations between groups. Even after such restructuring occurs, attitudes that are deeply embedded in the culture or have acquired functional utility for individuals may resist change; years, even decades, may pass before they catch up with the new social reality.

Nor is it true that attitudes between groups will change only if the groups' relations do. They may also be affected by education or indoctrination, and by change in other spheres. Thus, under the impact of general social tension or economic frustration, prejudice against one or another minority group may grow increasingly salient or intense, and with sufficient prodding by organized movements may flare up into open hostility; yet, all the time, the social, economic and political positions of the majority and the minority may remain as they were.

In our view, the connection between changes in intergroup relations and changes in intergroup attitudes is reciprocal. The latter may affect the former as well as vice versa. Thus, no over-all analysis of the problems of prejudice and discrimination is complete unless both factors are understood: the social structure of the environment, and the psychological structure of individuals, which is a cause as well as a product of that environment. In this sense at least, the American public's attitudes toward Jews remain an important area of scientific inquiry.

Research of the kind with which we are concerned has also been attacked from quite a different quarter. Certain theorists, influenced by what might be called a political bias, have questioned whether the beliefs and sentiments of the general public have any real significance. In their opinion, the attitudes of "strategic elites" in the society are what chiefly determines political and social processes. How we feel about such a hypothesis is plain from the very existence of this study, devoted as it is to the beliefs and sentiments of the American people as a whole. No leadership group, it seems to us, can veer far from the sentiments of those it leads and remain viable—not, at any rate, over a period as long as that covered here, nor in a society, such as ours, which permits a relatively wide range of political expression. It may well be that the attitudes with which we deal were in part formed by opinion leaders; but the leaders' ideologies must themselves have been shaped and circumscribed by the attitudes and beliefs of the public at large. Of the policies offered by various elite groups at any given moment, only those would seem to stand a chance of acceptance which accord in some degree with the public's own life experiences and resulting attitudes.

Finally, attitudes are sometimes disparaged by those with a particular psychological bias as merely a superficial manifestation of some more fundamental psychological entity, such as "motivation" or "personality." It seems to us that this criticism confuses attitudes with some of their psychological causes. An individual's motivations and their embodiment in his personality structure unquestionably help determine his particular attitudes and are often mirrored in them; but they are not the only determinants, nor do they include everything we mean when we speak of attitudes. That the concept of attitude remains indispensable has been underscored by Katz and Stotland:

Efforts to deal with the real world show our need for a concept more flexible and more covert than habit, more specifically oriented to social objects than personality traits, less global than value systems, more directive than beliefs and more ideational than motive pattern.[4]

There is at least one intensely practical reason why the study of attitudes needs to be continued. Assuming that outside influences (for example, legislation) succeed in altering overt behavior toward a minority, how extensive and durable is such a reversal in the absence of corresponding attitude change? We believe actions and sentiments cannot long remain out of tune with each other. Continued hostile feelings pose a danger to any minority group, however well integrated it may become. For example, progress in Negro integration achieved without commensurate change in popular sentiment would seem to be precarious unless the public's feelings catch up with reality.[5] Only when attitudes and actions move in parallel fashion can we speak of a change in social norms. In fact, since social institutions depend ultimately on public consensus, attitudes are a more reliable indicator of long-term normative changes than specific practices.

It is with these considerations in mind that we undertake the present study, as a necessary complement to the study of overt behavior among groups. That the Jews' position in the society and their relations to the non-Jewish majority have altered since the period of mass immigration (c. 1880–1920) is beyond question. What we need to know is whether these changes have been accompanied by modifications of the largely unfavorable attitudes which the non-Jewish majority held a few decades ago. If we observe such modifications on a substantial scale we may conclude, albeit cautiously, that Jews have begun to be truly integrated into the larger society. But if we find that, despite all the changes in the Jews' position and their relations with the majority, the public still views them essentially as it did in former days, we will have to conclude that their position in America remains insecure and subject to change without notice.

The Validity of Measurements

A second working assumption made in the present study concerns the measuring devices used. The validity of data collected by opinion-research agencies has been severely questioned by workers in the field, as well as by others.[6] With some of these critics and their arguments we agree wholeheartedly; yet we are convinced that public-opinion data, for all their imperfections, afford the most effective if not the only way of attacking the problem we have set for ourselves. In what follows, we shall seek to demonstrate that they can yield many valid insights if appropriately evaluated.[7]

It is obvious that attitudes cannot be measured directly, but must be inferred from behavior, either overt or verbal.[8] We cannot always generalize from the overt to the verbal or vice versa; as a number of studies have demonstrated, there is no necessary consistency between the two.[9] Nor, for that matter, are verbal responses elicited in different situations necessarily consistent with one another. Thus, if we wish to generalize about attitudes from measured items of behavior, whether words or actions, we must obtain our measurements under standardized conditions, and confine our generalizations to the type of behavior measured. And since it is plainly impossible to observe overt behavior under controlled conditions on a nationwide scale, measurement of the attitudes of the society as a whole must rely entirely on the verbal expression of opinions, feelings and beliefs.

If it were flatly true that "actions speak louder [that is, more revealingly] than words," this limitation would be crippling indeed. But, not infrequently, verbal behavior indicates attitudes as reliably as do overt actions or more so. The point has been persuasively argued by Murphy, Murphy and Newcomb:

Actions are no more inherently "valid" in the first place than words. . . . Actions are frequently designed to distort or conceal "true" attitude quite as fully as verbal behavior. . . . *All* behavior is subject to modification in the process of execution from considerations of courtesy, expediency or other social pressures. . . . When verbal behavior is used to distort or conceal "true" attitudes, the distortion commonly *conforms to everyday behavior*. The reasons for concealing "true" attitudes are the same for both verbal and "overt" behavior. If conditions of secrecy and preferably of anonymity are observed, there is more reason to expect free and complete expression of attitudes through words, thus freed from social pressures, than from behaviors which are open to all beholders. . . . Observable behavior presents a weaker case for validity than "merely verbal" behavior under proper safeguards. And, finally, it may be observed that a man's categorical agreement or disagreement with a rather strongly stated opinion . . . is in everyday life regarded (if the man is sincere) as a *significant* part of his behavior. There seems to be no reason why this behavior should suddenly become *non-significant* when it is made the subject of careful inquiry, particularly if motives for insincerity are reduced to a minimum.[10]

Since public-opinion studies generally maintain anonymity, we see no reason to doubt, in principle, that their findings indicate how people actually think about social issues. This is not to say, of course, that poll results are entirely accurate. All inquiries are subject to error, and opinion research, with its large numbers of investigators working, more often than not, under minimal supervision, may well yield less precise data than other methods. Our interpretations therefore will follow a conservative course. We will take percentage distributions of responses as approximations, not absolutes; only when differences between groups are especially compelling will we treat them as firm data. This procedure may strike some readers as overly skeptical; but, given the degree of possible (indeed, demonstrated) error in large-scale opinion polling, it would seem to be the only realistic way of dealing with the evidence.

The factor of polling error apart, how revealing are the poll questions themselves? Our data derive from questions of the most varied types. In our opinion, no one type possesses inherent virtues denied to others. At the same time, we recognize that the many formulations employed over the years are not equally meaningful; some come to grips with the issue at hand, while others may be vague or tangential. Therefore, whenever we believe a question to have been inappropriately or inconclusively framed, we will qualify our interpretation of the results.

Contemporary attitude research tends to rely on scales rather than single questions as a means of empirically assessing the unitary nature of the attitude investigated and of increasing the precision of measurements.[11] In nationwide studies, such scales have been only sparsely employed; they therefore are rare in our collection. This is hardly a serious defect, however. Superior as they are, even attitude scales can measure only specific aspects of a general problem, and attitudes toward the Jew, with their manifold dimensions, are not necessarily best measured by such devices. Indeed, many of our concerns are such that it is difficult to see how scales could have been employed at all. Since, however, the questions frequently approach the same issue from various directions, the data add up to an assessment of feelings at various levels not unlike those which are obtained elsewhere through the use of scales—quite possibly a more comprehensive assessment, since it focuses less single-mindedly on isolated aspects of a given problem.

Is there an Over-all Attitude?

The third and last working assumption requiring discussion is simply that the object of our inquiry exists. We are setting out to measure the American public's general attitudes toward Jews; but at this point in our explorations, the existence of such over-all attitudes is a mere hypothesis, not a proven fact. It is at least conceivable that Americans do not respond in a coherent way toward Jews as a group, but merely react in disjointed fashion to discrete aspects of the Jewish group as they encounter them.

What distinguishes an attitude, whether hostile or friendly, from such isolated reactions is that it consists of several components which can be measured separately and are more or less consistent with one another. In the case of attitudes toward ethnic groups, Harding and his associates distinguish three components: (1) the cognitive, consisting of perceptions, beliefs and expectations regarding the group; (2) the affective, comprising friendliness, hostility and other feelings which the group inspires; and (3) the conative, which contains prevailing opinions on how "members of the group should be treated in specific social contexts." [12]

To determine, then, whether an over-all attitude toward Jews exists in America—whether, for example, there is such a thing as generalized anti-Semitism—we must first measure separately the cognitive, affective and conative dimensions of attitudes toward Jews in a variety of contexts and then estimate how well they agree. We may hazard a guess that the measurements will turn out to be more or less in harmony, since most research to date suggests that intergroup attitudinal components tend to be congruent, especially where Jews are the object.[13] If so, we will be convinced that Americans' varied reactions to the Jew stem from a unified structure which we may designate as their general attitude. If, on the other hand, we should chance to find the components grossly inconsistent with one another, we would conclude that the American response to Jews was fragmented and confined to momentary reactions or isolated concerns.

The evidence assembled in the chapters that follow is well suited, in our opinion, to settle the issue. It is diversified enough to guarantee that we will in fact be measuring generalized attitudes toward Jews if such a thing exists.

The data cover a great variety of specific responses; altogether, there are over 250 questions, some of them asked more than a dozen times—a larger and more varied body of information on the subject than has been assembled in any other study we know. The cognitive, affective and conative aspects of the problem are all covered in ample if not equal detail, and the data for each are sufficiently broad to warrant generalizations from convergent findings, if any, to anti-Semitism as such.[14]

Like all attitudes, anti-Semitism varies in intensity and salience among individuals. Larger numbers subscribe to its mild than to its severe forms. This variation furnishes us with a useful criterion by which change may be measured. Quantitative shifts from the more to the less extreme positions or vice versa actually are our principal indices of change. This being so, we are fortunate to have at hand a wide variety of questions which gauge different intensities as well as different dimensions of prejudice—questions which provide, not only samplings of the population, but also a sampling of specific attitudes in various projected contexts and under manifold verbal stimuli. In our opinion, the variety and number of questions ensure that we are in fact measuring anti-Semitism, and are what chiefly gives our study its value.

Comparability of Samples over Time

The measurement of change over time, with which this book is mainly concerned, poses certain problems in comparability. If we were working under experimental conditions, we could easily maintain a uniform basis for our explorations. We would call on the same persons in poll after poll, ask the same questions each time, keep the psychological circumstances precisely identical and hope that most of the respondents would survive to the end of our twenty-five year experiment. Our data, however, having been collected for short-term practical use, are drawn from successive population samples; and if we are to arrive at an undistorted picture of attitude trends, we must be sure that the different samples were as nearly alike as possible in all relevant respects.

In fact, they are less uniform than we might wish. About halfway through the period under study, sampling procedures underwent two major improvements, which somewhat altered the composition of respondent groups. In our comparisons over time, we will have to consider how much these alterations may have impaired the comparability of the earlier and the more recent data.

The first of the two procedural changes involved the methods by which samples were obtained. Until 1948, opinion-research agencies did not employ probability sampling as a general method, but used what was known as quota sampling. The selection of individual respondents was left to the interviewers, who were merely instructed to fill specified quotas in various demographic categories. This method has been much criticized because the samples it produced were far less representative than those secured by probability methods—or even by partial probability procedures that were not followed down to the actual selection of respondents.

Quota sampling tends to overselect the more accessible households and persons. The very rich and very poor are usually underrepresented, as are reluctant or socially isolated individuals. In our opinion, these groups are likely to contain relatively high proportions of anti-Semites. If so, it follows that the prevalence of anti-Semitism in the nation as a whole may have been understated in the surveys up to 1948, causing subsequent increases in anti-Semitism to look larger in the statistics than they really were, and causing decreases to look smaller.

A second procedural change, occurring about 1950, had to do with the population from which respondents were drawn. Up to this time, they had been taken from among voters (specifically, from among persons who had voted in the last election before the particular survey); in the years that followed, they were selected from the entire adult population.

Voters as a group are not necessarily representative of the nation as a whole where attitudes toward Jews are concerned. As a number of studies have shown, people who vote tend to be more sophisticated, better informed and less isolated than others.[15] Given these qualities, it seems reasonable to assume that they also are less likely to be hostile toward minority groups. If so, it follows again that the prevalence of anti-Semitism in the nation as a whole may have been understated in the earlier data.

A further seeming complication stems from the circumstance that the voting population differs from the general public in purely demographic respects—for example, that it contains disproportionately few women, Negroes and uneducated persons. It might be thought that these peculiarities made the voter samples of the older polls seriously unrepresentative of the public as a whole where attitudes toward Jews were concerned; but a careful analysis prepared in 1940 for one of the poll-sponsoring agencies indicates that this was not so. The various segments of the population turned out to differ little in their attitudes toward Jews, so that the overrepresentation or underrepresentation of this or that subgroup did not appreciably distort the over-all picture:

. . . While the samples used in the various polls are not truly representative of the total population of the United States, the results have not been appreciably affected or biased. This is because, first, the variation of the sample is not in general very great, and is in one direction as much as in the other, and, second, and more important, the response to the questions does not vary appreciably by locality, age, sex, religion, nationality, income, employment, politics or section [of the country].[16]

Comparability of Questions and Questioning Methods

Variation in the choice of issues and the formulation of survey questions confronts us with added obstacles in assessing opinion trends over the years. As has often been demonstrated, even the slightest of changes in a question may produce an alteration in responses. Thus, when a question is differently phrased in successive surveys, we cannot tell whether discrepancies in the results indicate a real change in attitude or not. The surveys on which our inquiry is based, having been originally devised to serve shifting programmatic needs, do not always come up to the standards of uniformity desirable in trend analysis. Where they do, we will confidently accept the results as facts, not artifacts; but where the wording has been changed even slightly, we will have to estimate the effect on the response. Indeed, in many cases, the phrasing or substance of questions on a given topic has been so decisively altered from one survey to the next that we cannot safely draw any general conclusions from differences in the results.

Fortunately, this lack of uniformity in the stimuli is offset by an impressive degree of consistency in the settings in which responses were secured. It is axiomatic that a man may answer the same question in various ways, depending on who asks it, why and with what emphasis; replies are wholly comparable only if obtained in similar, carefully controlled psychological situations.[17] On this all-important test, opinion research scores high. In their essentials, the conditions surrounding the responses made—the chief variable intervening between a person's attitude and the opinion he expresses—are largely standardized. Consistently, an individual answers questions posed by a stranger who is trained to ask them in a particular way for the explicit purpose of taking a public-opinion survey.[18]

All of the data in this study have been elicited under these general conditions. True, they were gathered by different agencies, whose practices varied somewhat, particularly during the early days of opinion research; but in our estimation the similarities in the over-all psychological situation far outweigh these procedural discrepancies.[19] Where we have reason to believe that differences in method may have colored the results, we will so indicate.

The Problem of Frankness

Public-opinion researchers have often been criticized for trying to survey attitudes supposedly not measurable by survey techniques. According to this view, polls can probe only those issues which the public considers fit for discussion; they cannot make respondents speak out frankly on "sensitive" problems. Impersonal interviews, it is argued, produce only the most superficial and stereotyped replies, and only those deemed socially acceptable.

The argument deserves discussion, for polling admittedly is not a perfect procedure for assessing attitudes which respondents may hesitate to express candidly. Feelings about ethnic minorities are often of this kind; responses concerning Jews, for example, have repeatedly been found to bear marks of inhibition. Still, we remain unconvinced that our findings are materially distorted by this factor, because the direction of the error, if any, is probably fairly constant. While respondents may well disavow prejudices they do possess, they hardly are likely to voice hostilities they do not feel. Insincerity, in other words, consistently causes the prevalence of hostile attitudes to be understated, never to be exaggerated. Thus, comparisons of such attitudes at different times should not be vitiated by this factor.

It may be, of course, that inhibition of prejudiced expressions has fluctuated in extent if not in direction. That avowals of anti-Semitism should have become more acceptable than a generation ago seems most unlikely to us; not only do research findings cast doubt on this hypothesis, but so do the improved actual status of minority groups and their more favorable representation in the mass media today.[20] A change of the opposite kind seems more plausible; outright bigotry may well have been driven somewhat farther underground in recent years. If so, then recent figures may understate the actual level of prejudice in the society, making decreases since earlier days look larger than they are, and increases smaller.

A recent growth, if any, in the inhibition of prejudice could scarcely have been large; if it had been, the inconclusive kinds of response ("don't know," "uncertain," no answer) in which the less than candid presumably take refuge would have shown a steeper rise than they actually do in most of our data. But even a small increase would be of interest in two respects. First, by its very smallness and elusiveness it would illustrate our earlier warning that apparent reductions of hostility to the tune of a few percentage points should not be too readily interpreted as actual fact. And, second, growing reluctance to betray anti-Semitism to poll takers would in itself be a noteworthy signal of changed behavior—an acknowledgment that free expression of ethnic prejudices was increasingly frowned upon by the public. If this is what has happened, it should be viewed as a real gain, not merely as an artifact which distorts the data.[21]

To be sure, our findings do not fully illuminate latent anti-Semitism in all its forms, and do not always tell us whether it has changed in prevalence or only in overtness. Part of the public's feelings about Jews undoubtedly is beyond the reach of our methods and could be explored only through prolonged, intensive interviews conducted by highly trained investigators—a difficult and costly undertaking if attempted on a nationwide scale. But as long as we remain mindful of the limitations under which we work, we are in no danger of claiming too much for our measurements of change. To trace the American public's attitude toward Jews through a critical quarter-century is a worthwhile undertaking, we believe, even if it must rely on less than perfect data.

Analysis According to Population Subgroups

The chief purpose of these pages is to assess the trend of attitudes toward Jews among the American people as a whole. In the accepted mode of public-opinion research, an attempt has also been made to relate differences of attitude to the social and demographic characteristics of different population groups, because such analyses sometimes help to account for opinion changes. However, these explorations have been undertaken on a limited scale only.[22] Any exhaustive inquiry would have far exceeded the resources available for this project. Besides, tabulations of the older studies are no longer available for reanalyzing, so that any such inquiry must rely, for better or worse, on whatever subgroup analyses were prepared at the time of the polls. Most of the evidence, such as it is, will be found in Appendix I. In addition, some comparisons of other subgroups have been included in various parts of the text, notably in Chapters VII, VIII and IX.

NOTES

1. George Eaton Simpson and J. Milton Yinger, *Racial and Cultural Minorities* (rev. ed.; New York: Harper & Row, 1958), pp. 288–289.

2. This view has not remained without dissent. See Daniel Katz and Ezra Stotland, "A Preliminary Statement to a Theory of Attitude Structure and Change," in Sigmund Koch, editor, *Psychology: A Study of a Science*, III (New York: McGraw-Hill Book Co., 1959), p. 446.

3. Thus Earl Raab and Seymour M. Lipset declare: "Prejudiced attitudes do not form the substance of 'our national problem of prejudice.' . . . People who actually work with Negroes, especially as equals, develop attitudes favorable towards working with Negroes. People who actually are neighbors of Negroes develop attitudes favorable towards being neighbors of Negroes." *Prejudice and Society* (New York: Anti-Defamation League, 1959), pp. 3, 22. We need only add that persons with a favorable attitude toward Negroes obviously are more often willing to work with them or live near them.

4. *Op. cit.*, p. 466.

5. For data on progress thus attained, see Melvin Tumin, *Desegregation: Resistance and Readiness* (Princeton, N.J.: Princeton University Press, 1958). A report on civil-rights demonstrations at Jackson, Mississippi, in June 1963, stated: "Recent events indicate it is questionable that anything but token racial change can be achieved without considerable modification of the attitudes of whites toward Negroes" (Claude Sitton in *The New York Times*, Review of the Week, June 16, 1963).

6. See, for example, Lindsey Rogers, *The Pollsters* (New York: Alfred A. Knopf, 1949); Quinn McNemar, "Opinion-Attitude Methodology," *Psychological Bulletin,* XLIII: 289–374 (1946).

7. In our opinion, social science cannot limit itself to the study of problems for which it has precise methods of measurement. To do so, as Abraham Maslow has noted, is to adopt the posture of the drunk who looked for his wallet, not where he had lost it, but under a street lamp, "because the light was better there." *Motivation and Personality* (New York: Harper & Bros., 1954), p. 16.

8. Bert F. Green posits three attitude universes: "spontaneous verbal," "elicited verbal" and "action" attitudes. "Attitude Measurements," in Gardner Lindzey, editor, *Handbook of Social Psychology,* I (Cambridge, Mass.: Addison-Wesley Publishing Co., 1954), p. 340. It is, of course, the second of these that are represented in public-opinion studies.

9. Isidor Chein and Others, editors, "Consistency and Inconsistency in Intergroup Relations," *Journal of Social Issues,* V, No. 3 (1949).

10. Gardner Murphy, L. B. Murphy and Theodore Newcomb, *Experimental Social Psychology* (New York: Harper & Bros., 1937), p. 912.

11. See Matilda Riley, John W. Riley and Others, *Sociological Studies in Scale Analysis* (New Brunswick, N.J.: Rutgers University Press, 1954).

12. John Harding and Others, "Prejudice and Ethnic Relations," in Lindzey, *op. cit.,* II, 1073.

13. See Eugene L. Hartley, *Problems in Prejudice* (New York: Kings Crown Press, 1946), p. 117; studies by Donald T. Campbell, Bruno Bettelheim and Morris Janowitz, and Theodor W. Adorno, cited in Harding, *op. cit.,* p. 1031.

14. We have fewer explicit data on the affective component than on the others because they are less readily obtained in the typical opinion-poll situation. But feelings about Jews are incidentally manifested in the responses to many questions dealing with other matters.

15. Certain data from the 1950s and early 1960s indicate that voters did not differ greatly from non-voters in their attitudes toward Jews. See Charles Herbert Stember, *Education and Attitude Change* (New York: Institute of Human Relations Press, 1961), pp, 36, 67; Table 124 in Appendix I, below. But the same could hardly have been true two decades earlier, when the politically sophisticated were much more involved in the electoral process.

16. Maurice R. Davie, *Report on the 1938–39 Polls on Anti-Semitism* (unpublished typescript; American Jewish Committee, Department of Public Reaction, 1940), p. 60. However, the exclusive use of voters as respondents in the older polls creates certain distortions when early and recent attitudes *within a given population subgroup* are compared (see Appendix I).

17. "The individual's reaction to a given object is a dual function of (*a*) his enduring attitudes and beliefs about the object and (*b*) the nature of the immediate situation. As the situation varies, his reaction toward the object will also show variation, even though his belief or attitude toward the object may be thought of as invariant." David Krech and Richard S. Crutchfield, *Theory and Problems of Social Psychology* (New York: McGraw-Hill Book Co., 1948), p. 208.

18. The total error arising from differences among interviewers working for a given agency has been found surprisingly small. See Herbert H. Hyman and Others, *Interviewing in Social Research* (Chicago: University of Chicago Press, 1954), pp. 225–274.

19. For an estimate of the nature and extent of differences in data secured by different agencies, see Charles Herbert Stember, *The Effect of Field Procedures on Public Opinion Data* (dissertation; Ann Arbor, Mich.: University Microfilms, 1955).

20. During the prewar years, the support Nazi Germany found among certain Americans may have served to increase the acceptability of openly anti-Jewish feeling in this country, but this influence could hardly have survived America's entry into the war.

21. As Katz and Stotland have noted: "The fact that private and public situations with differing sanctions may permit initial differences in private and public attitudes toward the same objects has important implications for social change. The propagandist constantly seeks to add the sanction of the universality of opinion for the publicly expressed attitude. . . . If people can be made to express certain attitudes in public, then they will be under pressure to bring their private views into line." *Op. cit.*, p. 445.

22. In an earlier monograph, we undertook a comparable set of correlations in full detail. See Stember, *op. cit.*

II

Images of the Jew

HOW JEWS APPEAR to non-Jews has commanded more attention in public-opinion surveys than any other of anti-Semitism's many facets. Nearly half of all poll questions concerning Jews have dealt with this topic. Though discrimination and organized anti-Semitic activity have markedly decreased in recent years, concern with the prevalence of stereotypes regarding Jews has not; and future research on anti-Semitism is sure to remain devoted in large part to the ever-challenging task of trying "to see ourselves as others see us."

The attention lavished on the Jew as he looks to the public—rather than as he really is or as he may appear to experts—reflects the growing emphasis on the role of cognition in social psychology, both theoretical and applied. In recent decades, it has become clear that we cannot understand people's attitudes unless we know their perceptions. Thus, Jews and those who know them well are often unable to see why anti-Jewish prejudice and discrimination survive in certain quarters, when the Jewish group has changed so radically over the years as to become virtually indistinguishable from the rest of the population in many of its habits, manners, values and attributes; but as soon as we discern what might be called the publicly perceived Jew and the ways, if any, in which he differs from most real Jews, the survival of anti-Jewish attitudes becomes psychologically intelligible.

Krech and Crutchfield, in 1948, described beliefs and attitudes as parts of a single structure, viewing the former as the cognitive embodiment of the latter.[1] Four years later, Solomon Asch asserted: "There cannot . . . be a theory of attitudes . . . that is not grounded in an examination of their cognitive foundation. . . . There can be no change of attitude without a corresponding change in knowledge or belief." [2] By 1954, as noted earlier,

Harding and his co-workers were presenting cognition as one of the major dimensions of intergroup attitudes.[3] But in this, as in so many other cases, research had long preceded theoretical formulation: Back in 1933, Katz and Braly had sought to determine what stereotypes of various ethnic groups were current among college students,[4] and their effort was followed by many similar investigations.

Thanks to the precedents thus set, it has become normal practice in research about ethnic attitudes to measure how the groups under study are actually perceived. Questions designed to determine how Jews looked "from the outside" have regularly been included in the nationwide surveys of attitudes toward Jews which began in the 1930s, and have proved continually fruitful in accounting for the persistence of anti-Semitism. There have been more or less unstructured attempts to determine in what ways Jews seemed "different," as well as examinations of specific, highly charged images—some of them entrenched in Western culture for hundreds or even thousands of years, others transient in nature, deriving from the happenings and conditions of the moment. In the present chapter and the two that follow, we will focus chiefly on the underlying, relatively timeless concepts. The specific notions in which these concepts come to the surface will for the most part be examined in later chapters, against the background of actual events.

Race, Religion or Nationality?

In order to interpret prevailing notions of what Jews are like, we must know how the public views the nature of the Jewish group. During the period under study, were Jews defined primarily in religious terms, in ethnic ones or in some other way? Surveys took up this question about the time the war ended, and again in 1962. Not surprisingly, the issue turned out to be highly complex; the results plainly mirrored the difficulties of measurement.

In 1944 and again in 1945, respondents were asked whether they considered American Jews "a religious group, like Methodists, Catholics and Quakers," or "a nationality group, like Poles, Swedes and Italians" (Table 1). The two sets of responses were quite similar and thus would appear reliable. In both years, nationality was most frequently named, religion somewhat less often. Few of the persons questioned seemed to have any difficulty in defining Jews as the one or the other; fewer than 10 per cent said they did not know.

Quite a different result, however, was obtained in 1946, when three alternatives were offered: "a religious group, like Catholics or Methodists," "a nationality, like French or Italians" and "a race, like Negroes or Indians" (Table 2). From one-third to more than two-fifths now said Jews were a race, while "nationality" became the least frequently named category. Even more noteworthy, the perceptions reflected in the replies turned out to be

Table 1   Perception of Jews as Religious or Nationality Group (1944–45)

"Do you think of the Jews in this country as being a religious group, like Methodists, Catholics and Quakers—or as being a nationality group, like Poles, Swedes and Italians?"

	Per cent	
	1944	1945
Religious group	32	34
Nationality group	49	47
Both	6	8
Neither	4	2
Don't know	9	9

SOURCES: N9, 11. (For explanation of these keys and similar ones throughout the study, see Appendix II, pp. 231–234.)

Table 2   Perception of Jews as Racial, Nationality or Religious Group (1946, 1962)

"Some people think of the Jews as a race, like Negroes or Indians, others think of them as a nationality, like French or Italians, while others think of them as a religious group, like Catholics or Methodists. How do you usually think of Jews?" (Sequence of alternatives varied; see below.)

	Per cent				
	"As a race, as a nationality or as a religious group"		"As a religious group, as a nationality or as a race"	
	1946	1962	1946	1962
Race	42	23	33	21
Nationality	22	28	26	31
Religious group	35	45	44	38
Don't know	5	6	3	10
	104[a]	102[a]	106[a]	100

[a] Totals over 100 are due to multiple answers.
SOURCES: O17; G38.

highly unstable: Responses were found to fluctuate when the sequence of the alternatives was varied. Thus, either "race" or "religious group" would draw the largest number of replies, depending on which was mentioned first; and "religious group" was named considerably more frequently than in the 1944 and 1945 surveys when listed first but not when listed last.

Since the matter at issue did not directly relate to current events, the discrepancies between the data obtained in 1946 and those gathered only one or two years earlier could hardly have reflected actual widespread shifts of opinion. In 1962, however, the 1946 poll was repeated, and now the results registered an unmistakable change (Table 2). No matter how the alternatives were arranged, fewer than a quarter of all respondents thought of Jews as a race, while somewhat more than formerly described them as a nationality or said they did not know. Only the proportion who considered Jews a religious group remained substantially as before, still ranging around 40 per cent and, unlike the rest, still fluctuating with the sequence of possible answers. Even here, however, one change had occurred: The direction of the fluctuations had become reversed. "Religious group" now evoked the largest response when listed last; when it appeared at the head of the list, it drew fewer replies, and the other categories (including "don't know") showed an increase.

The fact that stands out most in the findings just reported is the marked decrease in the perception of Jews as a race between 1946 and 1962. In interpreting the data, we must therefore ask, first, why anyone should think of Jews as a race and, second, what positive or negative evaluations may be associated with this view.

In our view, respondents who defined Jews as a race are likely to have been prompted by a hidden difficulty in the question, which the reader may have noticed. Each of the three alternatives offered has a certain plausibility: Jews are predominantly of the same religion; they once were (and those who live in Israel again are) a nation; and a widely known if discredited ideology describes them as members of a "Semitic race." But other, more nearly accurate alternatives—for example, "an ethnic or cultural group"— are not mentioned; and by suggesting parallel examples the question obscures the fact that Jews constitute a category of a unique kind.

We believe that this omission accounts in large measure for the configuration of the findings. Some of the multiple answers and "don't knows" undoubtedly represent reactions to the unrealistic nature of the alternatives offered.[5] Even more important, respondents unable to choose between available categories in the abstract may well have found answers suggested to them by the illustrative examples furnished ("a race, like Negroes or Indians," and so forth).[6] Thus, if a respondent said Jews were a race, he may have meant: "Jews are not like Frenchmen or like Methodists; they are more like Negroes."

In what sense would Jews impress a substantial proportion of the population as being similar to Negroes? Physical appearance may be part of the reason; Jews frequently are dark-haired and swarthy, and are typically thought of as being so. But a more convincing hypothesis is that the respondent took his cue from society. He realized that in certain crucial respects Jews were treated, not like Frenchmen or Methodists, but like Negroes; he knew, for example, that the majority discriminated against them in various ways, avoided close personal relations with them and frowned on intermarriage. Having just been reminded that Negroes were a race, he concluded that Jews also were one. Thus the image many Americans held of the Jew would seem to depend in large part on the treatment he received.[7]

This brings us to second question: Are unfavorable images specifically associated with the racial view of Jews? In Western societies, the connotations of minority racial status are predominantly negative. Racial ideologies usually claim superior qualities for the prevailing majority, defined as "white," "Aryan," "Nordic" or "Anglo-Saxon," as the case may be, and assume that both superior and inferior "racial" attributes are biologically fixed, hence unalterable. Thus, the baneful pseudo-scientific theories which during the last hundred years have largely supplanted religion as the basis of anti-Jewish movements in Europe are almost invariably built around the myth of an "Aryan race" of inborn creative genius, contrasted with a spiritually inferior, degenerate or diabolical "Semitic race." In the United States the concept of race has long been bound up with the status of the Negro minority, particularly with the natural inferiority imputed to Negroes by way of rationalizing slavery or segregation.

Thus, we might reasonably assume that describing Jews as a race was equivalent, in at least some instances, to viewing them with a degree of contempt;[8] and to the extent that this was so, we might interpret the decline in the notion of a "Jewish race" as a sign of decreased anti-Semitism.[9] The question is: Just how valid is this assumption? How closely is the perception of Jewry as a race, religious group or nationality linked with anti-Semitism or its absence?

Our data for 1962 are the only ones that permit us to apply a test; and here the results are not conclusive. When we cross-tabulate the three categories of the 1962 response with certain measures of anti-Semitism, we do find respondents who thought of Jews as a religious group less often hostile toward them than those who considered them a race; but, contrary to what might have been expected, the differences for the most part are far from great (Table 3). They are smaller still between those who saw Jews as a race and as a nationality. Similar proportions of all three groups said Jews had only admirable traits; and even among those who viewed them as a race, almost three-fourths rejected the commonest of all anti-Semitic images: the stock figure of the dishonest Jewish businessman.

At least in 1962, then, the idea of a "Jewish race" was not markedly correlated with hostility toward Jews. We must note, however, that a stronger correlation may well have existed at the time of the earlier study. It is quite possible that the survey question did not carry exactly the same import in 1946 as in 1962. By the latter year, thanks to the dramatic lowering of anti-Jewish barriers during the interval, the public probably was a good deal more familiar with Jews and their ways. For the same reason, the status of Jews now differed much more obviously from that of Negroes. The respondents of 1962, then, may well have relied less on proffered illustrations of "race," "religion" and "nationality" than those of 1946, and more

Table 3 Perception of Jews as Racial, Religious or Nationality Group, by Various Measures of Freedom from Anti-Semitism (1962)

	Per cent of those who think of Jews as		
	Race (24 per cent of total sample)[a]	Nationality (32 per cent of total sample)[a]	Religious group (45 per cent of total sample)[a]
Do not think Jews have too much power	75	79	83
Think Jewish businessmen as honest as others	74	80	96
Would vote against anti-Semitic candidate	62	62	72
Say Jews have:			
Admirable traits only	29	34	33
Objectionable traits only	9	7	3
Both	17	18	25
Neither	45	41	39

[a] Percentages recalculated with "don't know" omitted.

SOURCE: G38.

on their own perceptions and experiences—a change which in itself might be counted as a gain against prejudice.

Alleged Objectionable Traits

The supposed typical qualities of Jews, both good and bad, were favorite topics of surveys throughout the period under study. During the prewar years, open-end questions were repeatedly asked to determine what were the salient characteristics associated with Jews in the mind of the public. About three-fifths of the population consistently thought Jews as a group had objectionable traits, according to five polls taken between March 1938 and April 1940 (O1, 2, 4, 7, 8).[10] Roughly the same proportion credited Jews with admirable qualities, though the figures were less consistent, varying from 67 per cent in March 1938 to 51 per cent the following November. Throughout the two sets of polls, no more than 5 per cent were unable to answer the questions.

Just which of the Jews' alleged characteristics were considered objectionable was the subject of two surveys undertaken in 1938, and one each in 1940 and 1946 (Tables 4–6). The two taken in 1938 used the same question and code and obtained similar results, indicating that the data are reliable. In 1940 the questions were put somewhat differently, and in 1946

Table 4 Qualities Found Objectionable in Jews (1938)

(March–May 1938:) *"What qualities do you object to in Jews?"*

(November 1938:) *"Are there any qualities about Jews to which you object?"* (If "yes":) *"What qualities do you object to in Jews?"*

	Per cent of those who say they object to certain qualities	
	March–May 1938 (65 per cent of total sample)[a]	November 1938 (58 per cent of total sample)
Greed	21	22
Dishonesty	20	20
Aggressiveness	16	15
Clannishness	11	12
Selfishness, lack of consideration	11	8
Loudness	9	5
Overbearing attitude	6	6
Discrimination against non-Jews	4	4
Uncleanness	4	2
Peculiar religious ways	3	2
Lack of culture	3	3
Drive for power	2	1
Poor standard of living	1	1
Other	5	3

[a] Two waves combined.

SOURCES: O3, 4.

Table 5 Qualities Found Objectionable in Jews (1940)

"Are there any objectionable qualities which you think Jews generally have to a greater extent than other people?" (If "yes":) *"What qualities do you object to in Jews?"*

	Per cent of those who say they object to certain qualities (63 per cent of total sample)
Unscrupulousness	51
Aggressiveness	19
Clannishness; discrimination against non-Jews	17
Lack of culture or good breeding	16
Selfishness	6
Appearance	6
Lack of respect for others' religions	1
Other	6

SOURCE: O8.

Table 6 Qualities Found Objectionable in Jews (1946)

"What is the main thing that people dislike about Jews?"

	Per cent
Domineering nature	32
Dishonest or unethical conduct	19
Money uppermost thought	17
Money-making ability	14
Control of business	8
General dislike	8
No dislike	5

SOURCE: O17.

differently again, so that the findings cannot be exactly compared with each other, nor with those of 1938.[11] Yet four distinct clusters of supposed objectionable traits recur plainly enough:

(1) Jews were thought to be overly concerned about money, unscrupulous about getting it and highly successful in doing so. Their greed, it was believed, led them to seek and frequently gain control of businesses by dishonest or at least questionable means.

(2) Jews supposedly were "pushy," that is, domineering, aggressive, obstinate, lacking in respect for the rights and status of others, selfish and self-seeking.

(3) Jews were believed to be clannish: to stick together, to cover up for one another and to discriminate against non-Jews. They were charged with being excessively conscious of their own group and its interests.

(4) Jews were said to be unrefined, ill-mannered and unclean. They supposedly lacked the middle-class virtues of gentility and good breeding. Their appearance, habits and religious customs were considered foreign and generally repellent.

According to a rough estimate based on the data in our tables, over half of the population during the 1930s and 1940s seems to have thought of Jews as greedy in more or less the sense just described; perhaps one-third— no doubt consisting partly of the same individuals—considered them "pushy"; something like one-quarter subscribed to some notion of clannishness among Jews, and another quarter to ideas of Jewish grossness.

What is perhaps most striking about these images, taken together, is their strongly traditional character. None is new or original; most if not all date back hundreds or even thousands of years. For example, the figure of the "greedy Jew" was already centuries old when Shakespeare gave it what became its best-known embodiment in the person of Shylock; the notion that Jews are loyal only to one another may be found in the writings of Tacitus; and the myth that they are somehow physically repulsive or unwholesome can be traced back to the third century B.C., when they were said to be descendants of lepers. In short, the common twentieth-century prejudices concerning the nature of Jews are only superficially specific to their time and place; they are essentially incarnations of beliefs that have always been present beneath the surface of Western culture and have periodically come into the open, with plausible modifications according to the conditions of the moment.[12]

"Admirable" versus "Objectionable" Qualities

Let us now see what traits supposedly characteristic of Jews were considered admirable by the American people. Our evidence derives from four surveys, three undertaken in 1938 and one in 1940 (Table 7). The data

Table 7   Qualities Found Admirable in Jews (1938–40)

(March 1938:) *"What qualities do you admire in Jews?"*

(May 1938 through April 1940:) *"Are there any admirable qualities which you think Jews generally have to a greater extent than other people?"* (If "yes":) *"What qualities do you admire in Jews?"*

Per cent of those who say they admire certain qualities

	March 1938 (67 per cent of total sample)	May 1938 (58 per cent of total sample)	November 1938 (51 per cent of total sample)	April 1940 (58 per cent of total sample)
Ability in business or finance	31	18	25	33
Persistence, determination, ambition	20	13	11	15
Intellectual attainments	18	10	13	13
Racial or religious loyalty	16	21	24	29
Thrift, financial independence	13	11	10	*
Loyalty to wife and family	12	21	15	16
Kindness, generosity, charitableness	5	9	8	*
Integrity of character	3	2	2	*
Loyalty	3	5	5	*
Personal neatness or good taste	2	1	0	*
Obedience to law	1	1	3	*
Other	2	10	2	16

* Not coded.
SOURCES: O1, 2, 4, 8.

seem to be less reliable than where objectionable qualities were concerned: The proportions mentioning various traits fluctuated more from survey to survey, and the range of traits mentioned was altogether rather wide, as is shown by the varied nature of the code categories. Still, certain clusters of ideas are plainly evident:

(1) Jews were believed to be successful in making money, capable in money matters generally, thrifty and financially independent.

(2) Jews were considered persistent, determined, ambitious, anxious to get ahead and successful at doing so.

(3) Jews were held to be intelligent, interested in things of the mind and intellectually competent.

(4) Jews were credited with being exceptionally loyal to their families and their fellow Jews generally.

The first and fourth of these beliefs each were encountered among roughly 20 per cent of all respondents, the second and third each among approximately 10 per cent. The other traits listed in the table presumably did not constitute widespread images; none of these was mentioned by more than 5 per cent of the total population.

If we now compare the so-called objectionable and admirable traits, we observe several clear parallels. What is perceived as clannishness or greed in one context, we find, may be seen as loyalty or business ability in another. Praiseworthy determination and unpleasant aggressiveness turn out to be two sides of the same coin. What this means is that, at least during the years just before the war, a great many Americans had a fairly uniform idea of the supposed attributes of Jews, though they evaluated them in different ways.

Most prominent among both "good" and "bad" images was that of the Jew as an "economic man"—an individual desirous and well qualified to get ahead financially, eager to compete in the race for economic success and willing to employ all possible means toward this end.[13] Second in frequency was the perception of the Jew as assertive, persistent or aggressive—a trait somewhat more frequently evaluated as bad than as good. The two ideas evidently were interdependent, and may well have been inseparable in the minds of many persons, whether for better or worse. The image of the "economic man" refers to the Jew's supposed goals, the image of the aggressive individual to means by which he pursues these goals; but it may be questioned whether goals and means were always sharply distinguished.

We may find some wry amusement in the fact that aggressiveness and business acumen, taken separately, are considered praiseworthy in our society, and yet may add up to an image that evokes strong hostility in many observers. The same is true of group consciousness, which, as we have seen, may be evaluated positively as loyalty or negatively as clannishness. The notion of the Jews as a self-segregated, strongly cohesive group—an image almost as prevalent as that of the Jew as "economic man"—adds a new dimension to the picture we have begun to discern. The Jew was apparently thought to seek financial gain for the benefit of his own group, without regard to the rest of society. He was believed to be neither a thorough individualist in the "rugged" American tradition nor an altruist, but part of a limited circle whose members were dedicated to one another's welfare and advancement.

The intellectual capacities and attainments with which Jews were credited in favorable evaluations have no direct negative counterpart in the present data. However, there is reason to believe that the common notion of the shrewdness and trickiness of Jews (included, presumably, with "dishonesty" or "unscrupulousness" in the present tables[14]) was a negative interpretation of these qualities. In the context of the Jew's perceived goals and means, the ample mental endowment attributed to him may well have been viewed as a weapon for self-interest or group advancement, rather than as a tool for purely intellectual pursuits—a notion which must have lent an additional threatening aspect to his image.

Conversely, the hostile perception of the Jew as an alien, unrefined or unrestrained person, with whom it is best not to associate, lacks an explicit favorable counterpart in our data. We may hazard a guess, however, that this counterpart might be found in the image of the Jew as a picturesque embodiment of solemn Biblical tradition amid the turmoil of the modern world[15] or, alternatively, as a worldly-wise cosmopolitan who confronts life with more sophistication and gusto and gives his emotions freer rein than non-Jews supposedly do.[16]

It may be asked why we have tried to reassemble into a composite portrait the discrete images laboriously separated in the public-opinion studies from which our data are taken. We believe that such separation, though necessary for analysis, is inevitably artificial and at variance with the actual process of perception; for "the moment we see that two or more characteristics belong to the same person they enter into dynamic interaction. We cannot see one quality and another in the same person without their affecting each other." [17]

For this reason, we believe the evaluation of a particular trait as "objectionable" or "admirable" to have less import than its mere perception. Indeed, the parallels between what was named as good and as bad, viewed against the background of a period in which anti-Semitism was fairly prevalent, suggest that the "admirable" qualities mentioned by some respondents may actually have been objectionable ones in disguise. When we ask a person who dislikes Jews to name "admirable Jewish traits," we make him do something he does not normally do: to take a trait out of its context for purposes of evaluation. The characteristic in question may be perceived as admirable only when thus isolated. Robert K. Merton has pointed up this paradox in a well-known passage, in which he showed that the supposed virtues of "Abe" Lincoln were identical with the supposed vices of a hypothetical Abe Cohen.[18]

Unlike Merton himself, who explains it in motivational terms, we believe this "moral alchemy" to be inherent in the nature of cognition. That the evaluation of any individual datum depends on the context in which it is placed has been repeatedly demonstrated, not only in visual but also in social perception. Dinnerstein, Haire and Grunes, and Mensh and Wishner all have obtained experimental evidence that the perceived meaning of an individual's attributes changes with the context.[19] Asch summarizes the import of these studies: "Each trait possesses the property of a part in a whole. . . . The isolation of a trait alters its character—tends to make it abstract. Only when a quality finds its place in the entire impression does it develop its full content and function." [20]

Thus the image of the Jew, as constructed above, is intimately related to then prevailing notions about the nature of Jews as a group. Our earlier finding that at least one-fifth of the population seemed to consider the Jews a race is of particular relevance here, explaining as it does several hitherto obscure points:

(1) The notion that Jews are a race provides some basis for the frequent references to peculiar appearance. If the Jew is a member of an alien race, it appears appropriate for him to have distinct physical characteristics.

(2) The racial perception of Jews implies that both the over-all image of the Jew and its components are biologically fixed, and therefore independent of cultural factors.

Herein, perhaps, lies the reason why actual changes in the Jews' cultural characteristics are not always reflected in popular imagery. As long as racial traits are popularly thought to be immutable, individuals who depart from the supposed norm are likely to be discounted as deviants, and even widespread cultural change may be viewed as no more than a superficial overlay on an unchanging character structure. The same probably is true, in less degree, when Jews are thought of as a nationality; for, despite the traditional concept of the "melting pot," in which all foreigners are supposed to be gradually Americanized, the popular mind tends to equip certain nationalities with "inherent" traits. Jews evidently are considered less likely to become acculturated than other groups; much of what figures in our data as "clannishness," "group loyalty" and the like apparently reflects the belief that they resist assimilation.

The accusation of "clannishness," then, interacts with other imputed attributes in such a way as to suggest that Jews are not only endowed with certain racial or national characteristics, but also perpetuate these characteristics through self-segregation and inbreeding. In this way, traits attributed to Jews may well come to appear more enduring than those of other groups supposedly readier to assimilate.

Prewar and Postwar Beliefs

Fluctuations in the prevalence and nature of anti-Jewish beliefs before, during and after the war are recorded in a series of surveys extending from 1940 to 1959 and including 14 trend points. The polls sought to identify current stereotypes through two questions: "Have you heard any criticism or talk against the Jews in the last six months?" and "What kind of criticism or talk was it?" (Table 8).

As we assess the results, we must bear in mind several limitations implicit in this measure:

(1) We do not know how many of the respondents who reported hearing anti-Semitic talk agreed with what they heard. The question was intended as a projective device, but does not appear to have worked entirely in this fashion.[21]

(2) From 1950 onward, only a relatively small proportion of respond-

Table 8 Reported Criticism of Jews (1940–59)

"Have you heard any criticism or talk against the Jews in the last six

	Per cent of those who report any criticism				
	August 1940	February 1941	October 1941	December 1942	May 1944
Unfairness in business, unscrupulousness	27	31	21	22	30
Control of business, property, finance	20	21	21	18	22
Wealth, shrewdness, miserliness					
Too much power	10	12	9	11	10
Too much political power					
Too many in government	3	5	6	8	9
Clannishness	5	5	3	5	2
Aggressiveness, pushiness	6	7	4	3	11
Warmongering	3	4	13	4	2
Avoiding army, getting soft jobs in army				18	21
Communist leanings; spying	1	1		1	
Loyalty to Israel					
Jewish "race" disliked	8	12	7	4	2
Jews favor integration, run NAACP[a]					
(Percentages of total samples reporting any criticism)	(46)	(47)	(50)	(50)	(62)

† Less than 1 per cent.   a Asked in survey on desegration.
Sources: O9–11, 13–15, 17; N24–25, 29, 31, 33, 36; G36.

ents—11 to 24 per cent—reported anti-Semitic talk, and the incidence of the various stereotypes reported was correspondingly small: less than 10 per cent of the total population in all cases.

(3) The surveying task was transferred from one polling agency to another in 1950—precisely the year in which reports of anti-Semitic talk took a sharp drop.

(4) There is reason to believe that such talk was not equally prevalent at all educational levels. The most educated persons reported it from two to three times as often as the least educated. Thus the data probably overrepresent those stereotypes which circulated among the better-educated groups.[22]

Notwithstanding the interpretative problems posed by these limitations, it is plain that the data in no way disturb our earlier conclusions. The notion of the Jew as "economic man" predominated: Throughout the period covered, most comments bore on the Jews' supposed wealth, business tactics and financial success, while other traits consistently received less atten-

months?" (If "yes":) *"What kind of criticism or talk was it?"*

		Per cent of those who report any criticism						
March 1945	February 1946	November 1950	April 1951	July 1953	November 1954	November 1955	November 1956	March 1959
14	11	39	29	19	20	21	18	10
13	17	16	13	20	12	20	20	6
		14	12	7	28	23	13	13
11	6							
		5	8	5	3	2	3	3
6	2							
2	3	4	8	4	9	10	5	3
3	6	11	5		4	8	6	8
2	1							
8	3	1	5					
	1	8	18	26	11	2	4	†
		2	2			5	14	†
4	3							
								5
(62)	(64)	(24)	(16)	(21)	(14)	(13)	(11)	(12)

tion. Evidently, the image we constructed from the data examined earlier underwent little change during the time span covered, though its prevalence had been much reduced.

Side by side with these persistent elements, certain short-lived criticisms turned up. Thus, depending on the trend of current events, Jews were scored as warmongers, draft dodgers or Communists or were charged with excessive attachment to Israel. Stereotypes of this sort emerged suddenly, sometimes achieved considerable prevalence and then vanished almost as quickly as they came. Yet, in our opinion, they were probably related to permanent images. For example, complaints of warmongering, though by definition specific to the years just before the war, seem to have sprung from the long-standing belief that a Jew's prime loyalty was to world Jewry (then threatened by Hitler), not to his own country.[23]

As pointed out above, the data just reported are of limited significance. They are valuable insofar as they identify the particular kinds of anti-Semitic ideas that were in the air at various times, but probably misstate their prevalence. For a truer picture of their incidence, we must turn to surveys in which specific questions were asked.

That Jews one decade ago were still widely perceived as a group with distinctive characteristics is apparent from two studies undertaken in 1954 and 1955 (Table 9). At that time, from one-third to nearly one-half of the

Table 9   Perceived Difference between Jews and Others (1954–55)

(1954:) *"Do you think there are any differences between Jews and other people?"*

(1955:) *"Do you think Jews are any different from other people in any way?"*

	Per cent	
	1954	1955
Yes	34	45
No	62	50
Don't know	4	5

SOURCES: N31, 33.

population said Jews were "different from other people." [24] On both occasions, a follow-up question asked what differences between Jews and others were perceived, and despite some differences in coding, the findings were quite similar (Table 10): Negative characteristics were cited with conspicuous frequency, though the questions were phrased in neutral terms. With similar consistency, just under half of the respondents mentioned traits associated with religion, while only a small minority specified cultural characteristics neutral in tone.

What evaluations, if any, are implied in these findings? Ready perception

Table 10 Perceived Distinctive Qualities of Jews (1954–55)

"In what ways are they [Jews] different?"

	Per cent of those who think Jews different	
	1954 (34 per cent of total sample[a])	1955 (45 per cent of total sample[a])
Religion, beliefs, church	37	33
Holidays	3	3
Eating and dietary habits	5	8
Nationality, race	4	3
Talk, language	*	2
Manners, customs, habits	6	*
Physical appearance	3	2
Shady, unscrupulous in business	16	10
Rich, shrewd, successful in business	25	30
Loud, pushy, arrogant, socially undesirable	6	8
Clannish, unsociable, sticking together	20	19
Ambitious, hard-working, smart, intelligent	b	7
Helping each other	*	6
Other (less than 3 per cent each)	10	10

* Not coded.
a See Table 9.
b Included under "Rich, shrewd . . ."
SOURCES N31, 33.

of differences *per se* is likely, it would seem, to be associated with unfavorable attitudes. There are, of course, indubitably real differences between Jews and non-Jews; but persons to whom they are salient are evidently more likely to entertain anti-Semitic notions than those to whom they are not. Besides, an individual who feels no hostility toward Jews may well deny the existence of group differences as a way of asserting his belief in equality. Theoretically, of course, mutual acceptance in a democracy does not depend on similarity; differences between groups are supposed to be recognized and respected, not used as a basis for invidious distinctions. But in actual practice, group differences have so often been misused in precisely this fashion that any reference to them is bound to be interpreted by many individuals as an expression of hostility or disapproval.[25]

These circumstances lead us to conclude that some of the ostensibly neutral responses in the 1954 and 1955 polls must have contained unfavorable overtones. Thus, "different religion" may have meant "rejection of Christ," "different race" may have meant "alien and undesirable," and so forth. Similarly, references to distinctive physical appearance no doubt often involved unfriendly feelings. Our conclusion is supported by a simple cross-tabulation with another set of data from the 1954 survey, which shows anti-Semitism and perception of differences to be definitely linked: Those who saw Jews as different from non-Jews turned out to be less likely than others to welcome them as next-door neighbors (Table 11). It must be noted,

Table 11   Perceived Difference between Jews and Others, by a Measure of Anti-Semitism (1954)

	Think Jews different from others	Do not think Jews different from others
Per cent who would be concerned about a Jew moving next door	20	4
Per cent who would not be concerned	80	96

SOURCE: N31.

however, that the total volume of anti-Semitism revealed by this criterion was not great. Even of those who referred to Jews as different, fully four-fifths voiced no objection to Jewish neighbors—presumably because the differences contemplated were of an unobjectionable kind.

The specific images recorded in 1954 and 1955 were largely identical with those of previous years, but their prevalence was not the same. Thus, the perception of Jews as unrefined or ill-mannered had apparently lost some currency during the interval. The comparison is less than conclusive, however, because the prewar polls specifically mentioned "objectionable traits," whereas those of 1954 and 1955 merely asked about "differences." To overcome this difficulty and determine more accurately whether or not the image of the Jew had changed over the years, some of the questions asked in 1940 (see Table 5) were repeated verbatim in 1962 (Table 12). The response indicates a massive reduction of overtly hostile attitudes. The percentage of respondents who said Jews had objectionable qualities shrank from 63 to 22 per cent, that is, by about 63 per cent of the earlier incidence—a phenomenal change for a time span of not much more than two decades.

The question whether Jews as a group had admirable traits, originally asked in the 1938 survey, was also repeated in 1962 (Table 13). Since unfavorable perceptions had so markedly declined by the latter date, we might expect favorable ones to register an increase. As it happens, this is not so. Responses naming admirable characteristics, too, had decreased, though much less: from 51 per cent in November 1938 to 44 per cent, that is, by about 14 per cent of the former incidence. The fact that both kinds of

Table 12 Qualities Found Objectionable in Jews (1940, 1962)

(*Question as in Table 5*)

	Per cent of those who say Jews have objectionable qualities	
	1940 (63 per cent of total sample)	1962 (22 per cent of total sample)
Unscrupulousness	51	27
Aggressiveness	19	27
Clannishness; discrimination against non-Jews	17	18
Lack of culture or good breeding	16	4
Selfishness	6	4
Appearance	6	*
Lack of respect for others' religions	1	†
Too much emphasis on money	*	23
Other	6	11

* Not coded. †Less than ½ of 1 per cent.
SOURCES: O8; G38.

Table 13 Qualities Found Admirable in Jews (1938, 1962)

(*Question as in Table 7*)

	Per cent of those who say they admire certain qualities	
	November 1938 (51 per cent of total sample)	June 1962 (44 per cent of total sample)
Ability in business or finance	25	30
Racial or religious loyalty	24	36
Loyalty to wife and family	15	9
Intellectual attainments	13	11
Persistence, determination, ambition	11	16
Thrift, financial independence	10	7
Kindness, generosity, charitableness	8	9
Loyalty	5	†
Obedience to law	3	2
Integrity of character	2	2

† Less than ½ of 1 per cent.
SOURCES: O4; G38.

perception were less prevalent in the early 1960s than in the late 1930s would seem to indicate that Jews had come to be viewed less stereotypically; and this in itself seems to us a clear gain.

A rough estimate of current attitudes toward Jews may be obtained from the over-all distribution of favorable and unfavorable perceptions within the total population. In the case of the 1962 data, it was possible to sort out the respondents according to whether they endowed Jews with admirable traits only, objectionable traits only, both or neither (Table 14). No such

Table 14   Distribution of Unfavorable and Favorable Perceptions of Jews (1962)

	Per cent[a]
Think Jews have:	
Objectionable traits only	7
Both objectionable and admirable traits	18
Neither objectionable nor admirable traits	43
Admirable traits only	32

[a] Exclusive of "don't know" responses.
SOURCE: G38.

operation could be performed on the older data; but even so it seems safe to assert that the 1962 figures represent a considerable change from earlier times. Judging by the replies to this question, Americans actually seemed to have become pro-Semitic: Over four times as many persons thought Jews had only admirable qualities as believed they had only objectionable ones;[26] almost half said Jews had no special traits; and another fifth saw both good and bad in the Jews. A meager 7 per cent who saw Jews as all bad were all that remained of the vast anti-Semitic potential of the 1930s and 1940s.[27]

On the face of it, we may find it hard to believe that a full 32 per cent of the American people in 1962 should have credited Jews with none but admirable group characteristics, while only 7 per cent endowed them with nothing but faults. Having suggested that some of the respondents who named "admirable" qualities in earlier studies were actually expressing hostile feelings in disguise, we might reasonably assume that the same was true of the 1962 findings. In the present instance, however, the data permit us to verify this hypothesis, and the skeptical interpretation turns out to be unwarranted as far as the recent figures are concerned.

When the four categories of respondents established in Table 14 are cross-tabulated with certain measures of attitudes, we find that those who said Jews had only admirable traits did show themselves less anti-Semitic than the rest (Table 15). True, in the first of the measures used, they scored about the same as those who believed Jews to have both good and bad distinctive traits, and in the rest they differed only slightly from those who thought Jews had neither. But nowhere did respondents who saw only favorable qualities resemble those who saw only unfavorable ones.[28] Thus, it appears that, as of 1962 at any rate, most respondents who attributed none but favorable traits to Jews meant what they said. Only relatively

Table 15 Unfavorable and Favorable Perceptions of Jews, by Various Measures of Freedom from Anti-Semitism (1962)

	Think Jews have			
	Objectionable traits only	Both objectionable and admirable traits	Neither objectionable nor admirable traits	Admirable traits only
Per cent who:				
Would vote against anti-Semitic candidate	54	72	64	76
Do not think Jews have too much power	46	68	88	85
Think Jewish businessmen as honest as others	41	62	85	92
See Jew as:				
Nationality	37	26	31	32
Race	35	19	25	21
Religious group	28	45	44	47

SOURCE: G38.

small minorities within this category seem to have meant otherwise: the 8 per cent (viz., 100 less 92 per cent) who thought Jewish businessmen less honest than others, the 15 per cent who said Jews had too much power, the 24 per cent who would not vote against an anti-Semitic candidate.

The perception of supposedly admirable qualities in Jews, then, would seem to have contained less hidden hostility as of 1962 than as of 1938–40. In our opinion, this contention, though not based on numerical comparisons, is reasonably safe, because all signals point to a massive increase in the acceptance of Jews during the interim. Some of the data already cited (for example, Table 8), as well as the overwhelming bulk of the evidence throughout this book, indicate that anti-Semitism has dramatically fallen off since the Second World War. This being so, the very decline in the proportion who profess to see admirable qualities in Jews may be a symptom of increased acceptance, to the extent that it reflects the falling away of hostility couched in euphemistic terms.[29]

It remains for us to see how much the relative, as against the absolute, incidence of specific characteristics attributed to Jews may have shifted. Here we find little change, by and large. Of the admirable traits, "ability in business" and "racial loyalty" headed the list in 1962 as they had done a quarter-century earlier. The stereotypes held by the shrinking number of hostile persons also die hard; thus, "clannishness" was mentioned by 17 per cent of persons who objected to Jews in some way during 1940, and by 18 per cent of those who still did so in 1962—though the former proportion represents about 11 per cent (viz., 17 per cent of 63 per cent) of the total population, and the latter a mere 4 per cent (18 per cent of 22 per cent).

Only the percentage under the head of "unscrupulousness" appears greatly
reduced, and this seeming change almost certainly is a mere artifact of coding: In 1962, "too much emphasis on money" was set up as a separate
category, whereas in 1940 responses of this kind evidently had been included under "unscrupulousness." The actual image, then, turns out to be
remarkably stable: We find no new elements, nor do we find old ones dis-
lodged. Decade after decade, the Jews are accused of the same traits by
those who do not like them.

The Shylock Image

In tracing the prevalence of various images of the Jew, we must bear in
mind that not all are equally important or influential. Certain long-
established notions seem to occupy a central location in the mind of the
public, forming a permanent nucleus; other ideas—some lasting, some
ephemeral—group themselves around these centers and are often modified
or colored in the process.

Perhaps the most significant of central images is the tenacious belief that
Jews as a group are mercenary, unscrupulous or dishonest. In the light of
this familiar notion, the alleged group loyalty and aggressiveness of Jews
appear more objectionable than they might by themselves; their alleged
craving for power acquires a convincing motivation; and charges related to
current events—for example, accusations of warmongering or profiteering
—gain added plausibility. We must therefore devote special attention to
what has been called the "Shylock image" of the Jew.

Though surveys over the years point unmistakably to unscrupulousness
or dishonesty in business as the quality most commonly attributed to Jews,
the nature of the accusation is not entirely clear. We can only guess, for
example, whether Jews were visualized in this context as great financiers or
humble corner merchants. The Western world's long-standing antipathy
against Jews in the role of moneylenders might suggest that the "crooked
Jew" was imagined as a rich capitalist or banker. On the other hand, the
Jews personally known to the bulk of the middle and working classes in the
United States are likely to be local merchants. If we may hazard a guess, the
prevailing concept was perhaps a composite of the two: The storekeeper
down the street may have been perceived in a vague likeness of the medieval usurer. Insofar as Jews were imagined to be a racial group, their alleged dishonesty may well have been viewed as an "innate" characteristic.

More important, we find ourselves on treacherous ground when we try to
determine the precise nature of the dishonesty or unscrupulousness visualized. The difficulty here is that in American society norms of honesty have
long been fuzzy. Since the last century, if not longer, legally or morally
dubious means toward laudable ends have been regarded with great toler-

ance. Williams' comment on the formation of norms in our society is to the point:

Emphasis on the goals of wealth, power, and prestige creates a "bombardment of interests" that tends to break down the restraining power of the institution- alized definitions of appropriate means to reach the cultural goals. As the extreme, the emphasis on "getting yours" in terms of individual success becomes so great that "anything goes"—action escapes from all normative regulation except the tests of technical efficiency in reaching the prized goals.[30]

Yet much criticism of Jews has centered precisely on their allegedly ruth- less pursuit of success, at least when the topic was explicitly mentioned in the question. Polls in which this was the case, taken during 1938 and 1939, found nearly half the respondents convinced that Jewish businessmen were less honest than others (Table 16)—more than twice as many as voiced the

Table 16 Beliefs about Honesty of Jews in Business (1938–39)

"Do you think Jewish businessmen are more honest or less honest than other businessmen?"

	Per cent			
	March 1938	May 1938	November 1938	September 1939
Less	47	44	42	49
More	2	3	3	2
Same	48	44	46	43
No opinion	3	9	9	6

SOURCES: O1, 2, 4, 7.

belief spontaneously in another survey undertaken about the same time (see Table 4). Well over a decade later, in 1952, about the same result was obtained with the following question: "Compared with most people of your religious beliefs, would you say most Jews are the same, better or not as good in being fair in business?" In this instance, the stereotype was found somewhat less prevalent among the lower class—possibly an indication that the local merchant was not the prime referent.[31]

By 1962, the stereotype seems to have become a good deal rarer. In a rerun of the 1938 question during that year, only 18 per cent said Jewish businessmen were less honest than others, while as many as before said they were more honest or expressed no opinion (G38). Perhaps most signifi- cant, fully 70 per cent of the population now asserted that Jewish business- men did not differ from others in this respect. This percentage is all the more striking in that the category "about the same" was not included in the question but had to be volunteered.

That the proportion of persons who thought Jewish businessmen less honest than their competitors has declined during recent years by more than half would seem to be a development of far-reaching significance. So marked a weakening of one of the central concepts of anti-Semitism appears certain to undercut various peripheral prejudices as well. Still, as we shall see, it would be rash to conclude that the notion of Jewish unscrupulousness has been altogether demolished.

Studies conducted in 1957 and 1959 bear on this issue (Table 17). The

Table 17   Beliefs about "Trickiness" of Jews in Business (1957, 1959)

(1957:) *"Here are some statements that people sometimes make about Jews and I'd like to know how you feel about them. Just tell me which statement on the card comes closest to your own feeling: . . . 'One trouble with Jewish businessmen is that they are so shrewd and tricky that other people don't have a fair chance in competition.' "*

(1959:) *". . . Please look at this scale and tell me how you feel about each of the following statements: . . . 'The trouble with Jewish businessmen . . .' [as above]."*

	Per cent[a]	
	1957	1959
Strongly agree	11	6
Agree	24	24
Uncertain	15	22
Disagree	37	38
Strongly disagree	13	10

[a] White Christians only.
SOURCES: N37; G36.

question here was focused somewhat differently from those in earlier polls: It asked, not whether Jews were "dishonest," but whether they were "shrewd and tricky." In 1959, only 48 per cent of respondents took issue with this negative image—as against the 70 per cent who were to reject the notion of "Jewish dishonesty" in 1962. Equally significant, over a fifth at this time expressed uncertainty. Since the conflicting data were obtained only three years apart, they cannot well be taken to signal a massive change in the acceptance of Jews. More likely, they indicate that a subtle shift in imagery had taken place: The idea that Jews were especially dishonest was no longer held by a majority, but the notion that they might be "shrewd and tricky"—that is, almost but not quite dishonest—remained widely current. Still, there can be no doubt that hostility toward Jews was less prevalent than before the war: Fewer respondents called them tricky in 1959 than had thought them downright dishonest in the 1930s.

We must, of course, bear in mind the inevitable difficulties of comparing replies to questions constructed as differently as the two just examined. One such difficulty is that the 1957 and 1959 surveys, unlike that of 1962, included "uncertain" among the proffered alternatives, which undoubtedly increased the percentages under this head.[32] Another is that the question asked in 1957 and 1959 added a dimension which was not present in other studies and whose effect is hard to estimate: the idea that "other people don't have a fair chance in competition" with Jews. In our opinion, the addition of this thought may have caused some respondents to reject the stereotype solely out of pride in non-Jews' competitive abilities. And, finally, as we pointed out earlier, shrewdness—unlike dishonesty—is an ambiguous concept in our society; it may have favorable connotations, which may have seemed to some respondents to conflict with the negative ones implicit in the poll question. For all these reasons, we believe that the data in Table 17 underestimate the frequency with which Jews are regarded as "tricky businessmen."

The present figures and earlier results, taken together, suggest the following conclusions:

(1) The belief that Jewish businessmen are dishonest has become markedly less current during the past 20 or 25 years. It has been largely replaced by the notion that they are merely shrewd or tricky.

(2) Even this less extreme image is less widespread than the belief in Jewish dishonesty once was, though only a minority of the population reject it outright.

The validity of these conclusions is not impugned by certain indications that perceptions of Jews as unscrupulous are to some degree a function of educational level. That this may be so is suggested by the results of an extended inquiry into the images of various ethnic groups held by students of Princeton University. Between 1935 and 1942, it was found, the students' ideas about Jews remained fairly stable, whereas their notions of Chinese and Japanese underwent changes.[33] In 1951, however, a replication of the survey uncovered shifts in prevailing ideas about Jews: "The trait of shrewdness is still the one most frequently mentioned, but it has been reduced to almost 50 per cent of its former frequency. More than in 1935, there is some emphasis in the 1951 group on such traits as intelligence, ambition, and loyalty to family ties." [34]

As will be noted, these changes do not correspond to the shifts we have observed in the attitudes of the general public. The students plainly differ in their beliefs from the population as a whole.[35] Thus "shrewdness," the trait named most often by students throughout the period studied, did not figure as such in the 1938 survey of the general public and did not become an important category until 1954 (see Tables 7 and 9). On the other hand, intelligence, ambition and family loyalty, which turned up in the general surveys all along, did not receive much emphasis among the students in 1935 and 1942; and if these qualities were more widely named in 1951, one of the reasons, according to Gilbert,[36] is that the Princeton student body had become more nearly representative of the general population by the latter date.

Gilbert comments as follows on the decreased incidence among Princeton students of the "Shylock complex," the image of the shrewd, industrious, mercenary, grasping Jew: "The overall change in the Jewish stereotype was one of a considerable fading of a highly negative group stereotype in accordance with the general anti-stereotype tendency which the comparison of these two tests uncovered." [37] That the "Shylock complex" of late has not been especially prevalent among educated persons has been confirmed by cross-sectional studies elsewhere.[38] Yet, certain other beliefs of the educated group seem to have remained unchanged. For example, a poll taken in 1952 indicated that college graduates still were just as likely as non-graduates to think of Jews as "clannish" and "aggressive." [39] In other words, educated individuals continued to agree with the less educated on the Jew's supposed methods and personality traits, though they may have developed their own notions of his goals. Just what goals, other than the traditional "mercenary aims," this distinctive view may impute to the Jews cannot be determined from the present data.

It remains for us to explain why criticism of Jews consistently focuses on "sharp dealing"—a form of conduct that is regarded with a good deal of tolerance elsewhere in the American culture. One possible explanation is that the same standards are not really believed to apply to all: *Quod licet Iovi, non licet bovi.* As noted earlier, the evaluation of an individual's attributes varies with the context. Thus, it may be that evading the ordinary norms of honesty and fair play is considered permissible for those of high status in the social system but not for others,[40] so that an action of dubious integrity will be viewed as "smart" or as dishonest, depending on whether it is performed by gentile or Jew. If so, it would follow that notions of business practices among Jews are bound up with their supposed place on the status ladder. When Jews are called unscrupulous, they are really accused of acting above their supposed station—of seeking advancement through methods reserved for their supposed betters. Implicit in this accusation is the idea that Jews, unlike other persons, ought to be confined to a fixed place in the social system, that is, that there are specific norms for Jews different from the norms for society as a whole.[41]

An alternative explanation is that the Jew may be perceived as unscrupulous even beyond the generous limits customary in the American culture. Jews are frequently thought of as rich, and financial ability is one of the qualities most often attributed to them (see, for example, Tables 10 and 13). Since riches and success, in America's Puritan tradition, are considered marks of true superiority, a reason must be found why these prizes should fall to persons of supposedly inferior human or racial quality—persons whose origin and proper place are thought to be in the lower classes.

The belief that Jews have achieved their position by dishonest, or rather by *excessively* dishonest, methods is not only sanctioned by tradition; it also provides a seemingly rational explanation for their otherwise inexplicable success, and therefore is almost impossible to dislodge by evidence to the contrary. As long as some people believe Jews to be simultaneously inferior and rich, a theory will be needed to reconcile the contradiction.[42]

NOTES

1. Krech and Crutchfield, *Theory and Problems of Social Psychology*, p. 152.

2. Solomon E. Asch, *Social Psychology* (New York: Prentice-Hall, 1952), p. 564.

3. Harding, in Lindzey, *Handbook of Social Psychology*, II: 1022.

4. Daniel Katz and Kenneth W. Braly, "Racial Stereotypes of One Hundred College Students," *Journal of Abnormal and Social Psychology*, XXVIII:280–289 (1933).

5. If this assumption is correct, the greater number of "don't knows" would indicate an increase in sophistication.

6. Indeed, the examples would seem to have been included precisely because such perplexity appeared probable.

7. Here, the cognitive dimension of the individual's attitude clearly appears to derive from norms of social behavior.

8. We would draw no such conclusion with respect to the characterization of Jews as a religious group, since differences of creed are much more acceptable in the American society than differences of race.

9. Such an interpretation would not rule out the possibility that the decline in the racial view also reflected, in some degree, the fading of memories of the Hitler regime, with its racist definition of Jewry. The increased perception of Jews as a nationality, too, may stem in part from the course of political events, such as the founding of the State of Israel in 1948.

10. Three of the surveys asked: "Are there any objectionable qualities which you think Jews generally have to a greater extent than other people?" In the other two, the question read: "Are there any qualities about Jews to which you object?" (For explanation of keys, here and throughout this study, see Appendix II, pp. 231–234.)

11. For example, while the 1938 surveys listed greed and dishonesty as separate categories, the 1940 poll named only unscrupulousness, and that of 1946 distinguished between dishonest or unethical behavior on one hand and excessive concern with money on the other.

12. One example of such modification in a former age: During the fourteenth century, the ideas of Jews' physical unwholesomeness and their hatred of non-Jews crystallized into the allegation that they had caused the Black Death by poisoning wells. Paradoxically, the Jews' relative immunity to the plague—in fact a result of their greater cleanliness—made this notion especially credible.

13. In our data, the Jew as "economic man" figures mainly as a businessman, that is, a producer or merchant; but some of the traits mentioned in other contexts (for example, "neatness and good taste," "lack of culture") suggest that he is also seen as a consumer, both of the refined and the ostentatious sort.

14. For explicit findings on the alleged "trickiness" of Jews, see Table 17.

15. Note, for example, Lincoln Steffens's recollections of Jewish life on New York's Lower East Side during the 1890s. *The Autobiography of Lincoln Steffens* (New York: Harcourt, Brace & Co., 1931), pp. 243–244.

16. What is perhaps the most striking literary embodiment of this image dates precisely from the time of the polls discussed here: the figure of Esther Jack in Thomas Wolfe's novel *The Web and the Rock* (1st ed.; New York: Harper & Bros., 1939).

17. Asch, *op. cit.*, p. 216.

18. Robert K. Merton, *Social Theory and Social Structure* (rev. ed.; Glencoe, Ill.: The Free Press, 1957), p. 428.

19. Dorothy Dinnerstein, *A Study of the Development of Certain Cognitive Structures* (unpublished Ph.D. thesis, New School for Social Research, 1941); Mason Haire and Willa Freeman Grunes, "Perceptual Defenses: Processes Protecting an Organized Perception of Another Personality," *Human Relations,* III: 403–412 (1950); Ivan Norman Mensh and Julius Wishner, "Asch on 'Forming Impressions of Personality': Further Evidence," *Journal of Personality,* XVI:188–191 (1947).

20. Asch, *op. cit.*, p. 216.

21. See Stember, *Education and Attitude Change,* p. 15.

22. *Ibid.*

23. See Chapter V.

24. The discrepancy between the two sets of results almost certainly was due mainly to differences in the wording of the question. Also, the 1954 survey, unlike that of 1955, included Jewish respondents—a circumstance which may have further increased the negative response, if we assume that Jews would take the question to refer to the supposedly immutable differences so frequently named as a rationale for anti-Semitism.

25. An analogous dualism prevails in the feelings of Jews toward their own group characteristics. Many if not most Jews cherish these distinctive qualities; yet at the same time they commonly wish to be considered "no different from anyone else." Marie Jahoda reports the following from an interview with an Orthodox Jewish woman: "While she wished her child to see Jews as the chosen people, she wished Gentile children to think 'that a Jew is just like everybody else.' " "The Problem," in Isidor Chein and Others, editors, "Consistency and Inconsistency in Intergroup Relations," *Journal of Social Issues,* V, No. 3 (1949), 7.

26. In 1938–40, the proportion must have been roughly 1:1, judging by the frequencies with which admirable and objectionable characteristics were mentioned.

27. See Chapters III and V.

28. It is worth noting, furthermore, that those who thought Jews had no special characteristics also tended to shun anti-Semitic views—a finding which supports our contention that any decline in stereotypy, whether derogatory or favorable, indicates progress against prejudice.

29. We would not claim, of course, that ostensibly favorable perceptions—notably those relating to the Jews' much-cited "ability in business"—are wholly free from negative overtones even now.

30. Robin M. Williams, Jr., *American Society* (rev. ed.; New York: Alfred A. Knopf, 1960), p. 378.

31. Stember, *op. cit.*, pp. 16, 26.

32. The meaning of the "uncertain" response is not entirely plain. It might appear, on the face of it, as a refusal to generalize about a group; but we know that educated persons, who might be thought most likely to oppose stereotyping, were least likely in this poll to declare themselves uncertain (Stember, *op. cit.*, p. 16). Therefore, the "uncertain" response probably represents, rather, unfamiliarity with the stereotype or evasion of the issue.

33. See Melvin M. Tumin, *An Inventory and Appraisal of Research on American Anti-Semitism* (New York: Freedom Books, 1961), p. 68.

34. *Ibid.*, p. 70.

35. The perceptions of educated and uneducated persons are known to differ markedly. See Stember, *op. cit.*, *passim*.

36. G. M. Gilbert, "Stereotype Persistence and Change among College Students," *Journal of Abnormal and Social Psychology*, XLVI:245–254 (1951).

37. *Ibid.* The "anti-stereotype tendency" is further confirmed by the fact that nearly all students protested spontaneously against the unreasonable task of generalizing about people. For other indications of a decrease in stereotyped perception, see discussion of Tables 3 and 13, above.

38. Stember, *op. cit.*, p. 42.

39. *Ibid.*

40. See Williams, *op. cit.*, p. 356.

41. The author has observed an analogous resentment against "privileged" behavior by "unprivileged" persons in the castelike society of the armed forces. Enlisted men of middle-class origin objected particularly to being treated as members of an inferior caste by officers with lower-class civilian backgrounds. The implication is that upper-caste behavior would be acceptable, or more nearly so, if exercised by the proper individuals.

42. Jewish organizations have occasionally attempted to combat the stereotype of the "rich Jew." Merton points out a paradoxical element in these efforts: Acceptance in the larger society is sought by disavowing precisely the attribute most respected there (*op. cit.*, p. 432).

III

Beliefs about the Position of Jews in America

SINCE THE BEGINNINGS of American society, minority groups of one kind or another have labored under special disabilities; but during most of its history the nation as a whole has failed to see the problem in its true proportions. Except for the disadvantaged groups themselves, the public has not often addressed itself wholeheartedly to the challenge of discrimination and group hostility. Even persons opposed to these evils have tended to assume that matters were bound to right themselves in time. As recently as 1947, this traditional "long-term" view was widespread: 61 per cent of the population thought racial and religious minorities either were treated as well as they should be or were approaching fair treatment as fast as practicable (R13).

We will observe a great deal of this superficial optimism as we examine the rather fragmentary data concerning popular beliefs about the status and treatment of Jews in the United States. But before we can focus on that topic, we must consider its cognitive basis. How large does the "Jewish problem" look to the public? Specifically, do most Americans have a reasonably accurate idea of the number of people involved?

Beliefs about the Size of the Jewish Group

In a survey undertaken during 1946 to determine what facts or supposed facts underlay popular ideas about the Jews, respondents were asked to estimate the proportion of Jews in the country (Table 18). Because of an ambiguous clause in the question, the response is not easy to interpet,[1] but there can be little doubt that the size of the Jewish group was not well known. Only about a third of the replies ranged between 2 and 7 per cent.[2]

76

Table 18 Beliefs about the Proportion of Jews in the Nation's Population (1946)

"Out of every hundred people in the United States, how many would you guess are Jewish? Would you say that one out of every hundred people is Jewish, 4 out of every hundred, 8, 25, 50 or how many, roughly?"

	Per cent of respondents
Estimated number of Jews per 100 people:	
1	14
2–3[a]	6
4[a]	22
5–7	7
8	15
9–15	8
16–24	2
25	10
26 or over	3
Don't know; no answer; unclassifiable	13

[a] Approximately correct estimates.
SOURCE: O17.

Most of the rest overestimated the Jewish share of the population. More than twice as many respondents guessed above 7 as below 2 per cent; and 25 per cent, a grossly exaggerated figure, was named nearly as often as 1 per cent, a much less greatly understated one.

Why was the percentage of Jews in the population so commonly overestimated? One reason, of course, is that their true number is small; there simply was not much room for underestimation. But the sampling procedures followed in early (as well as some more recent) research may have been an added cause. Though nationwide samples supposedly included rural and urban counties in true proportions, polling organizations then tended to select "rural" samples near cities, in counties that sometimes were suburban rather than rural. Thus, the sample in this instance may have contained a disproportionate number of individuals from the more populous areas; and these are precisely the areas with a larger than average number of Jews. Generalizing from their own neighborhoods, such respondents may well have arrived with seeming logic at inflated figures.

Even more important, the conspicuousness of Jews in the society may have caused their number to be overestimated. Jews are largely concentrated in a few highly visible occupations and industries, they play a fairly prominent part in local and national affairs, and their economic level is high.[3] That the latter fact is widely known may be seen in another set of data from the 1946 study: When asked whether the average income of Jews was higher or lower than that of others in the same community, 63 per cent of the population said it was higher (O17).[4] As for prominence, about half of the respondents in the same survey agreed, for example, that "Jewish scientists have played an important part in the scientific advancements of the last twenty-five years or so," while only 16 per cent said their role had been unimportant (O17).

Finally, misconceptions about the number of Jews in some instances are undoubtedly caused by anti-Semitic anxieties. A person fearful of Jews—whether as competitors or in some other role—might well develop exaggerated ideas about the size or power of the "enemy." This is not to say, of course, that in other cases the misconception may not be cause and the hostile attitude effect; thus, an individual who thinks Jews constitute as much as a quarter of the population would presumably be more susceptible to anti-Semitic ideas than someone better informed.

Facts versus Beliefs about the Prevalence of Anti-Semitism

The public's awareness of anti-Semitism was gauged by a series of variously worded questions begun in 1937 and continued through the 1940s (Table 19). The proportion believing anti-Jewish hostility to be on the increase grew steadily larger from the beginning of the series until the war, registered a sharp rise during June 1944 and did not fall off until some time between 1946 and 1950.

How do these beliefs compare with the true state of affairs? If we use willingness to support an anti-Jewish campaign as an index of actual hostility, we find no clear correspondence (Figure 20).[5] Unlike perceived anti-Semitism, this particular form of actual anti-Semitism showed no steady growth; there is indirect evidence that it momentarily rose to a high level about June 1944, but this sudden peak in no way parallels the progressive rise in the belief that hostility to Jews was increasing.

We might have expected closer congruence between the two sets of data, since popular ideas about the extent and trend of anti-Semitism presumably have some basis in reality. Evidently, readiness to join in anti-Jewish activity was not what respondents had in mind when they said hostility was rising. We therefore turn to two other measures, the prevalence of anti-Jewish talk (see Table 8) and the belief that Jews have too much power;[6] and when we plot these two against the trend of beliefs concerning the level of anti-Semitism, we do find a remarkably close correlation—notwithstanding the fact that available figures do not always date from the same months of the same years (Figure 21). All three curves start near the same point, rise to high levels in 1944 and in February 1946 begin a decline which continues until 1950 or beyond.

The public's ideas about trends in anti-Semitism, then, coincided consist-

Table 19 Beliefs about Trends in Anti-Semitism (1937–50)

    (a) *"Do you think anti-Jewish feeling is increasing or decreasing in this country?"*

    (b) *"Do you think anti-Jewishness is increasing or decreasing in this country?"*

    (c) *"Do you believe that in this country hostility toward the Jewish people is growing or not?"*

    (d) *"Do you think the feeling against the Jews is increasing or decreasing in this country?"*

    (e) *"Do you think the feeling against Jewish people is increasing or decreasing in this country?"*

	Per cent [a]						
	(a) August 1937	(b) November 1938	(c) December 1938	(a) March 1939	(b) September 1939	(d) April 1940	(d) February 1941
Increasing	29	37	33	45	42	48	48
Decreasing	23	18	46	17	11	13	15

	Per cent [a]					
	(d) October 1941	(d) December 1942	(d) June 1944	(e) March 1945	(e) February 1946	(d) November 1950
Increasing	43	47	56	58	58	16
Decreasing	16	12	10	8	7	20

[a] For studies using split ballots with more than one wording, only one set of results is reported here.

SOURCES: G2; O4; R3; G6; O7, 8, 10, 11, 13–15, 17; N24.

ently with the fluctuations of stereotyping and casual anti-Jewish talk, that is, of prejudice in its milder forms. In contrast, virulent hostility—viz., readiness to support a campaign against the Jews—usually ran at much lower levels. Only in 1944, a year of exceptional stress, did the index of virulent anti-Semitism rise to the level of the other indices.[7] In another way, too, extreme hostility ran parallel with popular beliefs about trends in anti-minority feeling during that atypical year: Jews and Negroes, in this order, were the most frequently named targets both of perceived increases in prejudice (Table 22) and of hypothetical anti-minority campaigns.[8]

To state these observations in general terms: Actual receptivity to anti-Jewish campaigns may fluctuate sharply without corresponding change in the incidence of milder manifestations of anti-Semitism or in the general public's notions about increases or decreases in prejudice. The actual prospects of organized hate movements may be in the process of evaporating even while widespread unfavorable talk or stereotyping suggest a rise in

Figure 20   Beliefs about Trends in Anti-Semitism Compared with Indices
of Actual Anti-Semitism, I (1937–46)

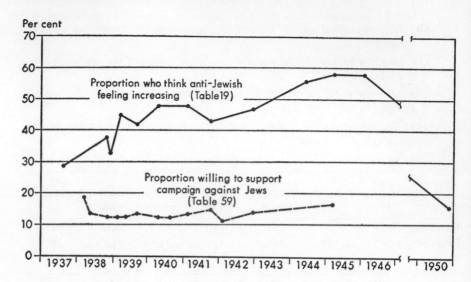

Figure 21   Beliefs about Trends in Anti-Semitism Compared with Indices
of Actual Anti-Semitism, II (1938–50)

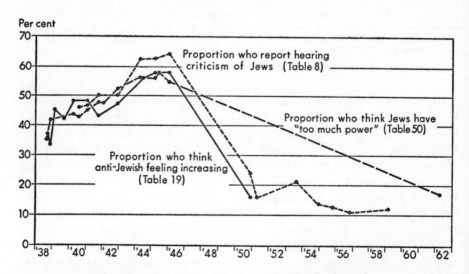

hostility. Conversely, an activist anti-Semitic mood might conceivably develop at a time when a lessening of anti-Jewish talk and imagery signaled a
seeming decrease in bigotry.

We are thus led to the conclusion that willingness to join concerted actions against Jews is largely an autonomous phenomenon. It is not necessar-

Table 22 Beliefs about Increases in Group Prejudice (1944)

"As you know, there are different religions and races in the United States which some people are prejudiced against—the Protestants, the Catholics, the Jews, the Negroes, etc. Against which one of these groups, if any, do you think prejudice or feeling has increased the most?"

	Per cent
Jews	37
Negroes	31
Catholics	3
Protestants	†
None	15
Don't know	16
	102ᵃ

† Less than ½ of 1 per cent.

ᵃ Percentages total over 100 because some respondents named more than one group.

SOURCE: P1.

ily just a stronger expression of attitudes also manifested in anti-Semitic talk or belief—no matter how insistently logic might demand such a connection.[9] For this reason, the potential strength of bigoted movements must be investigated in its own right; it cannot be deduced from these other indices.

Beliefs about the Reasons for Anti-Semitism

Though many studies have explored prevailing beliefs about increases or decreases in anti-Semitism, only a few have tried to find the reasons behind such beliefs. One of the earliest to do so was a study undertaken in December 1938, which found that 33 per cent of the population thought "hostility toward the Jewish people" was growing, while 46 per cent thought it was not. In the same poll, all respondents were asked why they felt Jews were objects of hostility in the United States and elsewhere. Reasons unfavorable to Jews were mentioned by 43 per cent of the total sample, reasons favorable to Jews by 13 per cent and neutral or external reasons by 16 per cent (Table 23).[10]

Between 1942 and 1946, the inquiry was continued in four surveys with virtually identical codes, which enable us to discern whatever trends there may have been (Table 24). A final study dating from 1950, with a more detailed code and reporting only white Christians' responses, rounds out the data (Table 25).

According to all these studies, perceived increases in anti-Semitism were blamed mainly on the Jews' own supposed characteristics. Most of the traits cited were identical with the "Jewish attributes" we encountered in explor-

Table 23   Beliefs about Reasons for Anti-Semitism (1938)

"What do you feel is the reason for hostility toward Jewish people here or abroad?"

	Per cent of total sample
Reasons unfavorable to Jews:	
Jews control or monopolize enterprise	13
Jews are unfair or dishonest in business, cheat or swindle	6
Jews are grasping, avaricious, covetous, cheap	6
Jews' manners, characteristics or attitudes are objectionable	5
Jews are clannish, do not mix with others, are interested only in own race	4
Jews are over-aggressive, too energetic, overbearing, forward, noisy	4
Jews are lazy, parasitic, won't do manual labor	1
Other	4
Total	43
Reasons favorable to Jews:	
People are jealous and envious of Jews	5
Jews are too clever and successful, have too much money-making ability	5
People are mean, narrow-minded, ignorant	2
Other	1
Total	13
External and neutral reasons:	
Religious and racial prejudice	4
Germany, Hitler, dictatorship	3
Fulfillment of Biblical prophecy, will of God	2
Propaganda, agitation	2
Other	5
Total	16

SOURCE: R3.

ing popular images of the Jew or prevailing anti-Semitic notions (see Tables 4–6, 16–17). The familiar complaints about greed or dishonesty and about excessive power, especially in the economic field, ranked at the head of the list. Two new items figured in the 1950 data: Small numbers of respondents now scored Jews as spies or Communists or said they were loyal to a foreign power, Israel.[11]

Probably the most intriguing aspect of the data is the ambiguous effect of the war. Alleged Jewish draft-dodging, profiteering and warmongering were often named to account for a perceived increase in hostility; but just as frequently the Jews' participation in the war effort was cited to explain a decline. Of particular interest is the assertion, recorded in the 1946 study, that anti-Semitism was growing because "the war made us conscious" of the

Table 24   Reasons for Supposed Trends in Anti-Semitism (1942–46)

"Do you think the feeling against Jewish people is increasing or decreasing in this country?" . . . "Why?"

	Per cent of those who think anti-Semitism increasing			
	December 1942 (47 per cent of total sample)	June 1944 (56 per cent of total sample)	March 1945 (58 per cent of total sample)	February 1946 (58 per cent of total sample)
Increase thought due to:				
Jews' power in finance	23	18	17	15
Jews' disagreeable traits	20	20	18	21
Jews' draft evasion, war profiteering	13	10	13	5
Jews' power in government	13	2	7	2
Propaganda	12	5	4	4
Jewish refugees	2	3	6	9
Jews getting United States into war	2	1	3	1
Jews' excessive power	*	13	15	12
War-induced consciousness of Jews	*	*	*	7
Other	4	15	2	7
Don't know; no answer	4	6	5	7
Decrease thought due to:				
Jews' troubles	48	37	30	18
War-induced tolerance	22	16	14	33
Jews' doing their share in war	10	10	10	6
Propaganda	8	6	0	8
Other; general or irrelevant	12	21	37	22
Don't know; no answer	9	12	10	14

* Not coded.
SOURCES: O13–15, 17.

Jews; it suggests that increased salience as such may be a factor in increasing hostility.

Equally challenging are the reasons mentioned by the small minorities who between 1942 and 1946 thought anti-Semitism was declining. Early in the war, this group of respondents cited sympathetic reactions to the German persecution of Jews far more often than any other reason; during 1942, 51 per cent referred to the Jews' sufferings. Later this explanation was offered far less often: by 18 per cent in 1946, and by a mere 8 per cent in 1950.[12] Meanwhile, a growing number of respondents were crediting perceived reductions in anti-Semitism to a general increase in tolerance,

Table 25 Reasons for Supposed Trends in Anti-Semitism (1950)

"Do you think the feeling against the Jews is increasing or decreasing in this country?" . . . "Why?"

	Per cent of those who think anti-Semitism increasing (16 per cent of total sample)[a]
Increase thought due to:	
Jews' unscrupulousness, greed	25
Jews' excessive business power	20
Jews' excessive political power	10
Jews' wealth	6
Too many displaced persons	6
Jews' clannishness	5
Jews' Communist leanings	3
Draft dodging by Jews	2
Jewish spies	1
Jews' aggressiveness, pushiness	1
Jews' allegiance to Israel	1
Other	27
Don't know	10

	Per cent of those who think anti-Semitism decreasing (20 per cent of total sample)[a]
Decrease thought due to:	
Increasing tolerance	41
Less talk against Jews	20
Persecution of Jews in European war	8
War, national emergency	6
Building of Israel	6
Too many other worries	2
Other	18
Don't know	10

[a] White Christians only.
SOURCE: N24.

supposedly induced by the war itself, not by the victimization of Jews during the war. By 1946, this theory was more widely current than any other.

The wartime revelations concerning Nazi persecution of Jews, then, seem to have had no lasting effect on the attitudes of the public toward Jews.[13] As the horrors receded in time, their impact, such as it was, evoked less and less sympathy for the Jews. Indeed, supposed decreases in prejudice were attributed to compassion only at a time when, as far as we know, prejudice actually was not decreasing at all; after bigotry had really begun to drop, the decrease was credited mostly to another cause.

This other cause, in turn, seems to have been largely illusory. The notion of war-induced tolerance is flatly contradicted by the observation—to be confirmed many times in later portions of this book—that resentments against Jews and other minorities increased during most of the war and reached a climax in the crucial year 1944. It might be argued that the rapid decrease of anti-Semitism after that time was a delayed reaction to the war, but we are more inclined to attribute it to the prospect and actual coming of peace—if only because our data tend to link anti-democratic sentiments with general tensions and frustrations in society.

Finally, we must note that the poll responses almost completely discounted anti-Semitic propaganda as a cause of increased bigotry. Indeed, "propaganda" was cited equally often as a reason for growing and for declining hostility toward Jews. This does not prove that the hatemongers' efforts actually wcrc ineffective, for, obviously, the persons most affected by propaganda are least aware of being its victims. The figures may, however, be significant in another sense. A great many persons habitually identify propaganda with notions not founded upon fact (for example, the reports of German atrocities in the First World War); therefore, the general disinclination to name propaganda as a cause of anti-Semitism may mean that many respondents thought hostility to Jews had some rational base.

Beliefs about Discrimination

Public awareness of discrimination against Jews in various phases of American life is a neglected chapter in opinion research. Only a few studies have grappled with the subject. The earliest, undertaken in 1938, dealt with individuals' knowledge of employment discrimination in their own companies. Respondents were asked: "So far as you know, would the fact that a man is a Jew hurt his chances of getting a job with your company?" (O3). The replies indicated that only a limited number of employees knew their organizations' practices; even in firms which employed no Jews, almost half the employees believed anti-Semitism was not a factor in hiring. In other words, as of 1938 the prevalence of job discrimination was not particularly well-known even in situations where first-hand evidence was available. Either the absence of Jews was not noted or it was assumed that Jews simply did not happen to engage in the particular trade or industry.

Further data on the same topic may be found in a study conducted in 1949 among a specialized sample: a nationwide cross section of college students (R18). Alternatives were proffered on how a Jewish college senior "with good grades and a good record in campus activities" would fare if he tried "to get a job in an industry owned and operated chiefly by Gentiles." The object was to compare the freshmen's responses with the seniors', but, as it turned out, there was hardly any difference between the two. We accordingly report the combined response of both groups.

Judging by the results, students at the time were well aware that job discrimination existed: Only 19 per cent maintained that a Jew would find employment in a gentile-owned firm as readily as a non-Jew "with the same personality and college record." [14] But the effect of these barriers was less well understood. A mere 6 per cent thought he would "never get a decent job in that industry at all," while 67 per cent believed he could ultimately succeed by "applying at many more companies than a Gentile." The latter response illustrates strikingly the unfounded optimism which has so often characterized Americans' beliefs about the treatment of minorities. The students simply do not seem to have known that a good many industries at the time were still flatly excluding Jews from some or all employment categories.

The same study also probed beliefs about the admission of Jews to colleges, with similarly rose-colored results. Most students were plainly ignorant of discriminatory quotas right under their noses. When asked to pass on a statement to the effect that a Jew would have a harder time getting into college than a non-Jew with equivalent high-school grades, over half of those answering thought this was "more false than true," while 40 per cent could not (or would not) express an opinion (R17).

Inconclusive as these data are, they strongly hint that as recently as the late 1930s and the 1940s discrimination against Jews was not seen in its true dimensions by the general public. A certain naive, wishful optimism seems to have distorted most persons' perceptions of the facts; evidently, the prevalence of exclusionary restrictions in institutional life was underestimated and their effect misunderstood. To what degree these tentative conclusions still apply is an open question. Both conditions and attitudes have changed in recent years: Restrictions against Jews have disappeared wholesale, and public opinion probably has become more sensitive to the disadvantages suffered by minority groups in general. Unfortunately, we have no data to verify whether large numbers of Americans today have a realistic notion of remaining anti-Jewish practices or how important they consider them.

NOTES

1. Part of the question read: "Would you say that one out of every hundred people is Jewish, 4 out of every hundred, 8, 25, 50 or how many, roughly?" The percentages were mentioned merely as illustrations, but seem to have been widely understood as multiple choices, for 1, 4, 8 and 25 per cent were named much more often than intermediate figures.

2. The actual proportion about this time was estimated at 3.5 per cent. *American Jewish Year Book*, L (1949), 717.

3. Although no precise data on the relative income level of Jews are available, all indirect evidence indicates a figure about average. See Donald J. Bogue, *The Population of the United States* (Glencoe, Ill.: The Free Press, 1959), pp. 705–709.

4. In a second version of the question, "about the same" was proffered as an alternative and chosen by 8 per cent; but, significantly, the proportion who said "higher" was not reduced.

5. Such willingness was frequently measured in opinion studies between 1938 and 1946. The findings are fully reported in Chapter V.

6. Data concerning this belief are also reported in Chapter V.

7. It seems likely that support for an anti-Semitic campaign would also have been found to coincide with the other trends during the period of unprecedently *low* anti-Semitism in the early 1960s, if the question had been asked at that time.

8. See Tables 58 and 60, Chapter V.

9. Indeed, it may be inspired not so much by specific anti-Semitism as by hostility to minority groups as such or by some other kind of generalized tension.

10. Multiple answers were permitted, so that some respondents undoubtedly gave replies falling into more than one category.

11. However, the founding of the Jewish state was cited more often as a reason for declining than for rising anti-Semitism. The charges of spying and Communism are fully discussed in Chapter VII, those concerning loyalty to Israel in Chapter VIII.

12. In another study, conducted during 1944, the Jews' treatment at the hands of the Germans actually heads the list of reasons given for *increased* anti-Semitism. Of those respondents who thought hostility toward Jews was increasing more than hostility toward other groups, 27 per cent cited this as the reason—almost twice as many as gave the next most frequent response, "Jewish power" (P1).

13. We have no public-opinion data on whether the subsequent revelations at the trial of Adolf Eichmann, in 1961, affected Americans' attitudes toward Jews to any substantial degree.

14. Whether the average respondent would ever think of a Jew and a non-Jew as having "the same personality" is open to doubt.

IV

Attitudes toward Association with Jews

THE AMERICAN PUBLIC'S feelings about association with Jews have been surveyed on a broad scale. Attitudes toward contacts with Jewish fellow workers and neighbors, encounters with Jewish vacationers and fellow students and intimate relationships with Jews in friendship and marriage have all come into the opinion researcher's ken. On the face of it, these would seem to be disparate issues. Ideas about the more public, formalized and impersonal kinds of association are plainly linked with the course of public affairs and policies, while feelings about more personal relationships might seem to occupy a purely private sphere, unaffected by outside events. There is no equivalent of fair-housing laws or fair-employment codes in the areas of friendship and the family. Yet, as our data will show, attitudes in the personal realm have undergone almost as much change in recent years as those in the public arena. The question thus arises whether the various issues examined are really separate variables or interconnected aspects of one phenomenon.

Jews as Employees and Fellow Workers

The subject of non-discriminatory employment has been bound up with public policy since 1941, a year of labor shortage, when Negro organizations began to press for fair-employment legislation, and a wartime Fair Employment Practices Commission was created by Presidential executive order.

Public-opinion studies carried out during the following decade revealed that a large portion of the public favored non-discriminatory employment practices, but did not think they should be prescribed by law. Thus, in

1944, a study found almost three-quarters of the population agreeing that "in normal times" the "wisest way for a large factory to do their [sic] hiring" was to "hire all those who apply for jobs and are qualified to do the work regardless of their race or religion" (R9), but during the next year, considerably less than half approved a hypothetical state law "which would require employers to hire a person if he is qualified for the job regardless of his race or color" (G14).

In 1945, the State of New York actually passed such a law—the first of numerous state enactments seeking, with varying degrees of success, to eliminate discrimination in private employment.[1] Simultaneously, however, Congress discontinued the wartime Federal Fair Employment Practices Commission. Though demands for restoration of the FEPC were voiced for several years thereafter, they do not seem to have been widely noted; in 1947, less than half of the people had heard about them (G28).

When confronted with the idea of Federal legislation guaranteeing that no person could be denied a job for discriminatory reasons, about 70 per cent of the respondents in the 1947 poll said they would like to have their Congressman vote in favor of such a law, but the issue probably was not especially salient to the majority of Americans, for only about half the population said they "felt strongly" about it one way or another. Moreover, there is reason to believe that the high rate of affirmative replies was prompted by the wording of the question: Unlike the 1945 poll cited earlier, which referred to "race or color," the present survey spoke only of "religion, color or nationality."

Reluctance to rely on legislation for fair-employment practices was unmistakably expressed in polls dating from 1948 and 1952 (Table 26). Here

Table 26 Opinions on Fair-Employment Legislation (1948, 1952)

"What would you like to see done about legislation that prohibits employers—when they are hiring people—from turning them down solely because of their race or religion?"

	Per cent answering "yes" to proffered alternatives	
	1948	1952
"Would you like to see laws passed by Congress to do this?"	25	31
"Would you like to see it left up to each state to pass their own laws if they want them?"	29	25
"Do you think it would be better not to have any laws at all of this kind and work the problem out some other way?"	37	31

SOURCES: R15, 19.

the alternatives to Federal legislation—state laws and methods other than law—were posed in rather attractive fashion, and the latter in particular drew considerable support. Changes during the four-year interval between the polls were not very marked, though somewhat more respondents wanted Federal legislation in 1952 than in 1948, and somewhat fewer favored "working out the problem some other way." Nor is any drastic change registered in the replies to another question, asked on three occasions in 1949 and 1950 (Table 27). The wording in this instance was vague and perhaps

Table 27 Opinions on Federal Fair-Employment Policies (1949–50)

(January 1949:) *"One of Truman's proposals concerns employment practices. How far do you yourself think the Federal government should go in requiring employers to hire people without regard to their race, religion, color or nationality?"*

(March 1949:) *". . . How far do you think . . ."*

(January 1950:) *"One of President Truman's civil-rights proposals concerns employment practices. How far do you, yourself, think . . ."*

| | Per cent | | |
	January 1949	March 1949	January 1950
"All the way"	34	34	34
"Part of the way"	8	7 [a]	14
"None of the way" (1950: "Take no action")	44	45	41
No opinion	14	14	11

[a] Includes "Leave it to the states."
SOURCES: G30–32.

somewhat slanted to invite negative replies; the results did not differ greatly from those just reported.

Legislation that would explicitly oblige employees to accept non-discriminatory policies was viewed with even more distaste than laws which would merely compel employers to institute such practices. Thus, in the 1945 study cited earlier, 43 per cent of respondents were for and 44 per cent against laws to assure non-discriminatory hiring; but when asked about a law which "would require employees to work alongside persons of any race or color," 56 per cent were opposed and only 34 per cent in favor.

It would be a mistake, however, to assume that such resistance to enforced proximity (and to fair-employment measures in general) was aimed principally at Jews. Both the wording and the context of the poll questions were such that respondents must have thought chiefly of Negroes. That this is indeed so may be seen in another study, dating from 1947, which found 94 per cent of respondents willing to work alongside a person of a different faith ("that is, a Protestant, Catholic or Jew"), but only 63 per cent ready to do so next to a person of a different race ("that is, white or colored"). Indeed, judging by this particular set of data, only a negligible fraction of the population objected to Jews as fellow workers (G28).

We may conclude, then, that the pattern we have observed refers typically to Negroes. Respondents were relatively willing to accept Negroes as long as the hypothetical relationship was that between an employer and an impersonally viewed employee; when personal association on the job was contemplated, acceptance declined. In the case of Jews, surprisingly, the reverse seems to have been true: A series of polls spanning the years from 1940 to 1950 consistently revealed more opposition to Jews as hypothetical employees than as hypothetical fellow workers (Table 28).

Within this general configuration, the data record certain actual or apparent shifts of considerable size. In 1940 and 1942, respectively, 26 and 29 per cent of the population said that having to work with Jews would make a difference to them; in 1950, only 6 per cent indicated that they would dislike it, while 19 per cent stated they would not care much. We cannot tell whether sentiment toward Jews on this particular issue actually became more favorable during the interval or whether the hostile opinions had been only weakly held in the first place; at any rate, by the time of the final poll, if not earlier, an overwhelming majority of the population was plainly ready to accept a Jewish colleague at the next desk or lathe.[2]

Other polls confirm that the public was a good deal more reserved toward Jews when hiring policies were considered from what was thought to be the employer's viewpoint. Figures to that effect were obtained, for example, by a study, dating from 1948, that asked respondents to state which of several listed policies they thought large employers should follow with respect to Jewish job applicants (Table 29). Over a quarter of the population endorsed some form of hiring discrimination, as against the mere 6 per cent who only two years later were to express dislike of working next to a Jewish colleague (see Table 28). The question asked probably constituted a more reliable index than the rather vague wording used in the latter poll ("Would it make any difference to you . . . ?"); on the other hand it may be that the listing of plausible alternatives, such as the quota system, caused respondents to give answers they would not otherwise have thought of.

If, during the 1940s, resistance to the hiring of Jews was more widespread than, and thus not merely an outgrowth of, opposition to working with Jews, what was the reason? Only one possible explanation, fear of "troublemaking" by Jewish employees, was explored through surveys, and the results were negative. In a poll taken during 1944, a mere 7 per cent of the sample mentioned Jews among "groups you think are sometimes apt to cause trouble when mixed in with other workers," whereas five times as many named Negroes (R9).

Lacking other specific data, we can only speculate about the causes of resistance to Jews as employees. In our opinion, the explanation lies in the

Table 28 Attitudes toward Jews as Employees and Fellow Workers (1940–50)

(1940:) *"If you were an employer hiring a new employee, would it make any difference to you if he were a Jew?"*

(1942, 1945:) *". . . if he were Jewish?"*

	Per cent		
	April 1940	December 1942	March 1945
Yes	43	37	42
No	51	57	50
No opinion	6	6	8

(1940:) *"If your employer hired a new worker tomorrow to work with you, would it make any difference to you if he were a Jew?"*

(1942:) *". . . if he were Jewish?"*

	Per cent	
	April 1940	December 1942
Yes	26	29
No	64	67
No opinion	10	4

(1950:) *"How would you feel about having a Jew work alongside you on a job, doing the same kind of work you do? Which one of these statements comes closest to your own feelings?"*

	Per cent
	November 1950
"Wouldn't like it"	6
"Wouldn't matter too much"	19
"No difference"	73
Don't know	2

SOURCES: O8, 13, 15; N24.

different demands made of fellow workers and employees. A colleague on the job is presumably judged for the most part by his personality traits, such as congeniality or ability to fit into a semisocial situation; and there is no reason to believe that Jews are found unacceptable on this score. More important, since Jews generally rank high on the socio-economic scale and are not held to menial jobs, as Negroes traditionally have been, it is safe to assume that no loss of status attaches to working with them as equals.

When an actual or imagined employer appraises a prospective employee, quite another set of criteria is invoked. The qualities that tend to make the

Table 29 Opinions about Employment of Jews (1948)

"Which of the things on this card do you think people who employ large numbers of workers should do?"

	Per cent
"Hire the most capable people whether they are Jewish or not"	65
"Hire Jews in proportion to the number that there are in the community"	7
"Hire Jews only when they are so outstanding that no one else could do the job as well"	9
"Hire no Jews at all"	11
Don't know; no answer	8

Source: R16.

Jew relatively acceptable as a hypothetical fellow worker probably have little bearing on his desirability as a hypothetical employee: The socioeconomic status of his ethnic group is almost a matter of indifference in this context, and his personality traits are much less crucial, except where professional or executive jobs are concerned. Managers and employers, it would seem to us, are more likely to be thought of as being concerned about character traits, and here, judging by our earlier data, considerable doubt about Jews prevailed at the time of the surveys. The common stereotypes probably came into play: the beliefs that Jews are dishonest, unscrupulous or tricky; that they are completely loyal only to one another; that their supposed aggressiveness and business acumen make them a threat to those who deal with them. Nowhere in our varied data are Jews credited with the typical workman's virtues: discipline, reliability, unquestioning obedience to orders.

How much of this distrust has survived since the 1940s? As we have noted earlier, unfavorable images of the Jew had lost much of their currency by 1962 (see Table 12). If opposition to hiring Jews is related to certain traditional stereotypes, as we have hypothesized, then we would expect the opposition to decline along with the stereotypes; and when we compare the trend of the former with that of the latter, we do find a remarkably close parallel (Table 30). As of 1962, expressions of hostility to Jews as employees had declined to the same nearly negligible level as references to Jewish "unscrupulousness," "overaggressiveness" and "over-emphasis on money."

Social reality, it must be noted, had not yet caught up with these newly enlightened public attitudes. Though job discrimination against Jews had lost nearly all its support among the general population by the early 1960s, Jews still were virtually absent from the executive echelons of many big companies (especially in the fields of heavy industry, banking, insurance

Table 30 Opposition to Employment of Jews Compared with Anti-Jewish Stereotypes (1940, 1962)

	Per cent of total sample	
	1940	1962
Say it would make a difference to them if a prospective employee were Jewish	43	6
Think Jews unscrupulous	32	6
Think Jews overaggressive	12	6
Think Jews overemphasize money	*	5

* Not coded separately; responses of this nature probably were included under "unscrupulousness." (See Table 12.)
SOURCES: O8; G39 (first 1962 item); G38.

and public utilities). Some firms, moreover, were still excluding them from white-collar employment in the middle and lower brackets.[3]

What should be done about job discrimination against Jews was the subject of one question in a study conducted during 1949 among college freshmen and seniors across the nation (Table 31). The results are of interest in

Table 31 College Students' Opinions on Combating Employment Discrimination against Jews (1949)

"If Jewish students do have trouble getting jobs in certain industries in some parts of the country, which, if any, of the things on this list would you like to see done about it?"

	Per cent
"Pass a law to prevent discrimination on the basis of religion in hiring people for jobs"	23
"Expose individuals and companies who practice religious discrimination in hiring people for jobs"	12
"Give publicity to the success many companies have had in getting Jews and Gentiles to work together congenially"	40
"Try to educate Jews to change their behavior so they will be less objectionable to non-Jews"	6
"Let Jews work for Jewish companies and let Gentiles work for Gentile companies"	3
"It's useless to do anything because human nature can't be changed, and you'll only stir up more trouble between Jews and Gentiles"	13
None of the above	4
Don't know; no answer	2
	103 [a]

[a] Total over 100 due to multiple answers.
SOURCE: R18.

that they illustrate the thinking then current among an educated segment of the population. Like the public at large, this group was at best lukewarm toward fair-employment legislation; a law banning discrimination "on the basis of religion" was much less often named as a remedy than publicity for companies that succeeded in integrating Jews and non-Jews. Only a small proportion of respondents thought it was up to Jews to change so as to make themselves more acceptable, and even fewer expressed approval of segregation by religion. On the other hand, a larger percentage than might be anticipated had little or no hope that conditions might be changed.[4] Unfortunately, there are no figures to tell us whether such pessimism has declined since. We are inclined to think so, because it seems to be generally understood that recent developments in the field of civil rights have radically altered the prospects of all minority groups.[5]

Jews as Neighbors

Dislike of Jews as residential neighbors is an attitude of long standing which has often expressed itself in restrictive measures. Yet, until the postwar period, the subject was rarely taken up in public-opinion studies—no doubt because other, more pressing concerns required attention.

In recent years, the pressure of minority groups on the housing market has led to the enactment of anti-discrimination laws or resolutions in at least 20 states and about 70 cities.[6] The first comprehensive Federal order on the subject, dealing with Federally assisted housing, was issued in 1962. But long before this time America's Jews had begun to break through the barriers of residential segregation.

During the last few decades, appreciable numbers of formerly all-gentile communities have abandoned their ethnic restrictions. Of late, this form of discrimination has so greatly diminished that it no longer constitutes a major source of frustration for Jews as a group. Though Jewish residents still are welcomed with something less than warmth in certain areas, Jewish middle-class and working-class families today have little trouble in finding adequate living quarters in either city or suburb. Where housing is available at all, it is usually available to Jews, except in some fashionable upper-class suburbs and in the most status-minded high-rent areas within cities.[7] White ethnic groupings in suburban communities and city neighborhoods are increasingly the result of voluntary clustering rather than restrictive practices; of the available areas within their means, members of each minority group spontaneously tend to choose those in which they expect to find fellow-ethnics, friends and business associates, as well as facilities or institutions they consider particularly important.[8]

But while the individual Jewish family as a rule encounters little hostility in middle-class areas today, there sometimes is considerable resistance to the idea of large-scale Jewish "invasion" and the implied prospect of social relations between newcomers and earlier settlers. Two polls, conducted in 1940 and 1942, illustrate the difference in the responses to the two situations.[9] The former study asked: "If you were moving to a new house and found that your next-door neighbor was Jewish, would it make any difference to you?" (O8). Only 25 per cent of the respondents said it would make a difference. On the other hand, the latter survey found 42 per cent naming Jews among the groups they would least like to see move into their neighborhoods (R4).[10]

Data gathered in the postwar period confirm that the thought of Jewish masses, not a single Jewish neighbor, is what provokes resistance. Thus, an oft-repeated poll question found only 10 per cent of respondents hostile to "a Jewish family moving in next door" in 1950, and in the 12 years that followed, the percentage gradually declined to negligible proportions (Table 32).[11] In contrast, studies conducted in 1957 and 1959 revealed

Table 32   Attitudes toward Jews as Neighbors (1950–62)

"Suppose a Jewish family were going to move in next door to you. Would you say you wouldn't like that at all, or that you wouldn't like it but it wouldn't matter too much, or that it wouldn't make any difference to you?"

	Per cent[a]						
	1950[b]	1953	1954	1955	1956	1959	1962
Wouldn't like Jewish neighbor at all	10	7	3	5	5	2 ⎫	3[c]
Wouldn't matter too much	20	12	8	6	7	8 ⎭	
Wouldn't make any difference	69	80	88	87	86	86	95
Don't know	1	1	1	2	2	4	2

a Christians only.

b Slight wording differences in 1950; alternatives chosen from card.

c Alternative responses limited to "yes" and "no."

SOURCES: N24, 29, 31, 33, 36; G36, 39.

substantial uneasiness about the effects of large-scale entry of Jews (Table 33)—a contrast perhaps heightened by the fact that the issue was phrased in vigorous language likely to bring latent bigotry to the surface. Whereas in 1959, for example, 86 per cent of respondents explicitly declared themselves willing to accept a Jewish family next door, only 63 per cent rejected the belief that "Jews spoil nice neighborhoods." Generally speaking, when Jewish newcomers were visualized in the mass rather than as individual families, substantially fewer respondents expressed acceptance, somewhat more (especially in 1957) voiced hostility and a considerable proportion declared themselves uncertain.

Reasons given by respondents for objecting to Jews as neighbors were recorded in three surveys, covering the period from 1940 to 1956 (Table

Table 33   Beliefs about Effect of Jews on Neighborhoods (1957, 1959)

(1957:) *"Here are some statements that people sometimes make about Jews, and I'd like to know how you feel about them. Just tell me which statement on the card comes closest to your own feeling: . . . 'The trouble with letting Jews into a nice neighborhood is that sooner or later they spoil it for other people.'"*

(1959:) *". . . Please look at this scale and tell me how you feel about each of the following statements: . . . 'The trouble with letting Jews . . .' [as above]."*

	Per cent[a]	
	1957	1959
Agree strongly	6	2
Agree	11	9
Uncertain	24	26
Disagree	43	46
Disagree strongly	16	17

[a] White Christians only.
SOURCES: N37; G36.

34). Since the replies were not uniformly coded, we cannot draw any conclusions about possible changes from one poll to the next; but, even so, the data are useful as supplements to our earlier insights. Little concern was expressed about the effect of Jewish residents on property values. The bulk of the replies reflected traditional stereotypes, such as the notions that Jews are clannish, aggressive, greedy or dirty; at the same time, they plainly mirrored the respondents' own clannishness ("prefer own group") and fear of differences ("they are a strange people"). It must be remembered, however, that all of these attitudes characterized only a small fraction of the total population; as we have noted, most respondents registered no objection whatever to the prospect of a Jewish family next door.

The near silence concerning property values even among persons hostile to Jewish neighbors strikes us as highly significant. True, this concern may not be quite so rare as the figures suggest, since some respondents may have hesitated to acknowledge that their attitudes toward ethnic or religious groups were determined by economic considerations. But even with due allowance for this possibility, it appears plain that Jews, having risen to middle-class status, are no longer thought to be a threat to property values by the socio-economic groups who inhabit nationwide population samples.[12] For all we know, their presence may on occasion even be considered beneficial.

Why the upper class, in contrast to the middle and lower classes, still surrounds its neighborhoods with anti-Jewish barriers is a question our data cannot answer, since the top bracket of society is barely represented in population samples; but there are no indications that the reasons differ ma-

Table 34 Reasons for Objecting to Jews as Neighbors (1940–56)

> (1940:) *"If you were moving to a new house and found that your next-door neighbor was Jewish, would it make any difference to you?"* (Data below from volunteered comments.)
>
> (1955–56:) *"Suppose a Jewish family . . . [as in Table 32]."*
>
> (If negative:) *"Why wouldn't you like it?"*

	Per cent of those objecting to Jewish neighbors		
	1940 (25 per cent of total sample)	1955 (11 per cent of total sample[a])	1956 (12 per cent of total sample[a])
Jews are arrogant, aggressive, noisy, dirty, clannish, greedy or loud	19	25	*
Prefer own group, have nothing in common with Jews	*	19	19
Not used to Jews, don't know them, they are a strange people	*	13	12
Jews are treacherous, money-grabbing, "out to beat you"	*	13	13
Entry of Jews decreases property values	4	4	6
(Unspecific and irrelevant responses omitted.)			

* Not coded.

[a] Includes both those who "wouldn't like a Jewish neighbor at all" and those to whom "it wouldn't matter too much" (see Table 32).

SOURCES: O8; N33, 36.

terially from those cited by the hostile minority among the population at large. The thought of social contact with a strange and supposedly repulsive group evidently brings snobbery and a sense of superiority to the surface, particularly in suburban environments, where nearness is most likely to lead to intimacy.[13]

Judging by the stated reasons for objecting to Jewish neighbors, fear of enforced intimate association is not the only reason why the idea of living in a predominantly Jewish district is resisted. The matter appears to have a symbolic dimension as well. Individuals do not necessarily select residential areas by practical criteria alone; a choice of neighborhood may also serve a socially identifying function, much as styles of clothing, types of houses and makes of automobiles have been held to do.[14] It has often been noted that many middle-class families move from neighborhood to neighborhood as their status changes. A man's address may thus help him validate his self-image (witness the associations called up by names and designations such as "the Gold Coast," "Sutton Place," "suburbia" or "the wrong side of the tracks"), and the arrival of supposedly strange or peculiar neighbors may appear to destroy the utility of a prestige location as an index of self-identification. Conceivably, this is what is really meant by the statement that "Jews spoil nice neighborhoods."

Social Relations with Jews

Many surveys before and during the war focused on the public's attitudes toward social intercourse with Jews. A wide range of possible situations was included, but systematically collected data covering the same situation over a period of years are not available in all cases, and the existing evidence is sometimes contradictory, as the following example will show. A survey conducted in 1938 asked, "Are there any Jews among your close friends?" and found about a third of the population answering in the affirmative (O1).[15] In contrast, a poll taken during 1945 indicated that less than half the population had frequent contacts with Jews, and that most of these encounters were of minimal intimacy: About a quarter each were reported to have taken place "at work" and "in stores," about one-sixth "in the neighborhood" and none in strictly social settings (O15).

Though there are no poll data that might serve as a basis for estimating how large a part of the general public has any close contact with Jews today, it seems reasonable to assume that the proportion is considerably greater than it was a few decades ago. True, the percentage of Jews in the population has declined somewhat, and even their absolute number probably has been fairly static; but social changes more than make up for this circumstance. Jews are much more integrated into institutional life than they were a few decades ago, as well as much less subject to residential segregation. Moreover, society as a whole has become increasingly urbanized, and contact with Jews is likely to be relatively frequent and close in cities and suburbs.

We do know that when the matter of familiarity with Jews was posed in hypothetical terms in 1950, the response was favorable to a striking degree: 69 per cent of the respondents said it "would make no difference to them" if a close friend were Jewish, another 20 per cent said it "wouldn't matter too much" and only 9 per cent categorically objected to friendships of this sort (N24). On the face of it, these figures suggest that social intimacy between Jews and others occurs less often today than the attitudes of the latter would permit; but this inference could hardly be put to the test, since there are too few Jews in the United States to provide 69 per cent of the nation with candidates for friendship.

Other crucial questions also remain unexplored for the time being. For example, can well-intentioned members of the majority approach members of a minority group undisturbed by ethnic differences or is social segregation so entrenched that self-consciousness inevitably intrudes? Is readiness for friendship likely to be communicated freely between persons of different backgrounds or does distrust stand in the way at first? Does concern about intermarriage limit the possibilities of friendship, and if so, how much? These and similar questions lie at the heart of the problem of social integration in general, but public-opinion research has not answered them.[16]

It seems probable that Jews sometimes shun or overlook available opportunities for friendly contact with non-Jews. One reason may be that they tend to underestimate the degree of receptivity they are likely to encounter. Like most or all other minority groups, Jews presumably refrain from making overtures to the majority, so as to avoid possible humiliating rejection. In addition, many probably feel that intimate social relations with non-Jews are likely to lead to intermarriage, which is frequently viewed as a danger. The tendency toward separateness fostered by these fears may lend color to the widespread notion that Jews tend to be excessively oriented toward their own group and hostile to others.

We believe nevertheless that self-segregation plays a much smaller role than the social segregation still imposed on Jews by others. It may be that most non-Jews really are as ready for close friendship with Jewish individuals as they proclaim themselves to be; but there is no denying that many of them still insist on ethnic segregation in precisely the institutionalized settings where intimate ties like friendship and courtship are formed [17]—for example, in vacation resorts and country clubs.[18] Of course, Jews for their part also tend to restrict intimate social interaction, including marriage, to their own group; but while this practice may sometimes be prompted by a wish to preserve the identity of the group, there are strong reasons to believe that it usually is at least in part a reaction to exclusion by non-Jews.[19]

That social self-segregation on the part of Jews is not the expression of a preference would seem to be confirmed by a study undertaken in 1948, which found them much readier to accept association with non-Jews in vacation resorts than vice versa (Table 35). Over two-thirds of the Jewish respondents said they would prefer a resort that did not discriminate; only one-third of the non-Jews did. A mere 6 per cent of the Jews, as against a full third of the non-Jews, preferred a completely segregated resort. And fewer Jews than non-Jews objected to a resort frequented entirely or predominantly by the other group. The greater readiness of Jews to mingle with the "others" did not extend to a desire to play the role of the lone outsider; when the clientele of the hypothetical hotel was described as including no Jews at all, 53 per cent of the Jewish respondents rejected the idea of staying there. But when "a few selected Jews" was specified, the rejection rate was only 12 per cent.[20]

In the light of our earlier observations concerning popular images of the Jew, these findings should occasion no surprise. As we have repeatedly noted, many non-Jews look upon Jews as strange, exotic creatures; and when they visualize a Jewish resort, they probably expect to find this strangeness there—whether in the imagined customs of the place, the diet, the forms of social life or in some other respect. The Jew, on the other

Table 35 Attitudes toward Jews in Vacation Resorts (1948)

"If you were going to spend a week at a vacation hotel, which of these different kinds would you want to stay at, assuming they all cost the same and provided the same quality of accommodations?"

	Per cent	
	Jewish respondents	Non-Jewish respondents
1. "A hotel whose guests were all non-Jews"	0	34
2. "A hotel that had a few selected Jews but mostly non-Jews"	1	20
3. "A hotel that might have any number of Jews or non-Jews depending on who applied"	68	34
4. A hotel that had a few selected non-Jews but mostly Jews"	10	†
5. "A hotel whose guests were all Jews"	6	†
6. Don't know; no answer	15	12

"Are there any kinds on this list that you definitely would not want to stay at?" (If "yes":) *"Which ones?"*

	Per cent	
	Jewish respondents	Non-Jewish respondents
Object to:		
None	27	16
Type 1 (see above)	53	3
Type 2	12	2
Type 3	0	5
Type 4	6	17
Type 5	5	69
Don't know; no answer	15	12

† Less than ½ of 1 per cent.
SOURCE: R16.

hand, is familiar with the ways of non-Jews, since they dominate the culture that surrounds him. He probably has eaten "American" food and mingled to some degree in the social world of the gentile; therefore, he is not likely to imagine a non-Jewish resort as quite so alien.

Social Contact among the Young

Uneasiness about friendship with members of minorities frequently centers on association among the young. A series of trend data on this subject, extending from 1938 to 1944, shows a tenth or less of the population opposed to having their children associate with Jewish youngsters, while from one-fifth to more than one-third object to contact with Negroes (Table 36).

Table 36 Attitudes toward Own Children's Association with Children of Other Backgrounds (1938–44)

"Do you like your children to associate with children of all racial and religious groups, or do you object to their associating with some? . . . Which?"

	Per cent of total sample			
	1938	1939	1942	1944
Object to some	44	34	37	47
Object to: [a]				
Negroes	36	28	21	35
Jews	10	9	6	9
Orientals	9	3	8	7
Italians	4	0	4	1

[a] Only most frequently named groups listed here.
SOURCES: O2, 7, 12, 14.

An open-end question was used in these polls, which may account for the infrequent mention of Jews; at any rate, twice as much opposition was registered in another survey, also in 1938, which asked explicitly, "Would you have any objection to your children associating with Jewish children?" (O1). It would seem that respondents deal with issues of this kind according to a pre-existing scale or hierarchy of preferred associations; when asked in general terms, without mention of specific groups, they tend to name only the group at the bottom, viz., Negroes, without registering their rejection of higher-ranking groups.[21]

Whether this explanation is correct or not, it is a fact that in 1938 as many as 20 per cent of respondents across the nation did not want their sons and daughters to associate with Jews and perhaps half that number felt strongly about the matter. Just what age group these individuals had in mind is not easy to determine. The actual wording of the questions clearly suggested childhood ("children of all racial . . . groups"; "Jewish children"). However, fear of association with outsiders usually focuses on adolescents and young adults, who might be led into sexual intimacy or marriage with members of the other group. This being so, some respondents may well have answered the question with the thought that childhood friendship spelled adolescent involvement or may actually have interpreted the words "your children" to mean "your offspring of whatever age," despite the context.

That young people themselves did not necessarily share this disapproval of association with Jews may be gathered from a comparison between two studies, one conducted in 1948 among the general population, the other in 1949 among a representative group of college freshmen and seniors (Table 37).[22] The question dealt with the desirability of anti-Jewish restrictions in

Table 37   Attitudes toward Jews as College Classmates (1948–49)

"If you were about to send a child of yours to college, which of these kinds of colleges would you prefer to see him or her go to?"

	Per cent	
	Adults, 1948	Students, 1949
"A college which admits the best students who apply, whether they are Jewish or not"	62	90
"A college which only admits Jewish students in the same proportion as there are Jews in that region"	6	4
"A college which only admits Jews if they are especially outstanding"	7	3
"A college which admits no Jews at all"	15	2
Don't know; no answer	9	1

SOURCES: R16, 18.

college admissions—an issue which may serve as an indirect measure of attitudes toward personal contact with Jews. A hypothetical college with a discriminatory policy found much less approval among students than among the general public. In some degree, this disparity undoubtedly reflects the differences between the population as a whole and one of its educated segments. But, as an earlier analysis of this particular poll has shown, educational level is only one part of the explanation, age level being another; the unfavorable response among college-educated people of all ages, though lower than in the total population, was not as low as among college students.[23]

Even among the general population, however, sentiment in favor of restricting the entry of Jews into colleges fell off phenomenally during the quarter-century covered by our data. In a poll taken during 1938, 26 per cent of respondents held that the number of Jewish students should be limited; when the question was repeated in 1962, a mere 4 per cent said so— notwithstanding the fact that competition for college admission had become

Table 38 Opinions about Limiting College Admission of Jews (1938, 1962)

"Do you think colleges should limit the number of Jews they admit?"

| | Per cent | |
	1938	1962
Yes	26	4
No	65	88
Don't know	9	8

SOURCES: O1, 2 (averaged); G39.

incomparably keener during the interval (Table 38). Insofar as colleges still maintain discriminatory barriers, then, they would seem actually to be lagging behind the general public in willingness to eliminate discrimination.

Intermarriage

We now turn to the most intimate form of association between Jews and non-Jews: marriage. The subject is of considerable timeliness, since the actual rate of intermarriage has been rising steeply in recent decades. No nationwide statistics are available, but the phenomenon is reliably documented on a narrower scale.[24]

A poll taken in 1940 asked respondents how they would advise a friend on intermarriage with Jews and found about two-fifths opposed (Table 39). Four years later, the question was repeated, but "your son or daugh-

Table 39 Attitudes toward Friends' or Children's Intermarriage with Jews (1940, 1944)

(1940:) *"If a friend of yours wanted to marry a Jewish boy or girl and came to you for advice, what would you say?"*

(1944:) *"If your son or daughter wanted to marry a Jewish boy or girl and came to you for advice, what would you say?"*

	Per cent	
		1944
	1940	("Son or
	("Friend")	daughter")
Two races or religions can't marry successfully	15	16
Advise against it; can't be done	26	46
Depends on the individual	5	6
Advise thinking it over	5	5
Individual must decide for himself	23	13
Marry; it's their own business	23	9

SOURCES: O8, 14.

ter" was substituted for "a friend"; the opposition now totaled almost two-thirds. In some degree, this discrepancy may be a function of actual attitude changes; as we suggested earlier, anti-Semitism seems to have reached a peak during 1944 (see Figure 21). Yet, we are inclined to attribute it chiefly to the difference between the issues posed. Fears and doubts naturally are stronger when a son or daughter than when only a friend is involved; there is less willingness to leave the decision to the individuals concerned, and more flat disapproval on the strength of parental authority.

Attitudes toward intermarriage are bound up both with deeply ingrained emotional responses to minority groups and with equally entrenched notions concerning marriage as such. The contradictions that may result are illustrated in a poll, dating from 1951, which asked whether "two young people in love who are of different religious faiths—Protestant, Catholic or Jewish—should get married." When the issue was put in these terms, the common belief in love as a sufficient condition for marriage evidently overrode religious considerations; a clear majority said yes (G33). A majority of the respondents also stated that they would not object to such a marriage for their own children. Yet, in the same study a majority of comparable size thought mixed marriages had at best only a fair chance of success.[25]

Implied in these responses is a viewpoint somewhat as follows: "If two people are in love, they should marry despite differences in religion, and if my son or daughter wanted to do so, I would not stand in the way. Just the same, they probably would be better off marrying someone of their own faith, since interreligious marriages are none too likely to work out well."

We believe most Americans today take an attitude somewhat like this toward interreligious marriages in general. Where marriage with Jews is concerned, feelings may well be even more mixed, because difference of religious faith is not the only problematic factor here, as it is likely to be between Protestants and Catholics. As we have observed on many occasions, Jewishness is frequently seen as something more than a religious attachment; it is also viewed as an ethnic identity with cultural, national and "racial" aspects. This dimension is not measurable in our data, however, since the polls available to us treat mixed marriage as a purely interreligious problem.

Within this limitation, highly instructive survey findings are available in addition to those already reviewed. Studies conducted during 1948–49 among cross sections of students and of adults posed the issue in terms of having a member of a minority group marry a near relative of the respondent. Among the students, 38 per cent mentioned Jews as objectionable in this context (R18, 1949); among the adults, 46 per cent did (R16, 1948). In another study, dating from 1950, 57 per cent of the respondents said they themselves would not want to marry a Jew (N24). These and earlier data, taken together, suggest that between 1940 and 1950 roughly half the population had fairly strong reservations about intermarriage with Jews, the particular proportion depending largely on how close to home this eventuality was visualized:

	Per cent
Would advise a friend not to intermarry (1940)	41
Would prefer not to have a close relative intermarry (1948)	46
Would definitely not want to intermarry themselves (1950)	57
Would advise a son or daughter not to intermarry (1944)	62

To assess possible changes in subsequent years, the 1950 question was repeated in 1962 (Table 40). Opposition to Jews as marriage partners turned out to have decreased notably during the interval: Flat rejection was less prevalent by 20 percentage points, while the proportion of individuals who would have no objection at all had risen by 8, and that of persons who

Table 40   Attitudes toward Own Intermarriage with Jews (1950, 1962)

"How would you feel about marrying a Jew? Which one of these statements [on card] comes closest to your own feelings?"

	Per cent[a]	
	1950	1962
"I definitely would not marry a Jew"	57	37
"I would rather not marry a Jew but it wouldn't matter too much"	16	25
"It would make no difference to me"	22	30
No opinion	5	8

[a] Christians only.
SOURCES: N24; G39.

would have only slight misgivings by 9. "No opinion" accounted for 3 percentage points more than formerly.

Since marriage would seem to constitute the ultimate degree of acceptance, the lessening resistance to Jews as potential wives or husbands probably is even more significant than the simultaneous lowering of barriers in other fields. Opposition to intermarriage remains much more widespread than any other form of rejection for which we have current data; but, significantly, it seems to have declined at about the same rate as hostility to Jews in the areas of work, residence and education (Figure 41).

Indeed, the trends in these key areas are so nearly parallel as to suggest that attitudes toward social relations with Jews are a unitary phenomenon. Once society admits the Jewish minority to full participation in some of the crucial areas of organized social interaction, growing readiness for intimacy —up to and including more frequent intermarriage—is apparently bound to follow.

Figure 41 Trends in Rejection of Jews (1938–62)

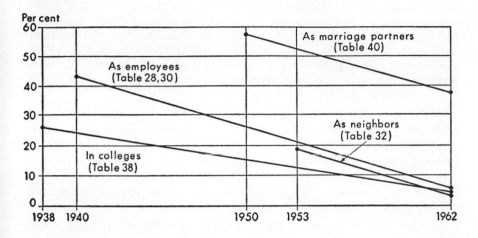

NOTES

1. Private codes, used in commercial employment agencies, have been a common means of evasion. As of 1958, over 72 per cent of the employment agencies in New York City accepted orders with discriminatory specifications; in the same year, only one of the 46 agencies in Denver refused illegal orders of this sort. American Jewish Committee: *Employment and Housing Discrimination Against Jews* (unpublished memorandum, March 6, 1962), p. 2.

2. A study undertaken during 1942 found "laborers" to be somewhat more ready than "farmers" to accept hypothetical fellow workers of Jewish or other white minority background (R5).

3. See Chicago Bureau on Jewish Employment Problems, *Memorandum on Management Opportunities in American Corporations,* January 1960; testimony of representatives of the Anti-Defamation League of B'nai B'rith before the Committee on Education and Labor, U.S. House of Representatives, November 3, 1961; American Jewish Committee, *Patterns of Exclusion from the Executive Suite: The Public Utilities Industry,* December 1963.

4. Data reported elsewhere indicate that seniors were less pessimistic on this score than freshmen, less likely to demand that Jews themselves change and more inclined to trust to publicity as a remedy. Other factors bearing on this question are assessed in Stember, *Education and Attitude Change,* pp. 155–167. The effects of college experience in decreasing prejudice are also discussed there.

5. For recent changes in attitudes toward Negroes, see Herbert H. Hyman and Paul B. Sheatsley, "Attitudes Toward Desegregation," *Scientific American,* CCXI, No. 1 (July 1964), 16–23.

6. To date, the effect of this legislation has been limited; fair-housing laws have been even more frequently evaded than fair-employment statutes.

7. In prestige neighborhoods, such restrictions still were widespread as of the early 1960s, being reported from virtually every major urban area in the United States. See Davis McEntire, *Residence and Race* (Berkeley: University of California Press, 1960), p. 71; American Jewish Committee, *Memorandum on Discrimination in Housing* (unpublished), March 1962. This applies both to certain upper-class suburbs and to a number of high-priced cooperative housing developments in large cities. See Jacob K. Javits, *Discrimination—U.S.A.* (New York: Harcourt, Brace & Co., 1960), p. 139.

8. There is some informal evidence, for example, that Jews are especially concerned about the quality of school facilities.

9. The 1942 poll was limited to factory workers, but its results differ so strikingly from those of the 1940 study as to suggest that a similarly distinctive result might have been obtained with a nationwide sample.

10. In the same poll, 72 per cent named Negroes, and only 13 per cent said it would make no difference to them what group moved in.

11. The 1950 survey, unlike the rest, employed a card containing a choice of possible answers. Conceivably, this is part of the reason why rejection of Jewish neighbors was registered most frequently in that year.

12. The upper extreme of the socio-economic scale is not likely to be adequately represented in nationwide samples of surveying agencies, because of its general inaccessibility.

13. Unwillingness to accept Jews as neighbors and in social situations generally has been found positively related to socio-economic status. See Stember, *op. cit.*, pp. 111–112.

14. That these commodities actually serve as marks of social identification is indicated by much advertising research.

15. This inordinately large response may be attributable, in part, to the wording of the question, which would seem destined to be answered in terms of the then widely voiced cliché, "Some of my best friends are Jews." The overrepresentation of urban areas and the use of voter samples in the surveys of the period may also have inflated the affirmative response. (See Appendix I.)

16. It would be comforting to assume that relationships between Jews and others would automatically improve with more frequent contacts of whatever kind. But we cannot take this for granted, since, as Deutsch and Collins have demonstrated, the effect of an encounter on attitudes depends largely on the conditions under which it takes place. See Morton Deutsch and Mary Collins, *Interracial Housing: A Psychological Evaluation of a Social Experiment* (Minneapolis: University of Minnesota Press, 1951). In surveys undertaken between 1944 and 1946, 12 to 15 per cent of respondents said they had "had unpleasant experiences recently with Jews," mostly in the course of business contact (O14, 15, 17). It is not hard to guess that at least some of the encounters in this common situation served only to validate the respondents' preconceived notions.

17. Tumin (*Inventory*, p. 91) suggests that Jewish-gentile intermixing might be expected to be "greater in the social than in the personal situation," but his thesis is based on data concerning participation in community affairs, which is never purely social in the sense that clubs and resorts are.

18. Barriers against Jews currently are much more prevalent in clubs than in such areas as education, employment, housing or public accommodations. In 1962, 67 per cent of a national cross section of 1,152 social clubs were found to practice religious discrimination; in nine cases out of ten, the practice was unofficial (Anti-Defamation League of B'nai B'rith, *Rights,* January 1962, January 1963). As for resorts discriminating against Jews, it was reported that their proportion had dropped from about 23 per cent in 1957 to somewhat under 10 per cent in 1963—a reduction amounting to about 60 per cent of the former figure (*ibid.,* February 1964). In this survey, however, information was obtained only from some 42 per cent of the 5,420 resorts queried; the rest may well have included a considerably larger proportion of discriminators.

19. "A consequence of the development of the Christian club has been the emergence of the 'Jewish club' " (*Rights,* January 1963). Of 90 Jewish clubs included in the Anti-Defamation League's study, 85 barred Christians (*ibid.*).

20. This finding parallels a situation observed by Asch, where an initially isolated member of a group found his confidence markedly bolstered by the emergence of a single ally. Asch, *Social Psychology,* p. 479.

21. Alternatively, the difference between the two sets of data may represent the difference between rabid and milder anti-Semites.

22. Our figures show the combined responses of freshmen and seniors, since the differences between the two groups were insignificant.

23. Stember, *op. cit.,* p. 107. It should be noted that college-educated adults from lower-class backgrounds showed an even lower level of prejudice than students (*ibid.,* p. 112).

24. In Washington, D.C., two generations ago, only 1.4 per cent of Jews married persons of other faiths; in the next generation the rate rose to 10.2 per cent, and in the one following to 17.9 per cent. Erich Rosenthal, "Studies of Jewish Intermarriage in the United States," *American Jewish Year Book,* LXIV (1963), 3–53. In Iowa, the proportion of Jews who intermarried rose from 36.3 to 53.6 per cent between 1953 and 1959 (*ibid.*).

25. These findings are not directly comparable with those in Table 39, since the latter specifically refer to marriage with a Jew rather than with someone "of a different faith."

V

Reactions to Anti-Semitic Appeals
before and during the War

SO FAR, MOST of our analyses have dealt with relatively long-term matters: with popular beliefs about the supposed nature of the Jew, and with the attitudes of Americans toward their Jewish fellow citizens in the interaction of everyday life. We now turn to another area of inquiry: the public's response to Jews in the shifting context of world events, beginning with the period before America's entry into the Second World War.

In the nearly nine years between Hitler's accession and Pearl Harbor, a host of anti-Semitic organizations sprang up in the United States;[1] and though the majority were hardly known outside their own circles of adherents, a few attracted nationwide attention and followings of some size. In the light of events in Germany, these movements appeared a good deal more threatening than they might have during calmer times. If a preposterous paperhanger could unleash terror and persecution on the Jewish citizens of one of the world's most advanced countries, then anti-Semitic movements everywhere—even in America—had to be reckoned with as an authentic menace, no matter how fantastic their aims or how slim their chances of success.

As the United States turned from isolation to increasing involvement in the affairs of Europe, and as the tensions between Germany and the West approached a crisis, American opinion slowly but steadily consolidated on the side of the Allies. The climate in America grew increasingly unfavorable to overt anti-Jewish agitation; hostility against Jews became irreconcilable, at least nominally and officially, with the developing national consensus. In the end, the United States' entry into the war placed the nation squarely on the side of Hitler's victims and among the avowed opponents of anti-Semitism.

But this pro-Allied consensus was not reached without formidable controversy. Until the last moment, it was strenuously opposed by a variety of groups—not only by the little bands of pro-Nazis and organized anti-Semites, but also by large numbers of German-Americans with pro-German if not pro-Nazi sympathies, and, most important, by a wide range of persons and organizations with isolationist or "anti-war" viewpoints (including, after the Soviet-German pact of 1939, the Communist-led left wing). Notwithstanding the differences in their ideologies, all of these groups found themselves wittingly or unwittingly echoing the propaganda Hitler was disseminating to keep America neutral—propaganda which was sometimes openly anti-Semitic. And even after Pearl Harbor put an end to these efforts, anti-Semitism continued to lead a vigorous life in the unofficial minds of many Americans. It was thus only natural that a great deal of public-opinion research, both before and during the war, focused on the American people's knowledge of anti-Semitic spokesmen or organizations, and on public responses to openly anti-Jewish appeals.

Familiarity with Anti-Semitic Groups and Individuals

Public awareness of overtly anti-Jewish groups and their spokesmen was measured between August 1940 and February 1942 by a series of four surveys (Table 42). At the time of the first, somewhat over a fifth of the population had heard of such agitation. Less than half this number remem-

Table 42 Awareness of Anti-Semitic Groups and Spokesmen (1940–42)

"Have you heard of any organizations or men who are trying to stir up feeling against the Jews in this country?" (If "yes": "Name it (them)."

	Per cent of those answering "yes"			
	August 1940 (22 per cent of total sample)	February 1941 (17 per cent of total sample)	October 1941 (19 per cent of total sample)	February 1942 (14 per cent of total sample)
German-American Bund	50	52	25	27
Ku Klux Klan	25	13	8	19
Charles E. Coughlin	20	15	7	14
Silver Shirts	10	17	6	14
Christian Front	9	5	3	4
Germans	5	9	7	5
America First Committee	0	0	20	8
Charles A. Lindbergh	0	0	32	7
(Scattering of other mentions)				

SOURCES: O9–12.

bered actually seeing or reading anti-Semitic books, pamphlets or periodicals; but this figure meant little, since propaganda was disseminated chiefly on the air, and demagogues like the Reverend Charles E. Coughlin reached large radio audiences week after week.[2]

In three of the four polls, the German-American Bund appeared as the best-known promoter of anti-Semitism. In 1940 and early 1941, it ranked far ahead of all other groups and individuals. But during the months that followed, the perceived locus of Fascist or Nazi-like tendencies seems to have begun a shift from the hyphenated fringes of American society toward its native core. For a brief period during the fall of 1941, the America First Committee became widely known as an anti-Semitic force.

The Committee was an aggregation of individuals with widely varying viewpoints, united by a common desire to keep the United States from going to war on the side of the Allies. Inevitably, Nazi sympathizers and other bigots joined, giving the organization an anti-Jewish cast. As if to deepen that taint, Charles A. Lindbergh, speaking at Des Moines under the Committee's auspices, accused the Jews, together with pro-British interests and the Roosevelt administration, of trying to draw America into the conflict.[3] Thanks to this speech, Lindbergh temporarily eclipsed the German-American Bund as the best-known purveyor of anti-Semitic propaganda. Soon afterward, however, America's entry into the war brought this shift to an abrupt halt. By February 1942, public opinion was once more thinking of anti-Semitic propaganda as the work of fringe groups—notably of the Bund, which actually had been outlawed by this time.

Frequent mention of the Bund was not the only indication that Americans during the early 1940s tended to view anti-Semitism as something German. Throughout another series of surveys, extending from 1940 to 1944, a majority categorically agreed that "the German *government* is trying to stir up feelings against the Jews in this country" (O9–14). The idea attained its widest acceptance in December 1942, with about two-thirds of respondents in agreement. By 1944, it was a good deal less common; evidently hostility toward Jews was no longer as widely considered an alien attitude.

If the Bund was, by and large, the best-known of anti-Jewish organizations, its leader, Fritz Kuhn, was also widely noted. As of 1940, his name was known to no less than 70 per cent of the public (O8). In the same poll, only 41 per cent reported having heard of General George Van Horn Mosely, a militaristic nationalist who charged Jews with promoting Communism through their alleged control of the mass media and power in international finance; and in 1944, only 36 per cent recognized the name of Gerald L. K. Smith, who was then attempting to organize a political party of his own and running for President in several states (O14).

To be sure, Kuhn was not, literally speaking, the most prominent anti-Semitic individual. That distinction fell to Father Coughlin, who was then arousing prodigious attention and enthusiasm, particularly among lower-class Catholics.[4] In a survey undertaken during 1940, over 90 per cent of the population said they had heard of Coughlin (O8); four years later, long after he passed his peak, his name still was familiar to more than four-fifths (O14). Beyond doubt, however, only a fraction of the respondents knew him in his capacity as an anti-Semitic agitator (see Table 43).[5]

The bulk of the large majorities familiar with Father Coughlin's name did not follow his radio broadcasts faithfully. According to surveys conducted in 1939 and 1940, only 6 per cent of the population listened to him "regularly" and a little over 40 per cent "occasionally" (O7, 8). Still, substantial numbers evidently did not need to hear the "radio priest" frequently in order to agree with him; an average of 37 per cent in the two surveys generally approved of what he said, which suggests that he gave voice to the ideas and prejudices of large numbers outside his immediate following. Moreover, those who agreed with Coughlin, though never more than a minority of the population, seem to have been fairly well united around a few central ideas; in contrast, those who disapproved of him based their criticisms on the most varied grounds, some of them far from democratic in spirit (Table 43).

Table 43   Reasons for Disapproval of Father Coughlin (1940)

"In general, do you approve or disapprove of what he [Father Coughlin] says?"

	Per cent
Approve	17
Disapprove	29
No opinion	54

"Why?"

	Per cent of those disapproving
Too radical, red	33
Rabble rouser	17
Clergy should not mix in politics	16
Logic unsound, opinionated	13
Disagree in principle	7
Creates race prejudice; fascistic	5
Fanatical, crackpot	5
Un-American	4
Makes personal attacks; criticizes President	2
Other	13

SOURCE: O8.

Charges of Warmongering and Profiteering

In the critical months just before Pearl Harbor, the allegation that Jews were seeking to draw America into the European war appears to have been widely noted. As poll results plainly show, Lindbergh's charge against the Jews attracted more public attention than the other parts of his threefold indictment. Just under half of the population knew enough about his speech to name one or another of the groups he had accused of warmongering. Of those who did, two-fifths, equivalent to approximately one-fifth of the total sample, recalled the anti-Jewish remarks (Table 44). The Roosevelt Ad-

Table 44 Familiarity with Lindbergh's Charges of Warmongering (1941)

"Lindbergh recently made a speech in which he mentioned three groups which he said are trying to get the United States into the war. Do you happen to know what three groups he mentioned?"

	Per cent of respondents naming any group (48 per cent of total sample)
Jews	40
The Roosevelt Administration	31
Pro-British groups	21
Other	15

SOURCE: O11.

ministration was mentioned a good deal less frequently, and pro-British circles only half as often.

When the famous aviator spoke, three months before Pearl Harbor, neutralism actually was well on the way out and pro-Allied sentiment had become widespread. It was therefore hardly surprising that only 22 per cent of the respondents in a poll taken during October indicated agreement with what "Lindbergh says about the war" (O11). What is more noteworthy is that a full 20 per cent expressed no opinion on this burning issue. Some of the latter, no doubt, were ignorant of what Lindbergh had said, but others may well have been reluctant to express approval, since his views were being scathingly condemned by a large part of the public. No less than 25 per cent of those respondents who disagreed with him referred to him as a traitor, Fascist or pro-German, while many others called him un-American or a troublemaker.

Most of the public would have no part of Lindbergh's accusation against the Jews, if we may trust the results of an open-end survey in October 1941. Only 6 per cent of the sample spontaneously named Jews as a group trying to get America into the war (Table 45)—much fewer than mentioned the Roosevelt Administration or big business. On other occasions,

Table 45   Beliefs about Warmongering by Certain Groups (1941)

"What persons or groups do you think are most active in trying to get us into the war?"

	Per cent
The Roosevelt Administration; the Democrats	19
Big business, capitalists, financiers	18
Foreign interests and agents	13
Jews	6
Pro-British groups	6

SOURCE: G7.

however, the issue had been put explicitly, and here the rejection was a good deal less clear-cut. In four surveys between 1939 and 1941, about a third of the population had answered "yes" when asked whether "the Jews in this country would like to get the United States into the European war" (O7, 9–11).

The motivations imputed to Jews by those who replied "yes" in this series of polls corresponded to the established images of the "clannish" and "greedy" Jew discussed earlier.[6] The largest number of comments mentioned the Jews' concern for their own group, and one comment in four said Jews hoped to make money out of the war. In surprising contrast to the latter finding, profiteering figured only as a minor theme of anti-Semitic feeling once the nation had actually entered the conflict. During March 1942, no more than 1 per cent of the population named Jews among "people or groups that are taking unfair advantage of the war to get money or power for themselves" (OP2). Even when Jews were explicitly mentioned in a prepared list, in an alternate version of the question, only 13 per cent charged them with profiteering, while 53 per cent accused labor leaders and 25 per cent businessmen.

Accusations of Shirking in Wartime

On the eve of American participation in the war and during its early phase, hostility toward actual or supposed shirkers was not focused on Jews to any appreciable degree. In November 1941, a survey asked which groups in a prepared list were doing "less than others for national defense" (OP1); only 7 per cent of respondents selected Jews. (Six times as many made the charge against labor leaders.) Spontaneous mentions were similarly sparse; thus, in October 1942 and June 1943, only 2 and 4 per cent, respectively, named the Jews among "groups of people who have gotten off easier than most others" (N2, 5).

During the same phase of the war, however, a more specific question yielded quite a different result. In December 1942, it was asked whether "there are any particular religious, nationality or racial groups who are not doing all they could to help win the war" (O13). One might have expected that persons of "enemy" descent would head the list of presumed slackers, and that Jews, being obvious enemies of Hitler, would be recognized for the strong supporters of the war they actually were. But the figures indicate otherwise: Jews were called shirkers twice as often as either Germans or Japanese.

The proportions involved in this set of findings were not large; less than a third of the population named any groups, and only a little over 10 per cent mentioned Jews. Yet, even so, the data confront us with a seeming contradiction. Before Pearl Harbor, Jews were suspected with some frequency of wanting to draw the United States into the war; but once we were in it, their support of the war effort was questioned, if not very often, at least more often than that of any other ethnic group.

The clue to this paradox probably lies in the changing meaning of the war itself. What had initially appeared as an ideological crusade may have come to be viewed increasingly as a patriotic national war against the German and Japanese people, not merely their totalitarian leaders. Under these circumstances, support for the war effort would naturally be viewed as a function of loyalty to the United States; and if Jews were widely charged with shirking, it was probably because their loyalties were often thought to be principally to their own group, not the larger society. The patriotism of Jews was consistently doubted by at least a quarter of the population between 1938 and 1942 (Table 46).[7]

Table 46   Beliefs about the Patriotism of Jews (1938–42)

"Do you think Jews in the United States are as patriotic, more patriotic or less patriotic than other citizens?"

Per cent answering "less"[a]

March 1938	May 1938	November 1938	September 1939	April 1940
31	31	26	30	30

Per cent answering "less" [a]

August 1940	February 1941	October 1941	February 1942	December 1942
25	28	25	24	25

[a] An average of about 5 per cent answered "more."
SOURCES: O1, 2, 4, 7–13.

Complaints about shirking by Jews centered chiefly on their alleged unwillingness to serve in the armed forces. Jews were specifically accused of draft-dodging at least as frequently as they were charged with lack of patriotism generally. Six surveys, conducted between 1941 and 1945 and based on two different questions, indicate convincingly that throughout the war many Americans thought Jews were particularly disinclined to enter the services (Table 47).[8] The notion actually seems to have grown in preva-

Table 47   Beliefs about Jews' and Others' Willingness to Serve in the Armed Forces (1941–45)

(February 1941:) *"Do you think that Jews today are generally more willing or less willing than other Americans to be drafted for military service?"*

(October 1941 through March 1945:) *"Do you think that Jews in the United States are generally   . . . [as above]."*

	Per cent			
	February 1941	October 1941	December 1942	March 1945
More	5	4	4	2
Less	33	37	36	42
Same	36	28	35	34
No opinion	26	31	25	22

"Do you think that any of these groups are less willing than other Americans to go into the armed forces?" (If "yes":) *"Which groups?"*

	Per cent of those answering "yes"	
	May–June 1944 (56 per cent of total sample)	March 1945 (51 per cent of total sample)
Jews	68 [a]	33 [b]
German-Americans	36	13
Negroes	14	7
Italian-Americans	12	4
Catholics	6	2
Irish-Americans	4	†

† Less than ½ of 1 per cent.
[a] Equivalent to 38 per cent of total sample.   [b] Equivalent to 17 per cent of total sample.
SOURCES: O10, 11, 13–15.

lence at least until the spring of 1944; thereafter, according to one set of data, it took a steep drop, though according to the other it continued to rise slightly (Figure 48). Since we cannot reconcile this discrepancy, we shall draw no firm conclusions about the exact trend of opinion. But in any event, two facts stand out clearly: About a third of the population thought Jews wanted to avoid military service; and Jews were far more frequently accused of such desires than any other ethnic group in the population, not excluding the German and Italian Americans, with whose kinsmen we were at war.

Figure 48   Beliefs about Jews in Relation to the War (1938–45)

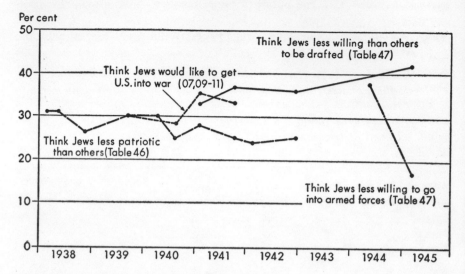

A related rumor current around 1944 accused Jews of avoiding danger-ous assignments. A poll dating from that year asked whether members of any particular groups were especially likely to shirk combat duty; of those who thought so, a full three-fourths, corresponding to 37 per cent of the total sample, named Jews (Table 49).

What are the sources of these accusations, which had no basis whatever in the actions or beliefs of Jews, and actually ran counter to their obvious desire to see Hitler defeated? Viewed against the traditional American re-spect for the fighting man, the talk about Jewish slackers might seem to

Table 49   Beliefs about Jews' and Other Groups' Desire to Avoid Com-bat Duty (1944)

"Once they are in the service, do you think any of these [groups] are more likely than other Americans to try to get out of actual fighting?" (If "yes":) *"Which ones?"*

	Per cent of those answering "yes" (49 per cent of total sample)
Jews	75[a]
German-Americans	26
Negroes	14
Italian-Americans	10
Catholics	4
Irish-Americans	2

[a] Equivalent to 37 per cent of total sample.

SOURCE: O14.

constitute a blanket indictment for cowardice. But there is reason to doubt that cowardice is the only or even the chief point at issue, since nowhere in our data, nor in any others we have seen, are Jews taxed with this vice *per se,* apart from wartime conditions. We believe charges of shirking by Jews to have a different basis; but in order to explore this avenue, we must first consider what military service meant to Americans during the Second World War.

From the time it was instituted, more than a year before the nation's entry into the war, the draft evoked an ambivalent public response.[9] On one hand, military service was considered an obligation or test of masculinity, as well as a kind of adventure for patriotic ends. On the other, it was seen as a hardship, involving as it did the breaking of family ties and the loss of jobs and income. Inevitably, there was much anger over actual or supposed injustice in the granting of exemptions and deferments, as well as widespread feeling that such privileges were being obtained by undeserving "smart operators" or those "on the inside." Similarly, within the armed forces, complaints about favoritism and about the seeking-out of advantageous assignments or positions were all but universal.

Jews, we believe, were predestined for such accusations by pre-existing popular notions of "Jewish characteristics." As happens so frequently, the established image determined specific percepts, creating a well-rounded, plausible stereotype calculated to justify popular notions independent of whatever the facts may have been. Jews were widely thought to be "greedy" and "shrewd," that is, both desirous and unusually capable of looking after their own interests; therefore, it was perhaps inevitable that they should be scored as seekers of exemption and special privilege or as especially loath to give up civilian life with its opportunities for making money.

In this context, then, Jews were considered nonconforming strangers with a self-centered morality of their own—a morality which supposedly permitted them to undercut the patriotism of the larger society without loss of self-esteem. Service in the armed forces and exposure to danger were frequently seen as the lot of the "suckers"; and insofar as Jews were accused of avoiding these situations, they were categorized as "smart operators" who know better than to get into hazardous situations for possibly dubious ends. This view would seem to agree with certain images observed or deduced by a number of investigators, though not documented in public opinion data: the perception of Jews as nonconformists whose values do not always correspond to those of the cultural majority;[10] as sophisticates and cosmopolitans with few ties to locale or position;[11] as dwellers in the hated and envied big city, living not by honest toil but by sharpness and slickness.[12] In addition, there are indications that Jews were widely thought of as non-physical types, as high-strung, introspective people—an image of considerable age, which probably cast further doubt on their readiness to enter the military life.[13]

Of all the accusations leveled against the Jewish group during the period we are studying, those concerning military service are probably the most virulent, the most charged with hostility and contempt. Like a number of other anti-minority ideas, discussed elsewhere in this book, they attained their widest currency in the spring of 1944. We can only guess at the reasons why bigotry should reach a peak at a time when America was fighting the persecutors of the Jews and when the Government was constantly stressing America's commitment to the democratic rights of peoples everywhere; but there are strong indications that the general fear, insecurity and economic frustration of wartime played a major part. Significantly, anti-Semitic feeling was highest during the Allied invasion of Normandy, perhaps the most precarious phase of the war. Soon after this crisis, various forms of anti-Jewish prejudice began to drop off; one year later, with peace in sight and tensions less acute, hostility toward minorities had been much reduced.

Beliefs about the Power and Influence of Jews

Criticism of Jews has often focused on their alleged power. For generations, the malevolent influence of the "hidden hand" has been a stock theme of anti-Semitic propaganda. Father Coughlin's Social Justice movement proved particularly adept at making political capital of this idea, as did Lindbergh, who said in his Des Moines speech, in September 1941, that the Jews' "greatest danger to this country lies in their large ownership and influence in our motion pictures, our press, our radio and our government." [14] Starting in 1938, many public-opinion studies explored this subject, sometimes seeking to identify any and all groups to which undue influence was attributed, but more often concentrating on ideas concerning "Jewish power."

A question asked in 14 polls between March 1938 and February 1946 found that one-third to one-half of the population considered Jews too powerful (Table 50). The proportion who subscribed to this idea grew, slowly but steadily, from a minority at the end of the 1930s into a majority during and just after the war. But when the same question was once more asked in 1962, the affirmative response dropped to less than a third of the 1946 level, the "don't knows" increased by about one-half and the proportion who said Jews did *not* have too much power was twice as large as formerly.

Similar trends are evident in other studies. A broadly focused poll taken in 1943 and 1945 asked about "any racial or religious groups that have too much power in this country"; a stable proportion of about 13 per cent named Jews in response to this open query, and about 10 per cent named Catholics (N6, 10). But in 1953, a comparable study conducted by a different agency revealed a profoundly changed picture; when asked

Table 50   Beliefs about Power of Jews (1938–62)

"Do you think the Jews have too much power in the United States?"

	Per cent				
	March 1938	May 1938	November 1938	February 1939	April 1940
Yes	41	36	35	41	43
No	46	47	49	48	40
Don't know	13	17	16	11	17

	Per cent				
	August 1940	February 1941	October 1941	February 1942	December 1942
Yes	42	45	48	47	51
No	42	41	37	38	33
Don't know	16	14	15	15	16

	Per cent				
	May 1944	March 1945	June 1945	February 1946	June 1962
Yes	56	56	58	55	17
No	30	29	29	33	66
Don't know	14	15	13	12	17

SOURCES: O1, 2, 4–5, 8–17; G38.

whether "any one racial or religious group" had "too much power and influence," only 1 per cent of respondents mentioned Jews, while Negroes were named twice as often and Catholics were cited by 11 per cent (P3). Even while allowing for a slight difference in wording, we can hardly doubt that suspicions of excessive Jewish power had fallen off precipitously at some time after 1945. Intense concern with this issue, then, evidently was in large part a transient phenomenon specific to the war years and the period immediately thereafter.

That fear of Jewish power reached a peak following the end of the war finds additional confirmation in still another study, carried out in 1942 and repeated in 1945 (Table 51). These surveys, unlike the others of the period, asked about Jewish "influence" as well as "power." The proportion of persons who believed Jews were too powerful or influential shows an even greater increase between 1942 and 1945 than do the corresponding proportions in Table 50.

From these generally consistent findings we must turn to a set of sharply conflicting data, obtained by an open-end question also asked in 1945, which read: "Are there any groups of people or organizations that you think have more to say about running this country than they should have?" (N10). Respondents who answered "yes" were asked to name the organizations or groups. Whereas, in the survey just described, 67 per cent of the

Table 51   Beliefs about Power and Influence of Jews (1942, 1945)

"Do you think the Jews have too much power and influence in this country?"

	Per cent	
	1942	1945
Yes	44	67
No	41	23
No opinion	15	10

SOURCES: OP3, 4.

population said Jews had too much power and influence when explicitly asked about them, a mere 4 per cent now mentioned them spontaneously among overly powerful "groups of people or organizations"—fewer than mentioned "the Government" (6 per cent)! Jews were named no more frequently than big business; labor unions were cited five times as often.

What, then, was the real feeling about "Jewish power and influence" in 1945? Is it reflected more accurately by the 4 per cent finding or the 67 per cent? To us, both seem significant. The lower figure indicates that Americans did not, by themselves, tend to be preoccupied with "Jewish power"; it accords with the fact that no widespread campaign against Jews materialized. The higher figure, on the other hand, shows how ready large numbers were to accept the myth of the all-powerful Jew when it was suggested to them. It thus illustrates the extent of latent or potential anti-Semitism at the time: While spontaneous resentment was focused in part on groups other than Jews, it could be refocused on the Jew with disturbing ease.

In this sense, the 17 per cent affirmative response to the 1962 question (see Table 50)—which, it will be recalled, explicitly mentions Jews—bespeaks a massive diminution of latent anti-Jewish attitudes, at least insofar as they were based on the Jews' presumed vast power. Evidently this particular *bête noire* has lost its appeal for the time being. Even so, we ought to note that the affirmative replies of 1962 plus the "don't knows" (which might be convertible into affirmatives) still make up one-third of the total.

In some polls taken between 1938 and 1942, respondents who thought Jews unduly powerful were asked: "What would you like to see done to reduce this power?" (Table 52). "Restricting Jews in business" and "keeping them out of government and politics" were the most frequently made suggestions, but "driving them out of the United States" was mentioned almost as often. Other replies envisioned curbs on Jewish immigration, laws to limit the rights of Jews, heavier taxes on Jews, segregation and boycotting. Menacing as this may sound, it must be borne in mind that the total proportion who thought Jews had too much power was never a majority, so that the incidence of such ideas actually was not very great. Thus, the highest percentage registered (the 28 per cent who during October 1941 would

Table 52   Actions Advocated to Reduce the Supposed Power of Jews (1938–42)

"Do you think the Jews have too much power in the United States?" (If "yes":) *"What would you like to see done to reduce this power?"*

Per cent of those answering "yes" [a]

	May[b] 1938	November[b] 1938	April 1940	August 1940	February 1941	October 1941	February 1942
Restrict Jews in business	18	25	31	28	24	28	16
Keep Jews out of government and politics	24	17	21	19	22	22	12
Drive Jews out of the United States	20	12	18	16	16	19	15

[a] For proportion of "yes" replies in total samples, see Table 50.
[b] Asked only of native-born with native-born parents.
SOURCES: O2, 4, 8–12.

"restrict Jews in business") represents only 13 per cent of the general population.

The ideas for curbing "Jewish power" show no particular trends. By and large, responses over the four years are stable, with perhaps somewhat diminished incidences after Pearl Harbor. Nor does any one prescription occur with especial frequency; the wide range of the replies illustrates the absence of a consensus—though it may be significant that an idea as crude as "driving the Jews out of the country" received almost as much support as far milder alternatives.

The Nature of the Jews' Supposed Power

One question left unresolved by the data so far presented is the nature of the Jews' presumed power. Having observed earlier that the popular mind viewed the Jew first and foremost as an "economic man," we would guess that the power envisioned was principally that of money. As it happens, this guess can be verified. In some of the surveys from 1938 to 1962, respondents who said Jews were too powerful were asked: "In what fields particularly?" (Table 53). The results leave no doubt that the economic realm is what most respondents had in mind. In each of the polls reported (except that of 1962), four-fifths or more mentioned business or financial pursuits, while a third or less named politics and government.

Within this general picture, some fluctuations are worth noting. Belief in the predominance of Jews in "finance" diminished during the war, while concern over their influence in what the polls rather loosely termed "busi-

Table 53   Beliefs Concerning the Nature of the Jews' Supposed Power
(1938–62)

"Do you think the Jews have too much power in the United States?" (If
"yes":) *"In what fields particularly?"* [a]

Per cent of those answering "yes"

	March 1938	February 1942	December 1942	May 1944	March 1945	June 1945	February 1946	June 1962
Economic fields:								
Finance	42	46	43	38	34	29	29	18
Business and commerce	47	45	41	43	49	41	43	47
Clothing industry	39	7	4	5	5	5	7	6
Manufacturing	5	4	2	2	7	5	9	1 [b]
Total	133 [c]	102 [c]	90	88	95	80	88	72
Other fields:								
Politics and government	10	16	34	30	33	21	24	12
Law and justice	3	3	2	3	2	1	2	1 [b]
Entertainment	21	12	9	10	9	7	9	6
Other	28	15	9	24	12	7	11	23
Total	62	46	54	67	56	36	46	42
Per cent of total sample who think Jews have too much power	41	47	51	56	56	58	55	17

[a] Wording in 1938 and 1962: ". . . *In what lines particularly?*"
[b] Approximated from data.
[c] Total over 100 due to multiple answers.
SOURCES: O1, 12–17; G38.

ness and commerce" remained high. As for Jewish political power, references were fairly rare before the war, increased markedly in 1942 and fell
off again after the war's end.

Subsequent studies undertaken in 1947, 1948 and 1949 shed further
light on these fluctuations, though the issue was framed in somewhat different terms and the results are not wholly comparable with those just presented. These polls asked whether Protestants, Catholics, Jews or Negroes
were getting too much economic or political power (Table 54). Much
fewer complaints than in earlier polls were registered against the Jews' role
in the former sphere—not necessarily because resentment had actually lessened, but perhaps only because the ill-chosen abstract term "economic
power" may have meant little to uneducated respondents.[15] A similar

Table 54   Beliefs Concerning the Jews' Supposed Economic and Political Power (1947–49)

"Do you think any of these groups [Protestants, Catholics, Jews and Negroes, listed on card] are getting more economic power anywhere in the United States than is good for the country?"

"Do you think any of these groups are getting more political power anywhere in the United States than is good for the country?"

	Per cent naming Jews		
	1947	1948	1949
Economic power	36	38	24
Political power	21	19	6

SOURCES: R13, 16, 18.

vagueness, though possibly in less degree, would seem to have been inherent in the term "political power" (as against "politics and government" in the older polls); the average respondent probably referred the term, not to the policy-making levels of government, but to political parties or machines —a sphere in which Jews have not been perceived as active to an objectionable degree.

But while these circumstances keep the two sets of data from being directly comparable, the trend within the three-year span of the studies is clear enough: Complaints about economic matters predominate as they did in the earlier figures; objections to economic power gradually lessen, as did those to financial (though not to "business") influence above; and concern about Jews in politics again shows a marked decline, dwindling to insignificance by 1949.

A poll conducted on six occasions between 1942 and 1945, asking whether Jews had "too much influence in the business world," "not enough" or "about the amount they should have," makes it abundantly clear—if clarification is still needed—that "Jewish power" was viewed first and foremost as economic (N1, 3, 6, 9, 11, 12). The "too much" responses, ranging from 50 to 58 per cent, were almost identical with those reported in Table 50, where the kind of power was not specified in the question.[16]

Beliefs about the political role of Jews during the New Deal were gauged by a question asked in three surveys during 1938: "Do you think there are too many Jews holding government offices and jobs?" An average of about 23 per cent said "yes" (about the same proportion as thought the government employed too many Catholics); roughly twice as many answered "no" (O1, 2, 4). In 1943, a somewhat higher affirmative response—33 per cent —was registered to the question whether Roosevelt had appointed too many Jews to jobs in Washington (G9). In the same poll, however, the proportion who expressed "no opinion" increased to 46 per cent from a previous average of about 30. In any event, we may conclude that Jews in government positions were less of a focus of anti-Semitism during those years than Jews in the economic world.

One other attitude toward Jews in politics has been explored by public-opinion research: willingness to vote for a hypothetical Jew seeking the Presidency (Table 55). Unfortunately, differences in question wording pre-

Table 55 Attitudes toward a Hypothetical Jewish Candidate for the Presidency (1937–59)

(1937:) *"Would you vote for a Jew for President who was well qualified for the position?"*

(1958:) *"If your party nominated a generally well-qualified man for President and he happened to be a Jew, would you vote for him?"*

(1959:) *"If your party nominated a generally well-qualified man for President who happened to be a Jew, would you vote for him?"*

Per cent answering "yes"

1937	1958	1959
49	62	72

(1958 replies concerning other hypothetical candidates:)

Per cent answering "yes"

A Baptist	92
A Catholic	68
An atheist	18
A woman	52

SOURCES: G1, 35, 37.

vent precise comparisons between the data obtained. What evidence we do have suggests that resistance to a well-qualified Jewish Presidential candidate declined markedly over the years: From over half of the population in 1937, the opposition shrank to not much more than a quarter in 1959. In 1958, a hypothetical Jewish candidate would have been almost as acceptable as a Catholic one; in 1959, he would have been more eligible than the Catholic the year before. Indeed, as of 1958 Jews appear to have been more popular than women, at least for Presidential purposes. By the end of the 1950s, then, not only had earlier concern about "Jewish political power" dwindled away; only a minority still opposed Jews even as top political leaders.

Taken together, our data confirm beyond reasonable doubt that the image of the Jew as a threatening power in politics was largely a passing phenomenon of the war years or perhaps, more exactly, of the Roosevelt

Administration's later years. Even then, this image failed to gain acceptance by a majority of the population, and after the coming of peace it declined to its earlier level of insignificance. In contrast, the view of the Jew as an "economic man" has proved extraordinarily tenacious. Throughout the period under study, resentment against Jews—insofar as it was a function of images—focused chiefly on the figure of the businessman successful beyond the point of acceptability to non-Jews. Even during recent years, when complaints about Jewish power in general had become less prevalent than formerly, Jewish power "in business and commerce" (though not "in finance") came in for unfavorable mention as frequently as ever.

The Idea of a Jewish Menace to America

Related to the notion of excessive Jewish power, though much vaguer, is the professional anti-Semites' perennial theme of an internal "Jewish threat to America." Popular fears of a Jewish or other domestic menace were assessed in a series of surveys begun in 1940. Of the resulting data, we present those concerning the groups most frequently mentioned as threats, including Jews, Negroes, Germans and Japanese (Table 56 and Figure 56A).

Up to America's entry into the war, the figures indicate little apprehension about Negroes or about Japanese living in the United States, and much about Jews and Germans residing here. After Pearl Harbor, as might be expected, uneasiness about Japanese and Germans rose, but within a year it began to subside, and by 1950 it had dwindled to the vanishing point. The notion of a Jewish threat, on the other hand, took a slight dip at the outset of the war, only to rise to a peak in June 1944. At the same time, fear of Negroes, which had been steadily increasing, outstripped concern over Japanese and Germans.

The figures for Negroes and Jews remained high and ran roughly parallel until after the end of the war, but by 1950 they had begun to diverge, and 12 years later they had moved far apart. The new, militant desegregation movement of the early 1960s sent apprehensions concerning the Negro even higher than in 1944–46, while notions of a "Jewish menace" had almost vanished.

That public concern in 1942–44 could shift so rapidly and decisively as to make the cousins of the Germans we were fighting appear less menacing than the cousins of their chief victims would seem to indicate that apprehensions about Germans (and Japanese) were never more than a momentary reaction to the outbreak of war, while anti-Jewish feeling was deeply rooted in the society. Only if we assume the latter can we explain why the belief in Jews as a threat remained at a high level until at least 1946 or why it actually became more prevalent after the most notorious anti-Semitic movements, such as the German-American Bund, were disbanded. Once

Table 56 Jews and Other Minority Groups as Supposed Menaces to America (1940–62)

"In your opinion, what nationality, religious or racial groups in this country are a menace [threat] to America?" [a]

	Per cent [b]				
	August 1940	February 1941	October 1941	February 1942	December 1942
Jews	17	18	20	15	15
Negroes	2	3	2	2	4
Catholics	6	5	4	5	3
Germans	14	14	16	18	14
Japanese	6	6	4	24	19

	Per cent [b]					
	June 1944	March 1945	June 1945	February 1946	November 1950	June 1962
Jews	24	19	20	22	5	1
Negroes	11	11	11	15	6	16 [c]
Catholics	5	3	3	9	6	0
Germans	6	4	3	1	1	0
Japanese	9	5	4	1	0	0

[a] In some surveys, the terms were presented in a different order ("religious, nationality or racial groups"), and in some (beginning with December 1942) the word "threat" appeared instead of "menace"—either on part of the ballots or exclusively. Split ballots of either kind are averaged here.

[b] Less frequently named groups are omitted here, as are irrelevant replies (those mentioning groups which are not national, religious or racial).

[c] Includes specific mention of Black Muslims.

NOTE: A different form of this question, not comparable with the above, found about 1 per cent naming Jews in 1954 and 1955.

SOURCES: O9–17; N24; G38.

established, the notion of a "Jewish menace" evidently did not depend for its survival on organized hate groups; the propaganda disseminated by Henry Ford in the 1920s and by demagogues like Father Coughlin in the 1930s remained effective until peace restored a cooler atmosphere. In subsequent sections we will present further evidence that the war years did not evoke favorable attitudes toward Hitler's victims but quite the reverse.

Somewhat less hostility toward Jews is evinced by a group of polls, dating in part from the same period, which asked what "groups of people . . . might be harmful to the future of the country unless they are curbed" or (in some of the replications) "cannot be trusted as much as others in time of danger" (R6, 7, 10, 16; N29, 31). In the replies, Jews were mentioned with decreasing frequency from 1943 on; in 1953 and 1954 no more than 1 per cent of the respondents cited them as untrustworthy. Negroes were named somewhat more often, but the response, by and large, was not so

Figure 56A Jews and Other Minority Groups as Supposed Menaces to America (1940–62)

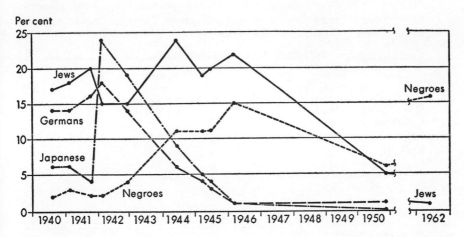

much in terms of ethnic as of organized groups, probably because of the rather vague reference to "groups of people" in the question.

The Outlook for Anti-Semitic Campaigns

The public's expectations concerning the possibility of an active anti-Semitic campaign in the United States were first gauged in 1938, and measurements were continued in one form or another until after the end of the war. The results are only roughly comparable because of a change in question wording; until 1942, the polls asked solely about a campaign against Jews (Table 57), whereas later Negroes, Catholics, Jews, "radicals" and

Table 57 Expectations of Anti-Semitic Campaign (1938–45)

"Do you think there is likely to be a widespread campaign against the Jews in this country?"

Per cent answering "yes"

March 1938	May 1938	November 1938	February 1939	May 1939	September 1939[a]	April 1940
26	19	20	22	19	21	30

Per cent answering "yes"

August 1940[a]	February 1941[a]	October 1941[a]	February 1942[a]	December 1942	March 1945
25	25	23	19	29	30

[a] Wording in these surveys: ". . . *against Jews* . . ."
SOURCES: O1, 2, 4–13, 15.

Table 58 Expectations of Campaigns against Jews and Other Groups (1944–46)

"Do you think there is likely to be a widespread campaign in this country against any of the following groups—Negroes, Catholics, Jews, radicals or foreigners?" (If "yes":) *"Which groups?"*

Per cent of those answering "yes"

	June 1944	March 1945	June 1945	February 1946
Negroes	41	26	29	22
Catholics	8	4	3	6
Jews	57	24	26	27
Radicals	33	9	10	15
Foreigners	16	9	9	10
Per cent of total sample naming Jews	35	12	13	13

SOURCES: O14–17.

"foreigners" were included as possible targets (Table 58). Yet, even so, the findings are instructive.

No marked change in expectations was registered from 1938 through 1942; the figures fluctuated from 19 to 30 per cent, without apparent direction. In June 1944, when the alternative target groups were mentioned for the first time, the percentage expecting an anti-Semitic campaign rose to 35. It might be thought that the change in the question caused this increased response, but the March 1945 poll, in which both versions were used, indicated the opposite: The new question evoked only two-fifths as many affirmative replies as the old. At this rate, if the old instead of the new question had been asked during the previous year, the response would have been in the neighborhood of 87 per cent! Extrapolated figures like these perhaps cannot be taken literally, but they should at least signal a trend; and the result in this case is nothing short of shocking, especially when we consider the apparent stability of the findings in the years preceding and following. Incidentally, the sudden peak was not limited to expectations concerning Jews; expectations of campaigns against other groups listed in the question were similarly high in 1944, only to fall off almost uniformly the following year.

Parallel with the inquiries into expectations went a series of questions designed to measure the support an anti-Semitic campaign might find (Tables 59–60). On the assumption that the two factors were related, though distinct, we may reasonably expect a momentary peak in potential support during June 1944, analogous to that observed in expectations. Accordingly, we again extrapolate the results of the new question to the terms

Table 59 Support for Hypothetical Anti-Semitic Campaign (1938–45)

"Would you support such a campaign [against the Jews]?" [a]

Per cent answering "yes"

March 1938	May 1938	November 1938	February 1939	May 1939	September 1939	April 1940
19	13	12	12	12	13	12

Per cent answering "yes"

August 1940	February 1941	October 1941	February 1942	December 1942	March 1945
12	13	15	11	14	17

[a] Wording in March and May 1938: *"Would you take part in such a campaign?"*
SOURCES O1, 2, 4–13, 15.

Table 60 Support for Hypothetical Campaigns against Jews and Other Groups (1944–46)

"Would you support a campaign against any of these groups?" (If "yes":)
"Which groups?"

Per cent of those answering "yes"

	June 1944	March 1945	June 1945	February 1946
Negroes	31	10	9	10
Catholics	7	2	2	2
Jews	43	11	13	9
Radicals	46	8	8	10
Foreigners	17	5	5	4
Per cent of total sample naming Jews	11	3	3	2

SOURCES: O14–17.

of the old, using the March 1945 data as a basis. The experiment confirms our expectation: If the old question had been asked in 1944, something like 62 per cent of the population probably would have declared itself willing to join a concerted anti-Semitic action.

The sudden rise and fall of hostility against Jews is once more paralleled in attitudes toward other minority groups. Whether Jews, Negroes, Catholics, "radicals" or "foreigners" were the hypothetical targets, June 1944 marked the highest point in the potential support for organized bigotry. A steep drop was registered in March 1945 and continued beyond the armistice. In February 1946, the level of potential hostility was found so low that questioning on the issue was terminated.

Besides measuring potential active support for anti-Semitic movements, several surveys attempted to gauge the proportions of potential passive sympathizers and active opponents—the former starting in 1939, the latter in 1940. The terms "support" and "sympathize" are not mutually exclusive and may not always have been understood precisely as intended; yet the recorded fluctuations, modest as they are,[17] present a reasonably coherent and, we think, reliable picture (Figure 61). While the opposition to anti-

Figure 61 Proportions Who Would Support or Oppose a Campaign against Jews, I (1938–45)

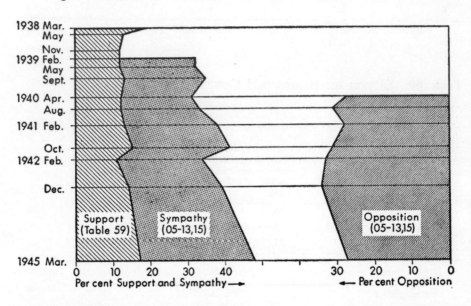

Jewish campaigns did not vary greatly, major increases in the anti-Semitic potential were echoed, during most of the period under study, by at least some waning of the opposed groups, and a decrease in anti-Semitism was accompanied by some slight increase in the opposed camp. In other words, as recruits flowed from the apathetic middle into the ranks of the active anti-Semites and their sympathizers, some others shifted from anti-anti-Semitism to apathy. Thus the small militant group at one extreme exerted an influence that extended, albeit indirectly, to the opposite end of the ideological spectrum. The opposition did not close ranks and opinion did not become polarized until anti-Semitism attained its high point in June 1944 (Figure 62); at this time, opposition also reached a maximum, and subsequently both fell off at comparable rates.

According to the data from April 1940 through March 1945 (see Figure 61), from 31 to 48 per cent of the population would have supported or sympathized with an anti-Semitic campaign, some 30 per cent would have

Figure 62   Proportions Who Would Support or Oppose a Campaign against Jews, II (1944-46)

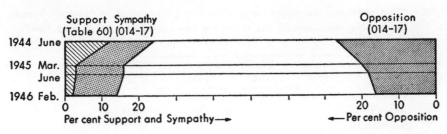

actively opposed it and the rest would have taken no stand. The data from June 1944 to February 1946 (see Figure 62), obtained through a question naming alternative target groups, indicate a somewhat lower anti-Semitic potential. The two sets of data are not strictly comparable because, as we have seen, a choice of targets may have deflected some hostility away from Jews; yet it would seem safe to say that from the prewar period until after the end of the war, between 12 and 30 per cent of the population would have joined or backed an anti-Semitic campaign, a similar number would have fought against it, and the rest would have remained indifferent.

Taken together, our findings suggest that willingness to join a campaign against Jews was not due in any large degree to German propaganda *per se,* or even to that of native anti-Semites. If it had been due to these causes, there is no reason why it should have been paralleled by readiness to take action against other minority groups or why it should have reached a sudden peak such as was actually registered in June 1944. It appears, rather, to have been part of a wave of general intolerance—a result of wartime frustrations and anxieties, already endured for two years and a half, and culminating during that crucial spring in the tensions and terrors of the Normandy invasion. Elsewhere in this book, we note analogous increases in various anti-Jewish attitudes during the critical period just before the end of the war came into sight.

If the issue of organized action against Jews was dead by early 1946, the same was by no means true of potential anti-Semitism elsewhere in the field of public affairs. As late as 1945 and 1946, well over half the population said they would not be influenced against a Congressional candidate by his being anti-Semitic, and almost a quarter declared they would find him more attractive for being so—considerably more than had expressed this view during the prewar period (Table 63). But when the question was repeated in 1962 (with a somewhat broader sample), the proportion who would be favorably impressed by anti-Semitism in a candidate had almost disappeared, while the proportion who would be repelled was nearly twice what it had been in 1945 and 1946—amounting now to well over half of the total. Though a little more than a quarter of the respondents remained in-

Table 63 Attitudes toward a Hypothetical Anti-Semitic Candidate for Congress (1940–62)

"If a candidate for Congress in this state should declare himself as being against the Jews, would this influence you to vote for or against him?"

	August 1940	March 1945	February 1946	June 1962
For	14	23	23	4
Against	45	31	32	60
No difference	29	35	39	27
Don't know	12	10	6	9

SOURCES: O9, 15, 17; G38.

different to the issue, there can be no doubt that by the early 1960s the balance had swung decisively against anti-Semitism as a potential vote-getting device, no matter what other forms of anti-Jewish sentiment may have remained alive.

NOTES

1. Donald Strong, *Organized Anti-Semitism in America* (Washington: American Council on Public Affairs, 1941), lists no fewer than 121 organizations (pp. 138–143) and examines 11 in detail.

2. Regular newspapers were published only by the Bund, Father Coughlin, the Silver Shirts and Gerald B. Winrod (*ibid.*, p. 148).

3. "Instead of agitating for war," Lindbergh threatened, "the Jewish groups in this country should be opposing it in every possible way, for they will be among the first to feel its consequences." (Quoted in *The New York Times,* September 12, 1941.)

4. Seymour M. Lipset offers the thesis that among the three major right-wing movements of the past 30 years, Coughlin's Social Justice movement represented the lower class, McCarthyism the middle and the John Birch Society the upper class. "Three Decades of the Radical Right: Coughlinism, McCarthyism and Birchism," in Daniel Bell, editor, *The Radical Right* (Garden City, N.Y.: Doubleday & Co., 1963), pp. 313–376. For an analysis of changes in American Catholics' attitudes toward Jews, see Appendix I.

5. That respondents may be familiar with the name of a man, yet unable to identify him correctly, was demonstrated by a study undertaken during 1944, in which only 79 per cent correctly identified Henry A. Wallace, then Vice-President (N8). Even smaller proportions were able to place such figures as Harry S. Truman (then a Senator), Sidney Hillman, Norman Thomas and John W. Bricker.

6. See Chapter II.

7. A dozen years after the end of the war, lack of patriotism had become much less of an issue. In 1957, only 10 per cent felt that Jews were "less loyal to our country" than other citizens (N37). But among these 10 per cent, the old images were as alive as ever: Jews were thought to be loyal only to one another and "to money." In addition, a substantial number now believed Jews were primarily attached to Israel.

8. This belief obviously was not based on the actual participation of Jews in military service. "A total of 550,000 Jewish men and women served in the United States Armed Forces during World War II. . . . Of the Jewish population of the United States, between 11% and 12% served in the armed forces of the country. This was about the average for the total population. Jews in service were about 3½ % of the total armed forces of the United States. This approximates their ratio in the total population." I. Kaufman, *American Jews in World War II*, I (New York: Dial Press, 1947), 349.

9. See Hadley Cantril and Mildred Strunk, editors, *Public Opinion, 1935–1946* (Princeton, N.J.: Princeton University Press, 1951), pp. 458–462.

10. Sidney Tarachow, "A Note on Anti-Semitism," *Psychiatry*, IX:131–132 (1946).

11. Robert Park, "Human Migration and the Marginal Man," *American Journal of Sociology*, XXXIII:881–893 (1928).

12. Arnold Rose, "Anti-Semitism's Roots in City Hatred," *Commentary*, October 1948, pp. 374–378.

13. Gertrude Abramson, *The Effect of a Stereotype on Judgment and Group Membership* (unpublished M.A. thesis, New York University, 1949).

14. The notion of the Jews' immense power has often been coupled with charges of a Jewish conspiracy to gain control of society—witness the *Protocols of the Learned Elders of Zion* (c. 1905), the notorious forgery from which Henry Ford, Father Coughlin and many other anti-Semites borrowed their ideas (Strong, *op. cit.*, p. 149). The Hitler regime in its later years based its anti-Semitic propaganda entirely on the myth of a "Jewish plot." When, thanks to expropriation and discriminatory laws, assertions about vast Jewish wealth and power in Germany "could no longer be backed up by even shreds of evidence . . . the emphasis . . . shifted to the thesis of a secret world conspiracy, an accusation no longer testable by the average German." Bruno Bettelheim and Morris Janowitz, *Dynamics of Prejudice* (New York: Harper & Bros., 1950), p. 32.

15. The inclusion of alternative target groups also may have helped to deflect hostility from the Jews; cf. Table 58.

16. It will be recalled that a follow-up question asked on several occasions found four-fifths or more of the affirmative response focusing on various economic pursuits (see Table 53).

17. The extrapolations for June 1944 made in the analyses of Tables 57 and 59 are not shown here.

VI

The Holocaust

OUR ANALYSES so far have dealt with the public's attitudes toward Jews in the context of American life and American affairs. We now turn to another aspect of public opinion concerning the Jews: the impact made on the minds of Americans by the persecution and ultimate destruction of European Jewry under Hitler. How clearly did Americans realize what was happening in Europe? What did they think of the Nazi policies? How did the new state of affairs affect their feelings toward Jews, and what obligations did they think it imposed? To each of these questions, opinion research supplies at least a partial answer.

By the beginning of 1938—the year in which our data begin—Germany's Jews were wholly or virtually excluded from civil service and the professions. Other occupations, one after another, were being closed to them. Those who held jobs in non-Jewish firms had for the most part been discharged; meanwhile, Jewish-owned businesses had been repeatedly boycotted or picketed [1] and were now being cheaply expropriated under transparent legal fictions. Exclusion of Jewish students from schools and colleges was far advanced. Local governments had begun to bar Jews from places of public accommodation. Most important, the Nuremberg Decrees of 1935 had written the second-class status of "non-Aryans" into law. Humiliation, physical abuse, secret arrests and unexplained disappearances of Jews occurred daily.

The year 1938 saw, simultaneously, the breakdown of whatever restraint still existed in Germany's anti-Jewish policies and the beginnings of the aggressive expansion process by which the greatest part of Central and East European Jewry was to come under German control. On March 13, Austria was annexed; at once, a campaign of overt terror, undisguised by legalisms,

136

was launched against the Jews of Vienna and spread rapidly into Germany proper. Arbitrary arrests and deportations to concentration camps were now put on a wholesale basis. On November 9, a government-inspired wave of destruction and violence, known as the *Kristallnacht,* or Crystal Night, swept the Reich, which by this time included the former Czech Sudetenland. The floodgates were now opened to unlimited persecution. Synagogues, previously spared, were burned; Jewish hospitals and orphanages were looted and their inmates driven out. In the days that followed, confiscations, fines and oppressive measures of every kind multiplied, while the quickening pace of deportations foreshadowed the "final solution."

It is against these events and the ensuing, all too familiar catastrophe that the reactions of the American public must be read.

Opinions about Early Nazi Policies

Support and sympathy for the policies of the Nazi government were repeatedly measured in order to determine the level of actual or potential anti-Semitism in the United States. This device was useful mainly before Pearl Harbor. Once America was involved in the war, the measure became less reliable, since respondents must have felt less free to express approval of what was now an enemy nation, and may even have come to condemn as the work of the enemy certain practices to which they had not objected on intrinsic grounds.

In what follows, therefore, we cite mostly findings dating from 1938 and 1939. At that time, the barbarism of the Jews' tormentors had long been plain to the world. Even if the Nazis had not conducted propaganda campaigns outside their own country, the Führer's speeches and the newsreels of the frenzied Nuremberg rallies would have been sufficient to reveal the ferocity and obsessive hatred that were sweeping Germany. Yet, the American response revealed a curiously inconclusive assortment of attitudes. In 1938, for example, 88 per cent disapproved of the treatment of Jews in Germany (G4), and 84 per cent said they would not like to see Hitler's "form of government" in this country (O4); but the former was by no means the most salient reason for the latter. Of the respondents who stated why they would oppose a Nazi-style regime in the United States, a mere 4 per cent mentioned persecution of minorities—a minute proportion compared with those who cited the loss of political liberties, expressed a belief in democracy or voiced a generalized dislike of Nazism.

Though willing to endorse enlightened principles in the abstract, the American public at this time appears to have been disconcertingly receptive to notions of the opposite kind when presented with some plausible rationalization. Thus, in March and May 1938, a majority was apparently seduced into condoning the persecution of European Jewry by the idea that it was at least in part the victims' own fault (Table 64).[2] In assuming that

Table 64 Opinions on the Cause of Persecution in Europe, I (1938)

"Do you think the persecution of Jews in Europe has been their own fault?"

| | Per cent ||
	March 1938	May 1938
Entirely	12	10
Partly	49	48
Not at all	23	31
No opinion	16	11

SOURCES: O1; G3.

Jewish behavior was of a kind to provoke hostile reaction, the bulk of respondents would actually seem to have been expressing their feelings about American Jews, since most of them probably knew little or nothing about those in Europe.

Opinions on the issue appear to have been vague, however. When, in the same year, the question was changed to mention "unreasoning prejudice" as an alternative reason for persecution, the proportion who thought the Jews themselves were to blame was less than a third (Table 65).[3] This propor-

Table 65 Opinions on the Cause of Persecution in Europe, II (1938–39)

"Do you think the persecution of Jews in Europe has been chiefly due to unreasoning prejudice, or do you think it has been largely their own fault?"

| | Per cent |||
	May 1938	November 1938	September 1939
Own fault	30	27	32
Prejudice	41	52	49
No opinion	29	21	19

SOURCES: O2, 4, 7.

tion remained about the same from May 1938 until September 1939. Simultaneously, "no opinion" responses declined somewhat, which suggests that the public's views may have undergone some slow crystallization as the Western nations closed ranks against the tormentors of the Jews. By the time of the last survey in the series, the Allies were already at war with Germany.

The earliest of the inquiries seeking to gauge anti-Semitism in the United States by surveying opinions about Nazism must be viewed with caution. A set of data extending from 1935 to 1939 may serve as an example. In the former year, an isolated poll had examined American reactions to Hitler's anti-Jewish campaign by asking whether, in the long run, Germany would be better or worse off if it drove out the Jews, and had concluded that anti-Semitism in America was a minor problem.[4] In 1938 and 1939, another series of polls repeated this rather leading question, minus the words "in the long run" (Table 66), and obtained a response which, on the face of it,

Table 66 Opinions Concerning Effect of Anti-Jewish Policies on Germany (1935; 1938–39)

(1935:) *"Do you believe that in the long run Germany will be better off or worse off if it drives out the Jews?"*

(1938–39:) *"Do you believe that Germany will be better off or worse off if it drives out the Jews?"*

	Per cent					
	November 1935	March 1938	May 1938	November 1938	February 1939[a]	September 1939
Better off	14	24	20	18	21	21
Worse off	55	46	42	52	46	46
No difference	*	23	16	13	14	15
Don't know	31	7	22	17	20	18

* Not coded.

[a] Wording in this survey: *"Do you think Germany . . . ?"*

SOURCES: R1; O1, 2, 4, 5, 7.

indicated that anti-Jewish feelings in America had somewhat increased during the interval. This impression may be deceptive, however, in that the 1935 survey had been conducted by another agency than the later one, was somewhat differently worded and made no provision for a volunteered answer of "no difference." In any event, the disparity between the 1935 figure and the average of the 1938 and 1939 figures amounts to only 7 percentage points.[5]

Far more conclusive were the results of eight polls, conducted between 1938 and 1941, which asked whether Hitler "was justified in taking the property of the Jews" (Table 67). Only a small proportion thought so; a large majority, not much below the 88 per cent who during 1938 condemned the Nazis' treatment of Jews in general terms, disapproved of confiscation. The findings are remarkable for their stability; except for a slight departure in November 1938,[6] they vary hardly at all. The issue evidently measured not so much the public's attitudes toward Jews or toward Germany as the fundamental American belief in the sanctity of property.

When, commencing in 1940, respondents were asked why they felt as they did about the confiscation of Jewish property, an overwhelming majority of those opposed actually cited the inviolability of property rights. But a similarly large proportion of those condoning confiscation gave as their reason that Jews had been "trying to run the country"—an echo of the theme of "Jewish power" we noted earlier (see Chapter V). Evidence from other

Table 67 Opinions on Hitler's Confiscation of Jewish Property (1938–41)

"Do you think Hitler was justified in taking the property of the Jews?"

	Per cent			
	May 1938	November 1938	February 1939	September 1939
Yes	10	7	13	11
No	77	87	80	83
No opinion	13	6	7	6

	Per cent			
	April 1940	August 1940	February 1941	October 1941
Yes	11	14	13	12
No	79	75	78	78
No opinion	10	11	9	10

SOURCES: O2, 4, 5, 7–11.

sources of the period leaves little doubt that the reference here was to the Jews' presumed economic rather than political power.[7]

Protest actions undertaken in this country evoked a surprisingly luke-warm response, considering the large numbers who in 1938 condemned Nazi persecution of Jews and the comparable numbers who registered opposition to specific acts of the Hitler regime about that time. Thus, only a bare majority expressed approval when the United States temporarily recalled its ambassador after the *Kristallnacht,* even though the poll question described this step as a "protest against the Nazis' treatment of Jews and Catholics." About a fifth of the respondents registered opposition, and another fifth expressed no opinion (G4).

Retaliation by American Jewry found somewhat wider approval than official protest action by the government. In a poll repeated several times between 1938 and 1940, about two-thirds of respondents said they did not object to boycotting of German goods by Jewish groups (Table 68). How-

Table 68 Opinion on Jews' Boycotting German Goods (1938–40)

"Do you object to Jews in this country boycotting goods made in Germany?"

	Per cent			
	May 1938	November 1938	September 1939	April 1940
Yes	26	20	20	22
No	60	70	69	65
No opinion	14	10	11	13

SOURCES: O2, 4, 7, 8.

ever, the proportion actually ready to participate was somewhat smaller (57 per cent), and one-third explicitly declared themselves unwilling to take part (G4).[8] Even apart from the latter figures, approval of anti-Nazi boycotts never was as widespread as condemnation of the Nazi persecutions.

To sum up: Even before America's entry into the war, Hitler's actions were disapproved by majorities of respondents, but the curbs he placed on Jews and the generally anti-Jewish policy of his regime encountered less widespread condemnation than the violations of property rights which occurred as a result of this policy. At least a sizable minority may have felt that Jews had more wealth and power than was proper, and some members of this minority evidently endorsed the Nazis' measures as a righting of the balance. The economic argument probably figured large in the minds of many of the respondents who early in 1938 said that the European Jews had brought persecution upon themselves. Insofar as these ideas were based on an extrapolation from the American scene, they tell us a good deal about the perceptions that underlay active and potential anti-Semitism in the United States. In judging the policies of Hitler without specific knowledge of European affairs and European Jewry, Americans evidently reasoned from the image that was dominant in their own society—the image of the Jew as "economic man."

Knowledge of the German Annihilation Program

As the war progressed, the Nazi policy of planned mass murder gradually became known, partly through Allied propaganda, partly through the efforts of rescue organizations seeking to save at least some of the prospective victims. Initially, Americans were unable to accept these revelations— perhaps because the unfounded atrocity stories of the First World War had left them skeptical. Thus, in January 1943, it was a known fact that two million Jews had been killed or deported in Europe since the war began,[9] yet less than half the population believed this report; the rest thought it was "just a rumor" or expressed no opinion (G8). Almost two years later, in December 1944, over three-quarters of the public believed that the Germans had "murdered many people in concentration camps," but, when asked to estimate how many, the bulk of those willing to make a guess named figures of 100,000 or fewer (G12). Not until the next year did more realistic notions become current; by May 1945, the median estimate of the number of victims had risen to one million, and 84 per cent of respondents thought the reports true (G13).[10]   The public almost certainly was not aware at first how large a proportion of the victims had been Jews. Even by the end of the war, when Hitler's policy of systematic murder probably was generally known in this country, the public does not seem to have realized the extent to which Jews were special targets of his wrath.

A genuine desire to learn or to have others learn about the extent and nature of the German atrocities would seem to be reflected in the results of a poll which asked during May 1945 whether films of "all the horrible things that have happened in prison camps run by Germans" should be shown to various audiences (G13). Only 10 per cent of the public at this time had actually seen such documentaries, but 39 per cent wished to see them; 60 per cent thought it would be a good idea to show them in theaters throughout the United States; and 89 per cent believed they should be shown to all Germans. Still, these findings do not tell us whether the American people had as yet comprehended the genocidal character of the anti-Jewish program. When we note how grossly the number of victims was underestimated before 1945, we may be tempted to answer "no." On the other hand, it may be argued with some justice that such estimates prove nothing, because mass murder in the hundreds of thousands is as far beyond imagining as mass murder in the millions.

There is, however, other evidence showing that even after the war some Americans failed to grasp the full scope of the tragedy or, even more disconcerting, that they were unmoved by it. In a survey undertaken as late as 1947, 21 per cent of respondents said some of Hitler's ideas were right, and 11 per cent expressed no opinion. About one person in 20 approved of Hitler's attitudes toward Jews, and similar proportions cited the economic improvements he brought about or his concern with the interests of his country (G25). Almost half believed that "in the years to come most of the German people" would regard Hitler "as a hero," though it is not clear whether this response represented a tribute to him or a condemnation of the Germans.

Effect of the War on Attitudes toward Jews

The appalling sufferings of European Jewry under Hitler, as well as the wholehearted identification of Jews everywhere with the Allied cause, might be thought to have made Americans more sympathetic toward their Jewish fellow citizens. The results of opinion polls make it clear that no such change took place. In two surveys, both dating from 1945, over three-quarters of all respondents said the mass killings in Europe had not affected their own attitudes toward Jews in America (Table 69).

The finding just cited is, of course, capable of various interpretations. It may be that many of the persons who reported no change in their attitudes were well disposed toward Jews in the first place. Alternatively, many or most of them may have distinguished between Jews here and abroad; though perhaps outraged by the catastrophe in Europe, they may have felt that American Jews were lucky not to be among the victims and could claim no special sympathy.[11] But, having observed how strongly many Americans in those years tended to look upon Jews as a special group with special loyalties, we are more inclined to believe that the general lack of

Table 69 Reported Effect of European Persecution on Respondents' Attitudes toward Jews (1945)

"Have the mass killings of the Jews in Europe caused any change in your attitude toward the Jews in this country?" (If *"yes"*:) *"How have you changed?"*

	Per cent	
	March 1945	June 1945
No, caused no change	77	79
Yes, caused change	19	14
More sympathetic	15[a]	12[a]
Less sympathetic	4	2

[a] Approximations from data.
SOURCES: O15, 16.

sympathy toward Jews in this country bespoke indifference toward people "not of our kind." Like the majority of Germans (though, it is true, with no comparable consequences), many Americans evidently refused to be their brothers' keepers. If in a poll taken during 1944 about 60 per cent of the population said the German people as a whole should not be blamed for "the cruelties to religious groups, the mass killings in occupied countries and the tortures in concentration camps," it is hard to avoid the impression that the respondents were vicariously defending their own unconcern (N9).[12]

Several of the surveys designed to assess the effect of the war on Americans' feelings toward Jews measured two distinct dimensions: respondents were asked what attitude change *was likely* to occur, and what change *ought* to occur. As a matter of pure logic, there is of course no reason why anyone should have given identical answers to the two questions; yet this is what seems to have happened, probably because respondents projected their opinions onto their expectations. Thus, in a poll taken during the early phase of the war, in February 1942, somewhat over half the sample felt no change in public opinion toward Jews was likely to occur, and a similar proportion thought none was called for (O12). Slightly over a third, on the average, expected a change, and about the same number advocated one.

In the survey just cited, only about 13 per cent predicted a decrease in the acceptance of Jews. Elsewhere the negative expectation was considerably higher. In a poll taken in 1944, 27 per cent of women 18 years or older expected more prejudice "against people of different races and religions" after the war than before, while about the same proportion foresaw the opposite (R8); in March 1945 only 14 per cent of the public expected more acceptance of Jews because of the war, while 41 per cent expected less (O15). The projection mechanism was not as clearly at work here as in the study mentioned previously; somewhat fewer respondents said their own attitudes

Table 70 Reported Changes in Respondents' Attitudes toward Jews (1945–46)

"Has your own feeling toward the Jews become more friendly or less friendly during the last few years?"

| | Per cent | |
	1945	1946
More friendly	10	12
Less friendly	26	23
The same	62	62
No opinion	2	3

SOURCES: O15, 17.

had varied in either direction "during the last few years" than were expecting analogous changes among the public at large (Table 70).

Unlike most of our data on other topics, the present figures do not show a peak in anti-Semitic feeling during the spring of 1944; they suggest, rather, that hostility toward Jews continued to increase at least until early 1945. The reason for this discrepancy may be that the question involved the respondents' awareness of changes in their own attitudes—an awareness which would not necessarily keep abreast of the changes themselves.

It probably is significant that contact with Jews during the war was named much more often as a reason for increased friendliness than were the Nazi persecutions. But it is equally significant that contact was named almost as often to account for increased dislike, contrary to the widely held belief that personal knowledge usually improves relations.

The Refugees

In the years prior to the war, before the policy of mass deportation and annihilation was fully put into effect, German and Austrian Jews desperately sought to save themselves through emigration. In the end, somewhat less than two-thirds succeeded; the rest remained trapped, and finally disappeared in the holocaust. Of the far larger number of Jews in the Eastern countries, who fell under Hitler's sway in the course of the war, virtually none were able to flee.

That greater numbers of the potential victims were not saved when it was still possible to do so is in part attributable to the reluctance of the free nations, plagued as they were with economic problems, to admit immigrants in sufficient numbers. "The world," Chaim Weizmann reportedly said during this critical period, "is divided into two groups of nations: those which want to expel the Jews, and those which do not want to receive them." The United States stood firm on its established restrictive immigration laws, notably the national-origins quota system; the admission quotas for persons born in Germany and Austria were not enlarged, though those for many other countries remained regularly unfilled. The rule requiring prospective immigrants to prove that they would not become public charges (by submitting "affidavits of support" from individuals in the United States) was applied with the utmost strictness. While the insistence on these policies impressed many observers as a mockery of America's traditional promise to the world's homeless, opinion research indicates beyond doubt that the nation overwhelmingly favored the restrictions during the late 1930s, and continued to do so during the war years, when the actual influx of immigrants slowed to a mere trickle.

The earliest of our exhibits concerning the subject dates from 1938. It consists of replies to two questions about the admission of refugees to the United States (Table 71). The response was emphatically negative; over 80

Table 71 Opinions on Admission of Refugees (1938)

"What is your attitude toward allowing German, Austrian, and other political refugees to come into the U.S.?"

	Per cent
We should encourage them to come even if we have to raise our immigration quotas	5
We should allow them to come but not raise immigration quotas	18
With conditions as they are, we should try to keep them out	67
Don't know	10

"If you were a member of Congress, would you vote yes or no on a bill to open the doors of the U.S. to a larger number of European refugees than are now admitted under our immigration quotas?"

	Per cent
Yes	9
No	83
Don't know	8

SOURCES: R2, 3.

per cent opposed any relaxation of existing restrictions. Whether the refugees were identified as "German and Austrian" or simply as "European" made virtually no difference.

Five years later, in the midst of war, attitudes still were about the same. In 1943, a survey asked whether it would be a good or a bad idea, once the war was over, to admit increased numbers of immigrants (Table 72). Virtually as many respondents as in 1938 went on record against any liberalization of existing policies—notwithstanding the facts that the refugees' plight meanwhile had grown far worse, that we were now at war with the

Table 72   Opinions on Liberalizing Immigration after the War (1943)

"Do you think it would be a good idea or a bad idea to let more immigrants come into this country after the war?"

	Per cent
Good idea	13
Bad idea	78
Don't know	9

SOURCE: N4.

nation responsible for this plight and that any opening of the gates was placed in an indeterminate future ("after the war").

Throughout the war and early postwar years, opinion polls continued to register widespread fear of foreigners who might come to these shores to live. However, the amount of opposition varied with the terms in which the issue was put. A poll taken in 1945 asked about permitting "persons from Europe to come to this country"; only 6 per cent of the respondents favored increased admission of such persons, 38 per cent wanted a reduction and 12 per cent were for closing the gates altogether (G15). Somewhat more sentiment for liberalized immigration was registered during 1946 in a survey which mentioned "Jewish and other European refugees" and pointed out that their admission was favored by President Harry S. Truman (G20). In the same year, a poll which employed notably sympathetic terms ("over 800,000 homeless people in Europe") found that more than a fifth of the respondents approved increased admission (N14). Sympathetic wording—plus, perhaps, a rather parenthetical mention of Jews—also would seem to account for the relatively favorable results of still another survey undertaken in 1946; the question read: "About a million Polish people, Jews, and other displaced persons must find new homes in different countries. Do you think the United States should take any of these displaced persons?" The positive response in this instance was uniquely high for the time. But it still fell short of forming a majority (G22).[13]

Alternative ways of dealing with the refugee problem were spelled out in a poll taken in 1948 (Table 73). Most respondents wanted the United States to do something for the refugees in one way or another, it was revealed; but few liked the idea of letting large numbers come here, even if "well and strong."[14] The most attractive plans turned out to be those which provided that other countries were to take either all or proportionate shares of the refugees.

On the face of it, the findings suggest that surprisingly few respondents differentiated between Jews (of no particular stated nationality) and Germans (a term which may or may not have been taken to include German Jews). Most of those respondents willing to see at least some refugees enter seem to have found the one as acceptable as the other. Parallel findings may

Table 73   Opinions on Providing for Refugees (1948)

"There are still a lot of refugees or displaced persons in European camps who cannot go back to the homes they had before the war. Which of these four statements comes closest *to what you think this country should do about these refugees?"*

	Per cent
"We should admit all of these refugees who are well and strong to the United States, no matter what other countries do."	10
"We should take only our share of these refugees and insist that other countries do the same."	43
"There are too many here now and we should not admit any more at all, but we should help to get them settled elsewhere."	23
"They are a problem for the European countries to worry about, and we should let these countries handle the problem."	17

"If most of these refugees should turn out to be [Germans/Jews] do you think that we should put a special limit on the number of them we take in?"

	Per cent of those willing to admit some refugees (53 per cent of total sample)	
	Limit Germans	Limit Jews
Yes	53	60
No	42	35
Don't know	5	5

SOURCE: R16.

be observed in earlier studies. Thus, a poll dating back to 1938 which specifically mentioned admission of "Jewish exiles" (Table 74) evoked roughly the same amount of opposition as a simultaneous survey specifying "German, Austrian, and other political refugees" (see Table 71).[15] A similar lack of differentiation is evident in a study undertaken during 1944, which sought in somewhat complicated fashion to unravel the public's notions of what ethnic groups were considered acceptable newcomers to America. In this survey, 60 per cent of the respondents said Jews should have the same chance as others to settle in this country; but when a list of ethnic groups was presented, Jews and Germans ranked together near the bottom in acceptability, above Japanese but somewhat below Mexicans and well below Chinese (Table 75).

As of 1944, then—the year which we have identified as the high point of American anti-Semitism in several other respects—Jews apparently were

Table 74 Opinions on Admission of Jewish Exiles from Germany (1938)

"Should we allow a larger number of Jewish exiles from Germany to come to the United States to live?"

	Per cent	
	March 1938	November 1938
Yes	17	21
No	75	71
Don't know	8	8

SOURCES: O1, 4.

Table 75 Opinions on Admission of Various Ethnic Groups after the War (1944)

"Here is a list of different groups of people. Do you think we should let a certain number of each of these groups come to the United States to live after the war, or do you think we should stop some of the groups from coming at all?"

	Per cent who say		
	"Let come"	"Stop from coming"	Don't know
English	68	25	7
Swedes	62	27	11
Russians	57	33	10
Chinese	56	36	8
Mexicans	48	42	10
Jews	46	46	9
Germans	36	59	5
Japanese	20	75	5

SOURCE: N7.

considered the least desirable immigrants except for members of what currently were enemy nations. But the hostility displayed toward potential Jewish newcomers was only partly inspired by bigotry. Much of it seems rather to have been generated by fear of mass immigration *per se*. Jews, it must be remembered, constituted the largest number of would-be immigrants throughout the prewar and war years, so that the terms "refugee" and "Jewish refugee" may well have been almost synonymous to at least a substantial portion of the public.

Both anti-Semitism and the assumption that most refugees would be Jewish are illustrated in a poll which, as early as 1939, explored popular attitudes toward admission of refugee children from Germany (Table 76). The question was asked in two forms, with and without the specification that most of the children would be Jewish; the results were about equally nega-

Table 76   Opinions on Admission of Refugee Children (1939)

    (a) *"It has been proposed that the government permit 10,000 refugee children from Germany to be brought into this country and taken care of in American homes. Do you favor this plan?"*

    (b) *"It has been proposed to bring to this country 10,000 refugee children from Germany—most of them Jewish—to be taken care of in American homes. Should the government permit these children to come in?"*

	Per cent	
	(a) ("Jewish" not specified)	(b) ("Jewish" specified)
Yes	26	30
No	66	61
No opinion	8	9

SOURCE: G5.

tive in either case. This finding might be taken to indicate that Jewish and non-Jewish youngsters were unwanted in approximately the same degree; but if so, we would be at a loss to explain why children, to whom the obvious objections against immigrants (for example, job competition, low living standard, subversive tendencies) did not apply, should be so unwelcome. We believe, rather, that a majority of the respondents thought of the children as mostly Jewish whether so described or not, and rejected them for that reason—a reaction that is at least psychologically intelligible, if thoroughly inhumane.

A survey dating from 1947 casts additional light on prevailing notions concerning the ethnic identity of refugees (Table 77). Here the questions did not explicitly refer to Jews; indeed, the wording did not particularly invite answers in ethnic terms, referring as it did merely to "kinds of persons." Yet 13 per cent of the respondents spontaneously defined the refugees as Jews (more than mentioned any other ethnic group), and when questioned further about the refugees' religion, 41 per cent said most were Jewish.

As noted above, the desire to let other countries share the burden of absorbing the refugees was widespread in 1948 (see Table 73). The wish to deflect immigration from the United States was echoed again and again. As early as 1938 (when, it will be recalled, over 80 per cent of respondents were opposed to letting increased numbers of refugees into the United States), about 38 per cent were willing to have "our government contribute money to help Jewish and Catholic exiles from Germany settle in lands like Africa and South America" (G4). Eight years and one world war later, just about the same proportion would have liked to see refugees distributed

Table 77   Beliefs about Nature of Displaced Persons (1947)

"What would be your guess as to the kind of person who makes up the majority of those people still in European refugee (displaced persons) camps?"

	Per cent who say
Homeless, unfortunate victims of war or political persecutions	30
Poor, lower classes	18
Jews	13
Undesirables, radicals	8
Eastern Europeans	7

(Other answers: no more than 4 per cent each)

"What would you say is the religious faith of the majority of these people?"

	Per cent who say
Jewish	41
Catholic	34
Protestant	4

(Other answers: no more than 3 per cent each)

SOURCE: G24.

Table 78   Opinions on a Plan for Distribution of Refugees (1946)

"Would you approve or disapprove a plan to require each nation to take in a given number of Jewish and other European refugees, based upon the size and population of each nation?"

	Per cent	
	June 1946	August 1946
Approve	40	37
Disapprove	49	48
No opinion	11	15

SOURCES: G18, 20.

among different countries (Table 78). In the years that followed, however, a marked alteration occurred in the tenor of the responses, reflecting, it would seem, changes in the actual nature of the refugee problem.

By the late 1940s, European Jews no longer figured as the chief group of potential immigrants, simply because it was now known that most of them had been killed. Meanwhile, the Iron Curtain had descended upon Europe. Huge numbers of people—ethnic Germans, Poles, Czechs, Hungarians and others—had fled from areas now under Soviet control; at the end of 1945, more than a million of them were in displaced-persons camps in West Germany, Austria and elsewhere. The United States, no longer beset by economic depression, helped substantial numbers to start a new life here—not through any major alteration in basic immigration law,[16] but through special executive and legislative action: a Presidential directive in 1945, the Displaced Persons Act of 1948 (amended in 1950) and the Refugee Relief Act of 1953.[17] Special commissions were set up in at least 20 states to help resettle the newcomers, and acceptance by the community followed rapidly, particularly in the case of settlers possessing skills that were in short supply.

Opinion data suggest that immigrants during this period appeared markedly more acceptable to the American public when described as victims or potential victims of Communism. Thus, as will be recalled, in 1948 only 10 per cent of the population favored unrestricted admission of "refugees or displaced persons in European camps" who were "well and strong" (see Table 73); but in the same poll fully 40 per cent approved the hypothetical entry of 200,000 persons who "are afraid to return to their old home because the Russians now control these countries." [18] By 1952, more than half the population (51 per cent) favored admission and ultimate citizenship for "people who have escaped from Communist countries in Eastern Europe in order to come over to our side" (N28). A mere seven months earlier, a question which did not mention Communism drew an affirmative response of only about one-third (Table 79).

However, broadened immigration was encountering a good deal more approval by this time than formerly even when flight from Communism was not specified—at least insofar as the potential newcomers were not described as refugees. When we compare the results of the 1952 poll with those of 1943 (see Table 72), we find a change of about 20 percentage points—an indication of a real shift in attitudes, even if we allow for the possible effect of differences in question wording. To what extent this change reflects the realization that only a modest proportion of the refugees from Communism were Jews must remain an open question.

The 1952 poll also inquired into the reasons for continued hostility to immigration and thus illustrated certain fears then besetting large segments of the American people. Opposition still focused chiefly on the immigrant as an economic danger: as a competitor for jobs and housing, a threat to native living standards or a potential burden to taxpayers. By comparison, concern over the possibility of political subversion by newcomers was a minor theme. And, as in other fields, overt anti-Semitism was far less in evidence than a decade earlier. Frank expressions of group prejudice were relatively rare; only the notion that there were "too many foreigners here already" could conceivably be construed as anti-Semitic.

Similar reasons for opposing liberalized immigration were voiced during 1955, in a poll in which two-fifths of the respondents thought too many immigrants were entering the country, while about one-half approved of the number being admitted or wanted it increased (Table 80). Opposition again centered on fears connected with jobs, housing or standards of living,

Table 79   Disapproval of Plan for Liberalized Immigration, and Reasons Therefor (1952)

"It has been proposed that over the next three years we should allow an extra 300,000 Europeans to enter the United States and become citizens. Do you approve or disapprove of this plan?"

| | Per cent | |
	April 1952	November 1952
Approve	36	31
Disapprove	57	63
Don't know	7	6

(April 1952:) *"Why?"*

	Per cent of those disapproving (57 per cent of total sample)
Not enough jobs for them, unemployment here	30
We are overcrowded now, no room for them here	17
They are radical, disloyal, politically unreliable	16
Not enough housing for them, no homes for our own people	13
Too many foreigners here already	13
They would depress our standards, work cheaply	7
They would be public charges, we would have to support them	6
(Other answers: no more than 3 per cent each)	

SOURCES: N26, 28.

with possible subversion a secondary theme. One new element was added: Of those who objected to current levels of immigration, about one-fifth now said newcomers would be "socially undesirable."

The assortment of ethnic groups rejected by respondents also had undergone some changes, according to the 1955 survey. The nationalities that had made up the refugee contingent—Germans, Jews, Southern and Eastern Europeans—still figured on a modest scale among the unwanted, together with Japanese and Asians generally. But in addition a new concern had emerged: The list of "undesirables" now included Puerto Ricans. The war had been over for a decade, the refugees had been taken care of somehow and the people of the United States were increasingly directing their attention to newcomers from within the New World.

At various times during the period under study, there were indications that refugees appeared more acceptable when the issue was brought down to the regional or local level. As early as 1947, 22 per cent of respondents across the nation declared themselves in favor of letting 10,000 "displaced"

Table 80 Disapproval of Immigration, by Ethnic Groups, and Reasons Therefor (1955)

"In general, do you think the United States is letting too many immigrants come into this country, or not enough?"

	Per cent
Too many	39
About right	37
Not enough	13
Don't know	11

"What particular groups or nationalities do you have in mind?"

	Per cent of those who say "too many" (39 per cent of total sample)
Those from Communist countries	14
Southern Europeans	10
Germans	10
Japanese	10
Puerto Ricans	8
Mexicans and Latin Americans	7
Asiatics	7
Slavs, Eastern Europeans	5
Jews	5

"Why do you disapprove of letting so many immigrants in?"

	Per cent of those who say "too many"
Not enough jobs for them	41
They are socially undesirable	19
They might be subversive	16
They work for less	12
Not enough housing for them	9
Enough here now	8
We must take care of Americans first	5
They go on relief	3

SOURCE: N32.

or "homeless persons from Europe" settle in their respective states, having first been informed that the Governor of Minnesota had proposed such a plan (G24). In 1955, a similar idea found wide acceptance; 63 per cent now were for letting "a few families from Europe come to this neighborhood to live" (G34). Thus, thanks to the passage of time and the fading of the refugee image, a majority of the nation at last found itself once more in harmony with America's traditional promise of asylum to the Old World's "huddled masses yearning to breathe free"—at least to the amount of "a few families" per community.

The fact that stands out in all this evidence is that, however willing Americans may have been to see something done about the victims of Nazism, most of them did not choose to take more than a token share of this burden upon themselves. In refusing to assume responsibility for the masses uprooted by Hitler, many seem to have been influencd in some degree by the realization that these masses were largely Jewish. They evidently were not ready to risk possible sacrifice for persons they did not consider members of their own group. In the years that followed, more sympathy and desire to help were expressed toward refugees from Communist regimes than had ever been bestowed upon those who were seeking to escape the Nazi holocaust.

NOTES

1. According to contemporary observers, such boycotts attracted more attention abroad during the middle 1930s than did any other aspect of the Nazis' anti-Jewish program, though in fact they were among the least effective forms of harassment. Gustav Warburg, *Seven Years of Hitler* (London: George Allen & Unwin, 1939), pp. 109–110.

2. The March and May surveys were conducted by different agencies; this probably is the main reason for minor differences in the findings.

3. Though the question does not explicitly mention Germany, it is probably safe to assume that most respondents thought of the German Government when giving their answer.

4. *Fortune,* January 1936, p. 157.

5. American Jewish Committee, *Summary of Polls on Anti-Semitism, 1938–1942* (unpublished report, March 1943), p. 31. The 1935 question seems to have been repeated simply in the hope of obtaining trend data.

6. Possibly in response to the *Kristallnacht.* However, the deviations were well within the range of possible sampling variation.

7. For example, in both August 1940 and February 1941 it was asked: "Why do you think the Hitler government adopted an anti-Jewish policy?" (O9, 10). Over half of the respondents cited Jewish wealth as Hitler's objective, while only about 15 per cent mentioned Jewish power as such. Again, less than two-thirds of the public, in a 1942 poll, disapproved Hitler's taking away the power (unspecified) of the Jews, and a substantial number expressed no opinion (OP3)—in marked contrast to the three-fourths or more who consistently condemned his taking of Jewish property between 1938 and 1941.

8. Several of the leading Jewish organizations in America refrained from supporting anti-German boycotts so as not to provide the Nazis with a pretext for further outrages against German Jewry. Whether the majority of the non-

Jews who declared themselves unwilling to take part were moved by similar considerations is open to question.

9. The figure of two million victims was mentioned, for example, by Rep. Emanuel Celler, in a speech to Congress. *Congressional Record,* January 21, 1943.

10. A slightly different question was used in the May 1945 survey.

11. In 1943, 66 per cent of the population supported the idea that "Germans should make up some of the losses suffered by the Jews," presumably in Germany (G9).

12. The proportion who thought many German civilians knew about atrocities committed had increased somewhat by 1945, but was still a minority (R12).

13. Positive replies to the question as stated above amounted to 43 per cent. In half the questionnaires, "let [them] enter this country" was substituted for "take [them] in"; here the affirmative response was 7 percentage points lower.

14. It is quite possible that the specification "well and strong," suggesting competition for jobs, increased the negative response.

15. In this particular instance, there actually was a little less opposition to Jews than to Germans—possibly because the term "exiles," applied to the former, sounded less threatening than "refugees," the word used to describe the latter, with its connotations of poverty and job competition. Alternatively, the difference might be attributed to sampling variations in the absence of probability sampling.

16. The McCarran-Walter Act of 1952, which replaced the Immigration Act of 1924, retained the national-origins system with its bias in favor of North and West Europeans, left the total volume of permissible immigration substantially unchanged and set no policy for pooling unused quotas.

17. The Act of 1948 permitted "mortgaging" of nationality quotas far into the future. These mortgages were subsequently forgiven. The 1953 Act placed the entry of refugees entirely outside the quota system.

18. The explicit limitation placed on the number to be admitted may have increased the favorable response to the latter question. The number given is almost identical with the one authorized by the original Displaced Persons Act, passed in that year.

VII

Jews as Alleged Radicals and Spies

IN CHAPTER II we attempted to synthesize prevailing stereotypes concerning Jews into a composite portrait. As will be recalled, the dominant image that emerged was of an "economic man": an individual either wealthy or at least devoted to the pursuit of wealth above all else; a sharp, ambitious dealer, thoroughly at home in the rough-and-tumble of free competitive enterprise.

In the context of American history, capitalism and radicalism would seem to be diametrically opposed forces. The United States knows no feudal tradition, no nostalgia for a pre-capitalist age, that might express itself in simultaneous rejection of plutocracy and Marxism, such as was voiced by the anti-Dreyfusards of the 1890s and by the Nazis. Popular stereotypy, however, is not noted for its consistency; and thus we will not be overly surprised to discover that images of the Jew as a dangerous radical have sometimes coexisted with the majority view of the Jew as a ruthless capitalist businessman. Thus, during the years just before the Second World War, one-quarter to one-third of the population said Jews tended to be more radical than other people; the proportions who thought them more conservative than others was somewhat smaller (Table 81).[1]

Why were Jews seen at the same time as capitalists preoccupied with success under the existing economic system, and as radicals bent on subverting the very foundations of society? The simultaneous presence of these two contradictory images may seem to underline the complexity of the Jewish image in American society. Yet, the contradiction is perhaps not as absolute as it appears at first sight; it probably derives in part from mere semantic confusion. In the intellectual's vocabulary, the term "radicalism" until recently stood for a particular political philosophy, characterized by

Table 81 Beliefs about Conservative and Radical Tendencies of Jews (1938–62)

"Do you think Jews tend to be more conservative or more radical in politics than other people?"

	March 1938[a]	May 1938	November 1938	February 1939	September 1939	April 1940	July 1962
			Per cent saying				
More radical	32	28	25	26	28	29	17
More conservative	44	19	18	23	22	22	22
Same as other people		24	30	30	31	30	28
Don't know; no answer	24	29	27	21	19	19	33

[a] Wording in this survey: *"Do you think they [Jews] tend to be more radical in politics than other people?"*
SOURCES: O1, 2, 4, 5, 7, 8; G39.

collectivism and a belief in government ownership or control. Among the American public as a whole, however, the word seems to have had no such specific meaning. A century ago, during the Reconstruction period, extreme Republicans were called "radicals"; and in later periods, too, the word has carried a connotation of deviation or extremism generally, rather than of leftism. A radical, in the popular language of recent decades, is one who is dissatisfied with the American system or out of tune with traditional values and beliefs—perhaps a troublemaker, but not necessarily an adherent of some particular collectivist doctrine.[2] Supposed "radicalism" in this sense does not necessarily conflict with other qualities commonly attributed to Jews, such as preoccupation with wealth. It would therefore seem that to describe Jews as "radical" (or even as "radical in politics") is not necessarily to label them as Communists, Socialists, or other leftist critics of American capitalism.

Quite apart from this semantic problem, the alternative posed between conservatism and radicalism is biased, in that the former is a respectable concept to most Americans, while the latter is beyond the pale. Conservatism's true opposite is of course liberalism, not radicalism. The false juxtaposition offered in the question thus left the best-informed respondents, those aware of the liberal inclinations of Jews, without a meaningful answer.[3]

Beliefs about Communist Tendencies among Jews

Whether Jews (as well as certain other groups) tended toward leftist ideologies was again asked in a survey conducted during 1940; but the wording of the question, while less vague than in the poll reported above, was still not wholly conclusive, including as it did both the specific term "communistic" and the vague adjective "radical" (Table 82). The results

Table 82   Beliefs about Radical or Communist Tendencies among Various Ethnic Groups (1940)

"What nationality, religious or racial groups do you think tend to be radical or communistic?" [a]

	Per cent naming
Russians	25
Jews	19
Germans	14
Italians	9
Foreigners	9
The German-American Bund	6
Communists	6
Nazis, Fascists	3
Organized labor	2
Other	19

[a] Order of terms altered on half the questionnaires (*"religious, nationality or racial groups"*); combined results reported here.
SOURCE: O9.

reflect the confusion implicit in this choice of words: Russians were named most frequently as a group likely to harbor such tendencies, and Jews ranked second; but Germans and Italians (that is, members or kinsmen of the then Fascist nations) came not far behind, followed by such far from communistic groups as the German-American Bund, and by Nazis and Fascists generally.

Poll questions concerning popular ideas of "Jewish radicalism" were repeated during 1944 and 1945, in an effort to test whether such notions were contributing to anti-Semitism. Among various approaches to this issue, an attempt was made to determine whether the images of certain Jewish public figures were tainted by supposed association with leftist causes. Thus, a series of surveys undertaken about the time of the 1944 Presidential election focused on Sidney Hillman, the head of the Political Action Committee set up by the Congress of Industrial Organizations to support Franklin D. Roosevelt's bid for a fourth term.

Republican propagandists throughout the campaign had pictured Hillman as a symbol of the menace of labor in politics, and of alleged communistic influence in the CIO.[4] The poll questions were designed to gauge how widely Hillman was identified as a Jew, how generally he was considered a "radical" and how much disapproval his activities were arousing. A high affirmative response to this trio of questions, it was assumed, would indicate that overt association of Jewish individuals with leftist causes was harmful to Jews as a group.

In August 1944, about 30 per cent of the respondents identified Hillman more or less correctly (G10). Of this group, about half were unfavorably disposed toward him, and two-fifths voiced no opinion. By October, with the election campaign reaching its climax, Hillman was known to 47 per cent of the public (N8). In November, after the election, two-thirds knew who he was, and unfavorable evaluations dropped to about two of every three (Table 83).[5] But even so, Hillman was by far the least liked of 11 prominent persons listed in the poll questions.

Table 83 Attitudes toward Prominent Persons, Including Sidney Hillman (1944)

"Will you tell me what you think of each of these people? Generally speaking, is your opinion of them favorable or unfavorable?"

	Per cent		
	Favorable	Unfavorable	Not familiar; don't know
Franklin D. Roosevelt	70	27	3
Thomas Dewey	62	30	8
Henry Wallace	58	23	19
Edward Stettinius	53	5	42
Herbert Hoover	44	45	11
James Byrnes	38	6	56
Harold Stassen	37	4	59
Clare Boothe Luce	32	32	36
Leverett Saltonstall	23	3	74
Sidney Hillman	22	43	35
Gov. Frank Lausche	11	3	86

SOURCE: G11.

Jewishness was not one of Hillman's most salient characteristics in the public eye, judging by a survey conducted only one month later (N9). A mere 13 per cent thought of him as a Jew, even when presented with this alternative on a list of identifying characteristics. Almost three times as many characterized him as a man who "cooperates with Communists"; similar numbers saw him as a labor leader and a supporter of the New Deal. Almost half of the respondents reported hearing criticism of Hillman during the campaign, but fewer than half of those who did so said they agreed with what they had heard.

A final set of three questions, asked in March 1945, sought to assess the connection between anti-Semitic attitudes and the perceived role of Jews in the Political Action Committee (Table 84). The poll found only 15 per

Table 84   Beliefs about the Jews and the CIO Political Action Committee (1945)

"During the last election did you hear anything about the activities of Sidney Hillman and the P.A.C.—that is, the Political Action Committee of the C.I.O.?"

	Per cent
Yes	64
No	36
	——
	100

(If "yes":) *"It has been said by some people that in the recent election the Jews were active in running the Political Action Committee. Do you think this is true, or not?"*

	Per cent of total sample
Yes	24
No	19
Don't know	21
	——
	64

(If "yes, true":) *"Do you think the activities of the Jews in the P.A.C. during the election have caused people to be unfriendly toward the Jews as a whole?"*

	Per cent of total sample
Yes	15
No	6
Don't know	3
	——
	24

SOURCE: O15.

cent of the population explicitly linking the two—indicating, it would seem, that ideas about "Jewish radicalism" were not a major source of anti-Semitic attitudes at the time. Even this modest percentage, if anything, over-states the facts because of the way the issue was presented. As will be noted, two preliminary questions were asked, the first connecting the P.A.C. with Hillman, the other with Jewish influence. On the strength of this juxtaposition, a certain number of respondents with no prior awareness about Jews in the P.A.C. must have guessed that Hillman was Jewish—which would naturally induce them to answer "yes" to the second question, that about the activity of Jews in the organization. Thus, part of the affirmative response to the second question probably was a mere playback of what respondents had learned from the first; and this inflated response may in turn have inflated the number of affirmative replies to the crucial third question.[6]

The issue was taken up again in 1948, this time with reference to the Presidential candidacy of Henry A. Wallace and the role of his Progressive Party. By September, over four-fifths of the population had heard about the new party; half of these thought Communists were its organizers or supporters, and only 11 per cent believed it to be backed by Jews (R16).

During the early 1950s, two major developments combined to heighten the interest of poll-sponsoring agencies in the question of "Jewish radicalism." One was the anti-Communist crusade that swept across the nation under the leadership of Senator Joseph R. McCarthy and his corps of investigators; the other was the trials and convictions of several Americans, some of them Jewish, who had served as spies for the Soviet Union. It seemed at this critical juncture that Jews might well suffer infinite harm from charges linking them as a group with Communism.

As it happened, no such eventuality occurred on a measurable scale; according to the polls, the image of the "Jewish Communist" did not grow in prevalence during this period of increasingly militant anti-Communism. In 1950, only 4 per cent of respondents spontaneously mentioned Jews when asked whether "any kinds or groups of people . . . [were] more likely than others to be Communists"; during 1953 and 1954, the response actually dropped to 2 and 1 per cent respectively (Table 85).[7] Parallel results emerged when respondents were presented with ready-made lists of

Table 85 Beliefs about Communist Tendencies among Various Groups, I (1950–54)

"Can you think of any kinds or groups of people in the United States who are more likely than others to be Communist?"

	Per cent naming[a]		
	1950	1953	1954
Poor people	14	10	14
The foreign-born	13	7	7
The uneducated	6	4	9
Union members	6	6	4
The unreligious	4	0	3
Jews	4	2	1
Negroes	3	4	4
Unhappy people	2	0	4
Italians	1	0	0
Intellectuals, the educated	0	6	4
Other	17	16	16
No particular groups; don't know	54	60	55

[a] White Christians only.

SOURCES: N24, 29, 31.

groups; in 1950, 11 per cent picked Jews as a group "likely to be Communists," in 1954 only 6 per cent (Table 86).[8] The corresponding figures for "Puerto Ricans in the United States" were 25 and 26 per cent. Even among the 11 per cent who in 1950 thought Jews inclined more toward Communism than other persons, only 4 per cent thought many and 1 per cent thought most Jews actually were Communists (N24).

Table 86 Beliefs about Communist Tendencies among Various Groups, II (1950–54)

"In this country do you think any of the people listed here are more likely to be Communists than others?"

	Per cent naming[a]		
	1950	1953	1954
"Union members"	30	25	25
"Puerto Ricans in the United States"	25	6	26
"Poor people"	21	15	21
"People in the government in Washington"	20	15	12
"Negroes"	14	12	10
"College students"	13	10	11
"Actors"	12	16	14
"Jews"	11	9	6
"New Yorkers"	11	6	4
"Italian-Americans"	9	9	5
"Teachers"	8	10	8
"Polish-Americans"	7	5	3
"Catholics"	2	3	2
"Protestants"	0	1	0
None of these	18	31	29
Don't know	17	12	12

[a] White Christians only.
SOURCES: N24, 29, 31.

What makes these studies particularly significant is that, unlike those of earlier years, they were not beclouded by the use of ambiguous terms such as "radical." They focused squarely on Communist affiliation, leaving the respondents much less room for doubt what the questions meant. True, popular definitions of "Communism" also are rather a mixed bag of goods;[9] but the term is at least understood to mean one or another variety of leftist doctrine—unlike "radicalism," which, as we have seen, may refer to deviation in any direction of the political compass. The majority of Americans during the early 1950s plainly refused to consider Jews as a group communistic, and this refusal was in tune with the facts. Only an insignificant portion of American Jews ever were enrolled Communists.[10]

The Jews and the Atomic Spy Trials

In November 1950, about three-fifths of the population knew that some individuals had been charged with spying on American atomic operations for the Soviet Union, and two-thirds agreed that spies were a serious danger; yet only half were able to name any of the accused (Table 87). Only

Table 87 Familiarity with Persons Accused of Spying (1950–51)

"As far as you know, has anybody in the United States been accused of atomic spying?" (If "yes":) *"Do you happen to remember the names of any of the persons accused? . . . What were they?"*

	Per cent of those who knew that some person had been accused	
	November 1950 (59 per cent of total sample)	April 1951 (67 per cent of total sample)
Harry Gold	16	13
Alger Hiss	13	12
Judith Coplon	7	6
Klaus Fuchs	6	8
Whittaker Chambers	6	1
David Greenglass	2	13
Rosenberg [unspecified]	2	12
Ethel Rosenberg	0	28
Julius Rosenberg	0	27
Morton Sobel	0	2
Sanford Lawrence Simons	0	1
Alfred Dean Slack	0	0

NOTE: A number of respondents in both surveys described individuals but could not name them. In 1950, these were insignificant in frequency, but in 1951 they included 17 per cent who described Ethel Rosenberg, 15 per cent who described Julius Rosenberg, and 12 per cent who knew Greenglass.

SOURCES: N24, 25.

Harry Gold and Alger Hiss were mentioned with even moderate frequency (by 16 and 13 per cent of the respondents, respectively). Judith Coplon, Whittaker Chambers, Klaus Fuchs and others received only a scattering of mentions.

By April 1951, the accused individuals had become much better known (Table 87). As in the previous poll, most of those mentioned had Jewish-sounding names; but there is no telling whether the Jewishness of these persons was salient or even known to the bulk of respondents. It might be argued that the assortment reflects, not selective remembering of Jewish names, but merely current publicity regarding particular spies who happened to be Jews, especially those involved in the Rosenberg case.

Some light is cast on this enigma by a follow-up question asked during 1950, in the course of which a prepared list of names was shown to respondents (Table 88). Harry Gold and Whittaker Chambers were now

Table 88 Actual and Spurious Recognition of Persons Accused of Spying (1950)

"Some of the people accused of atomic spying are included in this list. Can you tell me which ones they are? (You may remember some of these names when you see them)." (Names in order presented.)

	Per cent naming[a]
"Sanford Lawrence Simons"	2
"Alfred Dean Slack"	4
"Max Finkelstein" [b]	7
"David Dubinsky"	4
"Daniel Carpenter" [b]	1
"Harry Gold"	34
"William Brooks" [b]	1
"Julius Rosenberg"	19
"Whittaker Chambers"	34
"Isaac Shapiro" [b]	6
"Robert L. Phillips" [b]	1
"Samuel Levinsky" [b]	7
None; don't know	43

[a] White Christians only.
[b] Fictitious names.
SOURCE: N24.

identified by about one-third of the respondents, and Julius Rosenberg by about one-fifth. The chief interest of this poll, however, lies in the response obtained to fictitious names. Scattered through the list were the names of six imaginary persons—three Jewish-sounding ("Max Finkelstein," "Isaac Shapiro," "Samuel Levinsky") and three others ("Daniel Carpenter," "William Brooks," "Robert L. Phillips").[11] The nonentities with non-Jewish names, taken together, were "remembered" by 3 per cent of the sample, those with Jewish names by 20 per cent, or more than six times as often.[12] In addition, 4 per cent picked a real person bearing a Jewish name, who actually was one of the most prominent anti-Communists in the labor movement: David Dubinsky, President of the International Ladies' Garment Workers' Union.

How can we reconcile this outcome with our earlier findings, according to which nearly the entire public exonerated Jews from Communist leanings when explicitly asked (see Tables 85 and 86)? We are inclined to discount the possibility that large numbers of persons actually did think of Jews as communistic but concealed this belief from interviewers in direct questioning or hid it even from themselves. More probably, the names in at least some cases may have been identified, not as Jewish, but simply as "foreign," that is, non-Anglo-Saxon. Even if they were recognized as Jewish, this would not prove that the public associated Jews with Communism apart from contemporary realities; respondents may have responded to the fictitious Jewish names listed simply because they recalled that some of the accused spies were Jews. In this sense, the contradictory evidence may perhaps be viewed as an illustration of a conflict between established images and current fact: between the perennial stereotype of the Jew as a wealthy capitalist and the news about David Greenglass, Morton Sobel and the Rosenbergs.

Anti-Semitism and Anti-Communism

A relationship between anti-Communism and the belief that Jews tend to be Communists was demonstrated by Leo Srole on the basis of data gathered in 1950 and 1951.[13] Srole had observed a consistent relationship between anti-Semitic attitudes and belief in Communist leanings among Jews as a group,[14] which suggested to him that prejudiced persons, ready to pick up any new slur, found allegations of Communism a convenient addition to their arsenals. But he had noted at the same time that by no means all anti-Semites voiced this stereotype, while significant numbers of non-anti-Semites did—a circumstance indicating that some additional factor also was at work. Through a four-part analysis, he showed that intensity of anti-Communist feeling was this additional factor. The essentials of Srole's investigation are summarized in what follows.

First, strong anti-Semites, mild anti-Semites and non-anti-Semites among white Christian respondents were subdivided separately into strong, moderate and lesser anti-Communists, so that poll responses could be measured in relation to levels of anti-Communism, while strength of anti-Semitism was held constant.[15] The following sets of data were then analyzed according to these categories: (1) reports of talk accusing Jews of spying; (2) spontaneous references to Jews as likely to be Communists; (3) similar references in response to a proffered list; and (4) opinions on whether few, many or most Jews were Communists.[16]

(1) Anti-Jewish talk focusing on accusations of espionage was altogether rare, being reported by about 1 per cent of respondents. Reanalysis by categories shows this response, such as it was, to have been concentrated almost entirely within the strong anti-Communist column, particularly its highly anti-Semitic segment (Table 89); but the total incidence was too small to lend any conclusiveness to these subgroup differences.

(2) Spontaneous mentions of Jews as a group tending toward Communism were both more frequent and somewhat more patterned than sponta-

Table 89   Reported Criticism of Jews as Spies, by Strength of Anti-Communism and Anti-Semitism (1950)

"Have you heard any criticism or talk against the Jews in the last six months?" (If "yes":) *"What kind of criticism was it?"*

	Per cent within each category reporting talk of Jews as spies		
	Strong anti-Communists	Moderate anti-Communists	Lesser anti-Communists
Strong anti-Semites	4.1	0.0	0.0
Moderate anti-Semites	2.3	0.0	0.0
Non-anti-Semites	2.4	1.2	0.6

SOURCE: N24.

neous references to espionage as a topic of anti-Semitic talk. About 4 per cent of the total sample named Jews in this context. Among strong anti-Semites, the incidence of such mentions turns out to be markedly linked with strength of anti-Communist feeling, ranging from a mere 2 to 15 per cent, that is, from about half to about four times the sample average (Table 90); among moderate anti-Semites and non-anti-Semites, on the other

Table 90   Beliefs about Communist Tendencies of Jews, by Strength of Anti-Communism and Anti-Semitism, I (1950)

"Can you think of any kinds or groups of people in the United States who are more likely than others to be Communists?" (If "yes":) *"Which?"*

	Per cent within each category naming Jews		
	Strong anti-Communists	Moderate anti-Communists	Lesser anti-Communists
Strong anti-Semites	15	10	2
Moderate anti-Semites	5	2	2
Non-anti-Semites	4	5	3

SOURCE: N24.

hand, intensity of anti-Communist attitudes makes no statistically significant difference.

(3) A fairly conclusive result emerged from an analysis of responses to the same issue posed as an aided-recall question, a list of 14 groups being shown to respondents. References to Jews—voiced by 11 per cent of the population as a whole—now appeared to have been unmistakably distributed in accordance with strength of anti-Communist views, not only among the strong but also among the moderate anti-Semites (Table 91). In each of these subgroups, the notion that Jews are likely to be Communists is about twice as prevalent among strong as among moderate and lesser anti-Com-

Table 91 Beliefs about Communist Tendencies of Jews, by Strength of Anti-Communism and Anti-Semitism, II (1950)

"In this country do you think any of the people listed here [on card naming 14 groups] are more likely to be Communists than others?"

	Per cent within each category naming Jews		
	Strong anti-Communists	Moderate anti-Communists	Lesser anti-Communists
Strong anti-Semites	31	16	15
Moderate anti-Semites	14	8	7
Non-anti-Semites	10	9	7

SOURCE: N24.

munists; and a similar differentiation is noticeable even among non-anti-Semites, though not to a statistically significant extent.

(4) The most compelling finding in the series derives from the replies of persons who first named Jews as more likely than others to be Communists, and were then asked whether in their opinion only a few, many or most Jews were Communists (Table 92). The combined frequency of the last

Table 92 Beliefs about Frequency of Communist Tendencies among Jews, by Strength of Anti-Communism and Anti-Semitism (1950)

(Asked of respondents who thought Jews were more likely than others to be Communists:) *"Do you think that only a few, many, or most Jews are Communists?"*

	Per cent within each category saying "many" or "most"		
	Strong anti-Communists	Moderate anti-Communists	Lesser anti-Communists
Strong anti-Semites	14	10	8
Moderate anti-Semites	9	3	2
Non-anti-Semites	5	4	1

SOURCE: N24.

two responses, "many" and "most"—about 5 per cent in the total sample—is significantly linked with intensity of anti-Communist feeling, not only among strong and moderate anti-Semites but also, in less degree, among non-anti-Semites.

Taken together, these results leave no doubt that, as of 1950–51, inclination to view Jews as Communists was consistently related to intensity of anti-Communist feeling. Three of the four analyses find such a relationship among strong anti-Semites, two among moderate anti-Semites and one even among non-anti-Semites.

In the light of this outcome, the problem arises whether individuals at the time were likely to become more anti-Semitic if they were led to believe (by news of Jewish spies or otherwise) that many Communists were Jews.[17] It is at least conceivable that non-anti-Semitic or slightly anti-Semitic persons who grew intensely concerned about the menace of domestic Communists and came to think of them as largely Jewish might have transferred part of their fear or hostility to Jewry as a whole. As it happens, this hypothesis proves only partly verifiable with the data at hand. It would be supported by any evidence of a direct relationship between strength of anti-Communism and of anti-Semitism, and such a link is observable among the influential, if small, college-educated segment of the public: 60 per cent of the strong but only 40 per cent of the lesser anti-Communists in this bracket turn out to have been anti-Semitic in some degree (Table 93). But no similarly conclusive figures are to be found at lower educational levels.

Table 93 Relation of Anti-Semitism and Anti-Communism among the Educated (1950)

	Per cent [a]		
	Strong anti-Communists	Moderate anti-Communists	Lesser anti-Communists
Strong anti-Semites	15	14	7
Moderate anti-Semites	45	38	33
Non-anti-Semites	40	48	60
	100	100	100

[a] College-educated respondents only.
SOURCE: N24.

In the aggregate, then, our data strongly indicate that even during the early 1950s—a time of great concern over Communist infiltration and espionage—a large majority of Americans refused to associate Jews as a group with Communism. Though several of the Soviet spies then being tried and convicted amid the utmost publicity happened to be Jews, only small fractions of the public adopted the idea that Jews *per se* were more likely to be Communists than other people. Receptivity to this idea was greater among persons with strong than with moderate or weak anti-Communist concerns and convictions, particularly where a degree of anti-Semitism was also present; and within the educated segment of the public there were some indications of a direct linkage between anti-Semitism and anti-Communism. But only small minorities of the public held beliefs and attitudes of this sort.

The notion of the Jew as a congenital radical, never more than a minority opinion in America, actually seems to have come close to extinction in the postwar decades. It certainly would seem to have lost most of its usefulness as a propaganda device—which may account for the relative scarcity of anti-Semitic appeals among the extreme right-wing movements of today, compared with those of the 1930s. Present-day reactionaries, bent on attacking "radical" and "collectivist" causes, evidently realize both that anti-Semitism in general has declined, and that the theme of the "Communist Jew" will receive even less of a response than it did a generation ago.

NOTES

1. As of 1962, the number of "don't knows" had considerably increased, while the proportion who considered Jews likely to be radicals had diminished. Slightly more respondents now perceived Jews as inclined toward conservatism than toward radicalism. It must be noted, however, that throughout the series of polls, respondents who saw no difference between Jews and others or who professed ignorance made up at least one-half of the total.

2. As will be recalled, the noted right-wing agitator of the late 1930s, Father Charles E. Coughlin, was criticized more frequently for his "radical, red" tendencies than on any other grounds as late as 1940, when his ideas clearly had lost whatever collectivist tinge they possessed in earlier years (see Table 43). In recent years, ultra-conservative movements have become collectively known as "the Radical Right," even among some of the intellectuals ranging around the center of the political spectrum.

3. The existence of a "humanitarian ethos" among Jews has often been noted.

4. Roosevelt was reported to have said that the choice of a vice-presidential candidate should be cleared with Hillman. In the propaganda of the other side, the phrase "Clear it with Sidney," quoted out of context, was repeated and its significance magnified until the entire nation appeared "to be in instant peril of capture by 'Sidney Hillman, the pants presser.'" Matthew Josephson, *Sidney Hillman, Statesman of American Labor* (Garden City, N.Y.: Doubleday & Co., 1952), p. 631.

5. However, the question asked in November is not directly comparable with the earlier ones.

6. The outcome may also have been affected by the circumstance that respondents were asked to gauge other people's reactions—an unreliable measure of their own attitudes, it would seem, and one likely to inflate the affirmative response still further.

7. The 1954 response is the same as that in the calmer year 1959, when 1 per cent of the public spontaneously named Jews among groups supposedly "soft on Communism."

8. Stouffer observes apropos of the 1954 data: "In spite of the anti-Semitic propaganda which has made it a special point to identify Jews with Communist infiltration and in spite of the numerous Jewish names which actually have appeared in the news about suspected Communists brought before investigating committees it is of interest that only 5% of the national cross-section said that Communists were especially likely to be Jewish. The proportions of such men-

tions were somewhat larger among the local community leaders" than among the general public. Samuel A. Stouffer, *Communism, Conformity and Civil Liberties* (Garden City, N.Y.: Doubleday & Co., 1955), p. 174. The 5 per cent of a national cross section cited by Stouffer is equivalent to the 6 per cent of white Christians in our Table 86.

9. *Ibid.,* pp. 165–169.

10. Nathan Glazer, *The Social Basis of American Communism* (New York: Harcourt, Brace & Co., 1961), p. 130. Glazer asserts, however, that this tiny segment of American Jewry did constitute a disproportionately large part of the Communist Party (pp. 220–222).

11. Names identical with several of these are borne by individuals who received passing mention in government hearings on Communism during the early 1950s, but the resemblance is undoubtedly accidental. In devising fictitious personages, the designers of the survey would naturally choose fairly common names; and since the hearings involved thousands of persons, the chances of fortuitous duplication are high. The actual individuals, moreover, were far from prominent. None of them appear to have been mentioned in the press in connection with the hearings.

12. The 20 per cent total does not necessarily represent 20 per cent of the persons sampled, since multiple answers were invited. The average number of mentions per respondent in the poll as a whole was 1.6. Even so, it seems almost certain that the 20 per cent response represents a far larger number of individuals than the 3 per cent response.

13. Leo Srole, *The Perception of Jews as Communists and Spies* (unpublished report to the American Jewish Committee and the Anti-Defamation League of B'nai B'rith, 1951), pp. 57–65.

14. "Without taking the space for formal documentation of the evidence, we can report that . . . without exception, the higher is the position on the anti-Semitic scale the greater is the incidence of the anti-Jewish ['Communist'] stereotype" (*ibid.,* p. 58). The scale employed to measure anti-Semitism consisted of four questions, asking how the respondent would feel about a Jewish fellow worker, neighbor, friend and spouse (pp. 35–36).

15. Anti-Communism was measured with a scale compounded of three elements: belief or disbelief in domestic Communism as the chief menace to the nation; opinions on the degree of danger threatened by American Communists; and suggested ways of dealing with them (*ibid.,* pp. 2–3).

16. The overall data thus reanalyzed appear in Srole, *op. cit.,* pp. 9–12. Those for items 2 through 4 are also reported, respectively, in our Table 85 (first column), Table 86 (first column) and page 162.

17. The analysis that follows is taken from Srole, *op. cit.,* pp. 65–66.

VIII

The Impact of Israel on American Attitudes*

ISRAEL'S STRUGGLE for existence, from the final years of
the British mandate through the proclamation of an independent state in
1948 and the ensuing war with the Arab nations, confronted the United
States with an entirely new set of problems, and introduced a new, at first
totally incalculable, factor into public opinion concerning Jews. American
diplomacy in the Middle East found itself faced with the delicate task of
maintaining a balance between Arab and Jewish claims for support, with
actual military involvement threatening on several occasions. Nor were
hazards of this sort to remain confined to the 1940s; in 1956, Israel's invasion of the Sinai Peninsula, in defiance of American and United Nations
policy, put the United States temporarily in opposition to her allies, Great
Britain and France.

With a "Jewish problem" once more occupying the center of the world
stage, manifold anti-Jewish reactions were well within the realm of possibility. Through their strong support for the idea of a Jewish state in Palestine,
American Jews had come into open conflict with America's chief ally,
Great Britain.[1] There was no telling whether the spectacle of Jews joining
together in pursuit of this objective might not be interpreted as a new instance of Jewish "clannishness."

It seemed entirely conceivable, moreover, that by supporting Jewish interests America might strain her ties with her allies or get involved in an
armed conflict in the Middle East. Prospects like these, particularly disturbing just after a long and agonizing war, could be expected to give new life to
old charges of Jewish "warmongering" for selfish interests.

* Parts of this chapter reproduce studies by Benjamin B. Ringer. See notes
6, 9 and 13.

In addition, there was a real likelihood that the emergence of Israel would lay American Jews open to accusations of disloyalty or of allegiance to a foreign country, such as had often been raised against other ethnic minorities in the United States. In the past, Jews had been spared this slur because they had no "old country" of their own; but they could no longer count on such immunity now that an "old country" had been, as it were, retroactively created with their own help.

Finally, by endorsing unlimited Jewish immigration from Europe to Palestine, Jews in this country risked putting a damper on whatever hospitality toward refugees existed here. With a Jewish state available as a haven, Americans might well feel free to wash their hands of the problem; indeed, for all anyone knew, they might conclude that Jews in all countries, including this one, ought to remove themselves to Israel.

At the same time, the emergence of Israel bade fair to affect certain popular notions for the better. The struggle of the Jews in Palestine, from their successful defiance of the British to their victory over the Arab countries in 1948–49 and their triumph in the Sinai campaign, could reasonably be expected to counteract the old idea of the Jew as an introspective, feeble, unsoldierly creature, and to help recast him in the role of a hardy fighter and pioneer—a change which might indirectly enhance the image of Jews in other countries, including America. The treatment of Israel in the news, as well as the public response to fiction and entertainment dealing with the new state during subsequent years, might be taken to suggest that such a change was actually initiated.[2]

Opinion research, unfortunately, seems to have made no attempt to assess any such image change. In contrast, public opinion about political developments involving Israel was explored on a large scale; indeed, of our data, more deal with topics of this kind than with any other. We cannot report all of this vast body of information here, nor do we need to; much of it focuses on short-term aspects of the United States' fluctuating policy toward Israel during the formative years of that country, and thus is at most tangentially related to attitudes toward Jews in America. In what follows, we will deal chiefly with findings which do seem to bear, directly or indirectly, on such attitudes.

The Palestinian Problem

The end of the Second World War found Palestine in a seemingly unbreakable deadlock. The local Jewish community's efforts to create a national homeland there were vigorously backed by Zionist groups throughout the world, and its attempts to open the gates to the uprooted remnants of European Jewry found support among a wide segment of world Jewish opinion. These demands clashed head-on with the mounting opposition of Arabs both within and without Palestine's borders. The ruling power, Great

Britain, was committed to the idea of a Jewish national home through her Balfour Declaration of 1917 and the League of Nations mandate under which she governed the country, but had failed to carry out the commitment. Long unable to reconcile the claims of Jews and Arabs, she had closed Palestine to Jewish immigration early in the Second World War.

In November 1945, an Anglo-American Committee of Inquiry was created to seek a solution to these explosive problems. Five months later, this body recommended immediate admission of 100,000 refugees; a United Nations trusteeship to replace the British mandate; and eventual self-government as a multi-national state. The recommendations were endorsed by President Harry S. Truman; but Britain turned them down, pending a political settlement and assurances of American financial and military support.

During the months that followed, the possibility of dividing the country came to the fore. In August 1946, the Jewish Agency—the recognized Jewish body in matters concerning Palestine—accepted partition in principle. In April 1947, at Great Britain's request, the United Nations convened a special session to seek a solution and formed a Special Committee on Palestine (UNSCOP); in August, a majority of the Committee recommended partition of the country and prompt admission of 150,000 Jews from Europe.

This plan, endorsed by the United States and the Soviet Union, was adopted by the General Assembly of the United Nations in November 1947, and a U.N. commission was appointed to ensure an orderly transition. Great Britain, however, proved unwilling to cooperate with the U.N. commission, and as terror and violence mounted, the United States began to have second thoughts. In December, the United States put an embargo on arms shipments to the Middle East—a measure more detrimental to the Jews there than to the Arabs, who continued to obtain arms from Britain— and in February 1948, the American delegation to the United Nations suggested that the partition plan be set aside indefinitely for a U.N. trusteeship. But these reconsiderations came too late to alter the course of events. When British rule ended on May 14, 1948, and the State of Israel was proclaimed, the United States immediately accorded it *de facto* recognition. The sporadic fighting between Jews and Arabs now turned into a full-scale war, from which Israel ultimately emerged victorious and with a somewhat enlarged territory.

At the beginning of the period just summarized, few Americans knew what the Palestine problem was about or felt any concern with it. In December 1944, only about a third of the population was aware that Palestine was ruled by Great Britain (N9). In May 1946, persons who knew this were still a minority (N13); at the same time, almost three-quarters of the people said they had "little or no interest" in "news about our policy toward Palestine."

Levels of information and interest gradually rose as the struggle became more acute. Between late 1945 and 1947, about half the public claimed to have followed the developments there, and three-quarters or more said they had heard or read something about the situation (Table 94). But much of

Table 94 Familiarity with Developments in Palestine (1945–47)

	Per cent
Proportion who say they "have followed":	
"The discussion about permitting Jews to settle in Palestine" (December 1945)	55
"The news about disorders in Palestine" (January 1946)	58
"The discussion about the plan to allow 100,000 Jews to settle in Palestine" (May 1946)	50
"The problem of permitting Jews to enter Palestine" (August 1946)	54
"The discussion regarding the Jewish plans to make Palestine a Jewish nation" (September 1946)	51
Proportion who say they have "heard or read" about:	
"The establishment of a Jewish state or Jewish homeland in Palestine" (February 1946)	72
"The recent report by the Anglo-American Committee on Palestine" (May 1946)	28
"The problem of permitting Jews to enter Palestine" (August 1946)	80
"The trouble in Palestine" (February 1947)	83
"The trouble in Palestine" (April 1947)	83
"The United Nations committee's proposal to partition Palestine" (November 1947)	56

SOURCES: G15–17, 19, 21; O17; N13; G19, 23, 26, 27.

this awareness seems to have consisted merely of a general notion that a problem existed, not of familiarity with current specifics. Thus, while half the public in May 1946 knew of a proposal to admit 100,000 refugees to Palestine, not much more than a quarter had heard or read about the report by the Anglo-American Committee of Inquiry, in which this plan formed the central recommendation. Even the crucial, widely publicized partition plan of the United Nations Special Committee on Palestine was unfamiliar to nearly half the population in November 1947, when the General Assembly was about to debate it.

During the early stages of the Palestinian crisis, the American public seems to have favored the entry of Jewish refugees into Palestine and supported specific proposals to that end. In 1944, and even more in late 1945, endorsers of a Jewish state in the territory outnumbered opponents (Table 95). Among those who had followed the discussion, the proportion in favor

Table 95 Opinions on the Proposed Jewish State in Palestine (1944–45)

"There are over a million Arabs and over half a million Jews in Palestine. Do you think the British, who control Palestine, should do what some Jews ask and set up a Jewish state there, or should they do what some Arabs ask and not set up a Jewish state?"

	Per cent	
	December 1944	November 1945
The British should:		
Set up a Jewish state	36	42
Not set up a Jewish state	22	17
Follow neither Jews' nor Arabs' wishes; other solutions	10	10
Don't know	32	31

SOURCES: N9, 11.

Table 96 Beliefs about the Role of Jews, Arabs and British in Palestine (1946)

(January 1946; asked of the 58 per cent who say they have followed the news about disorders in Palestine:[a]) *"Who do you think is more to blame for these disorders—the Jews, Arabs or the British?"*

	Per cent of total sample
Jews	12
Arabs	10
British	33
Other; no opinion	12
	67[b]

(August 1946:) *"In Palestine, which group do you think the British have treated better, Jews or Arabs?"*

	Per cent
Jews	7
Arabs	38
No difference	18
No opinion	37
	100

[a] See Table 94.
[b] Some respondents gave more than one answer.
SOURCES: G16, 20.

of the Jews was particularly great; of 55 per cent who in December 1945 claimed to have followed the issue, three-fourths were in favor of "permitting Jews to settle in Palestine" (G15).[3] Similarly, in May 1946, the plan to admit 100,000 Jews (see Table 94) was favored by three-fourths of the 50 per cent who declared themselves familiar with it. But these sentiments turned out to be rather unstable and subject to the shifting winds of politics. By August, poll results had begun to reflect the thought—suggested in the British Government's rejection of the Anglo-American Committee's proposal—that a large-scale immigration scheme might involve the United States in a military operation to maintain peace; only one-half of those familiar with the problem at this time still favored admission of Jews to Palestine (G19).

Regardless of this change, responsibility for the impasse was laid, for the most part, at Great Britain's door. In January 1946, about three times as many of the better-informed respondents attributed the current troubles to the British as blamed either Jews or Arabs; in August, Britain was widely charged with playing favorites, 38 per cent of respondents asserting that she had treated the Arabs better than the Jews, and 7 per cent vice versa (Table 96). Since British policy was thus widely condemned by Americans familiar with the situation, we are probably safe in concluding that Jews in this country cannot have incurred much hostility through Jewish antagonism toward Great Britain in the years before partition.

Though outspoken in their sympathies and antipathies, Americans throughout the period were far from willing to see their own country involved. A series of questions, asked between 1944 and 1947, showed the public consistently critical even of minimal American intervention. No matter in what way the issue was raised, substantial majorities were opposed to letting the United States take a hand in keeping order, and even so mild a measure as calling on Great Britain to establish a Jewish state found favor with only a fifth of respondents (Table 97).

Table 97 Opinions on Suggested American Policies toward Palestine (1944–46)

(December 1944; asked of the 68 per cent of total sample not opposed to establishment of a Jewish state:[a]) *"Do you think the United States Government should officially demand that Palestine be made into a Jewish state, or don't you think so?"*

	Per cent of total sample
Should	20
Should not	30
Don't know	18
	—
	68

Table 97 (continued)

(November 1945; asked of the 73 per cent of total sample not opposed to establishment of a Jewish state:[a]) *Question as above.*

	Per cent of total sample
Should	20
Should not	35
Don't know	18
	73

(January 1946; asked of the 58 per cent of total sample who say they have followed news about disorders in Palestine:[b]) *"Would you approve or disapprove of sending United States soldiers to maintain peace there?"*

	Per cent of total sample
Approve	7
Disapprove	48
Don't know	3
	58

(May 1946:) *"The report of the Anglo-American Committee recommends that 100,000 Jewish refugees be admitted to Palestine in spite of protests by the Arabs there. President Truman has said that he thinks this ought to be done. Now England says that the United States ought to help her keep order in Palestine if trouble breaks out between the Jews and the Arabs. Do you think we should help keep order there, or should we keep out of it?"*

	Per cent of total sample
Help keep order	28
Keep out of it	61
Undecided	11
	100

(May 1946:) *"England has suggested that we send troops to Palestine to help keep order there if the Arabs oppose letting 100,000 Jews enter Palestine. Do you approve of our sending troops to Palestine to help England keep order there?"*

	Per cent of total sample
Approve	21
Disapprove	74
No opinion	5
	100

a See Table 95. b See Table 94. SOURCES: N9, 11; G16; N13; G17.

On the other hand, there was considerable support for intervention by the United Nations. In June 1946, when the possibility of a U.N. trusteeship was under consideration in the context of the Anglo-American Committee's recommendations, almost three-fourths of the population thought the U.N. should "handle the problem of letting Jews settle in Palestine" (G17). Again, in November 1947, when a peace-keeping force under the United Nations Commission on Palestine was being discussed, 65 per cent endorsed formation of "a United Nations volunteer army" to keep order, as against 3 per cent favoring the use of American troops and 18 per cent rejecting both alternatives (G27).

The Emergence of Israel

The adoption of the partition plan and the actual establishment of the State of Israel still found the American public in a mood of fairly widespread indifference, judging by polls taken in February, June, October and November 1948 (N15, 18, 20, 21). Only 16 to 24 per cent of respondents expressed strong interest in "news about our policy toward Palestine," while from 24 to 43 per cent said they took no interest in the problem at all.

Given this continuing apathy, it is not surprising to find that American opinion failed to crystallize, remaining content for the most part to follow the shifts and changes of United States policy. When told in November 1947 that the United Nations had worked out a plan for partition, 65 per cent of respondents registered approval and only 10 per cent disapproval; as the United States Government's support for this proposal began to waver, favorable reactions among the public fell conspicuously (G27). In February 1948, only 53 per cent of those who had heard of the partition proposal still favored it, while 26 per cent were now opposed (N15); in March, after the United States Government formally spelled out its objections to the plan, support among those who knew of this latest step dropped to 49 per cent, and opposition rose to 27 per cent (N16).[4] By April, only 26 per cent of a nationwide sample approved partition, while 31 per cent now thought the United Nations "should try to work out some other solution" (R14).

The shift in United States policy found general approval at this time; in two different surveys conducted during the spring of 1948, a majority of those respondents who took a position felt that the United States was justified in altering its stand (N16; G29). Large majorities also endorsed the American embargo on ammunition shipments to the area of conflict (P2). A possible loan to Israel was disapproved by a majority in 1948 (R16), and, as in earlier polls, most respondents opposed any police action by United States troops as such (N15). Again, however, large numbers of respondents favored a United Nations force to keep peace, and of those who did, few objected to American participation (N17).

But though American opinion, for the most part, followed in the footsteps of United States policy, it seems to have run ahead on at least one crucial issue. In March 1948, two months before the State of Israel was actually proclaimed, a poll question asked whether it should be the policy of the United States Government to encourage a state which the Jews might set up on their own, that is, presumably, without the backing of the United Nations, the United States or Great Britain (N16). Surprisingly, no less than half the population believed such a state should be encouraged. Only 10 per cent felt it should be opposed, and about a fifth thought the United States should take neither position.

Whatever the day-to-day vacillations of American policy and opinion, more Americans by and large sympathized with the Jewish than the Arab cause. From the fall of 1947 through the spring of 1949, about one-third of the population consistently sided with the former—twice as many as favored the latter (Table 98). The reasons for these sympathies were explored in the poll of July 1948 (Table 99). Among the supporters of the

Table 98 Sympathy with Jews or Arabs in the Palestine Conflict (1947–49)

- (a) *"If war breaks out between the Arabs and Jews in Palestine, which side would you sympathize with?"*
- (b) *"The United Nations has recommended that Palestine be divided between the Jews and the Arabs. The Arabs say they will not agree to have Palestine divided, and fighting has broken out between the Jews and Arabs. Do you sympathize with the Arabs or with the Jews in this matter?"*
- (c) *"In the conflict in Palestine, do you sympathize with the Arabs or with the Jews?"*
- (d) *"On the whole, which do you think has the most right on its side in the war in Palestine—the Jews or the Arabs?"*

	Per cent						
	(a) November 1947	(b) February 1948	(c) June 1948	(c) July 1948	(d) September 1948	(c) October 1948	(c) March 1949
Sympathize with Jews	24	35	34	36	29	33	32
Sympathize with Arabs	12	16	12	14	16	11	13
Neither; both; don't know	64	49	54	50	55	56	55

SOURCES: G27; N15, 18, 19; R16; N20, 22.

Table 99   Reasons for Sympathy with Jews or Arabs (1948)

"In the conflict in Palestine, do you sympathize with the Arabs or with the Jews?" . . . "Why?"

	Per cent of those who sympathize with Jews (36 per cent of total sample[a])
Reasons for sympathizing with Jews:	
It's their country by religious, historical, legal right	31
Jews are entitled to a home, need a country of their own	28
Jews have been persecuted, mistreated	27
Jews are more progressive, will develop the country	9
Respondent is Jewish, asserts natural sympathy for Jews	4
Other; don't know	24

	Per cent of those who sympathize with Arabs (14 per cent of total sample[a])
Reasons for sympathizing with Arabs:	
It's their country by religious, historical, legal right	43
Respondent does not like Jews (clearly anti-Semitic)	35
Respondent has no sympathy for Jews (not clearly anti-Semitic)	10
Other; don't know	23

[a] See Table 98.
SOURCE: N19.

Arab cause, the largest group cited the Arabs' traditional rights in Palestine; a considerable number indicated clearly anti-Semitic motivation. Of those who sympathized with the Jewish claims, the majority mentioned either the Jews' need for a homeland or the persecution they had suffered; historic or other "rights" to the area loomed less large than among the Arabs' friends.

The frequent references to the sufferings and the homelessness of Jews in this context agree with our earlier finding that Americans during the 1940s felt something should be done about refugees, yet were far from eager to see them admitted to the United States (see Chapter VI). The refugee problem may well have played a decisive role in rallying most Americans' sympathies to the Jews in their struggle with the Arabs. A Jewish state, capable of accommodating large numbers of refugees, seemed to offer a solution acceptable both to persons motivated by humanitarian considerations and to others. That at least some of the sympathy for the Palestinian Jews during this period grew out of a desire to deflect displaced persons from the United States is implied by two studies dating from 1944–45, which asked broadly whether "all Jews should be urged to live" in whatever Jewish state might come into existence. No less than 39 per cent of the public in 1944 and 42 per cent in 1945 thought so (N9, 11).

Once established and admitted to membership in the United Nations, Israel seems to have been accepted by the American public simply as one foreign nation among many—an understandable reaction, considering the dispatch with which the United States Government proceeded to normalize its relations with the new country.[5] Whatever hostility may have existed toward Jews as a group did not affect public opinion concerning America's relationships with Israel. So it would appear, at any rate, from a series of polls taken between 1950 and 1956, in which respondents were asked how important it was for the United States to cooperate with certain countries named in a prepared list (Table 100). For several years, about as many

Table 100 Opinions on the Importance of American Cooperation with Israel and Other Countries (1950–56)

"How important do you think it is for the United States to cooperate closely with [countries named]—very important, only fairly important, or not important at all?"

| | \multicolumn{5}{c}{Per cent answering "very important"} | | | | |
	1950	1952	1953	1955	1956
England					67
West Germany		55			
France	54	45			46
India	41		42		
Argentina			37		
Greece	37				
The Arab countries	34		32	47	30
Israel	31	34	34	34	35

SOURCES: N23, 27, 30, 33, 34.

persons considered Israel important in this sense as named the Arab countries; in 1955 her relative standing declined, but the next year it was back to its earlier level. Moreover, in 1950 Israel was thought almost as important to the United States as Greece, and in 1953 nearly as important as Argentina—both long-standing allies of this country in the conduct of foreign affairs.

Why did nearly a third of the public think it important for America to cooperate with a power as small and new as Israel? A survey undertaken in 1953 identifies some of the reasons (Table 101). As might have been antic-

Table 101   Reasons for Favoring American Cooperation with Israel (1953)

"Why do you feel it's very important for us to cooperate with Israel?"

	Per cent of those who think it very important (34 per cent of total sample [a])
The Israelis are a new nation, need help	17
We need them in the Cold War	16
Their trade is useful to us	12
Their country is the Holy Land	8
We must keep them from Communism	7
Jews have been persecuted	6
We are linked with Israel through American Jews	6
Israelis are friendly, democratic	5
Other; don't know	28

[a] See Table 100.
SOURCE: N30.

ipated, a large part of the response—about half—reflected sympathy for the new state or for Jews in general. But, significantly, the other half spoke in terms of Israel's usefulness to America, in the diplomatic or economic sphere. Evidently by this time the image of Israel as a struggling new nation in need of help had begun to yield to that of an established, functioning power.

In the aggregate, the data we have reviewed reveal little evidence that the establishment of Israel worsened the public's attitude toward American Jewry. Jews were not blamed for coming between the United States and her ally, Great Britain. Indeed, if any power was cast in the role of arch-villain during the Palestinian crisis, it was Britain. Though wary of possible involvement, Americans, by and large, favored a Jewish state; and soon after Israel came into existence, they began to view her as a useful ally. Throughout, most of the American people refused to condemn Jews for their efforts to create a nation of their own. On the contrary, a large portion of the public thought the long record of persecution and the unsolved refugee problem entitled them to a permanent homeland.

In part, this viewpoint may have derived from a selfish concern; a haven for homeless Jews outside the United States offered a painless solution to the refugee problem, which had nagged at the conscience of at least some Americans for years. Indeed, the existence of Israel may have served to reinforce the American public's hostile or at best lukewarm attitude toward admitting Jewish refugees to this country.

The Sinai Crisis

During 1955 and the first half of 1956, long-standing frictions between Israel and her neighbors, Egypt and Jordan, mounted toward a new crisis. For some time, Egypt had been intensifying her boycott, embargo and blockade policies against Israeli trade and shipping. In September 1955, the Egyptian Government, then being strenuously wooed by the Soviet bloc, concluded an arms deal with Czechoslovakia; the following month, Egypt induced Syria and Saudi Arabia to join her in a mutual-assistance pact providing for a joint command in case of attack, presumably by Israel; and, on July 26, 1956, Egypt nationalized the Suez Canal. In the ensuing months, stepped-up Egyptian commando raids in Israeli territory increased tensions to the breaking point.

On October 29, Israel invaded the Gaza Strip and the Egyptian Sinai Peninsula, and in less than a week, her forces wholly occupied these territories. Meanwhile, Great Britain and France entered the fray, ostensibly to separate the belligerents, and demanded a cease-fire at once. When Egypt refused, they bombed her from the air and proceeded to land troops, despite objections by a majority of the United Nations and by the United States. The "aggressive" action of France, Britain and Israel also was strongly condemned by the Soviet Union, in a statement which seemed to threaten a unilateral military move on behalf of Egypt, but was subsequently interpreted as a call for United Nations intervention with Soviet and American participation. Meanwhile, Egypt and Israel accepted a cease-fire agreement arranged by the United Nations, and on November 7 fighting ended. In the months that followed, Israel withdrew from Egyptian territory.

On the heels of these tumultuous events—between November 17 and 21—a survey was conducted to determine whether American attitudes toward Israel had been in any way altered by her recent actions.[6] Over several years, poll respondents had been asked to assess the blame for the conflict between Israel and Egypt. The question was now repeated, with some changes in the wording necessitated by recent events.[7]

Opinion was found to be more fully crystallized than before, with a larger proportion of respondents willing to express an opinion than in the previous poll, seven months earlier (Table 102). Responses critical of Israel increased from 7 to 19 per cent, that is, by 12 percentage points, and responses critical of Egypt from 18 to 29 per cent, or 11 points. The absolute increase thus was about the same on both sides, with Israel retaining an advantage of 10 per cent. At the same time, however, the ratio between the two countries changed significantly: In April there had been five critics of Egypt for every two of Israel; now there were only three for every two.

Table 102 Opinions on Who Is to Blame for Middle Eastern Conflict (1953–56)

(December 1953 through April 1956:) *"Have you heard or read anything about the conflict between Israel and the Arab countries?"* (If "yes":) *"Which side do you feel is more to blame in this dispute—Israel or the Arabs?"*

(November 1956:) *"Which of the two—Israel or Egypt—do you think is more to blame for the present trouble between the two countries?"*

	Per cent			
	December 1953	November 1955	April 1956	November 1956
Think blame falls chiefly on:				
Israel	8	5	7	19
Arabs, Egypt	11	15	18	29
Both	12	15	16	11
Neither	2	3	2	3
Don't know	67[a]	62[a]	57[a]	38

[a] Includes both those who have not heard or read about the conflict, and those who have but do not know who is to blame.
SOURCES: N30, 33, 35, 36.

Even so, the climate of opinion in America plainly remained more favorable to Israel than to Egypt—perhaps surprisingly, in view of the fact that Israel did initiate the Sinai attack, thereby laying herself open to charges of aggression. A supplementary inquiry into the respondents' reasons shows why Israel fared no worse than she did. Those who blamed Israel tended to focus on the attack itself, almost half citing this reason (Table 103). In contrast, those who blamed Egypt viewed the Israeli attack as a reaction against a crisis precipitated by the Egyptians, rather than as the cause of the crisis; most of them cited one or another of the events leading up to the attack, such as Egypt's provocative acts against Israel, her discrimination against Israeli shipping or her seizure of the Suez Canal (Table 104).

In providing critics of both countries with new ammunition, the Middle Eastern war drew attention away from some earlier points of contention. Thus, the charge that Israel had taken land belonging to the Arabs and had always been hostile to them was rarely heard in 1956, though in the preceding year this had been the most widely voiced criticism of all. Similarly, the Egyptians' refusal to recognize Israel's sovereignty and her right to the lands she held drew considerably fewer mentions in 1956 than in 1955. Even accusations taxing Egypt with aggressiveness underwent a change, from charges of underlying hostility toward Israel to mentions of overt provocative acts.

Table 103   Reasons for Blaming Israel in Middle Eastern Conflict (1955–56)

(Initial questions as in Table 102.) . . . *"Why do you feel this way?"*

	Per cent of those who blame only Israel	
	November 1955 (5 per cent of total sample)	November 1956 (19 per cent of total sample)
Israel attacked, invaded Egypt; was the aggressor		48
Israel was greedy, dissatisfied, expansionist, unreasonable; stirred up trouble	29	20
Israel took land which belonged to the Arabs in the first place; has always been hostile to the Arabs	58	11
Israel defied the United Nations; rejected attempts to negotiate; would not wait for a peaceful settlement		11
Israel plotted with England and France; knew in advance that they would support her		7
Anti-Semitic utterances	5	5
Other	6	3
Don't know specific reason	10	18

SOURCES: N33, 36.

The Sinai crisis served, then, to draw attention to the specifics of the moment and away from the underlying problems. Yet, in a sense, the earlier complaints and those of 1956 were variations on the same theme: that Egypt or Israel, as the case might be, was aggressive, immoral or both. Evidently, this idea lay at the heart of the case against each of the two countries.

Although most respondents felt that Israel was less to blame than Egypt for the conflict, a majority were unwilling actually to condone the military action she had launched. When asked, "Do you feel that Israel was justified or not in sending armed forces into Egyptian territory?" only 26 per cent replied "yes"; 40 per cent said "no." True, no less than 34 per cent, evidently feeling some uncertainty, responded "Don't know"—substantially more than gave Great Britain and France the benefit of the doubt in an analogous question (Table 105). But even so, it is evident that most Americans could see no justification for military action by any of the powers involved. Indeed, no less than half of the very individuals who thought the crisis in the Middle East was mostly Egypt's doing nevertheless objected to Israel's attack or were unsure (Table 106). Israel's critics were much

Table 104   Reasons for Blaming Egypt or the Arabs in Middle Eastern Conflict (1953–56)

(*Initial questions as in Table 102.*) . . . *"Why do you feel this way?"*

	Per cent of those who blame only Egypt or the Arabs		
	December 1953 (11 per cent of total sample)	November 1955 (15 per cent of total sample)	November 1956 (29 per cent of total sample)
The Arabs started the conflict, provoked all the incidents (1953, 1955). Egypt provoked, goaded Israel into attacking; had aggressive designs on Israel (1956).	35	44	36
Egypt started the whole thing by illegally seizing the Suez Canal.			25
Arabs are untrustworthy (1953, 1955). Nasser is a dictator, unreliable, ambitious, treacherous (1956).	10	0	19
Egypt was encouraged, influenced by the Soviet Union; received arms and took orders from the Soviet Union.	0	8	13
Egypt refuses to accept, recognize Israel; does not respect Israel's right to her land.	35	23	12
Egypt discriminated against Israeli ships in Suez Canal.			10
Egyptians are lazy, backward people, jealous of Israel's progress.	0	14	0
Other	4	3	4
Don't know specific reason	15	21	13

SOURCES: N30, 33, 36.

readier to condemn her than her supporters were to exonerate her; of those who held her responsible for the conflict, nine in ten refused to justify the invasion.

The pattern underlying this response becomes apparent when expressed willingness or unwillingness to condone Israel's invasion of the Sinai Peninsula is viewed against specific reasons cited for blaming the conflict on Egypt (Table 107). By and large, those respondents who assigned the fundamental blame to Egypt because of her hostility or provocative and discriminatory acts against Israel were relatively likely to consider Israel's action justified—more so than those who blamed Egypt on the grounds of the Suez Canal seizure as such, of subservience to the Soviet Union, of evil qualities attributed to the Egyptian President, Gamal Abdel Nasser, or for no specific reason. The more clearly Israel was seen as the prime target of

Table 105 Opinions on Use of Armed Force against Egypt in Sinai War (1956)

(a) *"Do you feel that Israel was justified or not in sending armed forces into Egyptian territory?"*

(b) *"Do you feel England and France were justified, or not justified, in using armed force against Egypt?"*

	Per cent	
	(a) Israeli action	(b) Anglo-French action
Consider use of armed force:		
Justified	26	25
Not justified	40	54
Don't know	34	21

SOURCE: N36.

Table 106 Opinions on Israel's Use of Armed Force in Sinai War, by Opinions on Responsibility for the Conflict (1956)

	Per cent of those who think blame falls chiefly on	
	Egypt (29 per cent of total sample [a])	Israel (19 per cent of total sample [a])
Consider use of armed force by Israel:		
Justified	50	10
Not justified	34	79
Don't know	16	11

[a] See Table 102.
SOURCE: N36.

Egypt's misbehavior, the greater was the inclination to condone her attack on Egypt.

This is not to say, however, that the presumed degree of Egyptian hostility to Israel was the only determinant. Closer inspection of some of the less specific reasons given indicates that other factors were also present. For example, respondents who referred to President Nasser as dictatorial, treacherous or otherwise evil were relatively unlikely to condone Israel's actions. No doubt a tendency to see political issues in moral terms was the operative factor here; the same moral standards that made Nasser appear reprehensible also made military action unacceptable, however grave the

Table 107 Reasons for Blaming Sinai War on Egypt, by Opinions on
Israel's Use of Armed Force (1956)

	Per cent of those who consider Israel's use of armed force	
	Justified (26 per cent of total sample [a])	Not justified (40 per cent of total sample [a])
[b] Egypt provoked, goaded Israel . . .	67	33
Egypt refuses to accept Israel . . .	63	37
Egypt discriminated against Israeli ships . . .	60	40
Egypt was encouraged, influenced by Soviet Union . . .	58	42
Egypt started the whole thing by seizing Suez Canal . . .	54	46
Nasser is a dictator . . .	53	47
Don't know	47	53

[a] See Table 105.
[b] For full wording of categories, see Table 104.
SOURCE: N36.

provocation, and however plain Egypt's basic responsibility for the conflict.

Still another factor seems to have been at work among respondents who assigned blame to Egypt because of her seizure of the Suez Canal or because of her Soviet connections—circumstances related not so much to the conflict with Israel as to the broader context in which this conflict occurred. Inclined as they evidently were to see particular events in a world perspective, these respondents may well have been concerned about certain larger consequences that might flow from the Israeli attack—specifically, the possibility that a third world war might be set off. This fear might well explain, at least in part, why they disapproved of Israel's attack on Egypt, even though they thought Egypt responsible for the trouble between the two countries.

No doubt the three factors just named frequently operated in conjunction with one another. At least some individuals must have been influenced by all three, with the result depending upon which seemed weightiest. Persons who condoned Israel's attack, then, were not necessarily blind to the moral questions involved in armed aggression and to the possibility of a larger conflict; rather, they may have felt that the guilt of Egypt outweighed these considerations and justified Israel's military action.[8]

We may sum up the findings as follows: Before Egypt's seizure of the Suez Canal and Israel's invasion of Egyptian territory in 1956, public opinion in the United States had tended to blame Egypt rather than Israel for the long-standing Middle Eastern conflict. A great many Americans, however, had remained undecided. The crucial events of 1956 served to crystallize public opinion about the issue. Roughly equal numbers of previously un-committed persons now began to blame Egypt or Israel, with the result that the margin in favor of Israel was somewhat reduced. Moreoever, even though the bulk of public opinion continued to sympathize with Israel, most Americans considered her attack on Egypt unjustified. In many instances, this judgment probably was based on moral considerations concerning the use of force; in others, it may have stemmed from fear of possible broader consequences, such as an enlarged war.

American Jewry and the Middle East Conflict[9]

What effect, if any, did public responses to the Sinai invasion exert on the status and security of Jews in the United States? Up to this point, our evi-dence suggests, Israel's existence had not materially impaired the senti-ments of Americans toward their Jewish fellow citizens, if only because her actions did not seriously conflict with American public opinion or govern-ment policy. But now that Israel had openly invaded neighboring territory against the expressed wishes of the United States and a majority of the United Nations, public opinion might well be expected to take an unfavora-ble turn. Indeed, it was conceivable that America's Jews would find them-selves accused of instigating or promoting the Middle East crisis, and sad-dled with whatever anti-Israeli feeling or anxiety concerning war or Ameri-can involvement might arise from the conflict.

As it happened, public opinion followed the opposite course. Before 1956, only 14 to 16 per cent of the public had linked American Jewry with the trouble in the Middle East, while from 43 to 59 per cent had denied any such connection. The latter group now grew even larger, to 67 per cent—a shift signifying a crystallization rather than a change of opinion, inasmuch as most of the increase was recruited from the "don't know," not the "yes," category (Table 108). More and more people were making up their minds,

Table 108 Beliefs about the Role of American Jews in Middle Eastern Conflict (1953–56)

"Do you think American Jews have anything to do with the trouble in the Middle East between Israel and the Arab countries?" [a]

	Per cent		
	December 1953	November 1955	November 1956
Yes	16	14	12
No	43	59	67
Don't know	41	27	21

[a] *"Between Israel . . ."* omitted in 1956.
SOURCES: N30, 33, 36.

and most of them adopted the view that American Jews had nothing to do with the troubles on the other side of the globe.

Meanwhile, an analogous consolidation of beliefs was taking place among the minority who did think American Jews were connected with the events in the Middle East (Table 109). Fewer than in 1953 or 1955 gave

Table 109 Beliefs about the Nature of American Jews' Role in Middle Eastern Conflict (1953–56)

(*Initial question as in Table 108.*) . . . *"In what way?"*

	Per cent of those who associate American Jews with trouble in the Middle East		
	December 1953 (16 per cent of total sample [a])	November 1955 (14 per cent of total sample [a])	November 1956 (12 per cent of total sample [a])
They send money to Israel	48	45	44
They encourage Israeli aggression	16	10	21
They have a stake in Israel	16	10	19
They provide money for arms for Israel [b]	5	9	13
They raise money for Israel [c]	6	10	6
They influence United States policy in favor of Israel	5	5	5
They influence, control Israeli policy	8	2	3
Anti-Semitic references	23	5	23
Miscellaneous	1	1	2
Don't know	25	25	12

[a] See Table 108.

[b] Includes only responses which mentioned that money raised or sent was being used to buy munitions.

[c] This category was not double-coded with "They send money to Israel." It includes only those who mentioned *organized* fund-raising efforts.

SOURCES: N30, 33, 36.

vague reasons or no reasons for this belief; more mentioned specific acts or attitudes ascribed to American Jews ("they provide money for arms," "they encourage Israeli aggression," "they have a stake in Israel"). Even anti-Semitic references, which had dropped from 23 to 5 per cent in the previous poll, regained their former level. On the other hand, the most frequently cited reason ("they send money to Israel") occurred neither more nor less often than formerly.

It must be noted that the small minority of respondents who believed American Jewry to be linked with the events in the Middle East did not necessarily consider such a connection improper, judging by the 1956 poll, the first to explore this question (Table 110). Opinions on this point turned

Table 110   Attitudes Concerning American Jews' Supposed Activities on Behalf of Israel (1956)

(Initial questions as in Tables 108–109.) . . . "From your own point of view, do you feel it is right or wrong for American Jews to do these things [those listed in Table 109]?"

	Per cent of those who associate American Jews with trouble in the Middle East (12 per cent of total sample)
Right	43
Wrong	47
Don't know	10

SOURCE: N36.

out to be almost evenly divided; similar proportions described the activities of Jews in this field as right and as wrong. American Jews thus were in a markedly favorable position; few of their non-Jewish fellow citizens associated them with the unpleasantness on the Egyptian frontier, and even of these few, barely half thought it a cause for blame.

What disapproval did exist of American Jewry's activities vis-à-vis Israel seems frequently to have been inspired by hostile feelings toward Jews generally, rather than by specific (actual or alleged) acts on their part. Among persons whose views of American Jewry's involvement in the Middle East appeared to be influenced by anti-Semitic notions, such as that of a Jewish world conspiracy, nearly three-fourths disapproved (Table 111). Being anti-Semitic in the first place, these respondents undoubtedly were convinced that anything American Jews might be doing must be evil. Disapproval was voiced by a much smaller proportion (less than one-half) of

Table 111   Attitudes Concerning American Jews' Supposed Activities on Behalf of Israel, by Presence or Absence of Anti-Semitic References (1956)

	Per cent of respondents whose replies concerning American Jews' role in the Middle East	
	Contained anti-Semitic references[a]	Did not contain anti-Semitic references[a]
Think what American Jews are doing is right	29	55
Think what American Jews are doing is wrong	71	45

[a] "Don't know" excluded.
SOURCE: N36.

presumably non-anti-Semitic individuals, who described the American Jews' concern in the Middle East in terms of specific activities, such as alleged political efforts in behalf of Israel or alleged collecting of funds for military equipment.

That American Jewry incurred little if any new hostility as a result of the events in the Middle East is underlined by findings concerning anti-Jewish talk in 1956. Not much more than one-tenth of the public reported having heard criticism of Jews in that year.[10] Furthermore, reports of such talk appeared to be more or less independent of the respondents' own attitudes toward the crisis, being roughly similar in frequency among those who blamed Israel for the conflict and those who blamed Egypt (Table 112). If

Table 112   Reported Criticism of Jews, by Opinions on Responsibility for Middle Eastern Conflict (1956)

"Have you heard any criticism or talk against the Jews in the last six months?"

	Per cent of those who think blame falls chiefly on		
	Israel	Egypt	Other
Have heard criticism	15	11	10
Have heard no criticism	85	89	90

SOURCE: N36.

the crisis had fomented anti-Jewish talk, there undoubtedly would have been an emphatic difference. Only one of the figures suggests an unfavorable effect, either actual or potential: Unlike all other anti-Jewish arguments reported, the idea that the first loyalty of Jews was to Israel was steadily becoming more frequent.[11] Unfortunately, we have no subsequent data to tell us whether this increase was a temporary phenomenon linked primarily with the tense situation of the moment or a more permanent change connected with Israel's generally growing prominence and her availability as a target for anti-Jewish sentiments.

Though the majority of Americans during 1956 refused to hold American Jewry responsible for troubles in the Middle East, the evidence suggested that they might respond differently in future situations. Between 1953 and 1956, references to American Jews as "encouraging Israeli aggression" had increased appreciably, and so had mentions of their "providing money for arms"—the activity most frequently described as improper in the replies to a supplementary question asked in 1956. Thus it seemed that, with changing conditions, public opinion might come to relate the fortunes of American Jewry more closely to those of Israel.

Looking back from the vantage point of today, we probably are safe in concluding—even without data for the intervening years—that no such development has occurred to date, and that the chances of its occurring are smaller in today's climate of opinion than they were in that of 1956. The only event likely to upset this expectation would seem to be a substantial worsening of Americans' attitudes toward Israel herself. In the past, what little disapproval of American Jewry's pro-Israel activities existed was voiced mostly by persons who saw Israel, not Egypt, as the villain on the Middle Eastern scene; in 1956, 13 per cent of the former and only 5 per cent of the latter objected to these undertakings (N36). Some future contingency in that part of the world, more threatening than the Sinai crisis, might conceivably enlarge this group enough to set off a reaction against such endeavors by Jews in the United States.

As for the events of 1956, we may summarize the findings and their implications as follows: Unfavorable reactions to Israel's policies exerted no perceptible impact on public opinion about Jews in the United States. Anti-Jewish talk did not increase, and only rarely was American Jewry linked in an unfavorable way with the trouble in the Middle East. However, some of the responses suggested that such a reaction might ensue if a more severe crisis in the future were to strain the American public's acceptance of Israeli policies or create widespread apprehension about a world conflagration arising from Israeli actions. This prospect was suggested by the circumstance that public opinion between 1954 and 1956 increasingly focused on the alleged loyalty of all Jews to Israel, and on objectionable kinds of aid said to have been rendered to Israel by American Jewry.

The Eichmann Trial

In May 1960, Israeli agents in Argentina kidnaped Adolf Eichmann, formerly one of the key functionaries in the Nazi genocide program, and took him to Jerusalem to be tried. At the time, it seemed more than likely that American attitudes toward Israel would be adversely affected by this step, since the abduction was plainly contrary to normal standards of due process. Nor could Eichmann's subsequent trial, in the spring and summer of 1961, be counted on to lessen such a reaction, inasmuch as the legality of the proceedings was widely disputed by legal scholars. For many months, the American public remained locked in debate on whether or not Israel had any jurisdiction for trying Eichmann, many jurists as well as laymen holding that he should have been turned over to an international tribunal or a German court.

Other observers at this time questioned the intent of the trial, as defined by Prime Minister David Ben-Gurion of Israel: "to see that the whole of this story [the annihilation of the Jews of Eastern Europe], in all of its horror, is fully exposed . . . as a unique and unexampled crime, unparalleled in the annals of mankind." [12] Expectations of what might be called a Christian backlash were voiced; the public had heard enough of the Jews' sufferings at the hands of the Germans, it was said, and further emphasis on the horrors of concentration camps and gas chambers would only be resented as an attempt to make the world at large feel guilty.

Public concern over these problems, which were provoking much excited debate among intellectuals and persons involved in Jewish affairs, was gauged through a nationwide poll about the time the courtroom proceedings began. Awareness of the trial was found to be widespread (G40); over four-fifths of the respondents said they had heard or read about the case. Fewer than one-third were strongly interested in the event; on the other hand, only about one-tenth declared themselves wholly uninterested—a surprisingly small group, considering that the issue in no way involved the United States or its concerns. The drama of the case probably did as much as its substance to engage public attention. As featured in the news media, Eichmann's abduction from Argentina had all the excitement of a detective or spy thriller; it is hard to imagine anyone remaining totally indifferent to this real-life story of undercover agents and their adventures.

The poll just cited did not measure public reaction to the controversial legal aspects of the kidnaping; but it did take up the question of jurisdiction, and here sentiment was found to be deeply divided (Table 113). Half the total sample approved of Israel's taking charge; more than a third said Eichmann should have been handed over to an international court, and 7

Table 113   Opinions on the Trial of Adolf Eichmann, by Levels of Education and of Interest in the Trial (1961)

"Which of these do you think would have been the right course for the Israeli Government to follow with Eichmann?"

		Per cent of respondents [a]					
	Per cent overall[a]	With high-school education or less, whose interest in the trial is			With at least some college education, whose interest in the trial is		
		High	Moderate	Nil	High	Moderate	Nil
Try him as they are doing before an Israeli court	50	60	56	45	45	42	23
Hand him over to an international court for trial	36	33	34	42	46	54	59
Hand him over to the Germans for trial	7	5	8	9	9	3	12
Let him go free	1	2	2	4	0	1	6
No opinion	6	b	b	b	b	b	b

[a] Non-Jews only.   [b] "No opinion" excluded.
SOURCE: G40.

per cent thought he ought to have been turned over to Germany for trial. Further analysis showed that the division of opinion varied with levels of schooling and with intensity of interest in the case.[13] The less educated and those with a strong interest tended to approve of the proceedings in Israel. In contrast, persons with at least some college training and those with less of a concern about Eichmann were more inclined to favor an international tribunal. Among educated persons with a moderate interest in the case or none, a majority would have preferred the international solution.

Despite these far-reaching doubts about Israel's right to try Eichmann, it was generally assumed that the proceedings would be properly conducted. Over 70 per cent of the respondents agreed that the defendant was getting a fair trial; fewer than 10 per cent took the opposite view, and about a fifth said they did not know. The trial's avowed purpose—to impress mankind with the horrors of Nazism—also found overwhelming approval among the American public, contrary predictions notwithstanding: Over 70 per cent of the sample said it was a good thing for the world to be reminded of the concentration camp horrors; only about a fifth disagreed (G40).

On the whole, then, the proceedings in the courtroom at Jerusalem seem to have stimulated little negative feeling toward Israel or the Jews generally.[14] Even Israel's taking jurisdiction, though considered improper by a substantial proportion of the public, was not believed to preclude the possibility of a fair trial.

NOTES

1. In 1945, four-fifths of American Jews were in favor of such a state and only 10 per cent were opposed (R11).

2. Note, for example, the remarkable success of Leon Uris's *Exodus* (New York: Doubleday & Co., 1958), a popular novel about the beginnings of Israel, which, in the words of an American observer, "accomplished the feat of supplying the world's Jews overnight with contemporary cowboy ancestors."

3. Other answers given were not necessarily hostile to Jewry. Among them were such solutions as giving the Jews some other homeland, letting them go anywhere they chose or admitting them to the United States.

4. Of the total population, 32 per cent knew at this time that the United States opposed the plan; 20 per cent thought the U.S. was in favor. Almost half did not know what America's position was.

5. In 1949, the United States granted Israel a loan and accorded her *de jure* recognition; in 1951, Israel became the recipient of a Point Four aid program and of a grant-in-aid under the Mutual Security Act. A treaty of friendship, commerce and navigation was also concluded in the latter year.

6. What follows (Tables 102 through 107 and analyses thereof) is a condensed version of part of an unpublished report on this survey, by Benjamin

B. Ringer (American Jewish Committee, Division of Scientific Research, *Report on the Nationwide Poll of November, 1956*).

7. The results probably were colored by simultaneous occurrences in the rest of the world. While Israel was invading Egypt, the Soviet Union was ruthlessly crushing a revolt against the Communist regime in Hungary. The tragic events in Budapest almost certainly distracted public attention from the Middle East and made Israel's actions appear less reprehensible than they might otherwise have seemed—particularly since Egypt was known to have cooperated with the Soviet Union. If Israel had been the only nation charged with aggression at the time, the test would have been more clear-cut.

8. It might also be conjectured that pre-existing images of the Jews and of Israel influenced appraisals of the Sinai campaign. As noted earlier, Jews— at least those in the United States—were believed during the war to be averse to soldiering (see Chapter V), and Israel was viewed in her early years as a country in need of help, sympathy and encouragement. The spectacle of the new nation's taking aggressive action against a neighbor must have appeared inconsistent with whatever remained of this imagery, unless a justification were found.

9. This section (Tables 108 through 112), like the one preceding, is a condensed version of data and interpretations from the unpublished report of the American Jewish Committee's 1956 poll (Ringer, *op. cit.*).

10. See Table 8 (Chapter II), which reports responses to this question from 1940 to 1956.

11. *Loc. cit.* In polls up to 1954, this criticism was mentioned too infrequently to warrant separate coding, or not at all. In 1955, it was reported by one respondent in 20 among those who reported any criticism of Jews, in 1956 by one in seven.

12. Quoted in *American Jewish Year Book,* LXII (1961), 208.

13. Benjamin B. Ringer, *The American Public and the Eichmann Trial: A Reanalysis of Data from the Gallup Poll of May, 1961* (New York: Division of Scientific Research, The American Jewish Committee, 1961), pp. 3–8.

14. There is no telling, in the absence of poll data, whether the same applies to Eichmann's abduction from Argentina.

IX

Jews and the Desegregation Crisis

BENJAMIN B. RINGER

From the late 1930s until well into the 1950s, most of the major issues bearing on Americans' attitudes toward their Jewish fellow citizens arose outside the United States. Neither the plight of the refugees from the Hitler regime, nor the threat of Soviet Communism, nor the struggle attending Israel's emergence—to name only the most obvious—was of America's making. But during the 1950s, it seemed, for a time, as if a purely domestic development might deeply affect public attitudes toward the Jews. That development was the Negro's struggle for equality.

As late as the Second World War and the years immediately following, efforts to ensure full civil rights for Negroes had commanded relatively little public attention. Outside certain liberal circles, racial segregation and discrimination were still seen primarily as concerns of the Negro minority, not of the nation as a whole. Yet during the same years a body of laws and court decisions designed to do away with such abuses was in the making; and in 1954 a legal ruling—the outlawing of segregated public schools by the United States Supreme Court—finally compelled the nation's citizens to recognize the "Negro problem" as an issue of direct concern to themselves.

From that crucial moment onward, the Negroes' demand for equality increasingly challenged and involved the nation as a whole. To no one's surprise, the mounting conflict between aspiration and privilege produced severe social tensions, and the question inevitably arose how these tensions might affect the status of other minority groups. The prospects of American

Jewry were particularly problematic because, as history has shown only too often, any serious strain in a society may become a threat to Jews. A varied assortment of anti-Jewish manifestations during the middle 1950s suggested that such a threat might once more be in the making: a flood of hate literature in the South; the momentary rise of anti-Negro, anti-Semitic demagogues like Asa Carter and John Kasper; continual attempts to brand desegregation and the organizations working toward it as part of a "Jewish Communist plot." Somewhat later, in the spring of 1958, bombings of synagogues and Jewish centers in several Southern cities seemed to signal the possibility of widespread trouble.

The immediate question during the 1950s, therefore, was what role in the civil-rights struggle was being attributed to Jews. If they were widely perceived as champions of Negro rights, they presumably would be viewed as potential enemies by the bulk of segregationist whites in the South and elsewhere. If they were not so perceived, then Negroes and integration-minded whites—their natural allies in the struggle for civil and social democracy—might accuse them of serving only their own narrow self-interest, of fighting discrimination against themselves while acquiescing in discrimination against others.

To what extent either of these prospects has come to pass can be only tentatively gauged with the opinion data at hand, since our information derives primarily from a single survey conducted in 1959 and focused, for the most part, specifically on school desegregation.[1] Concerning the opinions of Negroes, however, more recent information is available in a survey conducted by Louis Harris and Associates in 1963.[2]

Beliefs about the Attitudes of Jews toward Desegregation

As of 1959, religious groups were not widely viewed as major promoters of controversy over school desegregation. This fact is evident in the replies to the following question: "In those Southern communities where a serious dispute exists over the Supreme Court decision, which group or groups of people would you say have done the most to stir up trouble over the issue?" (G36). Large majorities in every category of respondents—segregationists and integrationists, Southerners and dwellers in other regions—identified supposed troublemakers in terms of race, place of residence or political persuasion ("extremists"); few referred to religious identity.

At the same time, however, many Americans thought of religious and racial groups as being committed to one side or the other. A further question in the 1959 survey asked, "In your local community, which of the following groups of people do you feel are in favor of, or opposed to, integrating the public schools in the South?" and proceeded to name specific groups, among them Catholics, Protestants, Jews and the National Association for the Advancement of Colored People.[3] Such perceptions as were registered in the replies turned out to be relatively uniform, no matter whether the respondents were Negroes, white Protestants or white Catholics; whether they lived in the South or elsewhere; and whether they themselves favored or opposed integration (Table 114). Among all these cate-

Table 114   Beliefs about the Attitudes of Jews and Other Groups toward School Integration, by Regions (1959)

"In your local community, which of the following groups of people do you feel are in favor of, or opposed to, integrating the public schools in the South?"

Per cent perceiving groups named as having views on school integration similar to their own

	Respondents favoring integration			Respondents opposing integration		
	White Protestants	White Catholics	Negroes	White Protestants	White Catholics	Negroes
Groups named						
In Deep South:						
Protestants	a	a	50	91	67	b
Jews			41	46	40	
Catholics			73	39	59	
NAACP			100	5	17	
In Border South:						
Protestants	29	50	53	75	b	55
Jews	55	92	56	35		50
Catholics	59	96	69	25		38
NAACP	98	100	97	6		20
In rest of nation:						
Protestants	71	72	57	39	20	b
Jews	73	81	71	32	14	
Catholics	71	85	75	12	24	
NAACP	94	95	96	5	2	

a Too few cases.   b Insufficient data on Jews available for comparison.
SOURCE: G36.

gories the NAACP was mentioned most frequently, and among nearly all, Protestants were named least frequently as integration-minded. Catholics were described as integrationists more often than were Jews; in fact, Negroes in the Deep South viewed Jews as even less integrationist than they did Protestants. Only white Catholic segregationists described Catholics (and, outside the South, Protestants) less frequently as favorable to integration than they did Jews.

To a degree, these perceptions agreed with reality. As of 1959, white Protestants were indeed less in favor of integration than the other groups named, notwithstanding the fact that outside the South a majority of Protestants were for it (Table 115). Where the opinions of Catholics and Jews

Table 115 Actual Attitudes of Jews and Other Groups toward School Integration, by Regions (1959)

"The United States Supreme Court has ruled that racial segregation in the public schools is illegal. This means that all children, no matter what their race, must be allowed to go to the same schools. In other words, this is integration. Please look at this scale and tell me how you feel about integrating public schools."

	Per cent		
	Approving	Uncertain	Disapproving
In Deep South:			
White Protestants	4	2	94
White Catholics	5	5	90
Negroes	42	19	39
Jews	a	a	a
In Border South:			
White Protestants	19	6	75
White Catholics	59	4	37
Negroes	64	12	24
Jews	a	a	a
In rest of nation:			
White Protestants	66	7	27
White Catholics	73	8	19
Negroes	90	5	5
Jews	96	2	2

a Insufficient data.
SOURCE: G36.

were concerned, however, the perceptions reported were generally out of tune with the facts.

White Catholics really were not much more in favor of desegregation than white Protestants, except in the Border South. Indeed, in the Deep South, the former opposed it about as frequently as the latter. If Catholics were so generally credited with more integrationist sentiment than they possessed, the reason probably is that, ever since the historic court decision, high-ranking members of the Church's hierarchy had publicly expressed support for desegregation or had actually taken steps to carry it out in parochial schools. These widely noted moves undoubtedly reflected on the

Church as a whole, making its lay members look more integrationist than they were—not only to the outside world, but in certain areas even to themselves: Substantial numbers of Southern Catholics who personally did not favor integration nevertheless believed Catholics as a group to favor it (Table 116).

Table 116 White Catholics' Own Attitudes toward School Integration, Compared with Their Beliefs about the Attitudes of Catholics Generally, by Regions (1959)

(*Questions as in Tables 114 and 115.*)

	Per cent of white Catholics	
	Who personally favor integration	Who think Catholics as a group favor integration
In Deep South	5	39
In Border South	59	74
In rest of nation	73	77

Source: G36.

Jews on the other hand (at least those outside the South) actually were more committed to integration than any other group, even the Negroes (see Table 115),[4] but they evidently did not convey to the public an idea of where they stood—or even of where they thought they stood, as the Catholics were doing. Not only was Jewish support for desegregation more widely underestimated than was the case with other groups; the number of "don't know" replies also was exceptionally large (Table 117). In short, most non-Jews did not know how Jews felt about integration; and if they thought they knew, they tended to be wrong.

At least two hypotheses suggest themselves as explanations of this misunderstanding. First, American Jews speak with many voices; they lack a recognized representative who might express, or be thought to express, their collective opinion. No rabbi or group of rabbis can speak for Jewry as the Catholic hierarchy does for the Church; no one organization occupies an unquestioned leading position among Jews.

Second, Jews constitute only a small part of the population, so that few non-Jews could have first-hand knowledge of Jewish opinion, even if contact between the two groups were more frequent than it presumably is. Thus, most of the poll respondents could have obtained such knowledge, if at all, only through mass communication channels. In all likelihood, not many were actually exposed to information of this sort. The coverage of Jewish topics in the mass media, besides being of necessity limited in volume and highly select in content, probably is not very salient to non-Jews; it is likely to be of greater interest to the Jewish than the general public. The average Ameri-

Table 117   Ignorance Concerning Attitudes of Jews and Other Groups toward School Integration, by Regions (1959)

(*Question as in Table 114.*)

	Per cent who say they do not know attitudes of groups named		
	White Protestant respondents	White Catholic respondents	Negro respondents
Groups named			
In the South:			
Jews	67	62	48
Catholics	56	24	40
Protestants	28	43	33
NAACP	19	10	19
In rest of nation:			
Jews	56	43	39
Catholics	55	16	33
Protestants	34	38	36
NAACP	34	18	9

SOURCE: G36.

can presumably feels little concern with the Jews' sentiments on integration or, for that matter, on almost any other issue; if the newspaper he reads were to carry a statement by a Jewish spokesman or organization, he would be quite likely to overlook it.

In the South, a third factor appears to have been at work. Though, as noted, we have no usable statistical information about the climate of opinion among Jews in that region, it is highly probably that they were much more divided and unsure than their cousins in other parts. In any event, the strategy of silence followed by important segments of Southern Jewry since the race crisis began makes it unusually difficult to gauge local Jewish sentiment with any degree of accuracy. In this connection, it may be significant that "don't know" answers regarding Jews were even more numerous in the South than elsewhere (see Table 117).

Given this lack of clues plus the low salience of Jews *qua* Jews in this context, widespread ignorance and misperception were perhaps inevitable. Lacking a firmer basis, many white respondents—both segregationists and integrationists—seem to have based their appraisals of Jewish opinion on their own feelings about Jews and about desegregation. Thus, in the South, whites who happened to be essentially free from anti-Semitism tended to assume that Jews agreed with whichever stand they themselves were taking on the race issue (Table 118).[5]

A comparable configuration could be observed among Negro integration-

Table 118 White Southerners' Beliefs about Jews' Attitude toward School Integration, by Respondents' Own Attitudes toward Integration and toward Jews (1959)

(*Question as in Table 114.*)

	Per cent of white Southern respondents			
	Who favor integration[a]		Who oppose integration[a]	
	Low in anti-Jewish feeling[b]	Moderate or high in anti-Jewish feeling[b]	Low in anti-Jewish feeling[b]	Moderate or high in anti-Jewish feeling[b]
Believe Jews favor integration	67	47	29	48
Believe Jews are neutral or have mixed feelings	20	38	25	18
Believe Jews oppose integration	13	15	46	34

[a] Index constructed from the question in Table 115, plus this: *"If the only way to resist integrating the public schools is to close the public schools, would you support this course of action?"* Replies to the first question were scored 0 (approve or strongly approve), 1 (uncertain), 2 (disapprove) or 3 (strongly disapprove); those to the second question were scored 0 (no), 1 (maybe or no opinion), 2 (yes if only temporarily) or 3 (yes even if permanently). Respondents with scores of 0, 1 or 2 for both questions combined were counted as favoring integration, others as opposing it.

[b] Index constructed from the questions in Tables 17 and 33. Replies to each question were scored 0 (disagree or strongly disagree), 1 (uncertain or no opinion) or 2 (agree or strongly agree). Respondents with scores of 0 or 1 for both questions combined were counted as low in anti-Jewish feeling, others as moderate or high in such feeling. "Moderate" and "high" were combined because the proportions under "high" were too slight to permit separate analysis (about 10 per cent).

SOURCE: G36.

Table 119 Negro Integrationists' Beliefs about Jews' Attitude toward School Integration, by Regions and Respondents' Own Attitudes toward Jews (1959)

(*Question as in Table 114.*)

	Per cent of Negro integrationist respondents			
	Outside the South		In the South	
	Low in anti-Jewish feeling[a]	Moderate or high in anti-Jewish feeling[a]	Low in anti-Jewish feeling[a]	Moderate or high in anti-Jewish feeling[a]
Believe Jews favor integration	76	62	45	50
Believe Jews are neutral or have mixed feelings	16	19	21	7
Believe Jews oppose integration	8	19	34	43

[a] Index as in Table 118.

SOURCE: G36.

ists outside the South: Persons relatively free of anti-Jewish feeling less often thought of Jews as segregation-minded than did anti-Semites (Table 119). Among Negro integrationists in the South, however, the pattern differed somewhat. Here, anti-Semitic respondents held a much more polarized image of the Jew than did individuals more or less free from anti-Jewish feeling: Much fewer of the former thought of Jews as neutral or undecided, while somewhat more believed them to favor integration, and substantially more to oppose it.

Recent Trends in Negroes' Perception of Jews

The passage of time seems to have done little to alter the way in which Negroes outside the South perceived the position of Jews in the civil-rights struggle. Responses in the 1963 poll were markedly similar to those of 1959, even though the content of the question was different (Table 120).[6] For

Table 120 Negroes' Beliefs about Jews' Attitudes toward the Civil-Rights Movement, by Regions (1959, 1963)

(1959: *Question as in Table 114.*)

(1963:) *"Now I want to give you a list of different people and groups that are run by white people."* (List contains 15 groups, among them Jews.) *"Do you think Jews have been more helpful or more harmful to Negro rights?"*

	Per cent of Negro respondents naming Jews			
	Outside the South		In the South	
	1959	1963	1959	1963
Believe Jews favor school integration (1959). Think Jews have helped Negro rights (1963).	46	49	27	37
Believe Jews oppose school integration (1959). Think Jews have harmed Negro rights (1963).	10	10	21	7
Don't know or not sure	44	41	52	56

SOURCES: G36; Brink and Harris, pp. 181, 232.

example, in 1963, as four years earlier, approximately two of every five respondents said they did not know where Jews stood in the controversy;[7] and among the rest, roughly five respondents in six thought Jews were helping, not hindering the Negroes' cause.

Among Southern Negroes, too, the proportion professing ignorance of the Jews' position showed little change; as in the earlier poll, "don't know" accounted for more than half of all answers. In contrast, a significant shift occurred among the minority who ventured an opinion: In 1959, almost as many persons had believed Jews to oppose school integration as believed them to favor it; in 1963, there were five respondents who thought Jews were helping Negro rights for every one who thought they were hindering them (Table 120).

Both in the South and elsewhere, it must be noted, responses favorable to the Jews' role constituted less than half the total sample. An actual majority who thought of Jews as backers of civil rights was found only among Negro *leaders* across the country, three-fourths of whom expressed this view in 1963.[8]

With respect to the Catholic group, Negroes outside the South responded almost exactly as they had done in 1959, despite the fact that the question now dealt with "Catholic priests," not local Catholics, and that its substance was different (Table 121). Again, just under two fifths said they did

Table 121 Negroes' Beliefs about Catholics' Attitudes toward the Civil-Rights Movement, by Regions (1959, 1963)

(1959: *Question as in Table 114.* 1963: *Question analogous to that in Table 120, with "Catholic priests" in lieu of "Jews."*)

	Per cent of Negro respondents naming Catholics			
	Outside the South		In the South	
	1959	1963	1959	1963
Believe Catholics favor school integration (1959). Think Catholic priests have helped Negro rights (1963).	55	54	42	57
Believe Catholics oppose school integration (1959). Think Catholic priests have harmed Negro rights (1963).	8	8	13	3
Don't know or not sure	37	38	45	40

SOURCES: G36; Brink and Harris, pp. 181, 232.

not know where the Catholics stood; of the rest, approximately seven-eighths again considered the Catholics' position favorable to Negroes. The close resemblance between the two sets of data, incidentally, would seem to support our contention that respondents in the 1959 poll thought of the Catholic hierarchy when asked about "local Catholics."

Among Southern Negroes, about as large a proportion as in 1959—roughly two-fifths—were uncertain about the Catholics' sentiments on integration. Among those who did express an opinion, however, a dramatic shift was registered. As of 1959, three of every four persons in this group had thought of Catholics as being on the Negroes' side; by 1963, the proportion was no less than 19 of every 20.

The Negroes' response to Jews and to Catholics, then, seems to have run parallel during the years spanned by the two surveys. In each case, the only material change occurred in the South, among persons who expressed a definite opinion. Even this change did little to alter the relative standing of the two groups in the perceptions of the Negro community at large; Catholics still were believed to be more committed to the cause of Negro equality than were Jews. Only the leaders of the Negro group named Jews as allies with the same frequency as they did Catholic priests.

Whether the white Protestants' and Catholics' perception of the Jews' opinions on civil rights remained similarly hazy by the 1960s cannot be determined from our data, but there is a strong presumption that such is the case. What might happen if this state of affairs were to change is an intriguing question. The present curtain of ignorance undoubtedly has served, in some degree, to protect American Jewry against segregationist attacks. If the far-reaching commitment of most Jews to the civil-rights cause were better understood, such attacks might not remain confined to the propaganda of the Southern lunatic fringe, and might become somewhat more effective than they apparently have been to date. Presumably, the more anti-Semitic of the segregationists would become still more hostile, and some of those who were normally well disposed toward Jews might also be expected to cool off toward them. Even in 1959, it should be noted, anti-Semitic attitudes were more frequently observed among segregationists than integrationists and, except in the Deep South, more often among extreme than moderate segregationists (Table 122).

Beyond these rather narrow boundaries, the continuing struggle for the Negroes' rights does not appear likely to strengthen anti-Semitism among either whites or Negroes—if only because of certain far-reaching changes in the movement itself. The desegregation issue has become increasingly po-

Table 122   Prevalence of Anti-Semitism among White Integrationists and Segregationists, by Regions (1959)

	Per cent of white		
	Integrationists [b]	Segregationists [b]	Extreme segregationists [b]
Persons moderate or high in anti-Jewish feeling:			
In Deep South	43	71	63
In Border South	49	60	66
In rest of nation	42	54	70

[a] Index as in Table 118; see footnote to that table concerning reason for combining "moderate" and "high."

[b] Index as in Table 118, except that combined scores were counted as follows: 0, 1, 2 "integrationist"; 3, 4 "segregationist"; 5, 6 "extreme segregationist."

SOURCE: G36.

larized into a conflict between black and white. In 1959, it may still have been possible to think of desegregation as a cause promoted largely by whites on behalf of the Negro; by 1963, leadership had unmistakably passed into the Negro's own hands. Under these circumstances, whites—perhaps even white segregationists—probably will concern themselves less than formerly with what Jews think, and more with what Negroes do. By the same token, the Negro community presumably will find the actual or supposed opinions of Jews on integration less and less important. Certainly, the anti-Semitism that exists in the Negro community today centers, not on misconceptions about the Jews' attitudes toward Negro rights, but on more traditional animosities.

NOTES

1. The 1959 data cited throughout this chapter are from two unpublished reports of the American Jewish Committee, Division of Scientific Research: *The Nationwide Poll of March 1959*, by Benjamin B. Ringer, and *Memorandum on the Nationwide Poll of 1959*, by Marshall Sklare.

2. These data were obtained from William Brink and Louis Harris, *The Negro Revolution in America* (Copyright Newsweek, Inc.; New York: Simon & Schuster, 1964).

3. "Labor unions" and "chambers of commerce" were also listed, but the results are irrelevant in this context.

4. Samples from the Deep South and Border South included too few Jewish respondents to yield significant data on Jewish opinion in these regions.

5. Among anti-Semitic, anti-integrationist respondents, the opposite tendency —to assume that Jews were on the other side of the issue—was apparent, though in far less degree. Among anti-Semitic integrationists it was not, perhaps because the sample contained relatively few respondents of this description.

6. The 1963 findings cited in what follows are from Brink and Harris, *op. cit.*, p. 232.

7. For purposes of comparison, we eliminate the "neutral or mixed feelings" response from the 1959 figures. There is no such category in the 1963 data.

8. No comparable data for 1959 are available.

X

Summary and Conclusions

THE PUBLIC-OPINION studies on which our analyses are based measure a broad assortment of public attitudes in all their dimensions: the affective, cognitive and conative. Taken together, they constitute what we believe to be a reasonably comprehensive representation of Americans' feelings toward their Jewish fellow citizens over the years. We are therefore in a position to assess the trend of attitudes during the last quarter-century with some degree of assurance.

The Trend of Attitudes

One fact consistently emerges from our analyses: Anti-Semitism in all its forms massively declined in the United States between the prewar or war years and the early 1960s. This conclusion is strikingly illustrated by (though by no means exclusively drawn from) those issues for which we have data spanning all or most of the period under study. Each of these measures registers a substantial diminution of anti-Semitism or of ignorance or stereotypy with respect to Jews, no matter whether it is the affective, cognitive or conative aspect that is gauged (Figure 123). Thus, as of 1962, significantly fewer people than formerly believed that Jews as a group had distinctive undesirable traits or considered them a "race." Fewer thought Jews were clannish, dishonest, unscrupulous or excessively powerful in business and finance. Fewer believed colleges should limit the number of Jewish students. Much fewer objected to Jewish neighbors or employees. And fewer opposed marriage between Jews and others than had done so as late as 1950.

At the outset, each of the 12 measures used to explore these issues drew

Figure 123 Long-Term Decreases in Anti-Semitism, According to 12 Measures (1938–62)

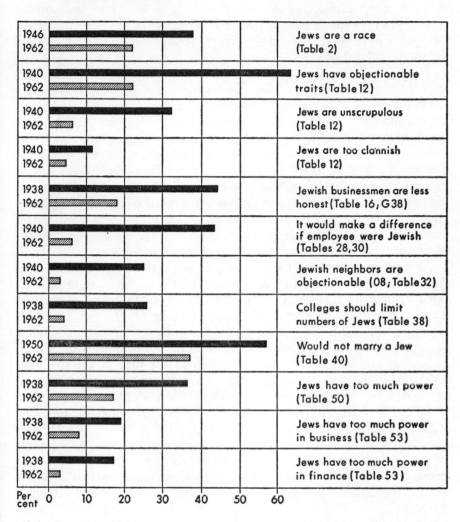

anti-Semitic responses from at least 10 per cent of the population, and all but four from more than 25 per cent. In 1962, only five of the 12 measures obtained such responses from as much as 10 per cent, and only one from more than 25 per cent. Of the remaining seven, four did not attain even the 5 per cent mark: the ideas that Jews are clannish, have too much financial power, are undesirable neighbors and should be denied unrestricted acceptance by colleges. Even with the most careful evaluation of the facts, we are bound to conclude that at least these four issues have ceased to function significantly as focuses of anti-Semitic feeling.

Though anti-Semitism was much less prevalent at the end of the quarter-century studied than at its outset, the trend during the intervening years was by no means uniformly downward. According to our evidence, hostility against Jews actually increased from the beginning of the period until the final phase of the war, turned down sharply toward the later 1940s and has consistently ebbed since.

That a steep drop in anti-Semitism should have occurred in the decade after the war is perhaps surprising. The early years of the Cold War, particularly the period of the inconclusive struggle in Korea, were a time of frustration and anxiety, comparable in some ways to 1944, the year in which anti-Semitism had reached a peak. In this climate, a number of emerging issues seemed more than likely to worsen the public's attitudes toward Jews. One was the birth of Israel, which according to some observers was sure to cast doubt on the loyalty of American Jewry. Another was America's growing concern about Communist espionage and subversion, culminating in the trial and conviction of several Soviet spies, some of whom bore Jewish names. A third was the Negro's mounting demand for equality—a development which heightened social tensions all over the United States.

As it happened, none of these developments produced the expected anti-Semitic reaction. The creation of Israel (1948) does not seem to have altered the public's perception of American Jews as Americans; neither did Israel's subsequent invasion of Egyptian territory (1956), an act which directly challenged policies of the United States Government. Longstanding fears that American Jewry might be linked in the public mind with political radicalism proved equally groundless; even at the time of the spy trials (1950–51), the nation showed little disposition to associate Jews as a group with radicalism, espionage or loyalty to the Soviet Union.

As for the civil-rights issue, which came increasingly to the fore following the U. S. Supreme Court's outlawing of segregated public schools (1954), Jews appear to have been objects of widespread ignorance. Large segments of the public remained unaware of how strongly Jews supported the Negro cause. Lacking this knowledge, integrationists and segregationists alike frequently based their appraisals of the Jews' position on their own attitudes: Persons reasonably free from anti-Semitism tended to view Jews as allies while, to a less marked degree, anti-Semites seemed inclined to think of them as taking a position opposed to their own. In any event, toward the end of the period under study the question became increasingly academic; leadership of the movement was so rapidly passing into the Negroes' own hands that what Negroes were doing became much more significant than what Jews or other whites were thinking. In sum, whatever forces caused anti-Semitism to wane during the postwar years remained virtually unaffected by this as by other seemingly ominous developments.

Changes in Imagery

In two distinct ways, traditional images of the Jew lost ground during the period we have studied. First, some particular prejudices very nearly disappeared. Thus, notions of "Jewish clannishness," "Jewish power" and "Jewish domination of finance" are no longer widespread; and many more individuals today state they would support a hypothetical Jewish candidate for the Presidency of the United States than said so two or three decades ago. Second and perhaps more important, far fewer persons than formerly think of Jews as having any distinctive traits or characteristics at all, whether good or bad. Jews, it would appear, are being perceived more and more as individuals, rather than as a special kind of people with fixed qualities.

Of the changes in the prevalence of particular stereotypes, perhaps the most significant is the waning of the "Shylock" image—the notion that Jews as a group are "greedy," "dishonest" or "unscrupulous." This image has long served as a nucleus around which other permanent and ephemeral prejudices (for example, "aggressiveness," "lack of refinement," "warmongering") have organized themselves. The "Shylock" image has not altogether disappeared, but has become both less prevalent and less extreme: Fewer persons today think Jews are merely "shrewd" or "tricky" than considered them downright dishonest a generation ago.

Though the currency of anti-Jewish stereotypes has been much reduced, their content—except in the case just cited—has undergone no marked change. Among persons who continue to see Jews as a group in an unfavorable light, the perennial accusations still hold sway, centering as always on the Jews' supposed economic preoccupations, their alleged aggressiveness in business and their success in that field. Certain accusations connected with the war ("lack of patriotism," "warmongering," "draft dodging" and "avoidance of front-line action") probably were mere variants of traditional stereotypes, adapted to the conditions of the moment. Since such adaptations require a reasonably well-structured pre-existing image, the recent weakening of the central "Shylock" concept should go far toward inhibiting their growth in the future.

That the various specific perceptions which make up the dominant stereotype of the Jew have all declined simultaneously is heartening indeed but not especially surprising in the light of our observations. As we have seen, ideas about a given group of people reinforce one another; each separate component attains its full significance only in conjunction with the rest. For example, the idea that Jews have certain unchangeable group characteristics undoubtedly depends to a considerable extent on the belief that they are a "race." Therefore, the recent weakening of the latter concept probably has helped to undermine the former. Similarly, the Jews' supposed aggressiveness presumably is linked with their "clannishness" and "dishonesty," being viewed as one of the means by which they are thought to pursue their allegedly selfish goals. Therefore, if Jews are less widely perceived as clannish or dishonest than formerly, we may count on them to appear less aggressive as well.[1]

Consistent with this observation, we note that new ideas about groups find acceptance only if they fit into whatever well-developed stereotypes may exist. It will be recalled that neither the actual participation of a number of Jews in left-wing movements nor the publicity surrounding accused Soviet spies with Jewish names gave added circulation to the notion that Jews generally tend to be Communists. The reason, we believe, is that in the context of the American culture this notion conflicted with the dominant image of the Jew as rich, not poor; as economically rather than politically oriented; as preoccupied with advancing his own group, not the working class or society as a whole.[2] Only among a relatively sophisticated segment of the public, which no longer believed the old stereotype, did the image of the Jew as a leftist hold any meaning, and even within this segment only a small minority embraced the idea during the 1950s.

If the future should bring a further weakening of the central stereotype, the image of the Jew as an "economic man," certain beliefs that contradict this image might gain readier acceptance. Thus, prejudices now of limited currency—such as the association between Communism and Jews as a group—theoretically could become the prevailing view. But of course this reasoning applies as much to "good" as to "bad" images. Favorable ideas about Jews will also enjoy increasing chances of public acceptance as the fabric of older prejudices crumbles.

Association with Jews

Unwillingness to associate with Jews has shown a marked decline in recent decades. The available data, for the most part, do not reach back to the 1930s; but as far as the postwar years are concerned, the general downward trend of anti-Semitism finds unmistakable expression in a growing willingness to mingle with Jews in a variety of situations. As early as 1947, nearly the entire public declared itself willing to work next to Jews. When respondents were invited, about the same time, to consider employment of Jews from an imagined employer's standpoint, acceptance was less general; but by 1962 even this rather hypothetical form of resistance had virtually disappeared.

The longstanding desire of many Americans to restrict Jews to segregated neighborhoods has similarly ebbed. By the early 1960s, an overwhelming majority appeared ready to accept individual Jews as next-door neighbors. As might be expected, however, fears of Jewish newcomers in massive numbers were somewhat stronger; as of 1959, a sizable minority still held that such "invasions" made neighborhoods undesirable.

Judging by some rather sketchy but intriguing figures, the reasons for whatever resistance to Jewish neighbors persists have undergone a change during recent decades. True, the belief that the presence of Jews lowers property values was rarely voiced even in the earlier years covered by our data; but while two decades ago alleged undesirable qualities of Jews still loomed large, the emphasis apparently has now changed to their supposedly strange or "different" ways. Possibly, this shift reflects the growing suburbanization of the country; for in the suburbs the neighborhood is much more definitely the arena of middle-class social life than in the city, where well-developed public transportation and a relative absence of localized community life combine to spread social associations over larger areas.

It must be noted that declared willingness to mix socially with Jews undoubtedly remains theoretical in most cases. In the past, actual social relations between Jews and non-Jews appear to have been relatively rare. Our figures do not tell us whether the picture changed during recent years, but they do suggest that many more people were ready to enter friendships with Jews than actually did so. The small number of Jews in the population may well have been the main reason, though reluctance on their part was probably a contributing factor.

Where institutionalized social settings, such as vacation resorts, were involved, the picture was not the same as when purely individual friendship was considered. In recent as in earlier data, Jews appeared more willing to fraternize with non-Jews in such settings than vice versa. But at least part of the reason, we believe, is simply that Jews are relatively well acquainted with the customs of the surrounding non-Jewish majority culture, while non-Jews are likely to be unfamiliar with what they imagine to be the peculiar ways of Jews.

Association of one's own offspring with persons of other backgrounds affords a crucial index of intergroup attitudes. Unfortunately, the data we have illuminate only a few of the numerous facets of this issue. Respondents generally expressed themselves as willing to let their children associate with Jews, but we do not know how many were thinking of young children in this context, and how many of adolescent or adult sons and daughters. Nor do the findings concerning college admission shed much light on the topic. Quotas to restrict the admission of Jews to colleges, still widely approved by adults (though not by students) in the 1940s, had almost completely fallen out of favor by the 1960s; but whether this change signals greater approval of social contact between young people of Jewish and other backgrounds remains an open question.

On the other hand, the data leave no doubt that sentiment against marriage with Jews has waned. Of course, rejection remains much more frequent here than in other contexts; as of 1962 intermarriage was the only issue covered in polls on which a majority of respondents expressed some degree of reservation. But this is hardly cause for surprise, inasmuch as intermarriage is not only the most intimate form of association, but one in which attitudes derive from a variety of ideological and practical considerations—obscured as often as illuminated by the belief that "love conquers all," and hedged about with expectations and theories concerning the chances of success. It is more noteworthy that between 1950 and 1962 acceptance of Jews as marriage partners increased at about the same rate as did acceptance of Jewish employees, fellow students and neighbors.

Attitude Components and Their Interrelations

In the polls which form the basis of this study, attitudes toward Jews are measured in all of their components: affective, cognitive and conative. We therefore may confidently conclude that we have indeed measured the attitudes themselves, not some incidental factors; and this conclusion is confirmed by the fact that the trends in all three components exhibit a high degree of consistency. Thus, over the years, the tendency to invest Jews with distinctive objectionable traits (affective) runs parallel with the prevalence of particular hostile stereotypes (cognitive) and with attitudes toward Jews in specific situations (conative).

Our data do not identify the particular component in which a change first occurred, but the parallelism among all three is such as to suggest that a major change in any one is bound ultimately to affect the other two. Even deeply embedded and rigidly held attitudes or beliefs—for example, opposition to mixed marriages or to the idea of a Jew's running for President— have lost ground as the acceptance of Jews in other fields has made conspicuous progress. Components of a given attitude are occasionally at variance over short periods of time, but in the long run they tend to revert to a common configuration.[3]

Active Hostility toward Jews

Our information about the potential support for organized anti-Semitism in the United States extends only from the prewar to the early postwar years. Before the war and during most of it, the idea of a large-scale anti-Jewish campaign drew a substantial response; at one time, perhaps as much as a third of the population felt ready to join or at least approve such an undertaking. This sentiment seems to have reached a peak in 1944, together with other kinds of anti-Semitic feelings; it had dropped rather sharply by 1946, at which point our data end.

At least during the war years, willingness to take organized action against Jews was in no sense an isolated phenomenon; it was part of a general anti-minority sentiment. When hostility toward Jews showed an increase in the opinion polls, so did hostility toward other minorities. This finding throws considerable doubt on the theory that ethnic prejudices necessarily displace one another—that when public resentment is centered on one group, others may expect to feel it less. On the contrary, our evidence suggests that hostile attitudes arising out of general social tensions like those of war are likely to encompass a variety of target groups, rather than to focus on one.

Whether such a comprehensive anti-minority climate develops and what groups become its objects would seem to depend also on the presence or absence of cognitive similarities among possible target groups. Thus, during the postwar years, hostility against political radicals increased drastically, while anti-Jewish feeling declined. Apparently the public does not, or did not then, react uniformly to minorities *qua* minorities; in the case just mentioned, a political minority evoked a response quite different from that to an ethnic one.

Another conclusion suggested by our analyses is that the degree of potential public support for anti-Semitic movements is not significantly related to public awareness of anti-Semitism. Such awareness appears to be much more closely linked to the circulation of anti-Jewish stereotypes.

The Effect of the War

The findings of opinion polls make plain how deeply the Second World War affected the American public's attitudes toward Jews. Anti-Semitism during those years evidently served as one outlet for the mounting aggressive feelings fostered by the tensions and deprivations of wartime. Other groups were similarly pressed into service as targets for this hostility—among them big business, organized labor and ethnic groups other than Jews.

Certain alleged reactions of Jews to the war crisis furnished a rationale to the growing numbers of persons willing to support whatever organized anti-Semitic action seemed likely to materialize. Between 1938 and 1942, over a quarter of the population described Jews as less patriotic than other citizens. During the months just before Pearl Harbor, a sizable minority of Americans accused Jews of seeking to involve the United States in the conflict. In the years that followed, Jews were more often charged than any other ethnic group with shirking their share of the war effort, with draft dodging and, once drafted, with avoiding front-line combat. As noted earlier, these widely accepted if transient images—held by well over a third of the population throughout the war—all were consonant with, and presumably derived from, the more general stereotypes current at the time.

Wartime antagonism against Jews, it must be noted, did not as a rule express itself in openly aggressive attitudes. Though widespread, it appears to have had little salience, remaining latent rather than becoming active. Still, it is paradoxical that such hostility should have existed at all in the midst of a conflict with the Jews' archenemy. Propaganda by the Axis powers does not seem to have played more than a minimal role in its formation. A more likely explanation is that Americans, by and large, interpreted the war against Germany, Italy and Japan not so much in ideological as in conventionally nationalistic terms. In any event, the wartime prejudices against Jews disappeared quickly at the end of hostilities, and so did most of the potential support for anti-Semitic movements.

The persecution and ultimate destruction of European Jewry by the Hitler regime exerted surprisingly little effect upon American attitudes toward Jews. While Hitler was in power, Americans for the most part remained ignorant of the dawning truth about the nature and extent of the annihilation program; and even the revelations of the early postwar years, which laid bare the crime in its whole enormity, do not seem to have increased whatever sympathy may have existed for the Jews as a people or affected public attitudes toward American Jewry. Whether the renewed and enlarged recital of the horror at the trial of Adolf Eichmann, in 1961, made any more of an impression on the American people is a question the opinion polls do not answer.

The plight of Hitler's victims and the obvious need to resettle hundreds of thousands of survivors failed to shake the nation's longstanding opposition to increased immigration. Indeed, the fact that most of the potential immigrants were Jewish seems to have strengthened the public's determination to keep the gates closed. Whatever sympathy existed for the refugees from the Nazi regime expressed itself, rather, in widespread approval of plans to settle the victims in other countries. Specifically, it may have strengthened opinion favoring Jewish immigration into Palestine and creation of a Jewish state there, even against the wishes of America's ally, Great Britain.

Distinctive Trends in Population Subgroups

We have undertaken only a limited analysis of population subgroups, summarized in Appendix I. What evidence we have indicates that present-day attitudes toward Jews differ little as between men and women, the old and the young, city dwellers and rural residents, Protestants and Catholics, Southerners and inhabitants of other regions or the well to do and those who are not. This homogeneity is the result of a leveling-out process, which has done away with differences that still were marked 20 or 30 years ago. The decline of anti-Semitism seems to have been greater among women, younger people, city dwellers, Easterners, Catholics and persons with high incomes than among their opposite numbers. However, these conclusions rest on a limited array of measures, and the differences observed are not always large or systematic.[4]

Concluding Observations

Anti-Jewish prejudice obviously is not yet a thing of the past, any more than anti-Jewish discrimination is, but both are unmistakably in a state of decline. As we have seen, hostile attitudes toward Jews are finding less widespread support in the 1960s than at any other time since the systematic study of public attitudes began. Actual discriminatory practices also have lessened to a marked degree during that period, so that we probably are safe in asserting that prejudice and discrimination today are not prevalent enough to reinforce or perpetuate each other significantly, as they formerly did. In both feeling and behavior toward Jews, our society has undergone a profound change within the span of one generation.

What of the future? Having come this far, American society may look forward to opportunities for even more fundamental rapprochements between gentile and Jew—opportunities which scarcely could have been foreseen two short decades ago, when it seemed conceivable that anti-Semitism might engulf a majority of the American people. Today, practitioners in the field of intergroup relations may reasonably strive to do more than help assure that hostility remains at the low levels to which it has fallen. Beyond the existing, largely accidental, relationships of Jews and non-Jews, more meaningful encounters—religious dialogue, friendship, shared civic enterprises—await increasingly intense cultivation.

Plans and hopes like these hinge, of course, on the assumption that the tendencies we have observed will continue in years to come. To take this for granted would be reckless as well as presumptuous, for throughout the long history of the Jews, periods of acceptance and security have alternated with periods of rejection and oppression. But we may confidently state that the current trend toward more and more complete acceptance of the Jew—both individually and in the abstract—appears unlikely to be reversed by anything short of a catastrophic crisis in American society. The longer such a crisis is averted, the more firmly will recognition of Jews as equal and respected fellow citizens become grounded in the mores of the American people.

NOTES

1. The decline in the perception of Jews as "clannish" may also explain why they were not widely viewed as primarily loyal to Israel.

2. These beliefs probably also account for the fact that Jews were not especially closely associated with the Negro cause in the public's mind.

3. This is one theoretical justification for the policy, followed by intergroup relations agencies, of concentrating on whatever attitudinal component may be

most open to change at the moment—for example, to work chiefly for acceptance of minority group members in employment, on the assumption that this will ultimately cause them to be differently perceived and less disliked. It must be noted that this theory is predicated on change in the components of attitudes, not merely in social relationships *per se*.

4. Formal education has been shown elsewhere to exert a limited effect on hostility toward Jews, serving to reduce some but by no means all types of anti-Semitic notions. For a detailed analysis of this factor, see Stember, *Education and Attitude Change*.

APPENDIX I

Differential Change among Population Subgroups

The bulk of the analyses and interpretations throughout this study has dealt with opinion changes among the public as a whole. We have found that, by and large, Americans' attitudes toward Jews have become more favorable during recent decades. But, obviously, we cannot assume that this change occurred at a uniform rate throughout the population. The over-all trends we have described may well be a composite of varied developments. Some segments of the public may have moved ahead faster than the national average, others may have stood still, and others yet may actually have swum against the stream.

In what follows, therefore, we will reconsider some of the opinion changes previously recorded, sorting out the respondents according to certain demographic criteria: sex, age, geographical region, rural or urban residence, income level and religion. We will not attempt to trace the fluctuations of opinion year after year, but will merely compare attitudes at the earliest and latest time points for which we have data broken by subgroups.[1] Our analyses will comprise nine questions asked during the early years of the period covered by this book, and repeated in 1962.[2] The questions and survey dates are as follows:

"Do you think Jewish businessmen are more honest or less honest than other businessmen?" (O7, 1939)

"Do you think Jews tend to be more conservative or more radical in politics than other people?" (O7, 1939)

"If a candidate for Congress in this state should declare himself as being against the Jews, would this influence you to vote for or against him?" (O9, 1940)

"Are there any objectionable qualities which you think Jews generally have to a greater extent than other people?" (O8, 1940)

"Do you think the Jews have too much power in the United States?" (O8, 1940)

"If you were moving to a new house and found that your next-door neighbor was Jewish, would it make any difference to you?" (O8, 1940) [3]

219

"If you were an employer hiring a new employee, would it make any difference to you if he were a Jew?" (O8, 1940)

"In your opinion, what religious, nationality or racial groups in this country are a threat to America?" (O17, 1946)

"Some people think of the Jews as a *race,* like Negroes or Indians, others think of them as a *nationality,* like French or Italians, while others think of them as a *religious group,* like Catholics or Methodists. How do you usually think of Jews?" (O17, 1946)

Resurvey of the foregoing (G38–39, 1962)

Comparability of Data

Even though our comparisons are expressed in numerical terms, they should be considered as no more than rough estimates, because the older and the recent subgroups are not precisely comparable in all cases.

As may be recalled, early public-opinion studies were confined to voters, whereas the 1962 survey drew its samples from the total adult population.[4] Insofar as over-all comparisons are concerned, this change in the samples probably does not significantly affect the accuracy of the data. We suggested earlier that during the 1930s and early 1940s persons who voted were more liberal than those who did not. But as of 1962, this probably was no longer the case; at least the two groups exhibited no consistent differences in their attitudes toward Jews (Table 124). Thus, even if the recent poll had been restricted to voters, as the earlier ones were, the outcome of comparisons over time would have been very little different.

When it comes to subgroup analyses, however, the change in sampling procedures distorts certain comparisons, the reason being that some population subgroups were underrepresented, and therefore somewhat misrepresented, in the early polls. Subgroup analyses by sex may serve as an example. Fewer women than men go to the polls; hence those women who do vote are less representative of women in general than men voters are of men in general. They are a more select group, and probably possess a greater concentration of the attributes that tend to distinguish voters from nonvoters: relatively high levels of income, education, information and civic involvement. We may reasonably assume that persons who have these qualities will show less group prejudice than others in answering most of our questions.

How does this circumstance distort the evidence about decreases in anti-Semitism during recent decades? If we are right in inferring that women voters are significantly less prejudiced than women in general, then our early statistics, being drawn from populations of voters, will understate the incidence of anti-Semitism among women, while the later ones, based as they are on the total population, will not. As a result, any reduction in prejudice among women will appear substantially smaller in the statistics

Table 124   Voters' and Non-Voters' Responses (1962)

	Per cent [a]	
	Voters	Non-Voters
Think Jewish businessmen more honest than others	2	2
Think them less honest than others	19	22
Think them about the same	79	76
Think Jews tend to be more conservative than others	34	27
Think they tend to be more radical than others	25	25
Think they are about the same	41	48
Would tend to vote for anti-Semitic Congressional candidate	4	3
Would tend to vote against him	68	61
Would not be influenced either way	28	36
Think Jews generally have objectionable qualities	26	18
Think they do not	74	82
Think Jews have too much power in the United States	22	17
Think they do not	78	83
Would mind a Jewish neighbor	3	5
Would not mind	97	95
Would mind a Jewish employee	6	6
Would not mind	94	94

[a] "Don't know" excluded.
NUMBER OF CASES: Voters, 2,342; non-voters, 788.
SOURCES: G38, 39.

than it really is. Among men, where voters are more nearly typical of the total population, there will be much less distortion of this sort.

Thus, when the figures indicate that anti-Semitism diminished less among women than among men, it may actually have diminished at the same rate; and when they show that it declined at the same rate among men and women, it may actually have declined more among the latter.

The same logic applies to two other subgroups, as represented in the early polls with their voter populations: Southerners and persons of low economic status. In each case the sample was more select and, presumably, less anti-Semitic than its counterpart in the survey of 1962. Therefore, the early incidence and subsequent decline of anti-Jewish prejudice in these subgroups are likely to be understated by the statistics. We will take this distortion into account when comparing trends in different groups.[5]

Men and Women

During the years spanned by our comparison, women by and large have moved away from anti-Semitism more than have men (Table 125). In the

Table 125 Men's and Women's Responses (1939–62)

		Per cent and (*proportionate decline*)[a]	
	Year	Men	Women
Think Jewish businessmen less honest than others	1939	52	50
	1962	21 (*60*)	18 (*64*)
Think Jews tend to be more radical than others	1939	36	33
	1962	23 (*36*)	26 (*21*)
Would tend to vote for anti-Semitic Congressional candidate	1940	17	12
	1962	6 (*65*)	3 (*75*)
Think Jews generally have objectionable qualities	1940	64	64
	1962	24 (*62*)	25 (*61*)
Think Jews have too much power in the United States	1940	52	50
	1962	23 (*56*)	17 (*66*)
Would mind a Jewish neighbor	1940	27	27
	1962	4 (*85*)	2 (*93*)
Would mind a Jewish employee	1940	38	37
	1962	8 (*79*)	5 (*86*)
Think Jews are a threat to America	1946	18	18
	1962	3 (*83*)	3 (*83*)
Think of Jews as a race	1946	38	36
	1962	34 (*10*)	32 (*11*)

[a] Amount of decline calculated as percentage of earlier poll figure in each instance.

NUMBER OF CASES: Men, 1,481—2,085; women, 867—1,678.

older polls, anti-Jewish attitudes were for the most part held with similar frequency by both sexes; in that of 1962, women showed somewhat less prejudice. Only one manifestation of anti-Semitism, the perception of Jews as radicals, had fallen off more among men, whereas women showed an unmistakably greater decline in four measures: the proportions of respondents who would vote for an anti-Semitic Congressman, who thought Jews had too much power and who objected to Jews as neighbors or employees. Moreover, for the reasons just outlined, it may be assumed that the decline of anti-Semitism among women was even greater than the figures show.

Age Groups

Comparisons between young, middle-aged and older respondents yield a rather mixed set of findings (Table 126). The early polls showed little

Table 126 Responses by Age Groups (1939–62)

		Per cent and (*proportionate decline*)[a]		
	Year	Young	Middle-aged	Old
Think Jewish businessmen less honest than others	1939	54	52	49
	1962	21 (*61*)	19 (*63*)	20 (*59*)
Think Jews tend to be more radical than others	1939	37	35	34
	1962	21 (*43*)	27 (*34*)	23 (*32*)
Would tend to vote for anti-Semitic Congressional candidate	1940	15	15	17
	1962	2 (*87*)	5 (*67*)	4 (*76*)
Think Jews generally have objectionable qualities	1940	66	65	60
	1962	16 (*76*)	25 (*62*)	28 (*53*)
Think Jews have too much power in the United States	1940	46	54	53
	1962	11 (*76*)	18 (*57*)	28 (*47*)
Would mind a Jewish neighbor	1940	25	30	24
	1962	3 (*88*)	3 (*90*)	3 (*87*)
Would mind a Jewish employee	1940	36	39	36
	1962	7 (*80*)	5 (*87*)	7 (*80*)
Think Jews are a threat to America	1946	18	21	15
	1962	3 (*83*)	5 (*76*)	2 (*87*)
Think of Jews as a race	1946	37	36	39
	1962	34 (*8*)	29 (*19*)	30 (*23*)

[a] Amount of decline calculated as percentage of earlier poll figure in each instance.

CLASSIFICATION OF AGE GROUPS: 1939, 1940 ("Congressional candidate"), 1946: 30 and under/31–45/46 and over. 1940 (other polls): 30 and under/31–50/51 and over. 1962: 21–29/30–49/50 and over.

NUMBER OF CASES: Young, 427—908; middle-aged, 1,020—1,412; old, 915—1,328.

differentiation by age groups. Differences nowhere exceeded 8 percentage points, and their direction varied; thus, the idea that Jewish businessmen were less honest than others was slightly more prevalent among the younger respondents, whereas the belief that Jews had too much power was found more often among the old. In contrast, some of the changes in subsequent years were plainly linked to age, usually with greater reductions in anti-Semitism among the younger respondents.

As of 1962, perception of Jews as radicals, willingness to vote for an anti-Semitic Congressional candidate, the belief that Jews as a group had objectionable qualities and the notion of excessive Jewish power all had declined more among the young than among the old; the middle-aged occupied an intermediate position in each of these instances except the second. The opposite configuration—a greater decline among the old—was registered only with respect to the perception of Jews as a race. No substantial age differentiation was evident in the items concerning Jews as businessmen, neighbors or employees nor in that about a "Jewish threat"; reductions were so large throughout (ranging around 85 per cent) that there simply was no room for wide variation among subgroups.

Regions

When the data are broken down by region, the South appears generally different from the rest of the country (Table 127).[6] In all but three of our

Table 127   Responses by Regions (1939–62)

		Per cent and *(proportionate decline or increase)*[a]			
	Year	East	Middle West	South	West
Think Jewish businessmen less honest than others	1939	53	53	52	48
	1962	17 *(67)*	21 *(60)*	26 *(50)*	14 *(71)*
Think Jews tend to be more radical than others	1939	46	30	25	26
	1962	23 *(50)*	24 *(20)*	24 *(4)*	30 *(+15)*
Would tend to vote for anti-Semitic Congressional candidate	1940	17	15	13	15
	1962	5 *(71)*	5 *(67)*	3 *(77)*	5 *(67)*
Think Jews generally have objectionable qualities	1940	64	63	58	71
	1962	26 *(60)*	22 *(65)*	27 *(54)*	22 *(69)*
Think Jews have too much power in the United States	1940	50	53	45	58
	1962	17 *(66)*	21 *(60)*	20 *(56)*	22 *(62)*
Would mind a Jewish neighbor	1940	29	27	24	27
	1962	1 *(97)*	4 *(85)*	5 *(79)*	2 *(93)*
Would mind a Jewish employee	1940	33	39	41	41
	1962	3 *(91)*	6 *(85)*	10 *(76)*	7 *(83)*
Think Jews are a threat to America	1946	20	14	10	7
	1962	6 *(70)*	0 *(100)*	5 *(50)*	2 *(71)*
Think of Jews as a race	1946	39	38	29	37
	1962	34 *(13)*	31 *(18)*	30 *(+3)*	28 *(24)*

[a] Amount of decline or increase calculated as percentage of earlier poll figure in each instance.

NUMBER OF CASES: East, 783—1,143; Middle West, 983—1,238; South, 302—842; West, 326—583.

nine measures, the South initially showed less anti-Semitism than the East, Middle West, or West; in all but one, the subsequent decline was smaller in the South than anywhere else.

The South, as noted earlier, is one of the subgroups whose responses probably are distorted in our statistics because the samples representing it in the early polls were highly select. The early studies, in which the South appeared less anti-Semitic than other areas, contained virtually no Negroes, since respondents were drawn from the voting population, and Negroes then were almost totally disenfranchised in most of the region. In the 1962 survey, with Negroes represented in their true proportions, Southern attitudes toward Jews strongly resembled those in the rest of the country,[7] except for slightly more hostility toward Jewish businessmen and Jews as employees. It is at least conceivable that this change may reflect a level of anti-Semitism among Negroes that is higher than among whites. We have no statistical data showing the former to be more hostile toward Jews than the latter, but a number of informal investigators have reported fairly widespread anti-Semitism among Negroes in recent years.[8]

In the nation as a whole, the changes registered over the years add up to a picture of what might be called de-regionalization. During recent decades, as American society has become more and more standardized, area differences in attitudes toward Jews—never large outside the South—have been increasingly leveled out. Thus, the Middle West registered what might by itself appear as a noteworthy decline (indeed, a total disappearance) of the notion that Jews are a threat to America; but the idea also lost most of its currency in other regions, notably in the East, where it had been especially widespread 16 years earlier. The de-regionalization of attitudes in the Eastern states is even more strikingly illustrated by the trend of ideas about "Jewish radicalism": In 1939, this stereotype was singularly prevalent in the East, in 1962 no more so than elsewhere.

Urban and Rural Dwellers

In the early polls, seven of our nine questions found rural residents less prejudiced against Jews than were city dwellers, and two found them equally prejudiced (Table 128). A slight underrepresentation of rural dwellers in the total sample can account only partly for the disparities; some real differences between urban groups and more or less rural ones seem to have existed at the time.[9]

It is all the more significant, then, that in 1962 the two groups differed hardly at all. Urban dwellers had turned away from anti-Semitism at an appreciably greater rate than rural residents—most markedly with respect to the alleged dishonesty of Jewish businessmen, the notion of "Jewish radicals," the image of Jews as a threat and the question concerning a Jewish neighbor—so that the gap between the two groups was as good as closed. Indeed, a few very small differences suggested that city people, if anything, were now more favorably disposed toward Jewry than their country cousins.

Table 128 Urban and Rural Dwellers' Responses (1939–62)

		Per cent and		
		(proportionate decline or increase)[a]		
	Year	Farm	Rural non-farm	Urban
Think Jewish businessmen less honest than others	1939	47	43	55
	1962	29 *(38)*	18 *(58)*	18 *(67)*
Think Jews tend to be more radical than others	1939	24	26	40
	1962	27 *(+13)*	23 *(12)*	25 *(37)*
Would tend to vote for anti-Semitic Congressional candidate	1940	13	12	17
	1962	6 *(54)*	5 *(58)*	4 *(76)*
Think Jews generally have objectionable qualities	1940	54	53	70
	1962	27 *(50)*	23 *(57)*	24 *(66)*
Think Jews have too much power in the United States	1940	50	43	54
	1962	23 *(54)*	17 *(60)*	20 *(63)*
Would mind a Jewish neighbor	1940	20	17	32
	1962	7 *(65)*	3 *(82)*	2 *(94)*
Would mind a Jewish employee	1940	39	35	38
	1962	9 *(77)*	10 *(71)*	5 *(87)*
Think Jews are a threat to America	1946	8	14	17
	1962	4 *(50)*	3 *(79)*	3 *(82)*
Think of Jews as a race	1946	36	35	38
	1962	33 *(8)*	28 *(20)*	31 *(18)*

[a] Amount of decline or increase calculated as percentage of earlier poll figure in each instance.

CLASSIFICATION OF COMMUNITIES: Farms/Places with less than 2,500 population/Places with population of 2,500 or more.

NUMBER OF CASES: Farm, 506—639; rural non-farm, 441—575; urban, 1,651—2,144.

Income Level

Comparisons according to income levels are complicated by two sampling difficulties. First, as we have noted, lower-income respondents were an underrepresented, hence relatively select, group in the early polls, which means that the statistics probably understate the initial prevalence and any subsequent decline of their anti-Semitic leanings. Second, income levels were divided in different ways at different times. Surveys undertaken in 1938 and 1939, for example, put an average of 14 per cent of respondents in the upper-income bracket,[10] whereas in 1962, 27 per cent ranked at this level.[11] Therefore, what was called the upper-income group in 1938–39 was more of an elite than what went by that name in 1962, even though its average annual dollar income was much lower.[12]

In the early polls, the upper-income group appeared more anti-Semitic than the rest with respect to most of the issues posed, and less anti-Semitic on only two, though the differences throughout were not great (Table 129).

Table 129   Responses by Income Levels (1939–62)

	Year	Per cent and (*proportionate decline*)[a]		
		Lower	Middle	Upper
Think Jewish businessmen less honest than others	1939	53	51	55
	1962	22 (*58*)	21 (*58*)	16 (*71*)
Think Jews tend to be more radical than others	1939	34	34	38
	1962	21 (*38*)	24 (*29*)	29 (*24*)
Would tend to vote for anti-Semitic Congressional candidate	1940	18	15	12
	1962	4 (*78*)	5 (*67*)	3 (*75*)
Think Jews generally have objectionable qualities	1940	55	67	72
	1962	23 (*40*)	22 (*52*)	31 (*57*)
Think Jews have too much power in the United States	1940	53	53	45
	1962	25 (*53*)	21 (*60*)	14 (*69*)
Would mind a Jewish neighbor	1940	23	27	36
	1962	5 (*78*)	3 (*89*)	3 (*92*)
Would mind a Jewish employee	1940	33	40	39
	1962	8 (*76*)	5 (*87*)	6 (*85*)
Think Jews are a threat to America	1946	14	15	17
	1962	2 (*86*)	5 (*67*)	1 (*94*)
Think of Jews as a race	1946	36	37	41
	1962	25 (*30*)	30 (*19*)	36 (*12*)

[a] Amount of decline calculated as percentage of earlier poll figure in each instance.

CLASSIFICATION OF INCOME LEVELS: 1939–46: not recorded. 1962: Under $3,000 p.a./$3,000–$6,999 p.a./$7,000 or over p.a.

NUMBER OF CASES: Lower income, 740—1,531; middle, 1,433—1,666; upper, 404—870.

During the years covered by our comparison, the upper-income group registered greater declines in anti-Semitism than the lower ones in five of the nine measures. The lower-income group exhibited the greatest reductions in only two measures, "Jewish radicalism" and the perception of Jews as a race; in five others, it showed less of a diminution than the higher groups.

How accurately do these data represent the true state of affairs? Where the figures indicate that anti-Semitism diminished most in the lower-income bracket we probably are on solid ground since, as explained, statistics tend to understate reductions at that level. Changes in the upper-income bracket are harder to assess; we cannot tell whether this group would have registered the greatest decreases in five measures of anti-Semitism if it had been limited to 14 per cent of the population, as it was in the older polls. We do know, at any rate, that as of 1962 the upper-income group was somewhat more likely than the lower strata to think of Jews as a race, as radicals and as having objectionable qualities, but less likely to think of them as excessively powerful or especially dishonest in business.

Protestants and Catholics

Comparisons according to religion, too, may appear to be somewhat flawed by imperfect comparability of the data. The early polls defined religion in terms of church membership, the 1962 survey in terms of religious preference. Thus the many individuals who consider themselves Protestants or Catholics without belonging to a congregation were excluded from the former and included in the latter. However, we have no evidence that the church members of the early polls differed in any significant way from the church adherents represented in the 1962 study, as far as attitudes toward Jews were concerned. Therefore, any differences we observe may be taken to indicate real changes.

Initially, members of the two major faiths seem to have differed little. Catholics were somewhat more likely than Protestants to consider Jews a race and to perceive them as radicals; on the other hand, Protestants were slightly more inclined to invest Jews with objectionable qualities and to reject them as hypothetical employees (Table 130). Greater differences ap-

Table 130 Protestants' and Catholics' Responses (1939–62)

		Per cent and (*proportionate decline*)[a]	
	Year	Protestants[b]	Catholics[b]
Think Jewish businessmen less honest than others	1939	52	53
	1962	22 (*58*)	15 (*72*)
Think Jews tend to be more radical than others	1939	32	42
	1962	26 (*19*)	22 (*47*)
Would tend to vote for anti-Semitic Congressional candidate	1940	15	18
	1962	4 (*73*)	5 (*72*)
Think Jews generally have objectionable qualities	1940	66	61
	1962	25 (*62*)	23 (*62*)
Think Jews have too much power in the United States	1940	51	54
	1962	21 (*59*)	20 (*63*)
Would mind a Jewish neighbor	1940	27	26
	1962	3 (*89*)	1 (*96*)
Would mind a Jewish employee	1940	39	32
	1962	7 (*82*)	4 (*87*)
Think Jews are a threat to America	1946	14	15
	1962	3 (*79*)	5 (*67*)
Think of Jews as a race	1946	36	42
	1962	31 (*14*)	32 (*24*)

[a] Amount of decline calculated as percentage of earlier poll figure in each instance.

[b] Other religions and "no religion" excluded.

NUMBER OF CASES: Protestants, 1,860—2,315; Catholics, 557—781.

pear in the subsequent developments. On four counts, Catholics registered a substantially larger decrease of anti-Semitism than did Protestants; the reverse was true in only one case. As of 1962, differences between the two groups showed Catholics less prejudiced against Jews than were Protestants.

Summary

The trends we have observed in pairs or larger sets of demographic subgroups do not always differ very emphatically. On several occasions, substantial disparities were noted in only one or two of the nine measures used. Still, the configurations observed seem distinctive enough to warrant certain generalized conclusions.

First, anti-Semitism in recent decades appears to have decreased most among women, younger people, the well to do, city dwellers, Catholics and residents of the Eastern states.

Second, where subgroups have differed greatly in the rate at which they changed their attitudes toward Jews, the effect has usually been to reduce old disparities rather than to create new ones. In 1962, only a handful of subgroup differences amounted to 10 percentage points or more (Table 131).

Table 131 Subgroup Differences of 10 or More Percentage Points (1962)

	Per cent	
Think Jewish businessmen less honest than others	South 26	West 14
Think Jewish businessmen less honest than others	Farm 29	Rural non-farm and urban 18
Think Jews generally have objectionable qualities	Young 16	Old 28
Think Jews have too much power in the U.S.	Young 11	Old 28
Think Jews have too much power in the U.S.	Lower income 25	Upper income 14
Think of Jews as a race	Lower income 25	Upper income 36

NOTES

1. For the earlier set of data in each case, we rely on cross tabulations made and reported at the time, since the tabulation cards are no longer available. The number of cases in each subgroup varies from survey to survey; rather than

give the specific number of cases in every instance, we indicate the range of variation at the bottom of each table.

2. Three other subjects which were resurveyed and broken down by subgroups in 1962 have been excluded from this comparative analysis. For two of them—attitudes toward intermarriage and toward admission of Jews to colleges —early subgroup data were lacking. A third—perceived desirable qualities of Jews—would have been difficult to interpret because the meaning of the responses appears to have changed considerably over the years.

3. Wording in 1962: "Suppose a Jewish family were going to move in next door to you. Would you say you wouldn't like that at all, or that you wouldn't like it but it wouldn't matter too much, or that it wouldn't make any difference to you?" (G39).

4. Since the older studies did not employ probability sampling, no tests of statistical significance can be applied to these comparisons.

5. Younger persons and residents of rural areas also appear to have been underrepresented in the early polls, but not in sufficient degree to warrant adjustment of the raw findings.

6. The term "South" here includes Alabama, Arkansas, Delaware, Florida, Georgia, Kentucky, Louisiana, Maryland, Mississippi, North Carolina, Oklahoma, South Carolina, Tennessee, Texas, Virginia, West Virginia and the District of Columbia.

7. Thus, in 1962, perception of Jews as a race was about as prevalent in the South as elsewhere; in 1946, it had been less widespread there, possibly because white Southerners tended to equate race with color. We have no way of telling whether the change is actually due to the inclusion of Negroes in the more recent sample or to a shift in the opinions of whites.

8. Negro spokesmen, writing in Jewish publications, have asserted that anti-Semitism is characteristic of only a fraction of the Negro population. Roy Wilkins, "Jewish-Negro Relations: An Evaluation," *American Judaism,* Spring 1963, pp. 4–5; Kenneth B. Clark, "What Negroes Think About Jews," *ADL Bulletin,* December 1957, pp. 5–8. Yet, even these statements imply a concern with the matter in the careful analyses devoted to reasons why Negroes might tend toward anti-Semitism.

9. As noted in Chapter III, the "rural" counties selected in early nationwide surveys were frequently located near urban areas, so that supposedly rural samples may actually have been more or less suburban.

10. The interviewers in the older studies did not actually ascertain a given respondent's income but merely estimated it as "upper," "middle" or "lower."

11. The proportion described as "lower-income" is more nearly constant: 33 per cent, on the average, in the older polls, and 26 per cent in 1962.

12. As of 1935–36, the upper 14 per cent of families in the United States comprised those with annual incomes down to $2,500, according to an estimate by the National Resources Committee. In 1962, the 27 per cent constituting the upper bracket had annual incomes averaging above $7,000.

APPENDIX II

Identification of Surveys Utilized

Agency	Key number in this study	Agency's survey designation	Date	Total number sampled	Population analyzed (unless total)
American Institute of Public Opinion (Gallup Poll)	G1	68	Feb. 1937	2,900	
	G2	94	Aug. 1937	2,950	
	G3	121A	May 1938	3,300	
	G4	139	Nov. 1938	3,150	
	G5	145A,B	Jan. 1939	c. 3,000	
	G6	151	Mar. 1939	3,150	
	G7	250K,T	Oct. 1941	c. 3,000	
	G8	287K	Jan. 1943	3,050	
	G9	308T:21	Dec. 1943	c. 3,000	
	G10	325K,T	Aug. 1944	1,160	
	G11	335K	Nov. 1944	c. 2,950	
	G12	335	Dec. 1944	c. 3,000	
	G13	346K,T	May 1945	c. 3,053	
	G14	349K,T	Sept. 1945	c. 3,137	
	G15	361K,T	Dec. 1945	2,542	
	G16	364	Jan. 1946	c. 3,000	
	G17	371K,T	May 1946	c. 3,000	
	G18	374K,T	June 1946	3,108	
	G19	376K,T	Aug. 1946	3,100	
	G20	377K,T	Aug. 1946	c. 3,000	
	G21	378	Sept. 1946	c. 3,000	
	G22	379K,T	Sept. 1946	c. 3,000	
	G23	390K,T	Feb. 1947	c. 3,000	
	G24	410K,T	Feb. 1947	1,550	
	G25	394K,T	Apr. 1947	2,984	
	G26	397K,T	Apr. 1947	c. 3,000	
	G27	406K,T	Nov. 1947	2,685	
	G28	408K,T	Nov. 1947	3,000	
	G29	416K,T	Apr. 1948	3,007	
	G30	433K	Jan. 1949	3,100	
	G31	439	Mar. 1949	2,184	
	G32	451K	Jan. 1950	1,400	

Agency	Key number in this study	Agency's survey designation	Date	Total number sampled	Population analyzed (unless total)
American Institute of Public Opinion (Gallup Poll)— *continued*	G33	482K	Nov. 1951	1,500	
	G34	547K	May 1955	1,500	
	G35	604K	Sept. 1958	1,500	
	G36	611K Supp.	Mar. 1959	1,946	
	G37	622K	Dec. 1959	1,527	
	G38	659K	June 1962	1,471	Total Christian
	G39	660K	July 1962	1,483	Total Christian
	G40	649K	May 1961	1,532	
National Opinion Research Center of the University of Chicago	N1	205	July 1942	2,650	
	N2	119	Oct. 1942	3,619	
	N3	210	Jan. 1943	2,450	
	N4	T18	Jan. 1943	1,071	
	N5	125	June 1943	2,160	
	N6	217	Nov. 1943	2,560	
	N7	228	Sept. 1944	2,549	
	N8	229	Oct. 1944	2,564	
	N9	231	Dec. 1944	2,500	
	N10	237	Sept. 1945	1,270	
	N11	239	Nov. 1945	2,540	
	N12	137	Dec. 1945	1,245	
	N13	142	May 1946	1,292	
	N14	243	Aug. 1946	2,504	
	N15	155	Feb. 1948	1,271	
	N16	156	Mar. 1948	1,289	
	N17	157	Apr. 1948	1,280	
	N18	158	June 1948	1,295	
	N19	159	July 1948	1,301	
	N20	161	Oct. 1948	1,257	
	N21	162	Nov. 1948	1,288	
	N22	164	Mar. 1949	1,301	
	N23	273	Jan. 1950	1,284	
	N24	294	Nov. 1950	1,273	Total White Christian
	N25	302	Apr. 1951	1,289	Total White Christian
	N26	323	Apr. 1952	1,250	
	N27	332	Oct. 1952	1,306	
	N28	333	Nov. 1952	1,258	
	N29	341–2	July 1953	1,291	
	N30	349	Dec. 1953	1,233	
	N31	365	Nov. 1954	1,201	
	N32	371	Apr. 1955	1,226	
	N33	379	Nov. 1955	1,276	

Agency	Key number in this study	Agency's survey designation	Date	Total number sampled	Population analyzed (unless total)
National	N34	382	Jan. 1956	1,238	
Opinion	N35	386	Apr. 1956	1,224	
Research	N36	399	Nov. 1956	1,286	
Center of the	N37	404	Apr. 1957	1,279	
University of					
Chicago—					
continued					
Psychological	P1	*	Apr. 1944	*	
Corporation	P2	*	Feb. 1948	*	
	P3	*	Nov. 1953	179	
Opinion	O1	*	Mar. 1938	*	
Research	O2	*	May 1938	*	
Corporation	O3	*	Mar.–	*	
			May 1938		
	O4	*	Nov. 1938	*	
	O5	*	Feb. 1939	3,052	
	O6	*	May 1939	*	
	O7	105	Sept. 1939	3,140	
	O8	105-D	Apr. 1940	3,219	
	O9	105-E	Aug. 1940	3,101	
	O10	105-F	Feb. 1941	2,732	
	O11	105-H	Oct. 1941	2,759	
	O12	105-I	Feb. 1942	2,549	
	O13	105-J	Dec. 1942	2,637	
	O14	105-K	May–	2,296	
			June 1944		
	O15	105-L	Mar. 1945	2,444	
	O16	105-M	June 1945	1,110	
	O17	105-N	Feb. 1946	2,619	
Office of Public	OP1	810	Nov. 1941	3,100	
Opinion	OP2	813	Mar. 1942	2,500	
Research	OP3	*	July 1942	3,000	
(defunct)	OP4	*	July 1945	1,054	Non-Jewish adult white males
Elmo Roper	R1	Fortune	Nov. 1935	c. 3,000	
	R2	Fortune	July 1938	c. 5,000	
	R3	Fortune	Dec. 1938	c. 5,000	
	R4	Fortune	Nov. 1942	c. 5,000	National cross section of factory workers

* Information not available.

Agency	Key number in this study	Agency's survey designation	Date	Total number sampled	Population analyzed (unless total)
Elmo Roper —*continued*	R5	NYHT	Dec. 1942	1,966	National cross section of laborers and farmers
	R6	NYHT	Sept. 1943	c. 5,000	
	R7	Fortune	Nov. 1943	c. 5,000	
	R8	Woman's Day 220	Apr.– May 1944	c. 5,000	Women, 18 years or older
	R9	Fortune 230B	Oct. 1944	5,142	
	R10	Time 300	July 1945	c. 3,500	
	R11	NYHT 301	Nov. 1945	c. 3,500	National cross section of Jews
	R12	Fortune	Dec. 1945	c. 3,500	
	R13	Fortune 417	May 1947	3,577	
	R14	Fortune 457	Apr. 1948	3,623	
	R15	Fortune 482A	Sept. 1948	3,506	
	R16	Fortune 69	Sept. 1948	2,508	
	R17	Fortune 76	Apr. 1949	c. 6,000	
	R18	ADL-B'nai B'rith 36	Oct. 1949	c. 2,000	
	R19	Commercial 59	May 1952	c. 3,000	

PART TWO

HISTORICAL AND
SOCIOLOGICAL PERSPECTIVES

American Anti-Semitism
Historically Reconsidered

JOHN HIGHAM

To GENERAL AMERICAN historians, anti-Semitism has never seemed a subject of major importance. No decisive event, no deep crisis, no powerful social movement, no great individual is associated primarily with, or significant chiefly because of, anti-Semitism. Accordingly, historians have shown scant interest in studying it. I myself became intrigued with the subject only in the course of examining the larger theme of nativism, and after I thought I understood the relation between the two, my attention turned elsewhere.

A single notable exception to the prevailing lack of interest occurred in the 1950s, but it was more apparent than real. A fierce little academic quarrel developed over the role of anti-Semitism in the Populist movement of the 1890s.[1] Though everyone tacitly agreed that anti-Semitism was at most a minor aspect of Populism, no other aspect received such anxious scrutiny. The specific issue was to what extent Populists had activated the myth of an "international Jewish conspiracy." The scholars' real concern, however, was not with the nature of anti-Semitism; it was with the integrity of Populist democracy. Young historians born and bred in the city were re-evaluating the "agrarian radicalism" that an older, less urbanized generation had fondly chronicled, and the charge of anti-Semitism lent a melodramatic touch to this new criticism of the rural, Midwestern mind. Further inquiry took the sting out of the charge, and the quarrel subsided with no one much the wiser as to where American anti-Semitism had its sources. For answering that question, a preoccupation with an essentially democratic movement supplied too narrow a basis.

Unlike historians, social psychologists have found anti-Semitism in

America enormously interesting and significant. A recent bibliography lists hundreds of research studies. One of the classics of American social science, *The Authoritarian Personality* (1950),[2] puts anti-Semitism at the very center of its conceptual scheme, on the assumption that critical attitudes toward Jews emanate from—and enable us to identify—a personality type that threatens the very survival of democratic society. Confronted with this literature, a historian must wonder at the embarrassing gap between his own priorities and those of an allied discipline, from which he would like to draw aid and comfort.

Part of the difference is doubtless inherent in the natures of the two disciplines. Social scientists operate in closer proximity to current action and policy than do most historians, and are therefore more easily involved in the action-oriented research encouraged by such concepts as "prejudice." In contrast, historical inquiry does not lend itself to sharp value distinctions, and historians tend to distrust the element of prejudice that may enter into the designation of certain attitudes as "prejudices." Moreover, a prejudice that is primarily latent rather than overtly mobilized—surely the case with anti-Semitism in America—seems more important to the psychologist than to the historian because the psychologist is far better equipped to deal with such phenomena. That which lurks in the hidden depths of personality offers him a special challenge and stimulus. The historian, having little access to the kind of material elicited through intensive interviews, must base his judgments largely on overt expression and behavior.

Yet the historian, with his more distant and impersonal perspective, need not shrink from criticizing social psychology's findings. Although the historical eye penetrates less deeply and registers categories less sharply, its angle of vision is wider. What counts in the long run in human affairs is not the latent potential of an underlying predisposition, but rather the visible impact of actual events. And of the long run, history most nearly provides a total assessment.

Recent events should help us put both anti-Semitism and the assumptions that have governed its study into clearer historical perspective. During the last decade, the Negro revolution has so vastly overshadowed the remnants of anti-Semitism in America that it is no longer easy to regard the latter as the representative type of prejudice. Rather than postulate a generic need to hate that fixates on any and all minorities, we now incline to interpret group prejudices as functions of specific conflicts. Indeed, the whole concept of prejudice, with its emphasis on the subtle, covert dimension of hostility, pales in the light of overt conflict between Negro and white today. It is now possible to suggest that the psychological approach to prejudice and the accompanying stress on anti-Semitism may have been outgrowths of a particular historical situation which is rapidly changing.

Pluralism and Its Alternatives

One of the great achievements of American social science in the second quarter of the twentieth century was its massive assault on racial thinking and ethnocentrism. Beginning perhaps with Walter Lippmann's elegant critique of stereotypes in *Public Opinion* (1922), with the sociological study of race relations by Robert E. Park and his associates and with the cultural relativism of Franz Boas and his disciples,[3] social scientists discredited the value ranking of ethnic groups. In the 1930s, psychologists joined the campaign, showing that ethnic prejudice was commonly interrelated with other illiberal attitudes such as militarism, imperialism and economic conservatism.[4] By the end of the 1940s, a standard encyclopedia defined race as an "obsolete division of humanity," [5] and virtually the entire intellectual community had been converted to a stanchly egalitarian view of minority problems.

While avoiding explicit value judgments, the egalitarian intellectuals took a highly sympathetic approach to minority cultures. Uncomplimentary facts about a given ethnic group were traced to environmental conditions over which it had little control. Desirable characteristics, on the other hand, were credited to the group's own cultural heritage. Thus, any antipathies it encountered could have had little to do with its actual qualities. The group in such cases was an innocent victim, a "scapegoat." Hostile feelings toward minorities accordingly had to be explained as irrational; they were thought to flow from aggression and mental rigidity in the dominant culture.[6]

The whole point of view was, in a word, pluralistic. The solution to ethnic problems was believed to lie in obliterating inequalities of condition, while fostering and praising differences of culture. Democracy was conceived as a system for conserving rather than liquidating cultural differences.[7] Any expression of a specific ethnic hostility, such as anti-Semitism, was to be understood as a manifestation of a generally anti-democratic temper. One could therefore expect to find all nationalistic and racial antipathies interrelated in a characteristically authoritarian "syndrome."

The pluralist outlook has comprised a generous and humane faith. Drawing upon our best traditions, it has helped in no small measure to make the United States a better homeland for many of its people, and few men of good will would want to impugn its basic values. Some affirmation of diversity, some pleasure in the sheer variety of the American people, would seem to be an essential element in the receptiveness and fluidity of our open society. Yet the improvement of ethnic relations during recent years has not occurred entirely in the way the cultural pluralists anticipated.

Whatever its normative value, pluralism is no longer an accurate description of ethnic processes. The remarkable advance of tolerance, decency and justice in every dimension of American ethnic relations since the Second World War has been accompanied by a steady decline of cultural distinctions. To be sure, ethno-religious activity flourishes, so that one may speak of "structural pluralism." [8] But communal customs, beliefs and aspirations have become more and more homogeneous. The trend toward equality has involved a hybridization of behavior and values, which resembles the old melting-pot theory more than it does the pluralists' vision of permanent minorities. Indeed, the very term "minorities"—that proud badge of underdogs asserting themselves against the dominant culture—is heard less and less often.[9] As the minorities of yesteryear participate increasingly in our mass society, they become more concerned about the quality of their own group life, and less able to maintain their identity by resisting a hostile majority. Prejudice, defined as a rigidly exclusionist frame of mind antagonistic to any and all "others," no longer seems to be the chief problem they face.

To put it differently, the concept of minorities as innocent victims of generalized prejudice had meaning only vis-à-vis an aggressive, insecure majority. In fact, this theory of prejudice—and the whole ideology of cultural pluralism—arose as a reaction against the inflamed racial nationalism of the early twentieth century. An immense, heterogeneous immigration, coinciding with war and other social dislocations, did indeed produce the highly generalized kind of prejudice that pluralists have described. On the eve of the First World War, and even more in the years immediately following, hostility toward various ethnic and religious minorities tended to coalesce into a sweeping rejection of all groups deviating from a conservative, Protestant, Northern European pattern. An unprecedented need for national unity and social conformity generated the spirit of "100-per-cent Americanism." Seeking to repress all deviant groups, the 100-per-centers indiscriminately assailed Catholics, Jews, Negroes, Japanese Americans and foreigners. The Ku Klux Klan of the 1920s embodied this convergence of anti-minority feelings, providing a single outlet for every racial and religious hatred and every defensive anxiety that festered among the nation's white Protestant majority. Instead of concentrating on a single adversary, the Klan proposed to "restore" the supremacy of the "old stock" and thus purify America of moral and racial pollution. In this milieu, anti-Semitism became part of a broader movement with a strongly racist ideology.[10] And social scientists quite rightly began to conceive of anti-Semitism in terms of a larger pattern of prejudice.

During the 1930s and 1940s, events in Germany placed anti-Semitism in the very center of attention. Hitlerism seemed to indicate the direction in which the "100-per-cent American" impulse was heading; and by its monstrous irrationality the slaughter of the German Jews further encouraged the view of prejudice as a scapegoating process. Anti-Semitism became the "classic prejudice": a sure indicator of the authoritarian personality, and a litmus-paper test of the racial nationalism that liberals were fighting.

By 1950, liberal intellectuals had nearly forgotten that a different interpretation of anti-Semitism had once commended itself to men of good will. They hardly remembered that until the early twentieth century anti-minority sentiments were not always so illiberal, so interlaced with one another in an authoritarian syndrome. Yet through most of America's history, ethnic tensions had been relatively discrete, and the prevailing theory of nationality had been consonant with that fact.

In the nineteenth century, American democracy was viewed primarily as a means of overcoming cultural distinctions rather than preserving them. This vision of an ultimate oneness fostered the belief that frictions such as anti-Semitism arose from temporary or special maladjustments between particular minorities and the rest of the population. So diverse were these tensions that no one tried to subsume them all under a single explanatory pattern. True, a wide range of hostilities, known as nativism, swirled recurrently around newcomers from overseas; but even this anti-immigrant sentiment was more selective and diversified than we ordinarily appreciate.

Accordingly, no considerable variety of anti-minority sentiments was strongly felt at the same place and the same time. The Alien and Sedition scare of 1798 produced much hysteria over foreign radicals but none over foreign Catholics.[11] A second nationalist crusade, the Know-Nothing movement of the 1850s, concentrated its fire on Catholics, ignored Jews and attracted many Northerners who sympathized with the plight of the Negro. The concurrent xenophobia of California, on the other hand, was racial and not at all religious. The anti-Chinese movement in that state hurt other minorities only in the sense that riotous Irishmen were often blamed for sparking the antagonism.[12] A strong revival of anti-Catholic sentiment in the Midwest during the 1890s bore no direct relation to the Anglo-Saxon nativism simultaneously developing in the East; and neither agitation threatened the Negro, whose situation in the North was actually improving somewhat.[13] While the Anglo-Saxon nativists of the East fretted about the Jews, the hard-hitting anti-Catholic movement ignored them. To avoid offending either the Protestant or the Catholic bloc, the Republican national convention in 1896 chose a rabbi to deliver the invocation.[14] Indeed, throughout the nineteenth century, the great diversity of minority groups and the relatively specific nature of ethnic tensions kept the members of any one group from feeling greatly involved in the welfare of another. It was not uncommon for Jews to join Anglo-Americans in disparaging the Irish or the Negroes.[15]

Under these circumstances, men of good will could consider anti-Jewish feeling in the United States to be in large measure a result of the Jews' real situation. It was thought that Jews encountered discrimination and prejudice partly because they were often foreign in manner and appearance, partly because their hard-driving pursuit of economic and social advancement made their foreignness especially salient. In 1923, this interpretation, still widely prevalent, was succinctly summed up by a contributor to the liberal weekly, *The Nation*. Anti-Semitism in America, Lewis S. Gannett argued, differed from the same phenomenon in Europe. Here it was largely an expression of a traditional dislike for newcomers. At the moment, nativist feeling concentrated on the Jews because of their prominence among the immigrants of recent years, and because of their distinctive ambition and assertiveness. The Jews' characteristic intensity, Gannett held,

. . . defeats us at our own game. Sometimes it leads new arrivals to intellectual or financial success before social adjustments have been made—while the voice is still uncouth, the accent strong, and the sense of tact and social relationship still in the stage of the suspicious push-cart peddler. The very rapidity with which the Jew adjusts himself to the primary conditions of life in America is his chief handicap.[16]

Many Jews had long agreed that conspicuously alien traits occasioned most of the rebuffs they met. In 1855, for example, an American Jewish periodical predicted the rise of a new respect, once Jews as a group "overleap the trammels of ages and become again what we were in olden days, noble, independent, laborious, instead of submissive, over-polite and scheming, living more by our ingenuity to turn everything to advantage, than by well-directed labor and persevering industry in some industrial and economical pursuit." [17] We need not accept this view literally to appreciate the urgent drive for assimilation which it reflects or the strong optimism with which Jews then looked forward to their future in America. They confidently expected the normal working of the melting pot to solve their problem; and they strove to adapt themselves to the process.

This assimilationist theory of anti-Semitism persisted into the 1920s, but in the following decade it collapsed. Jews now abandoned the hopeful idea that American anti-Semitism was a passing phenomenon, unlike the deep-rooted Jew-hatred of Europe. To attribute anti-Semitism in any considerable degree to the nature of the Jewish presence became, among decent and humane people, not just wrong but unthinkable. To do so was *prima facie* to proclaim oneself an anti-Semite.[18]

This *volte-face* can best be understood as part of the larger revolt against racism and 100-per-cent Americanism which so profoundly affected the intellectual and political life of the 1930s and 1940s. Intellectuals identified themselves with all the underdogs, who were simultaneously gaining power through the New Deal. Cultural pluralism and the scapegoat theory of prejudice became banners behind which a loose coalition of liberal intellectuals, ethnic minorities and urban politicians united and triumphed over the conservative defenders of the old-stock, Protestant order. The defensive Anglo-

Saxon Protestant majority of the 1920s was broken up, and in its place emerged an inter-ethnic establishment that has made tolerance an instrument of equipoise and adjustment.[19]

The victory has had its ironies, however. In struggling to change American culture, the immigrant minorities have become increasingly integrated into it. No longer reinforced by substantial immigration, they are settling into a congenial new status quo and losing the distinctiveness they sought to defend. In particular, anti-Semitism as a troublesome social issue has so generally faded that we can now perceive the intense irrational anti-Jewish feeling of the early twentieth century as a transitory rather than a permanent phase of American experience. Moreover, American Jews have become so much assimilated that we can once more seriously entertain the old hypothesis associating anti-Semitism with immigration and conspicuously foreign traits.

These reflections on recent changes in American culture offer a point of departure for examining the earlier history of anti-Semitism in America. Now that social science must explain the rapid decline (rather than the intensity) of a prejudice supposedly anchored in personality structure, the specific historical circumstances under which the prejudice arose in the first place acquire a fresh significance. To what degree has discrimination against Jews resulted from a real conflict of interest and cultures? What further conditions temporarily magnified anti-Semitism into a highly charged ideology and linked it with a whole complex of irrational feelings? The following pages will first examine the record of social and economic discrimination, the areas where tensions have been most persistent and keenly felt. We will then consider the emergence of anti-Semitic ideology, and finally return with some concluding remarks to the contemporary scene. Throughout, this essay will bypass the not unimportant subject of anti-Semitism among ethnic minorities, in order to focus on the predominant national culture.

Social and Economic Discrimination

The very few Jews who appeared on the North American mainland in the seventeenth century—perhaps 250 in all—at first encountered sporadic restrictions on their right to vote and to engage in certain kinds of trade. In practice, however, these restrictions survived no better than any of the other efforts to transplant medieval patterns of control and stability to the American wilderness. The peopling of a new society by voluntary means allowed capitalistic competition to overwhelm traditional privileges and prescriptions.[20] In early America, virtually from the beginning, there was no Jewish question.

By the middle of the eighteenth century, a regime of freedom flourished so profusely that intermarriage was frequent and socially acceptable. Well-to-do Jews joined the same clubs and private libraries as their Christian peers, attended the same dancing assemblies and sent their children to the same schools. Jews contributed to Anglican and Catholic undertakings and, on at least one occasion, solicited the aid of Christians for a synagogue. Full political rights lagged somewhat behind social integration: In a few states, religious tests for holding public office lingered into the early nineteenth century. These tests, however, were not distinctively anti-Jewish, and in any case they survived only where the absence of an active Jewish community left them unchallenged and inconsequential.[21] "In all the various intercourse of social life," concluded an American writer in 1833, "we know of no uncharitable barriers between Jews and Christians in our happy community." [22]

This is not, to say, of course, that unfavorable attitudes were unknown. In the folklore of Western civilization, the "Shylock traits" of avarice and dishonesty were too firmly associated with Jews to leave no imprint on the American consciousness. But such sentiments remained mild and often mixed with favorable stereotypes; they lacked the support of any real group antagonism. "Here you stand," a liberal Christian told American Jews, "on the same level with your fellow citizens of other sentiments; and if, in some cases, prejudices are still entertained against you, they are not stronger certainly than those which many denominations of Christians entertain against others." [23] Among "fellow citizens of other sentiments" a small, well-established American Jewish community created no social discomfort.

A change for the worse became perceptible in the 1840s. It stemmed, quite simply, from immigration. The hitherto stable, middle-class Jewish minority, numbering about 15,000 in 1840, entered a period of rapid growth with a substantial influx from Germany. From the literature of that day, one might still cull more favorable than unfavorable comments; no general pattern of hostility was as yet emerging. But the raw Jewish peddlers who swarmed southward and westward made a mixed impression. Terribly poor and often not very clean, they looked unappealingly alien and untrustworthy to some. In the worst section of New York the immigrants opened squalid second-hand shops, hardly more than cowsheds, their little windows broken and patched with old newspapers. A popular description of the sights of New York in 1849 comments on these shops and refers casually to the typical proprietor's hooked nose, "which betrays the Israelite as the human kite, formed to be feared, hated and despised, yet to prey upon mankind." [24] For many decades thereafter, assimilated Jews anguished over the bad reputation the immigrants were giving to their whole people.

The spread of such unflattering stereotypes prepared the way for a basic shift in social relationships. But what finally set off this shift and precipitated a pattern of social discrimination, in the 1870s, was not the arrival of immigrants; it was their rise. Though a remarkable number had prospered mightily, evidently few had as yet acquired much education or polish. Discrimination began where Jews as a group pressed most heavily upon a limited field of opportunity: at the social clubs and summer resorts in and around New York City.

Such institutions were then becoming increasingly important determinants of prestige. In a materialistic society troubled by its own clamorous mobility, many possessors of privilege—the Brahmin gentry, the leaders of bar associations, the founders of art museums, social registers and country clubs—were endeavoring to formulate a hierarchy of authority. Unfortunately, the very exclusiveness of clubs and resorts made them attractive to outsiders as well as insiders. Social mobility was the essential mechanism of social assimilation in the United States; and Jewish immigrants, more than any others, were eager and able to pay for acceptance into prestige circles. Thus, wherever standards of admission were not clearly defined, a crush of Jewish applicants inspired fears of invasion. Efforts to bar the Jews—in effect to retard their assimilation—generated real ethnic strife in the 1880s and 1890s. One may imagine the mutual frustration that occurred when Jews bought the hotels that tried to exclude them, only to find that the non-Jews fled to less accessible precincts. In time, the Catskills and the New Jersey resorts of Lakewood and Long Branch passed into Jewish hands.[25]

The crest of Jewish immigration, now flowing largely from Eastern Europe, came in the first two decades of the twentieth century. By its very size, the Eastern European influx obscured the increasing gentility of the mid-nineteenth-century immigrants' sons and grandsons. New kinds of resistance developed, notably in the areas of housing and education.

Even back in the 1880s, according to William Dean Howells, property values on a fashionable Boston street would drop after the first German Jew bought a house; but in the sprawling middle-income suburbs of that day, status rivalry had not yet become acute, and a heterogeneous ethnic democracy prevailed.[26] Around the turn of the century, however, the newer Jewish immigrants began to break out of the great urban ghettos, the original enclaves of settlement, and poured into better neighborhoods. This massive exodus, so much more concentrated than the earlier dispersion of German Jews, produced tensions on an altogether new scale. Jews encountered restrictive covenants, refusals by landlords to rent apartments and even a wave of hoodlumism. In one way or another, segregation generally resulted.

Eastern colleges and universities became another seat of conflict when Eastern European Jews revealed an extraordinary passion for higher education. As early as the 1880s, fraternities at the College of the City of New York were blackballing Jews. At Columbia University, where student societies soon followed suit, the first Jewish fraternity in America was founded in 1898. Around the time of the First World War, some of the colleges with large numbers of Jewish applicants instituted covert enrollment quotas.[27]

Discriminatory employment practices first became troublesome during the years just before the war. Until that time, Jews had not competed prominently for white-collar jobs that were in general demand. The Eastern European immigrants were petty tradesmen or workingmen, employed for the most part in a largely Jewish environment. But they wanted their children to get out of the factories, and now great numbers of Jewish high-school graduates, the immigrants' sons and daughters, were looking for jobs as clerks, stenographers and secretaries in non-Jewish firms. Their widespread debarment from such openings came to light in 1916, when Jacob Schiff resigned from the board of directors of a large employment agency because its mercantile branch discouraged Jewish applicants.[28]

The second-generation Jews' search for entry into urban middle-class life made its greatest impact between the two World Wars. All types of social and economic discrimination reached a corresponding peak. Stringent quotas regulated admission to medical schools. Public schools and colleges commonly hired only Protestant teachers; one study showed that during the 1930s Catholic colleges—with 3 per cent of their faculties Jewish—were considerably more receptive to Jews than were non-Catholic institutions.[29] Even the Jewish-owned *New York Times* accepted "help-wanted" advertisements specifying "Christians only"; other newspapers ran ads asking explicitly for Anglo-Saxons. The Depression made job discrimination more acute than ever. It was generally understood in New York that a Jew stood no chance of getting a white-collar job if a non-Jewish applicant was available. This led to many painful subterfuges; some Jewish girls, for example, joined in the vogue of wearing crosses.[30] A significant counterattack was now developing, but the intensity of conflict obscured the revitalization of ethnic democracy. Few could have predicted the advances that lay just ahead.

Anti-Semitic Ideology

To say that anti-Semitism in America sprang chiefly from the difficulties of integrating large numbers of first- and second-generation immigrants is, inferentially, to stress its similarity to other kinds of anti-immigrant sentiment—to put it in the same class with dislike of the Irish, Italians, Japanese, Mexicans and other transplanted minorities, while making allowances for the differential characteristics of each group. Likewise, this approach minimizes distinctions often made between different kinds of anti-Semitism, in that it relates all of them to a common root. Yet we must also consider the role of irrational anti-Semitic fantasies that had no direct connection with real problems of ethnic integration. The ideological hatreds spread by the agitator and the fanatic have had a place in American history, too.

Unlike the more ordinary social prejudices thus far discussed, ideological anti-Semitism condemns the Jews as incapable of assimilation and disloyal to the basic institutions of the country. In its more extreme forms, it portrays them as leagued together in a vast international conspiracy. The alleged plot usually centers on gaining control of the money supply and wrecking the financial system; sometimes it extends to polluting the nation's morals through control of communications and entertainment. The supposed eventual aim is to overthrow the government and establish a superstate. In America, anti-Semitism of this kind has not been so well organized or so productive of violence as other racial and religious phobias. But it has enjoyed an unusually rich and complex imagery.

Religious motifs, by and large, have not figured prominently in American anti-Semitic thought. Except among certain preachers spawned by the Fundamentalist movement of the 1920s (notably Gerald Winrod and Gerald L. K. Smith),[31] one looks in vain for a clearly religious animus. Though not entirely lacking in references to the treachery of Judas, ideological anti-Semitism has always dwelled mainly on the power of Shylock. Whether the Jew appears in his traditional role as exploiter or in his later incarnation as Bolshevik, his subversive influence supposedly flows from an unwillingness or inability to abide by the existing economic morality.

Born and bred in Europe, this indictment insinuated itself into the American value system at one responsive point. Americans have always put an exceptionally high premium on productivity: on the work of the hand and the machine in mastering the wilderness, creating abundance and achieving industrial efficiency. Many American heroes, from Franklin to Lindbergh, have been men skilled in making things; few have been men skilled in manipulating intangibles like money or ideas. The tradition of agrarian protest, from Jefferson through Jackson to Thorstein Veblen and beyond, rested on a fundamental distinction between the "producing classes" (the "bone and sinew of the country," in Jackson's telling phrase) and the unproductive creditors, speculators and middlemen. The former group comprised the industrious makers of things; the latter the parasitic makers of money.[32] Thus, in identifying the Jew as the essential parasite, anti-Semitic ideologues tapped a vein of indigenous thought. "He is not a producer," the argument ran, "but a buyer and seller, a profit taker, who makes his gains from the labor of others." [33] Henry Ford launched his widely noted propaganda campaign against the Jews by picturing a basic struggle between two great forces in the modern world: "creative Industry" and "international Finance." [34]

Significantly, this charge of non-productivity figures in the earliest faint foreshadowing of American ideological anti-Semitism that I have discovered. In 1820, exactly a hundred years before Ford's *Dearborn Independent* opened fire on the "international Jew," the editor of the famous news magazine, *Niles' Weekly Register,* discussed the need to eliminate officeholding restrictions from the Maryland Constitution. Wondering why the Jews in most countries were denied some part of the rights of other men, he concluded:

There must be some moral cause to produce this effect. In general, their interests do not appear identified with those of the communities in which they live, though there are some honorable exceptions to this remark. But they will not sit down and labor like other people—they create nothing and are mere consumers. They will not cultivate the earth, nor work at mechanical trades, preferring to live by their wit in dealing, and acting as if they had a home no where. . . . But all this has nothing to do with their rights as men. . . .[35]

What *Niles' Register* said so tranquilly, with so noticeable an absence of fear, could become a cry of alarm after immigration made Jews more numerous and visible in the United States. But this happened only in moments of crisis, when war or depression sharpened resentment at the trader and the profiteer. The first instance of something approaching explicit ideological anti-Semitism occurred during the Civil War, when Jews were accused of exploiting the war effort and occasionally of trying to destroy the national credit. The next manifestation took place during the socio-economic crisis of the 1890s, a time of searing depression, intense class resentments and widespread fears of an end to individual opportunity. A third, probably the sharpest, outbreak of ideological anti-Semitism began around the time of the First World War, and culminated during its immediate aftermath of domestic turbulence and disillusion.[36] A last flareup came in the 1930s, stimulated by the Great Depression and the example of European fascism.

In all these instances, the typical native American formulation of anti-Semitism may be described as pseudo-agrarian. The major anti-Semitic ideologues gave a special twist to the moral and economic biases deeply ingrained in the agrarian tradition. Shaped by the old producer ethic, they hated the soft materialism of an urban civilization and looked back longingly to a time when no idle exploiters lived in corrupting luxury. They had little understanding of the problem of industrial overproduction, attributing society's troubles primarily to the lords of finance and trade. Like other American agrarians, they turned their special animus against banks, moneylenders and bondholders. Where the pseudo-agrarian seems to have differed from his fellows was in a sourer view of human gullibility and a more cataclysmic vision of the future. The few Populists who gave vent to anti-Semitic diatribes were extravagantly susceptible to fears of anarchy, of a breakdown of the whole civilized order.[37]

In sum, the prophets of anti-Semitism were alienated and often despairing critics of the power of money in American society. Some, like Brooks Adams and Madison Grant, denounced the rule of greed from an aristocratic or martial viewpoint.[38] Others spoke as frustrated, embittered reformers, thwarted in various efforts to restore the imagined innocence of a Jeffersonian world. These included Tom Watson, the former Populist, John Jay Chapman, the quondam municipal reformer, and a succession of monetary cranks ranging from Henry Ford through the Reverend Charles E. Coughlin to Ezra Pound. Coughlin and Pound, like Ford, evolved into anti-

Semitic agitators after fixing on international bankers as the despoilers of America. "We were diddled out of the heritage Jackson and Van Buren left us," wrote Pound in 1935. "The real power just oozed away from the electorate. The de facto government became secret. . . . The people grovelled under Wilson and Harding, then came the nit-wit and the fat-face." [39]

With this kind of sponsorship, the "international Jew" as visualized from the 1890s to the 1930s was perhaps mostly a hobgoblin of the rural imagination, associated with all the insidious influences thought to emanate from faraway Eastern cities. Certainly the most concerted propaganda campaigns were aimed especially at rural and small-town folk. These were the people whom Tom Watson, in 1914, provoked to a spasm of race hatred during the struggle for justice to Leo Frank, a Jewish factory superintendent in Georgia, who had been accused of violating and murdering an adolescent girl in his employ. Anti-Semitism in this episode appears to have stemmed directly from popular indignation over the "outside interference" of influential northern Jews and urban newspapers in Frank's behalf.[40] A few years later, Ford's agitation against Jewish influence went out to a similar audience in the rural Middle West, the center of his popularity. *The Dearborn Independent* dwelled on the needs of the farmer and the soulless life of the big cities, as well as on the alleged machinations of the Jews. Again, in the late 1930s, Father Coughlin's anti-Semitic tirades received their widest approval in the small towns and the countryside of the upper Middle West.[41]

Thus, ideological anti-Semitism seems to have made its primary appeal to native Americans in areas of low Jewish density, where the supposed enemy was a remote and shadowy figure rather than a daily reality. This may be one reason why the agitation has never really amounted to much. The economic and status rivalries that strained Jewish-gentile relations in urban society did not ordinarily coalesce with the irrational fears of the hinterland. In fact, the rural dwellers' suspicions of Jewish power seldom attached to the few Jews who actually belonged to the local community. As a rule, the Ku Klux Klan's feeble efforts to boycott Jewish stores failed abysmally, because the townspeople were on good terms with the Jews they actually knew. Studies of small towns characteristically reveal complete acceptance of local Jews alongside negative stereotypes of "The Jew." [42]

We must ask, then, why the subjective and the objective aspects of anti-Semitism never fused in a major political movement or in a significant wave of violence. Why, for example, did anti-Jewish feeling never develop the organized power that anti-Catholic crusades acquired in the 1850s, the 1890s and again in the 1920s? The question leads us back from projective fantasy to social reality. If a nation can choose its enemies, it does so in terms of its own scheme of values. Between Jewish and American values, a general compatibility has always obtained. At the very outset of our history, the New England Puritans identified themselves with ancient Israel; later, Jefferson proposed for the seal of the United States a picture of the children of Israel fleeing from Egypt. In addition to specifically Biblical images, Americans acquired a very strong attachment to religious freedom and a profound distrust of centralized ecclesiastical authority. The Jews had always had these values, and as a religious group they readily accepted the voluntaristic and pluralistic pattern of America.

Perhaps the most important symbiotic link between Jewish and American values, however, lies in the very economic sphere that modern anti-Semitism has tried to exploit. As an ethnic group, Jews have traditionally emphasized the materialistic, competitive values of business life that are so deeply ingrained in American culture. The prestige America confers on the businessman—the man of thrift, enterprise and rational calculation—has ordinarily encompassed the Jew. Nowhere does this deference appear more vividly than in the immense respect Americans felt for the House of Rothschild during a great part of the nineteenth century. Aware as we are of the anti-Semitic potentialities of the Rothschild stereotype, we may find it hard to credit how cheerfully rank-and-file Americans once attributed vast power to that family. In 1856, a Know-Nothing newspaper, patronized largely by lower-class readers, concluded a worshipful sketch of "The Money Kings" with the statement that the Rothschild family "for forty years past has controlled the destinies of our century more than any other power." Similarly, the conservative editor of *Harper's Monthly,* in the course of praising the Jews, wrote quite casually that Rothschild was "the most powerful man in the world." Rudolf Glanz has perceptively attributed the mythic scale of the Rothschild legend to a "need to express the essence of capitalism in one great human example, that was, moreover, no individual fortune doomed to extinction, but a family undertaking, continuing from generation to generation." [43]

After the 1890s, admirers of the Jews no longer extolled Jewish wealth and power;[44] yet the continued vitality of a capitalistic way of life has surely remained a major roadblock to ideological anti-Semitism in twentieth-century America. In fact, the increasing integration of rural America into a homogeneous national culture has largely dissipated the old hostility to the city, and the rise of a consumption ethic has helped to shatter the ideological distinction between "producing classes" and the idle rich. With the decline of agrarian protest, the pseudo-agrarian perversities have withered, too. Ideological anti-Semitism has lost the narrow basis it once had in American economic morality.[45]

From Immigration to Integration

Although ideological anti-Semitism never cut very deep, antagonism to Jews as foreigners and *arrivistes* once did. The rise of social discrimination, beginning in the 1870s and reaching a peak in the 1920s, roughly paralleled the growth of national concern over unrestricted immigration; and the principal ideological outbursts against the Jew also occurred in an atmosphere charged with anxiety over foreign influence. Thus, the problem of anti-Semitism in America ultimately needs to be viewed in relation to mass immigration.

The same impulse propelled the movement to check immigration and the discriminatory drive to limit internal mobility and opportunity. Both types of restriction resulted from fear of being invaded and overrun. Both sought to stabilize a society caught up in bewildering flux. In the early twentieth century, the wildfire spread of discrimination and the mounting clamor for immigration controls reflected the increasingly beleaguered feelings of millions of Americans obsessed by fears of dispossession.

After the First World War, however, the parallel ended. Restriction of immigration now acquired the force of law and became a permanent feature of American institutions; domestic restraints on immigrant minorities for the most part did not. The measures that reduced Jewish immigration to a trickle acquired a legitimacy and respectability which anti-Jewish discrimination within American society never enjoyed. The reason, no doubt, is that practicing discrimination within a society is much more divisive than regulating admission to it. Americans wanted stability, but they wanted integration even more. Discrimination at home could only retard integration. Restricted immigration, on the other hand, though discriminatory in its own way, in the long run made for homogeneity at home. Indeed, it ultimately undermined the *raison d'être* of domestic discrimination. After secure barriers to immigration were finally erected in 1924, the strain and tempo of assimilation eased. The jerry-built structure of internal restrictions was destined gradually to crumble, as official restraints on immigration made informal restraints on assimilation superfluous.

To invest immigration restriction with the requisite legitimacy, it was essential not to carry the invidious ethnic distinctions in men's minds overtly into law. Although an ugly strain of anti-Jewish feeling ran through the restriction movement, it was seldom openly confessed. Even when restrictionists campaigned unabashedly for protecting the "Nordic race" from all lesser breeds, they devised a quota system cleverly contrived to rest on apparently impartial criteria. Only the Asiatic exclusion clauses made a frankly racial discrimination, and these were later repealed by Congressmen intent on strengthening the basic law.[46] If the laws had been more explicitly discriminatory, they might never have been enacted, and they surely would not have survived into the 1960s.

Only once was a serious effort made to strike especially at Jewish immigration, and the embarrassed slyness of the attempt reveals the powerful sanctions against any such scheme. In the winter of 1896–97, Congress passed by huge majorities a bill excluding adults unable to read and write their own language. (This literacy test, while looking impartial, would chiefly obstruct the "new immigration" pouring in from Southern and Eastern Europe.) At the last minute the restrictionist leaders, captained by Henry Cabot Lodge, tried to alter the proposed test so that it would fall with special severity on Eastern European Jews: The sponsors quietly changed the pending bill to require literacy, not in the immigrant's own tongue but in that of his native or resident country, so as to take advantage of the fact that few of the Yiddish-speaking Jews from Russia or Rumania could read the national language.[47] The maneuver came to light. Lodge resorted to bland double talk, but other Congressmen took alarm. To save the bill from possible defeat, the original formula was restored.[48]

Congress never again tried to discriminate specifically against Jews; in all likelihood, it seldom wished to do so. As a strong group consciousness crystallized among old-stock Americans, concrete hostilities fused into a broadly racist ideology. The great problem was not just the Jews but the outsiders of all kinds, alien in blood and heritage. In the early twentieth century, the United States was becoming so heterogeneous that every social strain could be interpreted in terms of ethnic subversion; and "100-per-cent Americans" tried desperately to impose unity and social stability by asserting against all intrusive groups their own sense of possession and preeminence in the land of their fathers. In this situation, Jews learned to think of themselves as allies of all the other minorities in a common front against racism.

Now the great wave of immigration has passed, the ethnic majority that rallied against it has lost cohesion and the generic prejudice it inspired is subsiding. The Nordic ideology, by which super-patriots once sought to justify their traditional ascendancy, cannot sustain today's right wing. Lacking a sense of proprietorship and doubtless aware of their own disparate origins, the members of the new Right are little inclined to construe Americanism in ethnic terms.[49] They rely instead on moral and constitutional dogmas. For them, the enemy is the "establishment"—an entrenched aggregation of power—rather than a rising tide of immigrants. Anti-Semitism has thus lost both its objective basis in the presence of the Jewish immigrant and its subjective support in the psychology of American nationalists.

Much the same account can be given of the decline of other prejudices since the Second World War: for example, the fading of "Yellow Peril" propaganda and of anti-Catholic crusades. These, too, have dissolved in the common process of ethnic assimilation. But the case of the Negro is significantly different. Although prejudice and discrimination against Negroes have also fallen markedly in recent years, the similarity in trend is somewhat deceptive. While social resistance to Catholics, Jews, Japanese Americans and even Puerto Ricans has been breaking down almost imperceptibly, with hardly any overt strife, the partial release of the Negro from oppression has excited the one live ethnic hatred of our time. The general weakening of ethnic barriers that has so greatly reduced conflict between groups of immigrant and of native white descent has intensified conflict between whites and Negroes. This difference between the experience of Jews, Catholics or Orientals and that of Negroes provides a final measure of the importance of immigration in defining the status of the Jew in America.

Cultural pluralists have taught us to think of all Americans, except possibly the Indians, as immigrants. Yet we have difficulty in so conceiving of early English colonists or African slaves. The difficulty, I believe, points to a fundamental sociological distinction. Colonists and their captive labor force constituted the original social order that took form in the seventeenth century. From the outset, it is now clear, prejudice and subordination marked out the Negro's sphere of life under this order;[50] both law and mores positively forbade his assimilation. In contrast, other racial and religious minorities entered the new society voluntarily and with no such clearly defined status. Their extensive integration during the eighteenth century established the reality of a society open to new arrivals. A presumption in favor of the assimilation of immigrants, whatever their race or origin, became embodied in the symbol of the melting pot. But neither the presumption nor the symbol included the American Negro.

Thus, the custom of the country sanctioned the aspirations of the peoples who arrived in the United States during the nineteenth and twentieth centuries. Any barriers to mobility and opportunity for immigrant groups had to be newly created, whereas resistance to the Negro had only to be maintained. No one told the Jew to stay in his place, for he had no historically appointed "place" in America. Typically, he was enjoined to become more "American"—*just not too fast*. Conflict arose when others moved to check his assimilation, not when they permitted it. In the case of the Negro, strife has typically come from efforts to make assimilation possible.

For Jews, we might say, the promise of America was never really lost, only temporarily deferred. For Negroes it has yet to be achieved. By one of the ironies of history, the breakdown of broad-spectrum prejudice—of the generalized hostility that taught Jews to think of themselves as a racial minority allied with the Negroes—is revealing the painful distance between the two.

NOTES

1. The opening salvo came from Daniel Bell in a general discussion of the indigenous sources of American anti-Semitism, "The Face of Tomorrow," *Jewish Frontier*, XI, No. 6 (June 1944), 15–20. The argument was elaborated in Oscar Handlin, "American Views of the Jew at the Opening of the Twentieth Century," *Publications of the American Jewish Historical Society*, XL:323–344 (1951); Richard Hofstadter, *The Age of Reform: From Bryan to F.D.R.* (New York: Alfred A. Knopf, 1955), pp. 77–83; and Victor C. Ferkiss, "Populist Influences on American Fascism," *Western Political Quarterly*, X:350–373

(1957). Rebuttals were offered in C. Vann Woodward, "The Populist Heritage and the Intellectual," *American Scholar,* XXIX:55–72 (1959–60); Paul Holbo, "Wheat or What? Populism and American Fascism," *Western Political Quarterly,* XIV:727–736 (1961); Walter T. K. Nugent, *The Tolerant Populists: Kansas Populism and Nativism* (Chicago: University of Chicago Press, 1963); and a spate of articles by Norman Pollack, including "Hofstadter on Populism: A Critique of 'The Age of Reform,' " *Journal of Southern History,* XXVI:478–500 (1960); "Handlin on Anti-Semitism: A Critique of 'American Views of the Jew,' " *Journal of American History,* LI:391–403 (1964); and "The Myth of Populist Anti-Semitism," *American Historical Review,* LXVIII:76–80 (1962). The whole dispute is recanvassed in a symposium, "Papers on Populism," printed in *Agricultural History,* XXXIX:59–85 (1965). Here Oscar Handlin defends himself by attacking the cyclical view I propounded in "Anti-Semitism in the Gilded Age: A Reinterpretation," *Mississippi Valley Historical Review,* XLIII: 559–578 (1957). No notice is taken of the distinction I drew between the ebb and flow of ideological anti-Semitism and the cumulative development of social anti-Semitism.

2. By Theodor W. Adorno and others. See also Melvin M. Tumin, *An Inventory and Appraisal of Research on American Anti-Semitism* (New York: Freedom Books, 1961).

3. Fred H. Matthews, "White Community and 'Yellow Peril,' " *Mississippi Valley Historical Review* L:631–633 (1964); Thomas F. Gossett, *Race: The History of an Idea in America* (Dallas: Southern Methodist University Press, 1963), pp. 409–430. Especially influential was Ruth Benedict's *Patterns of Culture* (Boston: Houghton Mifflin Co., 1934).

4. Gardner Murphy, L. B. Murphy and Theodore Newcomb, *Experimental Social Psychology* (New York: Harper & Bros., 1937), pp. 889–1046; David Krech and Richard S. Crutchfield, *Theory and Problems of Social Psychology* (New York: McGraw-Hill Book Co., 1948), p. 487.

5. *The Columbia Encyclopedia* (2d ed.; New York: P. F. Collier & Son Corp., 1950), p. 1632. The 1963 edition reinstated race as "one of the groups of populations constituting mankind."

6. Gordon W. Allport, *The Nature of Prejudice* (Cambridge, Mass.: Addison-Wesley Publishing Co., 1954), sums up a generation of research.

7. The key manifestoes of cultural pluralism were Horace Kallen's *Culture and Democracy in the United States* (New York: Boni & Liveright, 1924) and Benedict's *Patterns of Culture.* For a standard synthesis, see Francis J. Brown and Joseph S. Roucek, editors, *One America* (3d ed.; Englewood Cliffs, N.J.: Prentice-Hall, 1952).

8. Milton M. Gordon, *Assimilation in American Life* (New York: Oxford University Press, 1964).

9. As William Petersen has pointed out, a minority is "a relatively small group that is opposed by a relatively unified majority." "Prejudice in American Society," *Commentary,* XXVI:345 (1958). A decisive shift away from minority consciousness was registered in Will Herberg, *Protestant—Catholic—Jew: An Essay in American Religious Sociology* (New York: Doubleday & Co., 1955).

An official "Minorities Dinner" in Washington, customarily part of Presidential inaugurations, was held for the last time in 1957. Don Oberdorfer, "No Wonder Madison Said, 'I'd Rather Be in Bed,' " *The New York Times Magazine*, January 17, 1965, p. 38.

10. John Higham, *Strangers in the Land: Patterns of American Nativism, 1860–1925* (New Brunswick, N.J.: Rutgers University Press, 1955), pp. 194–299; Lee Levinger, *Anti-Semitism in the United States: Its History and Causes* (New York: Bloch Publishing Co., 1925).

11. James Morton Smith, *Freedom's Fetters: The Alien and Sedition Laws and American Civil Liberties* (Ithaca: Cornell University Press, 1956). Note, for example, the genial attitude of Federalist Boston toward Bishop John Lefebvre de Cheverus at this time. Frances S. Childs, *French Refugee Life in the United States, 1790–1800* (Baltimore: Johns Hopkins Press, 1940), pp. 41, 199.

12. Oscar Handlin, *Boston's Immigrants* (rev. ed.; Cambridge, Mass.: Harvard University Press, 1959), pp. 201–204; Leonard Pitt, "The Beginnings of Nativism in California," *Pacific Historical Review*, XXX:36–37 (1961); Mary R. Coolidge, *Chinese Immigration* (New York: Henry Holt & Co., 1909), pp. 40, 64–67.

13. Donald L. Kinzer, *An Episode in Anti-Catholicism: The American Protective Association* (Seattle: University of Washington Press, 1964), pp. 47, 90; Gilbert Osofsky, *Harlem, the Making of a Ghetto: A History of Negro New York, 1890–1920* (New York: Harper & Row, 1966), pp. 36–37.

14. *The Nation,* LXII:481 (1896). For a similar incident see *Jewish Messenger,* LXXIII, April 28, 1893, p. 17.

15. Robert Ernst, *Immigrant Life in New York City, 1825–1863* (New York: King's Crown Press, 1949), pp. 167–168; Bertram Wallace Korn, *Eventful Years and Experiences: Studies in Nineteenth Century American Jewish History* (Cincinnati: The American Jewish Archives, 1954), pp. 58–73; *Jewish Messenger,* LXXVIII, November 22, 1895, p. 4.

16. Lewis S. Gannett, "Is America Anti-Semitic?" *The Nation,* CXVI:330–331 (1923).

17. "Politics," *The Occident and American Jewish Advocate,* XIII:109 (1855). See also the sources cited in John Higham, "Social Discrimination against Jews in America, 1830–1930," *Publication of the American Jewish Historical Society,* XLVII:8–10 (1957).

18. Thus a highly respected research study classified as mildly anti-Semitic the type of respondent who merely expressed "stereotyped notions about the Jews, including some which were not necessarily unfavorable from his point of view." Bruno Bettelheim and Morris Janowitz, *Dynamics of Prejudice* (New York: Harper & Bros., 1950), p. 13.

19. E. Digby Baltzell, *The Protestant Establishment: Aristocracy & Caste in America* (New York: Random House, 1964), pp. 260–314; John P. Roche, *The Quest for the Dream: The Development of Civil Rights and Human Relations in Modern America* (New York: The Macmillan Co., 1963), pp. 144–207.

20. Ellis Rivkin, "A Decisive Pattern in American Jewish History," *Essays in American Jewish History* (Publications of the American Jewish Archives, IV, Cincinnati, 1958), pp. 28–34.

21. Jacob Rader Marcus, *Early American Jewry*, II (Philadelphia: Jewish Publication Society of America, 1953), 384–388, 494–501, 514–537.

22. Joseph L. Blau and Salo W. Baron, editors, *The Jews of the United States, 1790–1840: A Documentary History*, III (New York: Columbia University Press, 1963), 683.

23. "A Letter to the Jews of This Country," *Christian Examiner and General Review*, XV, September 1833, p. 39.

24. George G. Foster, *New York by Gas-light* (New York: Dewitt and Davenport, 1850), pp. 58–59. See also W. M. Rosenblatt, "The Jews: What They Are Coming To," *Galaxy*, XIII, January 1872, p. 47, and Higham, "Social Discrimination," *loc. cit.*, pp. 4–6.

25. *Ibid.*, pp. 8–13.

26. Kermit Vanderbilt, "Howells Among the Brahmins," *New England Quarterly*, XXXV:302–305 (1962); Sam B. Warner, Jr., *Streetcar Suburbs: The Process of Growth in Boston, 1870–1900* (Cambridge, Mass.: Harvard University Press, 1962), p. 79.

27. Higham, "Social Discrimination," *loc. cit.*, pp. 13–22; Baltzell, *op. cit.*, pp. 131–135.

28. Cyrus Adler, *Jacob Schiff: His Life and Letters*, I (New York: Doubleday, Doran & Co., 1928), 363; A. L. Severson, "Nationality and Religious Preferences as Reflected in Newspaper Advertisements," *American Journal of Sociology*, XLIV:540–542 (1939).

29. J. X. Cohen, *Jews, Jobs, and Discrimination: A Report on Jewish Non-Employment* (5th reprinting; New York: American Jewish Congress, 1945), pp. 20–21. See also *American Jewish Year Book*, XXVII (1925–26), 112.

30. Cohen, *op. cit.*, pp. 11, 16–17; *idem, Towards Fair Play for Jewish Workers: Third Report on Jewish Non-Employment* (New York: American Jewish Congress, 1938), pp. 2–3, 18. There is also much illuminating material in "Anti-Jewish Discrimination," Box B, Louis Marshall Manuscripts (American Jewish Committee Archives).

31. Ralph Lord Roy, *Apostles of Discord: A Study of Organized Bigotry and Disruption on the Fringes of Protestantism* (Boston: Beacon Press, 1953), pp. 26–91.

32. Marvin Meyers, *The Jacksonian Persuasion: Politics & Belief* (reprint; New York: Vintage Books, 1960), pp. 15–22; Carl N. Degler, "The Locofocos: Urban 'Agrarians,' " *Journal of Economic History*, XVI:322–333 (1956); Eric F. Goldman, *Rendezvous with Destiny: A History of Modern American Reform* (New York: Alfred A. Knopf, 1952), p. 49.

33. "Judaism in the 'Comics,' " *American Standard*, I, April 15, 1924, 7. See also Z. Ragozin, "Russian Jews and Gentiles," *Century Magazine*, XXIII: 919 (1882); Goldwin Smith, "New Light on the Jewish Question," *North American Review*, CCCCVII:128–143 (1891); Ku Klux Klan, *Papers Read at*

the Meeting of Grand Dragons (Asheville, 1923), pp. 121–123. From Hamilton York's *The Dawes Report and Control of World Gold* (New York: The Beckwith Press, 1925), p. 2, we learn that "the Nordic capitalist plays the game not so much for money as he does for the joy of constructing, the satisfaction of accomplishment."

34. "The International Jew: The World's Problem," *The Dearborn Independent*, May 22, 1920, pp. 1–3.

35. *Niles' Weekly Register*, VII, October 21, 1820, p. 114.

36. Bertram Wallace Korn, *American Jewry and the Civil War* (Philadelphia: The Jewish Publication Society of America, 1951), pp. 121–188; Higham, "Anti-Semitism in the Gilded Age," *loc. cit.; idem, Strangers in the Land*, pp. 265, 277–286.

37. Frederic Cople Jaher, *Doubters and Dissenters: Cataclysmic Thought in America, 1885–1918* (New York: The Free Press of Glencoe, 1964), pp. 104–128.

38. Nevertheless, Adams was also a kind of agrarian, not only in his inflationary schemes but even more in his social theory. The history of the nineteenth century, as Adams read it, did not turn on the Marxian theme of capital versus labor but rather on the agrarian lament: the triumph of the bankers over a preceding regime of "the producers." Brooks Adams, *The Law of Civilization and Decay* (reprint; New York: Vintage Books, 1955), pp. 257–282.

39. Ezra Pound, *Jefferson and/or Mussolini* (New York: Liveright Publishing Co., 1935), p. 97. See also Noel Stock, *Poet in Exile: Ezra Pound* (Manchester, England: Manchester University Press, 1964), pp. 143–219; Charles J. Tull, *Father Coughlin and the New Deal* (Syracuse: Syracuse University Press, 1965), pp. 10–12, 21, 35, 193–238.

40. Higham, *Strangers in the Land*, pp. 185–186; Charles and Louise Samuels, *Night Fell on Georgia* (New York: Dell Publishing Co., 1956), pp. 20–21, 27, 39, 168, 177–181, 191–193.

41. Seymour Lipset, "Three Decades of the Radical Right," in Daniel Bell, editor, *The Radical Right* (Garden City, N.Y.: Doubleday Anchor Books, 1964), pp. 384–385. On Ford's popularity, see: *Literary Digest*, LXXVII, June 30, 1923, pp. 5–7; Allan Nevins and Frank Ernest Hill, *Ford: Expansion and Challenge, 1915–1933* (New York: Charles Scribner's Sons, 1957), p. 315.

42. Samuel Taylor Moore, "Consequences of the Klan," *Independent*, CXIII:534 (1924); Omer C. Stewart, "Rural Anti-Semitism," *Frontier*, II:14–16 (1951); Toby Shafter, "Fleshpots of Maine," *Commentary*, VII:63–64 (1949); Peter I. Rose, "Small-Town Jews and Their Neighbors in the United States," *Jewish Journal of Sociology*, III:174–191 (1961).

43. *New York Dispatch*, November 23, 1856, p. 1; "Editor's Easy Chair," *Harper's Monthly*, XVII:267–268 (1858); Rudolf Glanz, "The Rothschild Legend in America," *Jewish Social Studies*, XIX:5 (1957). The passage in *Harper's* refers to a confrontation between Napoleon III and James Mayer, Baron de Rothschild, the head of the Paris house. See also the ecstatic report on the industry and abilities of the Rothschilds and other Jews in "The Jews—A Cursory Glance at Their Past and Present Status," *De Bow's Review*, V:694–

700 (1868). A rare sour note was sounded by the Governor of Mississippi in 1841 when the state defaulted on some of its bonds. Reginald C. McGrane, *Foreign Bondholders and American State Debts* (New York: The Macmillan Co., 1935), p. 93.

44. George H. Warner, *The Jewish Spectre* (New York: Doubleday, Page & Co., 1905), pp. 260–275, 300–307.

45. Matt Murphy, Imperial Counsel of the United Klans of America, still believed just before his death in 1965 that a group of "international Jew Zionists" had had financial control of the United States for the preceding forty years (*The New York Times*, April 20, 1965, p. 24). But even the Klan's spasmodic anti-Semitism seems only a weak reflex of its bitter-end resistance to the Negro. The bombing of several Southern synagogues in 1958, when pressure for change in the South still came largely from the outside, apparently backfired by increasing sympathetic attitudes toward the Jew in the South generally. Oscar Cohen, "Public Opinion and Anti-Jewish Prejudice in the South" (Paper delivered at the National Executive Committee meeting, Anti-Defamation League, September 25, 1959).

46. Higham, *Strangers in the Land*, pp. 308–323; Marion T. Bennett, *American Immigration Policies: A History* (Washington: Public Affairs Press, 1963), pp. 141, 176–177.

47. *Congressional Record*, 54 Cong., 2 Sess. (1897), 1219–1222.

48. *Ibid.*, 1430; Philadelphia *Public Ledger*, February 2, 1897, p. 16, and February 5, 1897, p. 6.

49. Bell, *op. cit.*, especially pp. 413–419, 442–445.

50. Carl N. Degler, "Slavery and the Genesis of American Race Prejudice," *Comparative Studies in Society and History*, II:49–66 (1959); Winthrop Jordan, "Modern Tensions and the Origins of American Slavery," *Journal of Southern History*, XXVIII:18–30 (1962).

Jews and the Character of American Life since 1930

MORTON KELLER

Charles Herbert Stember's study serves to remind us that an investigation of American attitudes toward Jews may proceed from either of two very different points of view. The first of these is primarily sociological or psychological; the inquiries it inspires are in effect reexaminations of anti-Semitism as a persistent kink in the makeup of Western man, or case studies in authoritarian and libertarian personality structure. The other focuses more on the culture that gives birth to the attitudes observed. Here the emphasis is on the specifics of time and place: on the conditions that induced Americans at a particular moment to look upon their Jewish fellow countrymen in the ways they did.

For the most part, Stember devotes himself to the first perspective. His initial interest is in "the underlying, relatively timeless concepts" of Jews held by Americans.[1] He then turns to attitudes more solidly grounded in specific historical contexts, such as the Second World War, the destruction of the European Jews, the rise of Israel, the Cold War with its attendant fears of internal Communism, and the Negro civil-rights movement. But again he seeks especially for the insights into the nature of intergroup attitudes which these topics provide. Except in Appendix I, which sorts out certain findings according to the demographic characteristics of the respondents, only passing references are made to the milieu in which the reported attitudes toward Jews developed and had their being. Thus it seems proper to dwell here on the culture that produced the attitudes Stember has so carefully analyzed.

It is true, of course, that in the American experience since 1930 attitudes toward Jews have not had a very conspicuous place. However, if historical perspective forces us to deal with a non-image as well as an image of American Jews, that does not make the subject less important. Rather, the very constraints evident in public attitudes raise questions of central importance to an examination of American life in recent decades. Why wasn't there more substantial, more vigorously articulated anti-Semitism in years as traumatic as these? Why did not the "international Jew," the supposed carrier both of atheistic Communism and of rapacious capitalism, become a prime scapegoat for the American people when confronted with the Great Depression? Why did "Jewish interventionism," "Jewish profiteering" and "Jewish shirking" fail to become potent rallying cries in the years of the Second World War? And finally, why have the postwar tensions in our national life—the strains of the Cold War, the welfare state, the alteration in race relations—prompted so few Americans to resort to the classic scapegoat of the Western world?

The Depression Decade

At the onset of the Great Depression, a substantial heightening of intergroup tensions might reasonably have been expected. From the vantage point of today, we can see that the native white Protestants' rejection of a culturally pluralistic society had reached a peak, not a plateau, in the 1920s; but at the time, the prevailing spirit might well have seemed destined to continue, perhaps for good. An elaborate system of restrictive covenants, exclusive private associations and Jim Crow laws, backed by racist beliefs about the wellsprings of human behavior, had been developing for several decades. During and after the First World War, there had been substantial, nationally organized and legally sanctioned repression of dissent. These attitudes prevailed after the issues of war had gone. A system of immigration restriction based on openly racist assumptions took form in the quota laws of 1921, 1924 and 1929. For a time, the Ku Klux Klan became a popular, politically powerful force in large areas of the nation. Prohibition remained the law of the land—a law so explicitly directed at the newer immigrants and their natural habitat, the city, that the countryman's hard cider was exempted from the restrictive provisions of the Volstead Act.

These institutional rejections of diversity in American life stemmed from deeply held assumptions about the nature of human personality and social structure. The postulates of racism, though losing ground, still occupied a respectable place in relevant intellectual disciplines. In addition, the national effort in the First World War had dealt a profound shock to traditional beliefs in the beneficence of a pluralistic society. For the first time since the Civil War, substantial portions of the population—chief among them the German-Americans—had been suspected of disloyalty. In 1919, the United States Commissioner of Education summed up the spirit of the preceding years: "The government recognizes no groups. It knows only individuals." Lewis Mumford noted that the war had "brought the individual face to face with the state and divested him of all associative interests." [2]

Disapproval of diversity weighed heavily on minority groups during the 1920s. Their isolation was emphasized even by their achievements, such as they were. Their success in sports or entertainment, or prominence in organized crime, were peripheral attainments, filled with imputations of separateness or servitude or violence.[3]

Against this unprepossessing background, the Great Depression offered additional incitements to group hostility. Widespread unemployment and want, the betrayed economic expectations of millions, the conspicuous role of the nation's financial institutions in the crash—all made a national search for scapegoats likely. Jews might well have been prime candidates. The stereotype of the "international Jew" was at hand, having been kept fresh in the 1920s by Henry Ford's anti-Semitic publications and the publicity they generated. The Hoover Administration was dramatizing the wrongdoing of financial leaders (for example, in the Pecora investigation of banking and the stock exchanges), and was stressing the central importance of international factors in the crash—a line of thought that might easily have fostered a public inclination to fasten upon the Jews as the cause of current troubles.

Yet, anti-Semitism did not become an important part of the American response to the Great Depression. Discrimination and hostility, though often evident, were no more prevalent than they had been during the relatively prosperous 1920s; and they were more likely to appear in the private than the public sector of American life.

The reasons for this state of affairs are deeply embedded in the nature of American society. The prevailing political tradition allowed little room for appeals to racial or religious animosities. Tolerance, however slighted in practice, was an important part of the American creed. In addition, the commitment to individualism and *laissez faire* that flourished in the 1920s had left its effect. These attitudes were strong enough to impede the Government's emergence as a positive force even in the area of economic recovery and reform. How much more difficult, then, for the state to enter the forbidding area of intergroup relations!

Furthermore, the archetypal anti-Semitic ideas of Jewish aggressiveness, materialism and greed could not evoke the same response in America as in European societies. The nation's admiration for entrepreneurial success was too deeply ingrained to be wiped away by the Depression. Even in the 1930s, the ambition and business ability of American Jews won as much admiration as disapproval from their countrymen.[4]

In any event, American minorities in general were not as defenseless as the events of the 1920s seemed to imply. The very heterogeneity of the American population had diffused and weakened the force of nativism. The absurdly large number of the Klan's hates—Catholics, Negroes, Jews, aliens, radicals, wets—ultimately was a measure of the protection afforded by diversity. At the same time, the self-awareness of the newer American population had been piqued and strengthened by the hostility of older groups. The Presidential nomination of Alfred E. Smith may have been delayed by the anti-Catholicism and anti-urbanism of the time; but that it did finally occur was testimony to the political power generated by the numbers and the self-awareness of newer Americans.

Finally, to the degree that members of minority groups had been excluded from significant areas of national power in the 1920s, they escaped responsibility for the great crash. The culpable men and institutions in politics, banking, finance and industry were almost universally old-stock American. Ethnic institutions such as the Jewish Bank of the United States, the Italian City Trust Company and the Irish County Trust Company went down with (and often before) their Anglo-Saxon counterparts; but their victims were their own people.[5]

How widely Jews or other minority groups might be blamed for the Depression did not, of course, necessarily depend on their actual share of the responsibility. They might well have been made to serve as the chief scapegoats in any case. But another factor came to their aid: the inclination of Americans to blame the economic collapse not on ethnic groups but on individuals (for example, Herbert Hoover, Charles E. Mitchell, Samuel Insull) or institutions (Wall Street, the banks, the Republican Party).

By the onset of the Depression, respectable scholarship in sociology, psychology, anthropology, economics, political science and history had substantially freed itself from racist explanations of human behavior, and had turned to environmental, socio-economic frames of reference. The change in intellectual climate may be gauged by a comparison of the Dillingham Immigration Commission's massive studies, issued between 1907 and 1910, with the work of the President's Research Committee on Social Trends from 1929 to 1933. The Dillingham report offered essentially racist analyses of many social problems: poverty, education, crime, vice, disease, insanity. *Recent Social Trends in the United States,* the report of the President's Research Committee, paid only scant attenton to "problems of biological heritage," and concluded: "The problem of the minority groups both within and without the continental United States is not so much racial as cultural." National problems that cut across group lines, and environmental rather than racial causes and cures, were the Committee's primary concerns.[6]

Far from bearing the brunt of the economic collapse, American minority groups came politically of age in the 1930s. But, again, considerations other than specifically ethnic ones were responsible. The alliance of minorities that became so important a part of the New Deal's political strength was not purposely constructed on ethnic lines. Franklin D. Roosevelt and the New Dealers usually thought and acted on behalf of the economically and socially dispossessed, only rarely in response to the aspirations of Negroes, Jews or Catholics as such. If distinctive ethnic allegiances to the New Deal developed, it was because minority groups were concentrated in the non-union factory, the hardscrabble farm, the city slum.

Nor did anti-New Dealers view the society and its problems otherwise. Political criticism of the New Deal was steeped in ideological and institutional arguments, but not in ethnic distinctions. Conservatives scored Communism, Socialism, radicalism, liberalism or planning, and warned of threats to the Constitution, to individualism, *laissez faire* or free enterprise; they did not attack the Jews, the Catholics or the foreign-born. Under these conditions, Jews were singularly free to play an active part in the New Deal without suffering overmuch from anti-Semitic aspersions. In alliance with their Christian fellow Democrats and liberals, they linked civil liberties and minority rights to the New Deal's social and economic reforms.[7]

The political extremists of the 1930s afford a final insight into the conditions that blocked anti-Semitism. Huey Long spoke to elements in the society that might have been expected to respond warmly to an anti-Semitic message. But he appealed to the poor against the rich, and to the South against the East; he did not incite his followers against Jews, Catholics or even Negroes. A native of a stanchly Populist Louisiana parish, Long drew mainly on the imagery and ideology of the Populist political tradition; and anti-Semitism was only a minor theme in the Populist critique of American life.[8]

The Reverend Charles E. Coughlin's low-middle-income, urban, primarily Catholic followers were even likelier subjects for an anti-Semitic appeal. Yet in the early and middle 1930s, Coughlin dwelt primarily on the faults of the economic system, picturing it as an assembly of devils among whom a Morgan was as important as a Rothschild. In 1936, he favored a boycott of the Berlin Olympics as a protest against the Nazis' treatment of the Jews, and anti-Semitism was not a major theme in the campaign of his National Union Party that year.[9]

The factors that kept anti-Semitism out of America's major political responses to the Depression were also present on the political fringes. Neither Long's dirt farmers nor Coughlin's city Catholics had traditions of organized, political anti-Semitism, no matter how much it may have been part of their social mores. Long and Coughlin perforce adopted the prevailing style of political dialogue. They emphasized the culpability of individuals and institutions, the need to preserve American liberties and the importance of securing equality of opportunity—themes in which anti-Semitism *per se* would have struck a false note.

The Eve of the Second World War

If the great domestic crisis of the decade failed to stir American anti-Semitism, foreign developments—the rise of Nazism and the possibility of American involvement in a European war—threatened to do so. The appearance of an overtly anti-Semitic regime in Germany encouraged the growth of fringe anti-Jewish organizations in the United States.[10] But the great majority of Americans found the anti-Semitism of the Nazis distasteful. Roosevelt's comment on the *Kristallnacht* of November 9, 1938 ("I, myself, could scarcely believe that such things could occur in a twentieth-century civilization") reflected the opinion of his countrymen. When in 1938 Americans were polled on the Nazis' treatment of the Jews, 88 per cent disapproved.[11]

As the international situation worsened toward the end of the decade, American involvement in a European war began to appear possible. A linkage of interventionism with American Jewry might well have appealed to the substantial portion of the American population that valued neutrality over the need to defeat Nazi Germany; and the extra-party protest movements now made anti-Semitism a major part of their programs. Gerald L. K. Smith, the inheritor of the Long movement, took up the theme in 1939. In July and August of the same year, Father Coughlin reprinted the spurious *Protocols of the Learned Elders of Zion in Social Justice,* the organ of his Christian Front, and by November he was bringing his anti-Semitic appeals to a radio audience of over three million.[12] The most important and respectable quarter to identify the Jews with the danger of American intervention in the European war was the America First Committee. At Des Moines, on September 11, 1941, Colonel Charles A. Lindbergh told a rally of the Committee: "The three most important groups who have been pressing this country toward war are the British, the Jewish and the Roosevelt administration. Behind these groups, but of lesser importance, are a number of capitalists, Anglophiles, and intellectuals who believe that their future, and the future of mankind, depends upon the domination of the British Empire."

Nevertheless, consciousness of Jewish interests played little part in the evolution of American attitudes toward affairs overseas. The most noticeable trend in public opinion on foreign affairs was the degree to which the isolationism of the early 1930s gave way to a growing commitment to the Allied cause. Popular sentiment from 1939 to 1941 was consistently, overwhelmingly on the side of the Allies, approving all aid short of war to Germany's opponents. And as the nation's detestation of Nazism grew, so did opposition to organized domestic anti-Semitism.

What is more, anti-Semitism had only a peripheral and uncertain place even in its most promising political home, the isolationist movement. Coughlin was not widely recognized as an anti-Semite in opinion polls during 1941; that distinction was reserved for the discredited German-American Bund. Lindbergh's remarks, too, were something other than strident, undiluted anti-Semitism when taken in context. Not only did he accuse several groups besides the Jews; he also acknowledged that "it is not difficult to understand why Jewish people desire the overthrow of Nazi Germany. The persecution they suffered in Germany should be sufficient to make bitter enemies of any race. No person with a sense of the dignity of mankind can condone the persecution the Jewish race suffered in Germany." And even with these significant qualifications, Lindbergh's statement was severely criticized by supporters of America First, such as John T. Flynn, Al Smith, the *Chicago Tribune* and the Hearst press.[13]

The fact of the matter is that Americans reacted to the coming of war, as they had to the Depression, in institutional rather than group terms. Perhaps the most revealing of the poll data from this period is the response to the question: "What persons or groups do you think are most active in trying to get us into the war?" The question was asked in October 1941, when a sense of imminent war must have been near its peak, and when a latent inclination to blame interventionist groups might have had its freest rein. Nevertheless, only 6 per cent of the respondents named the Jews and 6 per cent referred to pro-British groups—while 19 per cent specified the Roosevelt Administration or the Democrats, 18 per cent pointed to big business, capitalists or financiers and 13 per cent mentioned foreign interests or agents.[14] As with the Depression, so with the war: Americans visualized the forces controlling their destiny as political and economic entities rather than as ethnic ones. Among the significant transformations of American life wrought during the 1930s was the ascendancy of institutional over group conceptions in the national definition of, and response to, social issues.

The War Years

An impressive body of poll data suggests that hostile attitudes toward the Jews rose substantially during the war years, despite the presence of a common enemy.[15] Classic ingredients of intergroup tension were operating in full force. Sharp, sudden, widespread dislocation—economic, social, physical, psychological—was the lot of many Americans. Violence was on the rise from 1941 on. During 1943, group hostility repeatedly exploded: in the "zoot suit" outbreaks against Mexican-Americans in Los Angeles; the Detroit race riot (the worst since the time of the First World War), in which twenty-five Negroes and nine whites were killed and scores wounded; the New York riot, in which Negroes attacked the predominantly Jewish-owned shops of Harlem. Cities particularly caught up in the migrations, the social and economic transformations, the shortages and tensions of wartime were the locales of these incidents.[16]

The wartime animus against Jews, then, was part (and only a minor part) of a general increase in intergroup hostility. The most concrete expression of wartime anti-Semitism was the "Clear it with Sidney" episode—the attack on Sidney Hillman of the Congress of Industrial Organizations during the 1944 Presidential campaign. Critics often dwelt on Hillman's origins as the son of a Lithuanian rabbi and on his supposed mysterious role within the Roosevelt entourage. But the chief target of this obloquy was not some shadowy Jewish political power; it was the exceedingly tangible Political Action Committee, the CIO's agency for organizing labor and minority votes in the large cities.

When we examine more closely the data on wartime attitudes, we find ourselves in a spectral world of diverse and undirected animosities. A sample of the population was asked to name those elements that were using the war to gain money or power. Thirteen per cent mentioned the Jews; in contrast, 25 per cent pointed to businessmen and 53 per cent to labor leaders. When a series of questions attempted to probe the public's perception of Hillman, only 13 per cent of the respondents thought of him as a Jew. Many more linked him with Communists, with labor or with the New Deal. As might be expected, the substantial economic gains made by Jews during the war stirred resentment. But when asked in 1945 to identify people or organizations possessing too much power, only 4 per cent of a national sample referred to the Jews—as compared to 6 per cent who named the Government! [17]

Nor did voters respond to anti-Semitic appeals when presented with the opportunity. Several openly anti-Semitic Congressmen were defeated in 1944 or did not seek re-election. In 1942, Gerald L. K. Smith received 130,000 votes as a candidate for the United States Senate from Michigan; but in 1944, when he ran for President on the ticket of the America First Party, he won only 1,530 votes in that state.[18]

It appears, in sum, that the mode of national response to crisis remained during the war what it had been in the Depression and prewar years. Intergroup animosities flared up in response to the strains of wartime, but they did not substantially affect the way in which Americans perceived, and reacted to, the war itself.

The Postwar Decades

In recent decades, Americans have continued to avoid anti-Semitism as a mode of response to public issues. What is more, many traditional forms of hostility toward Jews seem to be withering away. Thus, despite the manifest rise in American Jewish wealth and influence, fear of "Jewish power" has declined. In February 1946, 55 per cent of a national sample thought that American Jews had too much power and 33 per cent did not, whereas by May 1962, only 17 per cent thought so and 66 per cent demurred.[19] In the mass media, Jewish performers and topics have been much in evidence since the war, but fewer and fewer Americans worry about them. Higher education has become the portal to professional and even to white-collar status, with colleges growing crowded and expensive; yet declining numbers of Americans wish to see the admission of Jews limited. Ever larger numbers of Jews have entered the professions, and have found it increasingly easy to do so. Formal quotas have disappeared, and *sub rosa* limitations have become less and less onerous. Even the most sensitive indices—acceptance of Jews as neighbors, as fellow workers, as in-laws—follow the same pattern.[20]

These trends confront us with a seeming paradox. Surely there has been much in recent American experience that might plausibly have fed anti-Semitic attitudes: the strains of postwar economic reconversion; the tensions of demographic and social mobility; uneasiness stirred by the Negroes' drive for equality; a spectacular rise in the economic standing of American Jews; suspicions of divided loyalty inspired by the rise of Israel; and, perhaps most of all, the frustrations and anxieties generated by the Cold War.

Plausible explanations are not hard to find. The principles of cultural pluralism continue to occupy a commanding place in the American scale of social values; Americans still define their problems in institutional rather than group terms. But the problem has another dimension, one suggested by Stember when he observes that both unfavorable *and* favorable American attitudes toward Jews are declining.[21]

The world events most important to the American Jewish community during the past twenty years have been the destruction of European Jewry and the rise of the State of Israel. As Stember observes, the American response to the revelations about the death camps was not commensurate with the enormity of the horrors uncovered. The relatively mild persecution of the German Jews during the 1930s seems to have evoked as much sympathy and concern among Americans as did the subsequent holocaust. In the 1950s, Americans apparently responded more strongly to the plight of anti-Communist refugees then they had done to that of the death-camp survivors. Yet when the Eichmann trial took place in 1961, interest ran high; a large portion of the public was willing to have the story of the death camps told again.[22]

Public reactions to the tragedy of the European Jews should not be used as a measurement of anti-Semitism or its opposite. The first shock of the Nazis' actions in the 1930s and the drama of the Eichmann affair naturally caught the public's attentions and stirred its sympathies; but otherwise the tragedy, however heavily it weighed on the American Jewish community, was only a distant, and later an ended, nightmare to most Americans.

Similarly dispassionate was the American reaction to the emergence of Israel—a reaction described by Stember as "continuing apathy." [23] A people whose international concerns were shaped by the Cold War had little attention to devote to the creation of new states. Opinions on the relationship of American Jews to Israel are even more revealing: Despite the substantial American Jewish contribution to the new republic, a large and growing proportion of poll respondents thought American Jews had nothing to do with the Israeli-Arab crises of the 1950s.[24]

Perhaps the best measures of the Jews' subordinate place in the American consciousness during recent years are the great domestic crises of the postwar period: the Communist scare of the early 1950s and the Negro civil-rights movement.

The absence of anti-Semitism in the movement led by Senator Joseph R. McCarthy has been widely noted. The Senator himself set the tone: He concentrated his attacks on Protestant, old-stock American men and institutions, and a lawyer named Roy Cohn was conspicuous in his entourage.[25] Nor was the great majority of Americans inclined to identify Jews with Communism even during the heated days of the early 1950s, when Jewish names often figured in revelations of spy plots. Only 5 per cent of a national cross section made the association—while 7 per cent of Jewish respondents did.[26]

By the same token, and for the same reasons, the Negro civil-rights drive has generated little anti-Semitism. A great many Jews sympathize with the movement or are active in it; racists often talk about an insidious trinity of civil rights, Jews and Communism. But the movement has been so widely supported by the major religious, educational, judicial and political institutions of the country that the involvement of Jews does not stand out. The prevailing tendency has been to see civil rights as an issue between two great American communities, the white and the black. This polarization has further lessened Americans' general perception of Jews as distinctive members of the society.

In recent years, the most substantial residue of anti-Semitism appears to have remained at the higher levels of American society. A decade ago, Samuel Stouffer noted that irrational anti-Communism, insistence upon conformity and indifference or hostility to civil liberties flourished most among persons of relatively little education, wealth and social standing, while tolerance of dissent was strongest at the higher socio-economic levels;[27] yet he found that 11 per cent of community leaders—more than twice the national proportion—identified Jews with Communism. Stember's data point in the same direction. The most educated respondents reported hearing anti-Semitic talk two to three times as often as did the least educated. Opposition to the employment of Jews was more likely when the relationship proposed was that of employer to employee than when Jews were visualized as fellow workers.[28] The beliefs that Jews are more radical than other people, that they are more likely to have objectionable qualities and that they constitute a separate race appeared most frequently among the well to do.[29]

That anti-Jewish attitudes have proved most tenacious among the more comfortable segments of the American people is not surprising, for that is where a large proportion of the Jews themselves now dwell. In income and education, Jews and Episcopalians far outstrip other religious groups.[30] As a consequence, Jews today are remote as real or potential competitors or peers from most of their fellow countrymen.

The Outlook

Jews today constitute less than 3 per cent of the population of the United States, and their exceptionally low fertility rate makes it certain that the proportion will decline further; but we doubt that the marked decline in the American public's awareness of Jews is due merely to this demographic fact—or, for that matter, to the Jews' cultural assimilation and their concentration in certain socio-economic brackets. In our opinion, the attitudes that prevail today have their sources less in what is happening to American Jews than in what is happening to American society.

What, then, is the broader, national context of the attitudes that now prevail? Do they simply reflect cultural pluralism come of age? Are we observing a new tolerance, extending to the unknown and unfamiliar as well as the known and familiar? Surely there is much reason so to argue. The principles of tolerance and equality have never had more intellectual, moral and social respectability than now. Seen in this context, the decline of anti-Semitism is indeed part of a general triumph of the principles and practices of cultural pluralism. It belongs, in this sense, with the current revolution in laws and public policies bearing on racial equality, and with the election of an Irish Catholic to the Presidency in 1960.[31]

Unquestionably, the legitimation of a pluralistic society has gone on apace in the years since the Second World War. Yet the American public's current indifference to Jews seems to require something more in the way of explanation.

We have been accustomed for some time to thinking of American life as ultimately divisible into two subcultures. One is the traditional way of life of the old-stock Americans: of native-born Protestants whose origins lie in small towns and on farms. The other, just as distinctive, is the culture of the newer Americans: of varied ethnic and religious groups whose background is European and whose style of life was molded in the cities. But today we may observe the rise of a third style of American life.

This new style has been shaped primarily by the tremendous economic, social and geographical mobility of recent years, and by the folkways which the mass media teach. It cuts across, and dissolves, the ethnic, religious and regional distinctions that once were all-important in determining the individual's place in American life. If the Old American culture was rooted in small towns and the countryside, and the New in the cities of the East, the third culture has its prototypal home in the suburbs. Yet it is not tied to locale, or to ethnic character or even to class. Its aspirations are defined by communications media which reach out to all with a fine impartiality, by an increasingly widespread, inconstant and unstructured way of life.

In this new American culture, older issues of social organization, notably group distinctions and the question of "cultural pluralism or melting pot," are of minor significance. That would seem to be at least part of the reason why the American public's awareness of Jews has declined so markedly of late, and why the steepest drop in anti-Semitic sentiment since the Second World War has occurred within the past few years. The idea of a Jewish President of the United States was acceptable to more people in 1960 than that of a Catholic President had been only two years earlier.[32] That the Republican convention of 1964 should choose as its candidates one man of partly Jewish descent and another of Catholic faith and Jesuit education illustrates not so much the triumph of ethnic acceptance as the rapidly diminishing importance of group distinctions, invidious or otherwise.

It is significant that indifference to ethnic identity should find such emphatic expression in conservative and ultra-conservative quarters. The fact is that the Radical Right, for all its traditionalist dogma, is more than the political voice of old-stock Americans yearning for a society that was. The coalition of malcontents that brought about Senator Barry M. Goldwater's nomination in 1964 also included a more dynamic element: *nouveaux riches* identified with the new style of life. Beset by complex insecurities and wants that derive from social and economic mobility, these elements find irritants and scapegoats in the structure of government, the Cold War and the Negroes' demands—not in Wall Street, the city, the foreign-born or the Jews. In 1962, the John Birch Society, the Christian Anti-Communist Crusade and the Christian Crusade all claimed to have Jewish members.[33]

What does the emergence of the new culture imply for the place of Jews in American life? If the general public's perception of Jews is dimming, the same is by no means true of the Jewish community's sense of itself. As long as Jewish group consciousness remains strong, problems of relationship to the society at large will persist, while the problems of maintaining group identity will increase.

Jews have long lived with anti-Semitism and are not unfamiliar with the rarer state of philo-Semitism. But now, as a self-defined ethno-religious group in a society where definition increasingly takes other forms ("How much does he make?" "Where did he move from?" "What does he read?"

"How educated is he?" "Is he white?"), they will have to cope with a new and difficult condition which might be called *asemitism:* indifference to, or unawareness of, their identity as Jews.

If Jews turn their attention to this latest phase in their relationship to American society at large, they will not merely be serving themselves. For the problem is not peculiar to them alone. In the past, the American people have had to face the problem of maintaining their national identity in the face of growing cultural diversity. In the future, they may have to cope increasingly with the no less difficult task of preserving their individuality from the oppressive weight of cultural sameness.

NOTES

1. See p. 49.

2. Lewis Mumford, "Patriotism and Its Consequences," *The Dial,* LXVI: 406–407 (April 19, 1919). Randolph Bourne's essay on "The State" is the most sustained and forceful comment on this consequence of American involvement in the First World War. It is most readily available in Bourne, *War and the Intellectuals* (Carl Resek, editor; New York: Harper Torchbooks, 1964), pp. 65–104.

3. Daniel Bell, *The End of Ideology* (Glencoe, Ill.: The Free Press, 1960), pp. 115–136, is germane to this point.

4. See pp. 54, 56.

5. Oscar Handlin, *Al Smith and His America* (Boston: Little, Brown & Co., 1958), pp. 147–148.

6. The Dillingham report is analyzed in Oscar Handlin, *Race and Nationality in American Life* (Boston: Little, Brown & Co., 1957), pp. 97–131; President's Research Committee on Social Trends, *Recent Social Trends in the United States,* I (New York: McGraw-Hill Book Co., 1933), xx, xli.

7. John P. Roche, *The Quest for the Dream* (New York: The Macmillan Co., 1963), pp. 130–183.

8. The relevant literature on the extent of Populist anti-Semitism is reviewed in Walter T. K. Nugent, *The Tolerant Populists* (Chicago: The University of Chicago Press, 1963), pp. 3–32.

9. Charles E. Coughlin, *Eight Lectures on Labor, Capital and Justice* (Royal Oak, Mich.: The Radio League of the Little Flower, 1934); *American Jewish Year Book* (hereafter *AJYB*), XXXVIII (1936–37), 184; David O. Powell, "The Union Party of 1936: Campaign Tactics and Issues," *Mid-America,* XLVI:133–138 (1964); Edward C. Blackorby, "William Lemke: Agrarian Radical and Union Party Presidential Candidate," *Mississippi Valley Historical Review,* XLIX:83 (1962).

10. Donald S. Strong, *Organized Anti-Semitism in America* (Washington: American Council on Public Affairs, 1941), pp. 14–15.

11. See p. 137.

12. *AJYB*, XLI (1939–40), 209; Strong, *op. cit.*, p. 63.

13. See p. 113; Wayne S. Cole, *America First* (Madison, Wis.: University of Wisconsin Press, 1953), pp. 144–148.

14. See pp. 114–115.

15. See pp. 80, 82–85, 115–116.

16. A survey of these incidents by Carey McWilliams, "What We Did about Racial Minorities," appears in Jack Goodman, editor, *While You Were Gone* (New York: Simon & Schuster, 1946), pp. 89–111.

17. See pp. 115, 159–161, 121–122.

18. *AJYB*, XLVII (1945–46), 268–270.

19. See p. 121.

20. See Ch. IV, pp. 88–109; Appendix I, pp. 219–230.

21. See p. 65.

22. See Ch. VI, pp. 136–155.

23. See p. 178.

24. See pp. 189–190.

25. Daniel Bell, editor, *The Radical Right* (Garden City, N.Y.: Doubleday Anchor Books, 1964), Chapters VII, XIII.

26. Samuel A. Stouffer, *Communism, Conformity, and Civil Liberties* (Garden City, N.Y.: Doubleday & Co., 1955), p. 174.

27. Stouffer, *op. cit.*

28. See pp. 61, 91–93.

29. See p. 227.

30. Donald J. Bogue, *The Population of the United States* (Glencoe, Ill.: The Free Press, 1959), pp. 701, 706.

31. Roche, *op. cit.*, pp. 234–257.

32. See p. 126.

33. *AJYB*, LXIII (1962), 196.

Anti-Semitism in the Perspective
of Jewish History

BEN HALPERN

IN A DISCUSSION of the meaning and etiology of anti-Semitism, the specialist who deals with the subject from the viewpoint of Jewish history enjoys a clear advantage over those who approach it from other disciplines and perspectives. From his vantage point it is obvious, not as an assumption but as an observed fact, that anti-Semitism exists—a fact which cannot be taken for granted by the interpreter of opinion polls, and which remains doubtful to the student of American history.

The position of the social psychologist interpreting poll data is clearly stated by Charles Herbert Stember:

The . . . last working assumption . . . is simply that the object of our inquiry exists. We are setting out to measure the American public's general attitudes toward Jews; but at this point in our explorations, the existence of such over-all attitudes is a mere hypothesis, not a proven fact. It is at least conceivable that Americans do not respond in a coherent way toward Jews as a group, but merely react in disjointed fashion to discrete aspects of the Jewish group as they encounter them.[1]

As Stember goes on to state, he would conclude that there is an "over-all attitude toward Jews" (that is, he would confirm the hypothesis that "there is such a thing as generalized anti-Semitism") only if he found separate measurements of "the cognitive, affective and conative dimensions of attitudes toward Jews in a variety of contexts . . . to be more or less in harmony."

The historians who, in the present book, examine anti-Semitism as part of American history do not begin with the same methodological skepticism about its very existence. Historians do not usually question the existence of anything referred to by name in reliable sources. Yet if we were to poll them, in Stember's terms, on whether Americans "respond in a coherent way to Jews as a group," the most likely answer would be that the people "merely react in disjointed fashion to discrete aspects of the Jewish group as they encounter them."

Thus, Morton Keller holds that since the 1930s Americans have reverted to their fundamental antipathy against group distinctions, and today express their partisanship or hostility in institutional rather than ethnic or religious terms. Not the Jews or Catholics, but big business or big labor are the villains now. Similarly, John Higham holds that during the most important of those spells when anti-Semitism briefly rose to a certain prominence on the American scene, it was only one aspect of a general nativist reaction against immigrants. In short, the students of American history seem to feel that anti-Semitism may be a fact of the nation's past, as it is referred to in documents, but that it has occurred only sporadically in this country, and has had neither major significance nor an independent, continuous tradition.

No such doubts or reservations arise when we study anti-Semitism in what is, after all, its natural habitat: the world history of the Jews. Moreover, in this context we should hardly limit investigation to the ninety years, more or less, during which the term "anti-Semitism" has been used. What goes by that name seems to us part and parcel of a group hostility which has appeared for many centuries wherever Jews were found. In the perspective of Jewish history, the object of our inquiry exists as a prime datum of observation, and has major significance as well as an independent, continuous tradition. Indeed, it is axiomatic, and a necessary presupposition of the whole field of Jewish history, that throughout the span of their existence Jews have been reacted to as a group, a continuing entity—not merely by themselves but also by others. Historians and historically oriented ideologists of the Jewish question have differed only on what elements in the nature or history of the Jews as a group constitute the fundamental cause of the perennial Jew-hatred most recently known as anti-Semitism.

Ideological and Moralistic Theories of Anti-Semitism

The theories most frequently advanced to explain anti-Semitism attempt to establish a universal law from which the Jews' long history of persecution might be logically deduced. A common-sense liberal view that was once widely held attributed violent Jew-hatred to ignorance, backwardness and prejudice, exploited by oppressive rulers or ruthless demagogues for their selfish ends. As Stember points out in his opening chapter, the rise of Nazism in Germany, a country with an advanced industrial civilization and a high culture, made this assumption hard to sustain.

The failure of the common-sense liberal theory led many to favor economic explanations, such as had been common in Socialist circles since the end of the nineteenth century. Anti-Semitism was now widely interpreted as a symptom of capitalism at its last gasp—a device of desperate reactionaries seeking to subvert an expected revolution by playing on the prejudices of embittered *déclassé* elements. That hostility to Jews is a function of economic collapse with its attendant frustrations is still a widely held theory, forming the basis of much current discussion. Both Stember and others represented in this book take off where they think this conventional materialistic theory fails, and offer their own explanations of various points as alternatives to it.

Zionist ideologists commonly explain anti-Semitism as an inevitable effect of the very structure of Jewish existence in the Diaspora.[2] According to this view, all aliens encounter hostility; but the Jews, as an unassimilable minority without a territory of their own, have remained aliens for so many centuries that hatred for them has assumed a peculiarly explosive, ingrained, frequently psychopathic form. The indicated remedy is to provide a national home for the Jews, removing enough of them from the position of alien so that the rest can be absorbed or tolerated by their environment as other minorities are.

Historical explanations are by their very nature inconclusive. Rival views fluctuate in popularity among historians, and the existing canon of historical science provides no method of resolving such major controversies decisively. But within a given type of theory, particular formulations are sometimes proved inadequate by subsequent events.

Thus, the creation of Israel as a Jewish state constituted a test of the Zionists' basic thesis, bringing into sharp focus certain apparent flaws. Anti-Semitism, according to the Zionist hypothesis, should be disappearing with its cause, Jewish national homelessness; but not only does it seem to be persisting—it has even made the new State of Israel one of its prime targets.[3] Our own interpretation, to be presented later, will take off from observations like these. The explanations we propose for various historical problems will often begin where conventional Zionist analysis seems to fail, and are submitted as an alternative.

If anti-Semitism stems from the structure of Jewish existence in the Diaspora, yet the end of Jewish national homelessness fails to eliminate it, then it would seem natural to reconsider as a possible cause another permanent feature of the Jewish exile: the Jewish religion. This will, indeed, be the point of departure for our own analysis. First, however, we must consider various other theories of religion as the cause of anti-Semitism which differ from our own in taking a moralistic rather than a structural approach. According to these views, religion produces anti-Semitism, not because of its structural relation to society, but because of its direct moral impact on individual behavior. Thus, Judaism or (for example) Christianity may be *blamed* for anti-Semitism because of specific religious beliefs, practices or attitudes which, it is thought, need only be altered in order to make Jew-hatred disappear. Arnold Toynbee's work, which somewhat incidentally but repeatedly and with marked emphasis refers to the question of Jew-hatred, has been a major source of such moralistic scholarly controversy.

Toynbee's own analysis is notably many-sided. He discusses Judaism as a fossil remnant of Syriac civilization; he describes the "distortions" of culture and character, the economic specialization and the social segregation that develop in a "penalized minority," producing friction with, and hatred in, the host society.[4] In his theory, the various separate analyses of economic rivalry, social alienation and religious antagonism fall into an integrated pattern; but by itself each of them resembles one or another of the traditional common-sense explanations of Jew-hatred, and fails to reveal the source of Toynbee's moralistic bias against the Jews. This bias unmistakably emerges only when he discusses what he regards as the root-cause: the Jewish religion.[5]

Monotheism produces a fanatical drive toward unity, says Toynbee (in terms which, by the way, describe his own ruling passion), and it is inherently predisposed to intolerance. When it succeeds—that is, when it dominates a universal state—it is more inhuman than pagan civilizations, until it learns that for practical reasons religious differences must be tolerated. When it fails, as Judaism did, it brings down persecution on its head, unless it adopts a gentle, quietist, Christlike way as its defense, instead of the violent way of the Maccabees. Though the Jews are not the only group whose fate Toynbee reviews in these terms, he reserves his harshest language for them. He comes close to blaming them for the existence of anti-Semitism insofar as he deduces religious hatred primarily from fanatical monotheism, of which they are the primary source; and he castigates them unmercifully for the ways in which, throughout history, they have chosen to respond to the outside world's hostility.

Stimulated by Toynbee's views, Rabbi Jacob B. Agus has defended at least one aspect of the Jewish reaction to defeat. What Toynbee calls Judaism's gentle response—exemplified, he believes, by Rabbi Johanan ben Zakkai and the Agudat Israel—Agus prefers to call its rational, universalistic tendency. Anti-Jewish feelings, according to Agus, are produced not by Judaism as such, but by the emotional, particularistic (that is, nationalistic) tendencies it contains.[6]

Another moralistic rejoinder to Toynbee's analysis has come from James Parkes.[7] In his opinion, Christianity—not monotheism with its Jewish origins—is to blame for anti-Semitism: ". . . Antisemitism is a unique expression of group prejudice, and arises out of a unique cause. That which changed the normal pattern of Jewish-Gentile relations was the action of the Christian Church. The statement is tragic but the evidence is inescapable." [8]

Parkes' explanation implies that the treatment of the Jews in Greco-Roman times or in Islamic countries cannot be called anti-Semitic, but is part of the normal range of relations, from hostile to friendly, that generally prevail between majorities and minorities. His view also implies that anti-Semitism can disappear without a radical change in the structure of Jewish existence amid the gentiles, given appropriate action by Christians—for example, abandonment of the "deicide" image.

Like all controversial historical views, these moralistic interpretations are convincing to their adherents on grounds over and above the specific evidence. Similarly, whoever rejects them does so, not merely because of the weight of contrary evidence, but also for more general reasons—for example, because he approaches historical questions from an ideological rather than a moralistic point of departure. The historian who takes an ideological attitude rules out, at the start, any interpretations that attribute major historico-social phenomena (such as anti-Semitism) to free choices of men, to their right or wrong decisions, their virtuous or sinful responses to challenges. At least, he will follow the methodological principle not to resort to such explanations before examining whether the phenomenon in question may be derived from structural features of the social history in which it is manifested. This is the principle followed in the present essay.

Anti-Semitism as an Historical Concomitant of Toleration

For such an approach, not Toynbee but the late Yehezkel Kaufmann is the major source in recent historical analysis. His description of anti-Semitism, like Toynbee's, is many-sided:

Its grounds are general, but their composition and combination have made Jew-hatred ("anti-Semitism") a unique historical complex. Religious fanaticism, national rivalry, hatred of aliens, economic and social competition—all these are general phenomena. But in Jew-hatred all these have been joined in permanent (and hence intensified) combination and have become historically fixed. . . . Wherever there is contact between [different] religious, ethnic, and economic groups there necessarily develop irritations and quarrels that breed enmity. Through the dispersion [of the Jews] the areas of contact between Israel and other peoples grew immeasurably. It was contact with a society differing in religion and racial stock, alien in the land, and beyond any hope of being merged in a common union. The irritants of hostility toward this society were intensified by continuous contact with it, by the multiplicity of areas of contact with it, and by the multiple grounds of difference. It was not a local but a universal hatred, encompassing almost all the nations, for Jews came in contact with everyone. These intensified irritants of hostility converged on a single object, were borne by one people, and accumulated around them generation by generation. Through the continuity of its object, this hatred became a sort of idea, a conception, a system.[9]

While Kaufmann stresses the multiple grounds of anti-Semitism and its historic continuity and growth, he also states unequivocally what he regards as its primary, universal and fundamental cause. Jew-hatred, in his view, is a universal response to Judaism and its specific history; it is the hostility necessarily evoked by the monotheistic faith of a defeated people. As a monotheistic religion, Judaism was inherently fanatical and developed a universal conversionist drive. But as a politically defeated and exiled people, the Jews were in no position to make mass conversions. Prospective proselytes were called upon, not merely to brave sanctions and penalties imposed by gentile authorities, but to join a cause that history seemed to have declared lost. Thus Judaism was doomed to remain the exclusive faith of native Jews; and the few who joined them merged indistinguishably with them.[10] This historic fatality, which joined the Jews and their religion in an exclusive union, consolidated the Chosen People as an ideologically recalcitrant, adamantine minority—a minority widely scattered, persisting through centuries, and subject to a hostility that became traditional.

It will be noted that Kaufmann *blames* neither Judaism nor any other faith for anti-Semitism. He *derives* anti-Semitism from religion as a structural element in the social relations of Jews and gentiles. The point will perhaps become clearer if we reformulate the theory in more abstract terms.

The generalizations that seem to underlie Kaufmann's views may be stated as follows: The monotheistic faith of the Jews is an ideological, not a mythic, form of culture.[11] Mythic value systems readily adjust to each other in syncretistic unions; ideological systems have an inherent tendency to submerge (or, as Nikita S. Khrushchev once put it, to "bury") differing value systems. If victorious, a people committed to an ideology tends to convert its unbelieving subjects forcibly; if defeated, it will resist stubbornly any pressure to conform, even to the point of challenging martyrdom. Therefore, a defeated people of this kind can be included in a greater society with different beliefs only by special measures of toleration; and such an exceptional tolerated status is inevitably accompanied by a special irritable animosity. In the case of Judaism, this state of affairs has prevailed so long and among so many societies that it has developed a specific, ancient and protean tradition of its own: an ambivalent syndrome compounded of simultaneous or alternating toleration and hostility. Only the term "anti-Semitism" for the hostile aspect of this perennial syndrome is new.

The view just outlined implies that anti-Semitism already existed in pre-Christian times, and that Islam as well as Christendom shares in the anti-Semitic tradition. Here again, one's agreement or disagreement depends on one's general position in the area of controversy as much as on the weight of the particular evidence. Thus Parkes, being initially inclined to see anti-Semitism as the fruit of a tragic error on the part of Christendom, attributes the evidence of hostility toward Jews in pre-Christian times and non-Christian areas to the merely normal frictions between groups that differ significantly. (The telling qualification, "significantly," of course begs the question.) In contrast, our own analysis, disposed from the outset to trace anti-Semitism to the specific history and structural relation of the Jews and Judaism, interprets the evidence from pre-Christian times and non-Christian areas as weighty confirmation.

It has often been noted that ancient complaints about the Jews bear a conspicuous family resemblance to the anti-Semitic stereotypes of medieval and modern times. The basic objection of anti-Semites in all generations is implicit in the charge of Haman, as we know it from the Book of Esther (3:8): "There is a certain people scattered abroad and dispersed among the peoples in all the provinces of thy kingdom; and their laws are diverse from those of every people; neither keep they the king's laws; therefore it profiteth not the king to suffer them." Now, the imperial civilizations of antiquity generally allowed subject peoples and religions to live according to their own laws. What is important here is that in the case of the Jews this meant express exemption from duties required of all others—for example, from participation in the imperial cult, from payment of debts or appearance before law courts on the Sabbath and, occasionally, from military service.[12]

Since the earliest times, then, Judaism has had to be allowed special privileges if its existence was to be tolerated at all. Not only were these privileges, granted by the central power, resented by other subject peoples and local authorities; the central power itself, in the very act of giving the Jews an exceptional status, necessarily adopted a wary and suspicious attitude toward them. The privileges were accorded only to Jews by birth; Jewish proselytes and gentiles who practiced Jewish rites were severely repressed. Thus, the specific toleration extended to the Jews had as its reverse side, from the very beginning, a specific hostility and suspicion.

When Christianity became dominant, it could not help accepting the established status of the Jews, just as Rome and Parthia had done in their time. But the dilemma inherent in the Jews' equivocal status was now seriously sharpened. Whatever *raison d'état* may have inspired the pagans' recognition of Judaism as a permissible religion, Christian authorities were able to accept it only on homiletical grounds. In the pagan Roman Empire, Judaism had been one of many tolerated minority religions; under Christianity it ultimately became the only one. Such an exceptional status was justified on the basis of proof texts in the Old and New Testaments and of other religious ideology. So, too, where the Romans repressed proselytizing out of a mere wariness of Judaism, the parallel Christian policy was designed to make the status of the Jews symbolically demonstrate that Judaism had been supplanted in God's favor by the new Israel: the Christian *ecclesia*.[13]

When Islam conquered the Byzantine and Sassanian realms, it adapted to its own uses some of each empire's institutions for the treatment of tolerated religions. The way in which toleration was justified particularly resembled the Byzantine model. A special position was accorded to the Peoples of the Book and by analogy to a few similar religions, but was denied to paganism. Islam took the privileges, restrictions and demonstrative subordination which Christian Europe had applied to the Jews, and extended them to Christians and Jews alike, on the basis of specific injunctions in the Koran. Samaritans, Zoroastrians and others were dealt with in similar fashion.[14] The *raison d'état* in this case was clear and compelling: The relatively small nomadic Arab bands might conquer weakened and demoralized empires by force of arms, but they could govern them only by enlisting the collaboration of the established, numerous sedentary populations. The result was that the ambiguous position of tolerated unbelievers was not occupied by the Jews alone, as in Christian Europe, but shared with Christians and certain other religious dissidents.

The special status of the Jews has always depended on the rulers, and has repeatedly been challenged by the ruled. When Roman or Gothic or Frankish monarchs tolerated Jews in a Christian society under secular laws, priests and bishops were their most vocal antagonists. Later, when bishops and popes established their rule over secular society, the special status they conferred upon Jews on the basis of Roman precedents was resisted by their subjects, both peasants and town dwellers. In these and later ages, such hostility often broke out into anti-Jewish violence when established rulers were suddenly overturned, or sought desperate means to prevent revolution, or were forced to make far-reaching concessions to their subjects. In these ways came about the expulsions and massacres of Jews, from the persecutions in the late Middle Ages through the Cossack uprisings and the Czarist pogroms to the Nazi terror that began with the overthrow of the Weimar Republic.

Where Jews were the sole tolerated religious minority, they enjoyed this exceptional status on two grounds, both precarious. First, toleration afforded certain practical advantages to the ruler—advantages which the ruled felt had been illegitimately extorted from them. Second, it was justified by a sophisticated interpretation of texts which was perhaps intellectually satisfactory to the higher regular clergy, but failed to sway the emotions of fanatical monks or laymen. In times of social upheaval, rebels had no patience for quibbles or calculations by which the establishment might seek to justify the Jews' special status. Thus, when anti-Semitic violence erupted, the Jews were thrown back even more on the good graces and support of the rulers. They remained with no recognized rights of their own, as mere protected dependents of their patrons.

As the central control of monarchs became fortified in Western Europe, the responsibility for keeping Jews in residence fell more and more on the rulers' heads alone. Among all other elements of the population, opposition grew and eventually proved irresistible. Each epidemic of Jew-hatred intensified the endemic hatred against the Jews who survived; each outbreak of violence spawned rationalizations for new crimes against the victims—until the Jews' royal protectors found it more advantageous to expel them than to bear the burden of keeping them. Jews *en masse* were finally driven from England at the end of the thirteenth century, from France at the end of the fourteenth and from Spain at the end of fifteenth.

In Central Europe, authority remained more fragmented, so that no single sovereign was solely responsible for protecting the Jews or capable of effectively driving them away. The Jews therefore remained, living in ghettos, engaging in occupations not pursued by Christians or forbidden to them as sinful. The survival of Jewish communities on these fundamentally illegitimate terms bred an endemic anti-Semitism of unparalleled virulence. The demonology of Jew-hatred in Europe was like a toxin: Injected during the period of the Crusades, it proliferated luxuriantly in the central regions, where Jews continued to live, and from there it spread into neighboring countries.[15]

At this point, what toleration existed was no more than inability to get rid of the Jews, and hostility, balked of full, genocidal expression, was at its height. Only when occupations considered sinful and therefore "Jewish" were commonly practiced by Christians, as occurred with moneylending in Italy, was endemic anti-Semitism moderated; cynicism, if not humane tolerance, often tempered Jew-hatred. In analogous fashion, the rise of Protestantism served to diffuse the hostility previously concentrated on the Jews—by providing other dissident religious minorities that could serve as targets.

Early mercantile capitalism, however, did more than dilute or dim antagonism against the Jews. It foreshadowed a new social structure and value system which placed a positive instead of a negative value on the Jews' characteristic economic functions and considered their religious dissidence irrelevant. After long absence, the Jews returned to a society which had abandoned former anti-Jewish institutions based on actual contact and retained only a legendary tradition of Jew-hatred. They settled in France during the era of Jean Baptiste Colbert, as well as in the Netherlands, England and the American colonies. In the late eighteenth and nineteenth centuries, their acceptance as equals in the trading community was widened by liberal bourgeois revolutions, and new doctrines of the separation of church and state qualified them for admission to full citizenship.

The sequence and form of these historic changes varied from country to country, producing distinct national histories. Distinctive literatures and cultural traditions defined the character of the various peoples. But, simultaneously with this basically aesthetic differentiation, a common Western civilization, founded on science, came into being. And while the new secular culture arose by freeing itself from theology and moralistic religion, the nations were yet united in their fundamental ethical orientation by a common Christianity, which helped bridge the differences in cultural tradition.

A similar partial diversification occurred in the balance of tolerance and hostility regarding the Jews. In all countries, a fundamental antagonism remained; wherever Jews lived among Christians, they were merely tolerated, that is, they existed in a milieu of endemic anti-Semitism. But in addition, each nation had its own specific experience with the Jews. In some of the national cultures or consciences they became a central concern, in others a peripheral one—depending mainly on the ways in which critical issues bearing on the question of toleration arose in the particular nation's history. Among issues of this sort were: the development of general religious toleration; the rise of the secular state, and the separation of church and state; the growth of the general franchise and of popular sovereignty.

Thus, in France and Germany the Jews won citizenship in the course of revolutionary struggles and national wars which set one part of the nation against the other, establishing patterns of political hostility and partisanship that still endure. Their status, while not a cardinal question in these struggles, evolved into a prominent secondary issue, so that they became closely identified with the liberal, secular, rationalistic, "progressive" side. In England, Jewish emancipation was involved in no such national crises, and the Jews gained no prominence as symbols of a particular political orientation. In Russia, Jewish emancipation had to wait for a social revolution which was inherently hostile to all forms of religion and nationalism, even when it provisionally tolerated them; and the Jews were prime examples of both the religious and nationalist "evils."

The development in America has been distinctive in a number of ways. As in England, Jewish emancipation was not related to major national political crises. It had even less political impact here, since it was accomplished not by specific measures in favor of Jews, but by the introduction of general religious toleration before a significant Jewish community was present. Moreover, America from the outset was characterized by religious pluralism, and early in its history instituted a far-reaching, quite firm separation of church and state.

Each of the factors mentioned above—the multiplication of religious minorities, the development of religious toleration culminating in the separation of church and state, the emerging conceptions of citizenship and the secular state—qualified and mitigated the Jews' exceptional position. As long as they were the only religious minority tolerated in Christian Europe, the myth of Cain, the eternal, indestructible outcast and wanderer, seemed to fit them precisely; unbelieving and unconverted ("perfidious"), they were expected to dwell as a tribe apart from the gentiles until Doomsday. When other religious dissidents began to be tolerated, and even more when church was separated from state, or secular national citizenship established, the myth lost its literal applicability. The ancient themes now persisted, rather, in continuous transformations to fit the visible facts, in an unending series of stereotypes.

Still, whether Judas Iscariot became Shylock the usurer, or Rothschild/ Trotsky, the international webspinner and wirepuller, or even Lessing's Nathan the Wise, attitudes toward the Jew remained something special. If the imagery kept within the range of ambivalent, partly hostile, partly tolerant attitudes that are encountered by all ideological or religious dissident minorities who are not completely suppressed or submerged, it also retained the specific themes derived from the myth-history of the Jews—a people uniquely associated with its own monotheistic faith, and suffering exile because it could not convert others.

The situation of the Jews in America, however special its character, is not fundamentally different from what it has been elsewhere; and the configuration of Americans' attitudes toward them, however unique it may be, remains confined within the traditional framework of ambivalence between anti-Semitism and toleration. These facts are sometimes disputed on the grounds that America lacks a feudal tradition, or that everyone's ancestors (except the Indians') were immigrants or that pluralism and diversity are part and parcel of American life—in short, that "America is different" even in regard to anti-Semitism and the Jews. But this is not the assumption underlying the present symposium. We are discussing, not whether anti-Semitism is foreign to America *ab initio,* but whether the findings of recent public-opinion polls signal its demise.

To answer this question we should, of course, have to define at what point we would consider the tolerance-hostility syndrome, in which anti-Semitism is inherent, to have been overcome. But two preliminary questions obtrude themselves: First, how can we assess the historical significance of opinion-poll findings generally; and second, what is the concrete historical significance of Stember's particular findings?

Historical Criticism and the Interpretation of Polls

How difficult it is to apply a comparative historical perspective to contemporary poll findings becomes obvious when we approach the problem from the poll taker's point of view. To compare the public's attitudes in the last few decades with attitudes in earlier times, we ideally should have comparable survey findings from each of the eras under study. Lacking such information for the earlier periods, we could only take the available poll results, extending from the 1930s to the 1960s, as our standard, and search historical sources for earlier data that might be comparably objective, representative and verifiable.

We know from the outset that this search would yield dishearteningly little. The historical sources which record attitudes toward the Jews—such as books, pamphlets or newspaper articles—are subject to such biases in sampling that comparing them directly with poll results would yield no usable conclusions. If we tried to estimate how a representative population sample at a given time and place might have answered questions like those asked in present-day polls, we would be at the mercy of our own or someone else's subjective and unverifiable interpretation of the sources—not to mention the varied form and often fragmentary condition of the sources themselves. To take a random example: The Jewish question was debated in the French National Assembly in 1791; the debates are available and could be supplemented by contemporaneous pamphlet material. But we would be hard put to estimate from these materials how a representative sample of Frenchmen at the time might have responded to today's poll questions—for example, whether they had heard any criticism or talk against the Jews recently, or which group in the population they believed had too much power or influence.

In practice, such a comparative analysis would be totally useless. If we must be cautious even in comparing responses to identical questions asked at brief intervals, merely because the polls were conducted by different agencies, how dare we compare responses that are separated by centuries and, for the most part, are purely hypothetical constructs? To interpret poll results on Americans' attitudes to Jews from the 1930s to the 1960s by reading them against truly analogous data about other periods is a job we obviously could not even begin now; we would have to wait, perhaps for several centuries, until the American Jewish Committee and other agencies had built up suitable indices and time series upon which such a longitudinal study could be based. Until that happy time, any analysis of the poll findings in the perspective of Jewish history must ignore the standards of reliability and representativeness according to which polling agencies collect their data. The historical materials at our disposal simply do not meet these requirements.

Historical data, however, are subject to their own standards of reliability. They must meet specific criteria of credibility and significance, worked out by a long-established tradition of so-called scientific or critical history. The historian's critical methods are not usually applied to opinion polls and their findings, mainly because historical criticism takes effect at a point where the collection of data is closely involved with, not sharply distinguished from, their interpretation. Just the same, in the present case it is essential to do so. Unless we use the historian's critical methods of evaluating data— the normal standards of credibility and significance—on poll findings and ordinary historical evidence alike, we cannot compare the two at all.

Some critical problems, such as timing, attribution and authenticity, are taken care of quite satisfactorily by the known methods of polling. But before we arrive at the "real" or *historically significant* attitudes the data imply, there remains the major task of determining bias, that is, of judging what the respondents meant to convey to their questioners in their replies, what impression they sought to create, and why.

Deceit and deliberate ambiguity or rhetorical concealment probably did not seriously distort the poll responses.[16] But a historian would assume, as a general rule, that the answers reflected primarily what the respondents thought they *should* feel or believe about the issue at hand—not how they would react if faced with an actual situation rather than a hypothetical question.

The *caveat* is familiar to anyone who deals with polls; yet analysts of public opinion are reluctant to apply it in interpreting their findings. They tend to assume that, by and large, responses directly indicate attitudes. Thus, Stember discusses in general terms the argument that "impersonal interviews . . . produce only the most superficial and stereotyped replies, and only those deemed socially acceptable"; but I have noted only one important instance where he considers a possible interpretation of the data along these lines.[17]

The case in point is as follows: When tested by various questions for a tendency to identify Jews as a group with Communism in the early 1950s, strikingly low and decreasing proportions of respondents made the identification; when asked to volunteer the names of Communist (or "atomic") spies, a large and increasing number mentioned Jewish names. The contradiction might be resolved, Stember suggests, by assuming that current publicity about the Rosenberg case made the names of actual Jewish Communist spies especially salient. However, when *fictitious* Jewish and non-Jewish names were inserted in a checklist, the respondents identified imaginary Jews as Communists more than six times as often as imaginary gentiles. Stember arbitrarily discounts the obvious explanation that "large numbers of persons actually did think of Jews as communistic but concealed this belief from interviewers in direct questioning, or hid it even from themselves"; he then offers several rather inconsistent alternative interpretations, including a notably far-fetched one at the end.

In our view, *all* poll findings—not only those which resist alternative interpretations—must be considered in terms of the respondents' willingness or unwillingness to reveal anti-Semitic attitudes. Until this factor has been taken into account, the kind and degree of underlying, historically significant anti-Semitism cannot be estimated. If we adopt this standpoint, we will conclude that the striking changes shown in the poll findings register, not necessarily the prevalence of anti-Semitism in America, but perhaps only its respectability, as it may have been affected by the historic events of the period.

Semantic analysis is another historico-critical technique sometimes used in interpreting poll data. Thus Stember in some cases explains away difficulties by supposed semantic changes, suggesting that identically worded questions asked at different times may have carried different connotations. He does so, for example, in discussing the question, asked in 1946 and repeated in 1962, whether Jews are a race, nationality or religious group. In 1962, the perception of Jews as a race (presumably an index of anti-Semitism) did not correlate well with other indices of anti-Jewish attitudes in the questionnaire. Stember then argues: "It is quite possible that the survey question did not carry exactly the same import in 1946 as in 1962." [18]

Other examples arise from Stember's general principle that underlying attitudes do not stand in a simple one-to-one relation with individual questions, but are complex, systemic phenomena. He holds that each question reveals one or more facets of a composite which comprises cognitive, affective and conative responses, and that, therefore, poll responses can be fully interpreted only when correlated with one another. As a consequence of this principle, a response favorable to the Jews is sometimes interpreted as an inverted index of anti-Semitism. It is argued that a respondent who is explicitly asked to name admirable traits of the Jews is being artificially induced to isolate specific facets of his attitude from their systemic coherence; he often betrays his true feelings by choosing "admirable" characteristics that correspond cognitively to traits commonly mentioned in response to questions about objectionable qualities of Jews.[19]

As a rule, interpreters of polls resort to semantic analysis only where specific difficulties arise. Furthermore, while they may occasionally introduce information about the usage of terms from the outside,[20] they prefer, as Stember's usual practice suggests, to seek clues to the significance of responses in cross-references among the poll items themselves. But if we are to abide by the standards of historical criticism, we may not employ semantic analysis merely in exceptional cases or as a last resort, nor may we limit it to the questionnaire items. We must interpret *all* responses semantically, if only to make sure that the meaning of identically worded questions has not changed; and we must consider *all* evidence, from whatever source, that might help determine their probable significance.[21]

The historian's explanatory assumptions, moreover, differ inherently from those held by most interpreters of opinion polls in what is considered to be of enduring rather than of transient significance. To be sure, Stember consistently distinguishes between lasting and transitory attitudes. In part, his doing so reflects a difference among the polls themselves, some of which ask the same or similar questions at intervals, while others deal with particular contemporary events. But he draws the distinction even among the regularly repeated polls; he holds that some questions reach more fundamental levels of attitude than others, and often interprets the supposedly shallower items as transformations of the profounder ones. For example, he repeatedly explains responses to apparently unrelated questions as reflections of what he considers the dominant American anti-Jewish image: the stereotype of the Jew as an "economic man." [22]

Stember derives this enduring and fundamental stereotype from the poll

findings themselves, where it appears with relative frequency. In this connection, he sometimes refers to historical precedents for anti-Semitic images
built around the economic activities of Jews. But he makes no systematic
effort to explore the storehouse of history in order to relate the poll findings
to those anti-Jewish images which have proved enduring in history's longer
perspective.

A historian bent on critical analysis of the poll findings, and thus obliged
to weigh the enduring or transitory character of the attitudes revealed,
would begin by systematically taking the semantic route through history.
He would seek to interpret the changing significance and relevance of verbal
symbols, turning to every kind of available record for his definitions, and
appraising every important term in its full historic context. Take, for example, the key conception: "the Jews." For the comparative historical analyst, attitudes toward the Jews are attitudes toward a single changing entity
and must be read against the respondents' continually shifting total background of Jewish associations: against their notions of centuries past, together with their impressions of recent or current events.

The social psychologist, on the other hand, pays little attention to the full
historical significance of key terms such as "the Jews." The chief underlying
assumption of poll analysis as practiced by Stember and others is that particular, discrete attitudes and attitude changes are the most important independent variables in determining the rise or decline of anti-Semitism.
Changes in the more enduring anti-Semitic attitudes are in turn attributed to
major shifts in the demography and socio-economic distribution of the Jews
within the changing American social structure; not the historical Jewish
entity as such but the social position it occupies are thought to be the important factor. Transitory anti-Jewish sentiments are traced to wars, de-
pressions or other general disturbances—that is, to events which stir up
public feeling against large groups including non-Jews as well (for example,
against the foreign-born generally). In this interpretation of the poll data,
the student of American history is likely to concur.

To a Jewish historian, other factors suggest themselves as more directly
pertinent. He will derive his view of the enduring elements in anti-Semitism
from the structure of the Jewish situation in world history; and he will refer
transitory variations to crucial historical events specifically related to the
Jews. Accordingly, he will cast a skeptical eye on prognostications such as
Stember's broadest appraisal of the poll data—an appraisal which envisions
the possible demise of anti-Semitism merely on the basis of trends observed
over a few decades and extrapolated into the future:

. . . Since social institutions depend ultimately on public consensus, attitudes
are a more reliable indicator of long-term normative changes than specific practices. . . . That the Jews' position in the society and their relations to the non-
Jewish majority have altered since the period of mass immigration (c. 1880–

1920) is beyond question. What we need to know is whether these changes have been accompanied by modifications of the largely unfavorable attitudes which the non-Jewish majority held a few decades ago. If we observe such modifications on a substantial scale we may conclude, albeit cautiously, that Jews have begun to be truly integrated into the larger society.[23]

In keeping with our earlier discussions, our own interpretations and prognoses will insist on certain distinctions within the vast historical panorama of the gentile world's reaction to the Jew—of the manifold attitudes down to modern anti-Semitism that constitute the longest-lasting and most universal social problem in history. Whatever the "fundamental" nature of these attitudes, they obviously are not all of one piece. Hostility against Jews does not form a continuum leading smoothly up to and including the motivations that prompt genocide. (Stember implicitly warns against this misconception when he notes that organized or political anti-Semitism and the usual run of anti-Semitic poll responses are separate phenomena following distinct courses of development.)[24] Nor do attitudes favorable to Jews constitute a continuum up to and including the motivations that produce "integration." There is a discontinuity that separates Jew-hatred from genocide, and another that separates toleration from integration.

In our opinion, the negative response to Jews known today as anti-Semitism appears in inversely varying proportions with its positive correlate, which we may call tolerance. The two are opposite aspects of a single ambivalent attitude, extending through a continuum of relationships that stops short of genocide on one hand and of integration on the other. When this sphere of ambivalence is exceeded and either hostility or acceptance is no longer balanced by its opposite—that is, when either genocide or integration occurs—we are dealing with new phenomena which cannot be understood in the same terms as the traditional syndrome of anti-Semitism and tolerance.

What factors may cause attitudes toward Jews to exceed the limits of that syndrome is fairly evident to the Jewish historian. At the negative end, we have seen how the usual ambivalence yielded to mass persecution because of general social upheaval and of the Jews' isolation as sole religious dissidents during the Middle Ages. In characteristic transformations, similar factors have produced genocide during our own times. At the positive end, we can conceive of a state of affairs in which Jews might no longer be an ideological dissident group that has to be tolerated, and thus might become "truly integrated."

As for variations of endemic anti-Semitism *within* the range of the tolerance-hostility syndrome, the Jewish historian will seek their sources among critical events of contemporary national history in which Jews were saliently involved.

The Historical Significance of the Poll Findings

Which historical events constitute the framework for an analysis of the poll data in these terms is clear enough. During the period under study, the Second World War broke out and was eventually won. In addition, salient occurrences like Hitler's rise to power in 1933, the ensuing stream of Jewish refugees, the Nazis' program for annihilating the Jews, the problem of displaced persons, the rise of Israel through a diplomatic and military struggle and the subsequent stormy history of the Jewish state must certainly have impressed themselves on the public's consciousness. In fact, the impact of some of these events is directly mirrored in the poll findings.

Thus, from 1940 to 1942, about one-fifth of the public was found to be familiar with anti-Jewish organizations and spokesmen in America. Between January 1943 and December 1944, the proportion who believed reports of the German annihilation program rose from less than half to over three-quarters. At the latter date, most respondents still greatly underestimated the number murdered ("100,000 or fewer"), but by May 1945 the median estimate was one million, and 84 per cent of the respondents now thought the reports true. In the mid-1940s, the struggle to establish a Jewish state and resettle Jewish refugees in Palestine was accompanied by a significant rise in information levels and interest. The same was true, during the following decade, of the growing friction between Israel and the Arab states: In 1953, one-third of the respondents expressed an opinion on the issue; by the end of the Sinai fighting in 1956, almost two-thirds did.[25]

In brief, the major historic events that affected Jews from the 1930s until the 1960s were fairly well known to the public. That some of the facts would at first be widely disbelieved or underestimated should not have been surprising, since the events were incompatible with Americans' ideas of what is to be expected or can be tolerated in majority-minority relations. As Stember points out, poll respondents were generally inclined to feel that Jews and other minorities were as a rule treated well in this country or as well as they deserved.[26] One may hazard the guess that majorities anywhere, at any time, tend to think a given minority deserves the treatment it gets—except when they are ethnic brothers of the minority in question. If someone is mistreated, it will be assumed that he has misbehaved, and that his punishment is more or less in proportion. Genocide, however, is out of proportion with any misbehavior conceivable in the context of an enduring majority-minority relation, since it deliberately destroys the relationship. Hence, the fact of actual or intended genocide is hard to believe—incidentally, not only for the majority but, as we have all had occasion to observe, also among the prospective victims.

In any case, the facts about the annihilation of European Jewry were eventually accepted as true, even though they went far beyond the limits of

Americans' prior experience with Jews and thus left the public without a ready pattern of responses. Later, as already noted, the emergence of Israel was widely noted and followed with interest, although this historic event, too, was without precedent in traditional Jewish status patterns and beyond the range of pre-existing gentile responses. How did Americans adjust or adapt their conventional attitudes toward Jews to deal with these new facts? And how, if at all, did they alter their attitudes toward *American* Jews as a result? Let us examine the poll findings as leads toward an answer.

Stember takes up the American reaction to the Nazi genocide program as reflected in a poll dealing explicitly with this subject and with related issues. In his opinion, the revelations of horror did disconcertingly little to diminish American anti-Semitism—a conclusion he draws from the facts that many respondents said the wartime events warranted no increased sympathy for Jews in this country, and that many also declared the German people as a whole should not be blamed for the atrocities. In giving the latter response, Stember believes, Americans were "vicariously defending their own unconcern." He also notes that until the end of the war and even later, polls designed to elicit sympathetic or unsympathetic responses to Jews continued to find negative attitudes widely prevalent.[27]

One may doubt whether these responses really prove the public to have remained unaffected by the wartime atrocities against the Jews. If the respondents chose to disbelieve and discount as propaganda the reports of persecution which had reached them, this in itself clearly indicates an immediate effect on attitudes: It reflects at least a suppressed sense of guilt. That this effect did not take the expected form of increased sympathy for Jews in America proves only that such expectations were based on incorrect premises concerning the anti-Semitism–tolerance syndrome. In any case, we do not think the major effect of the holocaust should be sought in the responses to questions which attempted to measure it immediately and explicitly; to do so would be to revert to the assumption that poll responses are necessarily direct indices of attitudes. In our opinion, certain poll findings of the 1950s and the 1960s, on seemingly unrelated issues, clearly indicate that the holocaust left a huge and lasting impact.

There is no single standard questionnaire, administered at regular intervals by the same agency over the entire period, that would enable us to pinpoint the moments of change. But it is obvious that broad shifts in attitudes—as revealed by the polls, at any rate—took place during and after the war. The earliest survey findings date from the years up to 1940, when America was not yet actively involved in the war, when Hitler's anti-Jewish program had not reached the stage of mass murder, and when anti-Semitic organizations were becoming increasingly noticeable in America. In those days, about two-thirds of the respondents said Jews had objectionable traits; from half to one-third stated Jews were unscrupulous or less honest than gentiles, or had too much power; from one-fifth to one-sixth declared they had too much power in business or finance specifically; and one-tenth held that they were too clannish. During the same time, over half the respondents would not have married Jews, almost half would have preferred not to employ them, over a fourth felt that colleges should limit their admission and almost a fifth objected to them as neighbors. As of 1962, however, all these indices had been cut by at least one-half, except for rejection of marriage with Jews, where the decline was smaller.[28]

This terminal result was a trough in a cycle which had previously mounted from prewar levels to a peak in the mid-1940s. In the period just before Pearl Harbor, propaganda against the Jews had considerable saliency for the general public; and it was coming increasingly from native quarters. Initially, its most prominent source had been groups considered alien, like the German-American Bund, but now nativist anti-war circles, led by so noted an American hero as Colonel Charles A. Lindbergh, became its best-known purveyors. True, only a strikingly limited proportion of persons familiar with organized anti-Semitic propaganda actually agreed with some of its specific charges, for example, that of "Jewish warmongering." [29] Also, certain stereotypes identified with the extremes and excesses of Nazi anti-Semitism were already disreputable here, and became more so with America's growing involvement in the conflict. But some anti-Jewish stereotypes which did not bear this stigma, far from declining, grew increasingly popular during the war and its immediate aftermath.

Thus, Jews were named as particularly prone to dodge the draft by 33 per cent of respondents in 1941, by 42 per cent in 1945; and when asked to choose likely draft dodgers from a list of groups including German and Italian Americans, respondents in 1944 and 1945 named Jews twice as frequently as any other group. Between 1938 and 1945, a rising proportion said Jewish power and influence in America were too great; more than half so stated between October 1942 and February 1946. (After the latter date, the question was not asked again until 1962, by which time the positive response dropped to one-sixth.) When asked which nationality, religious or racial groups in this country were a menace to America, respondents during 1942 most frequently named Germans and Japanese, but from June 1944 until February 1946 Jews were named more often than any other group. In contrast, Jews no longer headed the list when the question was asked once more in November 1950; all other groups also were now mentioned far less often.[30]

How are these figures, and others like them, to be interpreted? Why, in particular, did German and Japanese Americans, the kinsmen of the nation's foes, serve as the main targets of suspicion, fear or perhaps resentment only during the early part of the war, and then fall far behind the Jews, while the Negroes began to share the Jews' perilous eminence as a supposed national menace? Stember explains these phenomena as part of "a wave of general intolerance—a result of wartime frustrations and anxieties, already endured for two years and a half, and culminating during that crucial spring [of 1944] in the tensions and terrors of the Normandy invasion." [31] In other words, he believes the failure of sympathy or rise of antipathy toward the Jews to have been caused by a wartime hysteria, resulting from strain and directed not specifically against them but against all available scapegoats.

Again, how significant was the rise in antagonism? Was it simply an increase of ill feeling within the limits of an established relationship, or did it signal the rise of that extremist hostility which seeks to destroy the relationship? To put it differently, did wartime hysteria produce what we have referred to as epidemic anti-Semitism or did it merely heighten the endemic kind? Stember's argument implies that the two types were not sharply distinct, but were bridged by a continuum, at least for a certain period. Thus, before the explanation just quoted, he describes a set of findings intended to show that potential support for and opposition against organized anti-Semitic campaigns exerted a push-and-pull effect on each other during most of the war:

While the opposition to anti-Jewish campaigns did not vary greatly, major increases in the anti-Semitic potential were echoed, during most of the period under study, by at least some waning of the opposed groups, and a decrease in anti-Semitism was accompanied by some slight increase in the opposed camp. In other words, as recruits flowed from the apathetic middle into the ranks of the active anti-Semites and their sympathizers, some others shifted from anti-anti-Semitism to apathy.

This generalization, he feels, holds until 1944:

The opposition did not close ranks and opinion did not become polarized until anti-Semitism attained its high point in June 1944; . . . at this time, opposition also reached a maximum, and subsequently both fell off at comparable rates.[32]

By June 1944, then, the range of attitudes from anti-anti-Semitism to organized anti-Semitism no longer formed a continuum in which a shift at one end could be felt all the way to the other. Opinion now was "polarized"—that is, discontinuous—so that increased or decreased Jew-hatred was matched by increased or decreased resistance to Jew-hatred.

I am unable to find the supposed inverse relationship between anti-Semitism and active opposition to it in Stember's figures for the period from April 1940 to June 1944 (or March 1945). The most striking aspect of the polls, to me, is the consistency with which some 30 per cent of the respondents throughout the war said they would "actively oppose" organized anti-Jewish activity. Now it is true that the questionnaire allowed respondents to choose between degrees of feeling only in voicing anti-Semitism ("support" or "sympathy" for a campaign against the Jews), not in expressing opposition to anti-Semitism; but it would seem that, as long as active support was distinguished from mere sympathy on one side of the issue, the single available choice on the other side, "active opposition," must have been taken literally by the respondents. If so, then about 30 per cent of the people, throughout the war, really were not just tolerant of Jews —they were hostile to anti-Semitism and willing to fight it. Given the circumstances of the Second World War, they must have been consciously anti-Nazi, must have believed the news of Hitler's genocide program and probably supported the demands for a second front in Europe.

In our opinion, anti-Jewish feeling culminating in the spring of 1944 was a specific reaction to these and similar demands on the American conscience. Principled anti-Nazism aroused resistance, which stiffened with the prospect of sacrificing additional American lives in opening a second front; and this resistance inevitably became associated with hostility against the minority that seemed most clearly interested in getting America deeper and deeper into the war: the Jews. Even though hostility against other minorities was also increasing, there is no mistaking the special animus against the Jews at that time. They became the target, not because they were a classic scapegoat, but because they, of all minority groups, appeared most involved in the critical issue of the moment—the chief source of current anxiety and irritated ambivalence.

Following the end of the war, the polls noted a sharp decline in potential support and sympathy for anti-Semitic campaigns. Professed willingness to oppose such campaigns actively showed a similar drop; but though the American foes of anti-Jewish agitation were becoming less militant, opposition to anti-Semitism was by no means decreasing. On the contrary, there are clear indications that anti-Semitism was being far more widely rejected as discreditable than ever before. Fewer and fewer Americans were willing to voice support or sympathy for organized Jew-baiting, and precisely for this reason, expressions of militancy against potential Jew-baiters came to appear less and less necessary.

After 1946, the direct evidence for this conclusion thins out, because new problems began to interest the American Jewish Committee and other sponsors of polls. Most of the old questions—for example, about the objectionable traits of Jews, their alleged excessive power or the prospects for organized anti-Semitism—were now replaced by items focusing on immediate political issues. However, a few questions, those about current criticisms of Jews, were continued during the 1950s, and the results showed a sharp, continuing decline of anti-Semitism from the level of the 1940s. Furthermore, by 1962 no less than 60 per cent of respondents said they would vote against a professed anti-Semite running for Congress—double the proportion of the 1940s. Organized anti-Semitism had become quite disreputable, and poll respondents obviously took this fact as their cue in choosing what they thought proper answers.[33]

The moment of change seems to have been the end of the war, and the reasons for the shift, given the immediate historical context, seem fairly clear. With the war won, no resentment of impending sacrifices "for the benefit of the Jews" remained to inhibit the public's awareness of what genocidal anti-Semitism really meant; and the successive revelations of horror in the postwar years hammered the point home. The new issues that arose in relation to the Jews, such as the struggle to create the State of Israel, did not directly impinge on America and demanded no significant sacrifices from the American conscience. (In contrast, Great Britain, being directly involved in Palestine, appears to have experienced a sharp rise of anti-Semitic feeling after the war.)

As we noted earlier, neither Hitler's destruction of the Jews in Europe nor the creation of Israel fitted into the accustomed framework of attitudes toward the Jews, the traditional balance between hostility and tolerance. This was even more true of the latter than of the former. The Nazis' "final solution of the Jewish problem" was, of course, vicious in a unique degree, but at least it has its analogues in a long history of expulsions, forced conversions and massacres. Such disruptions of established Jewish-gentile relations were familiar enough in Christian experience, with the result that a pattern of response had been set. To be sure, ordinary gentiles condemned excesses of epidemic anti-Semitism, so that even a mere agitator like the Reverend Charles E. Coughlin was described by poll respondents as a "radical." [34] Yet a degree of understanding was implied in such disapproval; for the same hostility was present in normal Jewish-gentile relations, though here it was checked and counterbalanced by tolerance.

Thus, when the Nazi persecutions were first reported, there was a natural predisposition to regard them as merely another outbreak of epidemic anti-Semitism—deplorable, of course, but hardly unfamiliar. This very sense of familiarity may have been one of the reasons why so large a part of the public could only gradually bring itself to believe the news of Hitler's annihilation program, a phemomenon quite different in scope and kind from any Jew-hatred that had gone before.

In contrast, the rise of Israel was understood from the beginning to be an event unique in kind as well as magnitude. It challenged existing attitudes toward Jews in a form for which there were no analogies to fall back on, at least none that had ever been applied to Jews.

The poll questions put to the American public suggest that the sponsoring agency did not wholly recognize the unprecedentedness of the Israel issue. On the contrary, they imply the fear that the rise of Israel might evoke a response according to the traditional stereotypes of political anti-Semitism. The same implicit assumption underlies Ringer's analysis. He sounds as if he were pleasantly surprised that the rise of Israel caused few Americans to suspect their Jewish fellow citizens of disloyalty; that American Jewry's sympathy and support for Israel were only rarely blamed for that country's clashes with the Arab states; in short, that old accusations were not extended to the new case, except among the shrinking band of confirmed anti-Semites.

The data might have been interpreted in a different way, also within traditional patterns of response to the Jews. It could have been argued that public opinion was swinging from the hostility component toward the tolerance component of the established syndrome; for, as Stember notes, favorable responses of Americans toward Zionism and Israel often were plainly motivated by sympathy for Jewish refugees and survivors of the holocaust. But he also points out that the public, at the same time, was quite cool to proposals for letting Jewish refugees into the United States. Thus the strong positive response to Israel could not well be attributed simply and solely to general good feeling toward Jews.

Some light is indirectly thrown on the Israel issue by the public's complex responses to questions associating Jews with Communism in the early 1950s. As we have noted, respondents refused to identify the Jews collectively with Communist espionage, even though the news at the time of the Rosenberg case could have been interpreted to support such an association. The recent history of genocidal anti-Semitism evidently had created definite and conscious inhibitions against anti-Jewish propaganda of this type. Extreme right-wing groups of the postwar era, such as the cohorts of Senator Joseph R. McCarthy, seem to have avoided the theme deliberately, as have their more recent successors, for example, the John Birch Society. Indeed, McCarthy for a while seemed able to perform the astounding feat of identifying Communist anti-Americanism with old-stock, liberal, Protestant, Ivy League, striped-pants Americans. Yet simultaneously, there was at least a negative indication that the publicly tabooed equation of Jews with Communism was still at work below the surface. In the late 1940s and early 1950s, Americans showed considerable willingness to admit to these shores European refugees who were described as victims of Communism. These victims may well have been specifically identified by the respondents as non-Jews, for simultaneous questions about refugees identifiable as Jews elicited a far less hospitable response.[35]

The theory that sympathy for Israel reflected a decline in anti-Semitism thus needs to be qualified. As the polls show, identical issues evoked widespread sympathy when raised apropos of Palestine or Israel, but little when brought up in connection with America. Specifically, readiness to see Jewish refugees admitted to Palestine was combined with reluctance to let them come to America. We can easily explain these reactions as expressions of a single attitude, modified in relation to different situations; but in doing so, we acknowledge that the long-established ambivalence between anti-Semitism and tolerance was still present, notwithstanding the evident decline or disrepute of Jew-hatred. The dual finding just cited suggests a mixture of humanitarian sympathy with hostility, such as one might expect within the traditional syndrome.

At the same time, however, a bifurcation of attitudes was evidently emerging: Respondents were beginning to distinguish between American

Jews and Israelis. Sentiments toward the former still remained within the accustomed ambivalent syndrome, whereas for the latter, analogies would have to be found not in traditional feelings toward Jews but in attitudes to foreign nations.

Such a development is not directly reflected in the polls, but elsewhere there is ample evidence of a general tendency to distinguish between Israelis and American Jews. The distinction is deliberately fostered by Jews in both countries. Gentiles, too, make a point of it; they do so, for example, when criticizing actions or policies of Israel, and thus escape the stigma of Jew-hatred. Furthermore, studies among Jewish college students show that images of the Israeli differ considerably from traditional stereotypes still prevalent in descriptions of American Jews.[36]

Indeed, some of the poll findings themselves reflect a differentiation of attitudes toward Jews in the two countries. Thus, during the 1950s, respondents refused to identify American Jews with Israeli policies. More important, conceptions of the Jews as a "race," "nationality" or "religious group" appear to have been influenced by the emergence of Israel: The definition of Jews as a religious group had become markedly shaky by 1962 (the number of persons who affirmed it varied with the sequence of the alternatives offered), while significantly more respondents now regarded Jews as a nationality "like French or Italians," or answered, "Don't know." The emergence of a Jewish polity in Israel, together with declining hostility toward Jews, may also have contributed to another poll finding: In recent surveys, far fewer individuals than formerly were ready to name ways, either objectionable or admirable, in which they perceived Jews as different from other people.[37] Presumably, particular stereotypes have been affected, too, though no questions were asked that might prove it.

This, obviously, is not to say that reactions to Israelis have become totally separated from reactions to Jews elsewhere. Even though Israel realizes a form of Jewish existence which, according to traditional myth, should have not come into being until the transhistorical millennium, the historic image of the Jew still applies to both Israelis and Diaspora Jews, and responses to the one undoubtedly affect responses to the other in at least some degree. When, for instance, a large proportion of respondents during the 1950s felt that America had a substantial interest in cooperating with little Israel, this somewhat unrealistic appraisal certainly reflected a current humanitarian concern with Jews generally.[38] Or, to take an example from the hostile camp: When extremist anti-Semitism in its traditional form became disreputable, many Jew-baiting organizations and the Arab propagandists with whom they cooperate chose to concentrate their fire on Israel which, as a power engaged in political conflict, could be depicted as fair game, and proceeded to apply all the old negative stereotypes to the new state. Yet, for all that, the existence of Israel seems bound to affect permanently the relations between Jews and gentiles, in that it establishes a fact not easily comprehended within the accustomed syndrome of hostility and tolerance.

What of the Future?

What remains is, of course, the prognostic question. Do the poll findings, especially the marked decline in apparent anti-Semitism since the war, foretell a radical change in the basic structure of Jewish-gentile relations? Stember's final paragraph answers this question rather tentatively. To take for granted that the observed improvements of attitude will continue in years to come, he writes,

. . . would be reckless as well as presumptuous, for throughout the long history of the Jews, periods of acceptance and security have alternated with periods of rejection and oppression. But we may confidently state the the current trend toward more and more complete acceptance of the Jew—both individually and in the abstract—appears unlikely to be reversed by anything short of a catastrophic crisis in American society. The longer such a crisis is averted, the more firmly will recognition of Jews as equal and respected fellow citizens become grounded in the mores of the American people.[39]

Before attempting a summary judgment, let us examine more closely what elements in the poll findings and in other pertinent experience would suggest such a conclusion. First, Hitler's attempted "final solution of the Jewish problem" has cast extremist anti-Semitism into deep and lasting disrepute in the Western, Christian world. Other atrocities have produced revulsion in their time and left their mark on history; but none would seem to have stirred such pervasive, enduring, profound feelings of guilt. And second, the rise of Israel has cast doubt on the entire myth of the eternal exile and punishment of the Jews.

Yet, however much attitudes toward the Jews may respond to salient, crucial immediate experiences, they also relate to the entire historic background of the Jews as perceived at the particular time. The striking and traumatic events of our own time do not erase this background. Even the rise of Israel, the most drastic of challenges to the conventional image of the Jew, is bound to become assimilated into a total pattern that will accommodate both the old and the new.

A radical departure from the past patterns of Jewish history might conceivably be caused by certain changes in the situation of the Jews in America—changes which have appeared on the horizon during the last generation, and which might eventually compel a thorough reorientation of conceptions and feelings. Some significant developments have actually occurred or are now occurring; others, less substantial, are being advocated for the sake of better communal relations or even viewed (mainly by Jews and their friends) as *faits accomplis*.

Among the changes of actual conditions we may mention a sharp decline in discrimination. Since the New Deal days, both law and public opinion have backed this development; industries and universities have opened up to Jews on a large scale. We might also record a recently noted sharp increase in mixed marriages, and observe that the effects of such unions are compounded, as an economist would say, by a multiplier: Not only does each marriage of a Jew with a gentile result in a more or less thoroughly integrated new family; it also exposes larger circles of relatives to one another's values, and thus helps penetrate the ideological barrier between Jews and gentiles in the intimacy of their homes.

Whatever the ultimate effect of these developments, they are far from unprecedented in Jewish experience. A similar mingling of Jews with gentiles, a similar blending of ideas and values, was known in ancient Alexandria and Rome, in modern Europe and in early America no less than in our day. In fact, wherever Jews lived in exile—at least until Hitler—the option of submergence by conversion or assimilation was open to them, and on rare occasions entire Jewish communities may actually have vanished in this way. But this is not likely to happen in America. Here, no matter how wide the fringe of absorption, a substantial nucleus of identifiable Jews will certainly remain. They will retain, in essence, their old minority status, and will continue to encounter attitudes fluctuating from anti-Semitism to toleration.

We must not let this conclusion be obscured by certain fashionable definitions, slogans and tags that have been promoted for the sake of communal harmony. Americans have grown accustomed, with striking readiness, to speaking of their "Judeo-Christian" civilization, as though the two religions were really on a par in our society. Within a few years, the notion of the "triple melting pot" (Catholic-Protestant-Jew) has become a cliché. This may sound like an improvement over the older claim that America "had no minorities"; for what that claim really meant was that a tyrannous majority would not recognize the nation's actual diversity. But on closer inspection, we find that the "triple melting pot" theory also denies the existence of minorities, though in a different way. It does not and cannot refuse to recognize diverse religions, for religious toleration is an explicit principle of the American idea; instead, it denies that any one of the three standard religions is the dominant and most "authentically American" faith.

The prevalence of conceptions like these confirms only that contemporary Americans are reluctant to countenance any form of religious strife and are particularly averse to blatant anti-Semitism. The conceptions themselves are in fact quite conventional and have little meaning or effectiveness. Sociologists have often observed that Americans expect one another to identify themselves as Catholics, Protestants or Jews (though self-definitions by nationality, like "Italian," "Swede," or "Jew" in the ethnic sense, also would raise no eyebrows). But this does not necessarily imply that Judaism can claim an equal share in American mores; and to assume that it can is to stir up certain uncomfortable questions.

When we try to visualize such an all-American Judaism, we conjure up a vague panorama extending from Ethical Culture to liberal Reform and a rather lax Conservatism. Orthodox Judaism does not fit in; it certainly would never be thought of as a force in the founding of American civilization or as an authentically American religion. What is worse, from time to time one is reminded that the whole acceptance of Judaism as validly American is rather provisional. Witness, for example, Robert M. MacIver's recent suggestion that Judaism stress its universal message and abandon or at least play down its distinctive, peculiar rites[40]—an echo, in milder tones, of certain disconcerting words Heinrich von Treitschke once flung in the face of "Germans of the Mosaic persuasion."

In cold fact, the acceptance of Judaism as an American faith, when voiced by Christians, frequently implies a degree of confidence that Judaism is progressing toward submergence. Similarly, in Jewish mouths, talk of a Judeo-Christian civilization or of a peer relationship among Catholics, Protestants and Jews often tacitly anticipates an eventual merger in a joint American religion. An unspoken premise of this anticipation is that the merger will occur in neutral territory inoffensive to Jews, perhaps in something like Unitarianism; but that is obviously an unfounded hope.

For all its novel appearance, this whole ideology is anything but new in Jewish history. It is a classic gambit to which Jews have resorted ever since the eighteenth-century Enlightenment, in an attempt to escape their position of religious dissent without undergoing conversion. What really distinguishes our present from our earlier position is something quite different: Hitlerism and, above all, the emergence of Israel have radically disoriented our sense of historic direction. The world of Jewish possibilities is no longer neatly confined between the beginning of our exile and a transhistorical end to this exile in the millennium. The most significant novel element in the Jewish experience today is not the relatively limited changes which these developments have so far wrought in gentiles' attitudes toward Jews; it is the attitude changes that now are needed among the Jews themselves.

NOTES

1. See p. 40.

2. For a convenient selection of the many varieties of Zionist theory, see Arthur Hertzberg, editor, *The Zionist Idea* (Garden City, N.Y.: Doubleday & Co., 1959), especially pp. 184–188, 215–216, 235–241, 262–269, 333–340, 355–366, 471–473.

3. For a fuller discussion of this point and other pertinent observations, see Ben Halpern, "Israel as a Zionist State," *Hazut (Forum for the Problems of*

Zionism, World Jewry and the State of Israel, Hebrew edition), IV:156–162 (1958); or *idem, The Idea of the Jewish State* (Cambridge, Mass.: Harvard University Press, 1961), pp. 214–216, where the same analysis is given in substance.

4. Arnold J. Toynbee, *A Study of History* (London: Oxford University Press, 1934–54), II, 234–248; IV, 236; but cf. XII, 209–217.

5. *Ibid.,* VI, 222–229; V, 657–659; VI, 103–107; VIII, 278 (note).

6. Toynbee echoes Agus' views with approval: *op. cit.,* XII, 87–88, 511–517, and especially 209–217. Agus has now set forth his theories in a book, *The Meaning of Jewish History* (New York: Abelard-Schuman, 1963); cf. the review of this work in *Midstream,* X, No. 4 (June 1964), 96–101.

7. The most recent version of Parkes' thesis appears in his *Antisemitism* (Chicago: Quadrangle Books, 1963); cf. the review of this work in *Commentary,* XXXVIII, No. 4 (October 1964), 84–87.

8. Parkes, *op. cit.,* p. 60.

9. Yehezkel Kaufmann, *Gola v'Nekhar* (Tel Aviv: Dvir, 1954), I, 525–526.

10. *Ibid.,* I, 175–256, 507–515, 525–558.

11. I hope the terms as used here will be readily understood. For an extended, technical elucidation of this usage, see Ben Halpern, "The Dynamic Elements of Culture," *Ethics,* LXV:225–249 (1955).

12. Jean Juster, *Les Juifs dans l'empire romain* (Paris: Librairie Paul Geuthner, 1914), I, 221, 245, 338–390, *et passim;* Salo W. Baron, *A Social and Religious History of the Jews* (2d ed.; Philadelphia: Jewish Publication Society, 1952–1960), I, 188–195, 379–383.

13. Juster, *op. cit.,* I, 248–290, *et passim;* Baron, *op. cit.,* II, Chapters XII and XIII.

14. Baron, *op. cit.,* III, Chapter XVIII; H. A. R. Gibb and Harold Bowen, *Islamic Society and the West* (New York: Oxford University Press, 1957), I, Part II, Chapter XIV; S. D. Goitein, *Jews and Arabs: Their Contact Through the Ages* (New York: Schocken Books, 1955), Chapter V.

15. See Joshua Trachtenberg, *The Devil and the Jews: The Medieval Conception of the Jew and Its Relation to Modern Anti-Semitism* (New Haven: Yale University Press, 1943).

16. See pp. 38–39. However, one gets the impression that the public is conditioned to cooperate with the polls, so that a large number of people who really are uncertain or undecided give positive or negative responses. It might be well to establish the facts by subjecting the polling situation to psycho-social experiment and observation, such as have been applied to the psychoanalytic interview. To correct any bias, questionnaires should normally include measures to gauge the intensity of the respondents' beliefs or feelings.

17. See pp. 43–45, 163–165. George Salomon has drawn my attention to the footnote on page 108, which similarly deals with inconsistent responses.

18. See p. 52.

19. See pp. 56–59, 64–67.

20. See pp. 55–56, 58.

21. Hence, the socio-psychological and the historical critic would disagree on what each considers the defects of available polls. The social psychologist might object to differences in question wording, changes in polling agencies, insufficient or irregular replication of studies—that is, to circumstances which would hinder him in constructing a reliable index and time series. The historian would be more likely to complain that certain questions were not asked at all. For example, the sponsors of polls may have refrained from exploring such matters of acknowledged importance as the image of the Jew as deicide, for fear of stimulating anti-Semitism by their very study. Again, questions of significance to historians may never have been asked because the sponsoring agency with its particular ideology remained unaware of their importance, while others which the sponsors considered vital may turn out to be historically irrelevant.

22. See pp. 68–73, 119, 123–127, 165, 211–212.

23. See p. 38.

24. See pp. 79–81.

25. See pp. 111–115, 141, 174, 184,

26. See p. 76.

27. See pp. 141–144.

28. See. p. 209.

29. See pp. 111–115.

30. See pp. 117, 121, 128.

31. See p. 133.

32. See. p. 132.

33. See pp. 60–61, 134.

34. See p. 113.

35. See pp. 151, 147.

36. See Simon N. Herman, *A Social Psychological Study of Chalutziut (Palestine Pioneering) in America* (unpublished doctoral dissertation, University of the Witwatersrand, Johannesburg [1949]).

37. See pp. 50, 62–66.

38. See pp. 181–182.

39. See p. 217.

40. Statement in the panel discussion, "The Individual vs. the Jewish Establishment," at the Annual Conference of the American Council for Judaism, May 8, 1964.

The Changing Image of the Jew and
the Contemporary Religious Situation:
An Exploration of Ambiguities

THOMAS F. O'DEA

CHARLES HERBERT STEMBER'S study, based upon polls taken between 1937 and 1962, records a marked change in American gentiles' expressed attitudes concerning Jews. According to his findings, both predispositions to anti-Semitic activity and expressions of anti-Semitic sentiment have declined. Specifically, four features of the traditional hostile image of the Jew have lost much of their currency: unscrupulousness and consequent success in money matters; "pushiness" or aggressiveness in the pursuit of careers and in social relations; clannishness or excessive in-group loyalty, outweighing allegiance to the general community; and uncleanliness or uncouthness. Certain ostensibly favorable ideas about Jews which, on closer inspection, turn out to be variants of the unfavorable ones just noted also are less widely accepted than they were.

The last fifteen of the years covered in the polls have not been without occasions of a kind which in earlier times probably would have given rise to anti-Semitism: the phenomenon of McCarthyism; the arrest of Soviet spies with Jewish names and Jewish backgrounds, at a time of strong anti-Communist feeling; the emergence of the State of Israel, vigorously supported by many American Jews; and the rise of a militant movement for Negroes' rights. Yet none of these developments elicited an anti-Jewish response. Indeed, it was precisely during these years that anti-Semitism underwent its sharp decline.

No data are presented in Stember's study for the years since 1963—a period of increased rightist activity and influence, culminating in the taking-over of the Republican Party by its extreme right wing during 1964, and of some hostile reaction ("backlash") on the part of whites against the growing agitation and protest among Negroes. Evidence other than polls, however, affords little reason to think that the extremist trends of these years at last produced the "usual" rise of anti-Semitism which the experience of many generations might have led us to expect. On the contrary, a man of Jewish antecedents (though himself a member of the Episcopal Church) became the spokesman, symbol and standard-bearer of the new vociferous right, the very movement that refused to repudiate "extremism."

The question thus arises whether anti-Semitism in America is dying— whether some deep and permanent alteration has begun in the public's outlook on this vexed problem. The polls, together with recent events, might be taken to indicate that such is the case. Yet, we cannot discount the possibility that the observed changes of attitude and sentiment may be merely superficial fluctuations, which might be canceled out at any time by abrupt and far-reaching shifts in the opposite direction.

We do not doubt that the polls accurately reflect the expressed attitudes of the moment, that is, that the populations sampled were representative and the persons interviewed sincere. We question, rather, whether survey responses can be accepted as evidence of deeper sentiment when they deal with a phenomenon of the psychological depth and historical longevity of anti-Semitism. To put it bluntly: Dare we trust the plain evidence of the polls? Do the attitudes voiced by the respondents faithfully reflect the deeper ground of the public's sentiment?

To help answer these crucial questions, we shall first seek to appraise the reported decline of anti-Semitism in the light of the religious situation in America, past and present. As we do so, we will discover significant differences between European and American traditions in the relationships between Christians and Jews. We also will observe important changes apparently taking place in American religious life today. But these investigations will leave us with merely tentative conclusions. They will not tell us definitely to what extent current changes on the American religious scene are actually religious in nature, nor just what the distinctively American tradition in Christian-Jewish relations proves for the meaning of Stember's poll data.

For deeper insights into the meaning of reported changes in public opinion, we will have to enter a second, far larger area of inquiry: the long-term sociological and historical significance of anti-Semitism. Our explorations in this field will first define the nature and the overt causes of modern political anti-Semitism as it has manifested itself since the late nineteenth century. Later, we will go back over the long centuries of Jewish history, tracing to its origins the accumulated heritage of animosity and bias from which modern anti-Semitism stems and to which it appeals.

It may be well to state at the outset that our investigations will be studies in ambiguity. We have no choice but to proceed cautiously to highly tentative conclusions; for not only do the poll findings themselves permit more than one reading, but so do some of the events and conditions against which the findings must be viewed. In particular, the present-day religious situation in America, as throughout the world, is equivocal. The ambiguity that prevails in this area is reflected in a series of questions which the American Jewish Committee prepared as a set of agenda for the present paper:

Are the shifts in attitude toward the Jew related to a growing secularism, which frees older individuals from traditionally held notions about the Jew which have their origin in religious teaching or practice, and prevents younger individuals from learning these notions?

Or can the shifts be explained by a growing religiosity on the part of the American public—a religiosity which influences people toward holding a benign attitude toward religious differences?

Why in fact has the Jew fared so well during a period of religious revival? Must one take the position that this revival has, in effect, been a secular revival and it is because of this secular element that the Jewish position has changed?

How has Judaism come to be regarded as one of the three major faiths and how has this conception reduced hostility?

The hypothesis on which we proceed and which we hope to confirm may be summarized as follows. We believe that relationships of Christians and Jews throughout the long centuries of European history have remained similar in their basic structure, changing only on the surface, and that out of this experience a rich and varied hostile imagery was precipitated in the minds of Christians. These images furnished the terms in which the Jew was usually perceived and defined; in addition, they were capable of arousing emotions, serving as symbolic organizers of feeling and triggers of action. Jews for their part developed a complementary imagery of gentiles that was perhaps less rich but no less unfavorable.

This background of hostile imagery, we submit, was transmitted from generation to generation as a subtle ingredient in cognition, value orientation and attitudes. It was constantly reinforced and "proven" in encounters between Jews and Christians, occuring as they almost always did in essentially analogous situations. Inevitably, the accumulation of emotion-laden hostile images grew ever deeper, more elaborate and less amenable to counterinfluences. This, we believe, is why anti-Semitic ideas have been such a long-lived and psychologically vigorous phenomenon in Western civilization.

It follows that traditional hostile images of Jews can be destroyed only when the context from which they sprang is changed, that is, when the unhappy Christian-Jewish relationships typical of the European past are replaced by more auspicious kinds of interaction. What concerns us in this paper is whether this has actually occurred or can be counted on to occur in America.

The American Religious Background: Protestantism plus Secularism

Seen in the long range, Western history shows an undeniable trend toward secularization. From the thirteenth century to the twentieth, more and more people became more and more concerned with worldly values, goals and pursuits. Unbelief increased; important, indeed dominant, spheres of life—government, industry, commerce, education—were largely removed from the sacral context in which they had been embedded during the Christian Middle Ages. Intermittent periods of religious revival caused the trend to fluctuate, but failed to alter its general direction.

For a century and a half, roughly from 1770 to 1920, secularization coincided with a great improvement in the condition of the Jew; in fact, the two developments were intimately related. Yet, nativist reactions against secularization at times gave anti-Semitism a new prominence during this era; and the years that followed—a time when Western civilization seemed more secularized than ever—saw the worst outbreak of anti-Jewish fanaticism in the history of Europe.

In this country, secularism has been a major force and has affected the condition of the Jew since early days. It played a significant role in the adoption of the Bill of Rights, the first legal document in the West to grant full emancipation to the Jew—emancipation on grounds so broad that he was not even mentioned by name. The Jew's equality and security in America were guaranteed, not by special legislation, but by Constitutional safeguards for the rights of all. In an ethnically diverse new nation, his ethnic identity was treated like that of any other group, at least as far as the law was concerned. His actual experience proved less clear-cut; but until social mobility enabled Jews in sizable numbers to become rich, while large-scale immigration from Eastern Europe brought masses of additional, almost uniformly poor, Jews to these shores, his condition was quite tolerable. Compared with most of his experience in the preceding centuries, it was unbelievably good. Thus it seems to us that, from the nation's beginnings onward, relations between Jews and Christians were not the same here as in Europe: They were such as to make the background of traditional hostile attitudes less relevant. That, in our opinion, is why anti-Semitism, though usually alive in the American imagination and at times widespread, never assumed the same proportions or significance here as in Europe.

Nor were the religious and social conditions of the United States in the nineteenth century suited to make the Jew an appropriate target for animosity, as were those in Europe. True, Civil War America was less secular, more markedly religious and manifestly Protestant, than revolutionary America had been; unbelief was less widespread or at least less popular.

But in the decades after the Civil War, many areas of American life, notably the universities and intellectual life generally, once more became markedly secularized; and, most important, group hostility and distrust on the part of the nation's Protestant majority were finding a target more suitable than the Jews.

Both before and after the Civil War, Catholic immigrants from Ireland and Germany arrived in large numbers, setting off a hostile (at times violent) reaction. It was these Catholic newcomers who were destined to become the prime objects of hostile nativism—not the Jews, who were a smaller, less ubiquitous group and who seemed to fit in better, if only because their values were more like those of Americans. During the nineteenth and early twentieth centuries, anti-Catholicism came to fill the role in America which anti-Semitism played in Europe after 1870. As late as the 1920s, hatred of Catholics was a more important part of the revived Ku Klux Klan's message than hatred of Jews; it appealed more genuinely and more deeply to nativist sentiments.

The Catholic was a significant symbolic figure in the Protestant imagination. Anti-Catholic sentiment and its attendant imagery, dating from the period of the Reformation and the Wars of Religion which followed, formed an important set of inherited attitudes in the American Protestant pre-conscious. This hostility found a tremendous resonance among the older elements of the American culture. The Reformation had been the great event of the European past; "No Popery" had been an important slogan during the American Revolution, in response to Britain's Quebec Act of 1774, with its favorable terms for the Catholic Church in North America. Thus, mass immigrations of Catholics could easily be interpreted in terms of an already accumulated apperceptive symbolism.

Moreover, in many places from about 1850 on, the Catholic was typically an Irishman; the words "Catholic" and "Irish" became nearly synonymous in common speech. This meant that he was perceived in terms, not only of religious difference, but also of outright religious conflict. The Irish came to America from the scene of the perennial struggle with their English rulers— a struggle which had reached its full bitterness as a result of the Reformation. In America, residues of this old-world battle between Catholics and Protestants became the chief organizing symbols of thought and sentiment in what Ray Allen Billington has called a "Protestant crusade." [1]

The immigrant from Ireland, in short, was apperceived in terms of certain long-inherited, widely current modes of cognition and feeling, which had become incorporated with the imagery of American Protestant popular tradition. Furthermore, he responded to the hostility and suspicion with which he was received according to ready modes of thought and feeling which *he* had brought with him, and which his entire previous history had precipitated into *his* consciousness. Thus, his relations with the dominant Protestant group were essentially analogous to those he had known in Europe, with the same deep substratum of mutually hostile images and attitudes.

The Jew, as we have seen, was in a different position. An America compounded of denominational Protestantism and secularism offered a significantly altered context for his relations with gentiles—a context more favorable than he had known in Europe. The contrasting nativist reactions to the Irish and the Jews thus support our hypothesis that intergroup hostility is likely to persist where relations are structurally analogous to those which prevailed when the emotion-laden imagery of the conflict was originally precipitated into the culture.

The American Religious Situation Today

Today more Americans, absolutely and proportionately, are affiliated with churches than ever before. Polls as well as membership rolls reveal this fact: In surveys, more than 75 per cent of Americans call themselves church members. Moreover, between 95 and 97 per cent say they believe in God; some 73 per cent claim to believe in an afterlife, and in God as the judge of human behavior. An overwhelming majority hold religion to be something of importance, most believe in prayer and some 90 per cent say they pray on some occasions in their lives. As Franklin H. Littell points out, America is more churched today than ever before in her entire history.[2] These facts might be taken to mean that a religious revival has occurred in the last decade or two.

Whether the recent growth of church membership and attendance really represents an increase in belief is another question.[3] In the polls just cited, 80 per cent of the respondents also stated that they were most serious, not about the otherworldly concerns of the religions in which they said they believed, but in living as well and comfortably as possible in this world. When those who had described religion as something very important were asked, "Would you say your religious beliefs have any effect on your ideas of politics and business?" 54 per cent replied that such beliefs had no real effect, while 37 per cent said they had and 7 per cent gave no answer. In contrast, 91 per cent of the respondents declared they were really trying to lead a good life, 78 per cent thought they measured up more than halfway to their own standards of goodness and over half said they completely obeyed the counsel to love their neighbors as themselves. If, as Edward Sapir observed four decades ago, genuine religion is everywhere the enemy of self-satisfaction, such findings suggest that perhaps there has been no religious revival at all.[4]

Seymour M. Lipset, mustering the relevant statistics, has shown that increases in church membership and practice have been at best moderate, and that among some groups there has been an actual decline.[5] He and many others suggest that the apparent increase in religiosity masks what is in fact advancing secularization. In a somewhat related vein, Littell concludes that while the churches in America have achieved a new popularity, they still face the task of Christianizing and converting their new members. What took place in the 1950s, he holds, was only a "pre-religious revival": a renewed interest in churches, occasioned by a quest for values and community, but not yet a resurgence of religion.

Will Herberg has proposed the hypothesis that Americans, now three or more generations removed from their European cultural backgrounds, and often third-generation city dwellers, have turned to religion in their search for identity within our mass society with its characteristic social mobility. The old ethnic identities are being outgrown; the nation as a whole is too large, and the fact of being an American too indefinite, to serve as meaningful sociological reference points. According to Herberg, religious affiliation comes to fill this need, providing the individual with a significant reference group. To be an American today means to be identified with one of the "three great religions of democracy": Protestantism, Catholicism or Judaism. Religious identification and membership in the religious group have taken over what used to be the ethnic group's role as intermediary between the individual and the nation as a whole.

That the theory interprets correctly much that we see about us would seem clear enough. Gerhard Lenski reports that it was tested in Detroit and, with some modification, held up: Increasing church attendance was found positively correlated with increasing Americanization. Yet all this merely points up the ambiguousness of the situation. Robin Williams notes that religion in America has been losing its otherworldly character, and Herberg himself sees little deepening or intensification of genuine faith. The new religiosity which he thinks is developing does not seem to him to be deeply infused with the spirit of prophetic Judaism or New Testament Christianity.

Beneath the distinctive creeds of the three "religions of democracy" lurks a consensus on secular values, according to Herberg. America, he suggests, really has a common religion in the "American way of life"—the familiar constellation of beliefs and values based upon the Constitution, so-called free enterprise, a formal egalitarianism (accompanied by a belief in competition and social mobility), respect for the individual and a commitment to striving and achievement. It is an idealistic but not an otherworldly creed, compounded of beliefs and values that have long been operative among the American people. As affluence increases, as structural changes in business, education and technology create new opportunities, as the dying-away of ethnic differences and the expansion of the mass media strengthen egalitarianism, these values seem destined to achieve wider currency and an ever more central position on the American scene.[6]

We may reasonably assume that these developments are affecting the position of the Jew and the structure of Jewish-Christian relations. To the degree that adherence to a particular creed becomes less important than membership in one (any one) of the three religious "establishments," Judaism attains an equivalence with Christianity which it has not achieved elsewhere; the dichotomy between the two religions loses some of its salience, and acceptance of Jews is facilitated. The process parallels changes in other areas—for example, the fading of the old-world ethnic awareness that used to make Jewishness appear as something alien and uncouth, or the new social mobility fostered by education, which is breaking down the Jews' concentration in certain socio-economic sectors and thus weakening the notion of the Jew as a moneyman. In this fashion, the common American way of life wears down the stereotypes of the old inherited imagery.

Whatever its spiritual state, religion in present-day America seems to have achieved a new respectability among intellectuals, while a serious concern with contemporary issues appears to have significantly increased in religious circles. One of the most striking illustrations of this trend is the rise of an articulate intelligentsia among Catholic laymen—a development closely related to the *aggiornamento* initiated by Pope John XXIII. How developments like these might affect the public's attitude toward the Jew is a matter for speculation. They certainly would seem suited to make Christians increasingly aware of the horrors of anti-Semitism; the memory of the Nazi era presumably would be a major factor, perhaps the leading one, in any such sensitizing process. Albert Schweitzer has suggested that both Catholics and Protestants "became guilty, by simply accepting the terrible, inhuman fact of the persecution of the Jews." This guilt is felt in many places, as can be seen in the statement on the Jews adopted by the Second Vatican Council.

Some observers nonetheless foresee continuing religious conflict in America. Thus, Earl Raab suggests that, even though religious bigotry has considerably declined, religious controversies may actually have become sharper.[7] Issues such as state aid and bus service for parochial schools, or Christmas celebrations, Bible reading and prayers in public ones have provoked widespread discussion in the years since the war—a by-product of new social mobility and suburbanization. The record clearly shows that such controversies provide occasions for revived anti-Semitism, at least in the short run. Whether they will increase or subside, persist or disappear, remains to be seen.

Finally, international developments no doubt will continue to bear indirectly on Christian-Jewish relations in this country. During recent times, American solidarity has been strengthened by the existence of a hostile alien ideology and a hostile foreign power complex. Foreign-policy issues have become much more significant for America than formerly, and far more salient in the consciousness of the public. As a result, frustrations and aggressions which formerly would have found an outlet in anti-Catholicism or anti-Semitism have been achieving catharsis through the symbols and imagery of anti-Communism.

To sum up: We noted earlier that Christians and Jews in America have from the beginning confronted each other in situations which, unlike those traditionally found in Europe, did not continually reinforce traditional hostile images and sentiments. Since the Second World War, the conditions of Christian-Jewish encounter have been further broadened and diversified by social change—especially by alterations in the significance of religion, such as the replacement of ethnic by religious identity in the popular consciousness; the weakening concern with creed and with differences in creed; the emergence of a single, more or less secular consensus within the framework of varied religious groupings; and the recognition of Judaism as one of the nation's major faiths. Combined with other trends, such as the growing role of education in fostering social mobility, these developments may be creating a structural basis for genuinely new intergroup learning.

That such a process has actually been going on can hardly be doubted; yet it would seem neither sound nor safe to assume that the resulting changes have lasted long enough or reached deep enough to assure the demise of anti-Jewish hostility. Before we can draw a firmer conclusion, we must consider the sociological meaning of anti-Semitism itself.

The Sociological Significance of Manifest Political Anti-Semitism

Modern political anti-Semitism began in Germany and Austria during the 1870s. In Russia and elsewhere in Eastern Europe, it found an echo almost at once, in France somewhat later. During the twentieth century, it was to become a major political force. The end of the First World War, which saw formal emancipation of Jews enjoined by treaties and covenants, also marked the beginning of a large-scale growth in anti-Jewish agitation—a growth destined to culminate in the rise of Nazism and the horror of Hitler's "final solution."

The anti-Semitic outbursts in various parts of Europe during this era were usually related to events that upset domestic tranquillity, economic prosperity or general stability. They were often part of pronounced nativist reactions to change. The eruption in Germany and Austria during the 1870s followed upon the heels of the ruinous financial crisis of 1873. The beginning of the Russian pogroms in the early 1880s had for its background the economic effects of the emancipation of serfs barely a generation earlier; at the same time, Slavophile sentiment and ideology were rising in a Russia uncomfortably confronted with the culture of Western Europe. The French outbreaks of the 1890s, centering upon the case of Captain Alfred Dreyfus and his monarchist and militarist foes, occurred soon after the scandalous bankruptcy of the Panama Company, which had ruined half a million members of the middle class. And the tragedy of Hitlerism began in a Germany afflicted successively by defeat in the First World War, disastrous inflation and the Great Depression.

As has often been pointed out, a scapegoat was a functional necessity on these occasions, and a manifest connection between the Jews and the crisis was easily established. In Russia, Jews played an important economic role within the Pale of Settlement, the western provinces to which they were confined. In France, Jewish agents had helped bribe Parliament to authorize a bond issue that was to stave off the Panama Company's collapse; the net effect had been to enlarge the ranks of the ruined when the Company foundered after all. In Germany, Jews had long been involved in state finance and in a few industries; furthermore, they were prominent in the arts and sciences, and were entering public-service careers in somewhat increasing numbers under the Weimar Republic.

Yet, do the surface events explain adequately why in each case the Jew was chosen to be the scapegoat, and why anti-Semitism, once aroused, was so virulent? One cannot but agree with Hannah Arendt that the reaction in these and similar situations has been so out of scale with the actual involvement of Jews as to affront common sense. Distrust of cultural and religious differences, buttressing of in-group loyalty by hostility against others are fairly constant human phenomena, however reprehensible they may be; though they outrage any enlightened conscience, they do not surprise the social scientist. But even the expert is shocked by political anti-Semitism's savage terror against a powerless minority, which was not guilty, and would not have deserved such frightful treatment if it had been.

If we are to understand modern political anti-Semitism, we must go below the level of manifest events to the underlying sentiments. Forces deeper than momentary excitement were at work when Wilhelm Marr gained notoriety in 1873 with his pamphlet, *The Victory of Judaism Over Germanism;* when a fight in a provincial Russian tavern could set off anti-Jewish riots that engulfed 167 towns and villages in a few weeks; when the cry of "Kill the Jews" echoed through the streets of enlightened Paris; when a democratic Germany handed the reins of power to a racist demagogue.

In each instance, emotionally charged images and attitudes concerning Jews lay beneath the surface of the collective consciousness, waiting to be activated. That deeper level of cultural reality was the product of a long, still seemingly relevant history. Christians and Jews in Europe, like Protestants and Catholics in America, were facing each other from the vantage points of their respective experiences. They lacked a common background, a common interpretation of the past, and thus could not arrive at common viewpoints in the present.

To what extent emancipation failed to create such a common ground between Christians and Jews is further illustrated in the peculiar nature of friendships between them. Such friendships have occurred for at least two centuries, but they have frequently exhibited a peculiar gingerliness, a well-meaning stereotypy. For example, when Jews first gained entree to some of Germany's fashionable salons during Moses Mendelssohn's time, they were received as specimens of the "universal humanity" which the Romantic age thought it had discovered; and a century later, the *haut monde* of Paris—the society described by Marcel Proust—welcomed the Jew as an intriguing representative of a kind of spiritual underworld. In neither case were the members of the majority ready to accept the Jewish visitor simply as an individual, to be viewed and judged by the same standards as others.

Nor has America, for all its greater progress toward mutual acceptance between Jews and Christians, remained free of this self-consciousness among the well-disposed. One striking example is a peculiar taboo current as recently as the postwar years among presumably objective sociologists and social psychologists. It was then unthinkable to suggest that anti-Semitism must be studied in a reciprocal context; that all stereotypes are products, however distorted, of historical experience; that it is fruitless to seek the key to anti-Semitism in gentile "pathology" alone, neglecting the attitudes of Jews. In this hands-off policy, as in the arm's-length acceptance practiced by European high societies of yesteryear, a residue of the old mutual alienation still lingers.

Underlying Images: The Pagan and Early Christian Eras

We must now trace the historical origins of the various emotion-laden images of the Jew—the components of the latent substrate of feeling which makes manifest anti-Semitism possible. In what follows, we schematically distinguish four phases: (1) the pagan centuries of the Roman Empire and the emergence of Christianity; (2) the Christianized Empire and the Middle Ages; (3) the era of rising secularism and nationalism; and (4) the epoch of modern political anti-Semitism.

Throughout the early years of Imperial Rome, Palestine was torn by a nationalist struggle. The Roman rulers dealt severely with this movement; their policy of repression reached a climax in 70 A.D., when the Second Temple was destroyed and Jerusalem was barred to Jews. Long before these events, however, large numbers of Jews had left Palestine. They established communities in many of the Empire's urban centers, lived much like other ethnic minority groups and apparently experienced the same conditions of accommodation and conflict. The Roman authorities usually treated the scattered Jewish communities with forbearance, even granting them such unusual concessions as exemption from military service and recognition of their Sabbath. From time to time, public disturbances upset or reversed these policies; thus, in 19 A.D., the Emperor Tiberius expelled the Jewish community from Rome, and in 38 A.D., at Alexandria, a visit by

Agrippa I, the King of Judea, occasioned what can fairly be called a pogrom. But the Constitution of Caracalla (212 A.D.) gave Jews the privileges and responsibilities of citizenship, and from that time on their position seems to have been better than that of other dissenting religious groups.

Considerable cultural assimilation took place in pre-Christian antiquity —witness the Septuagint (the oldest Greek translation of the Hebrew Bible), which dates from this period. Yet, in the general thinking of the pagan era, Jews were viewed largely in terms of their ethnic differences, of which their religion formed an important constituent. Social segregation developed at this time, and with it a sense of cultural and religious otherness. Gentiles began to feel suspicious of, or superior to, Jews, and to perceive them as mysterious aliens. In centuries to come, these sentiments were to be reinforced by ever richer imagery.[8]

Meanwhile, Christianity was starting out on its meteoric rise. Though the Church began as a Jewish sect, it was to bring about a significant change in the Jews' status. Hostility between Christians and Jews began early. At first, controversy centered on the question whether or not Jesus of Nazareth was the Messiah—a conflict fought in terms of the implications of the Jewish Scriptures. Soon the Jews came to be perceived as the leading challengers of the claim that Christianity was "the true, original, universal religion of humanity, that it predated and outshone all that the poets, philosophers and lawgivers of Greece and the East could offer. It could make such a claim only on the basis of the possession, as exclusively part of its own history, of the story of Israel as revealed in the Old Testament." [9]

From the beginning of their relationship, then, the Christian perceived the Jew as a living rejection of, and challenge to, his faith. A new image came into being: the Jew as doubter. Indeed, the Christian, viewing the Old Testament through the interpretive prism of the New, saw him as the descendant of those who had slain the prophets and put Jesus to death. The scorn which Roman satirists like Petronius and Juvenal had heaped upon the Jews as a cultural minority was thus augmented by religious animosity. St. Ambrose, for example, denounced their synagogue as a home of insanity and unbelief, condemned by "God whom they have insulted . . . Christ whom they have crucified." [10] Minority alien, distrusted and resented; repudiator of the true faith; doubter and deicide—the accumulation of hostile imagery had begun. Begun in circumstances, moreover, where real interests were involved, and where the images could be learned again and again, acquiring ever deeper connotations. The foundation for differential apperception, mutual suspicion, antagonism and institutionalized segregation had been laid.

The Growth of Imagery in Christian Europe

The Edict of Milan (313 A.D.) recognized both Christianity and Judaism as lawful religions; in effect, however, it heralded the official Christianization of the Empire. The Jews' condition now suffered a radical transformation and deterioration. The later Christian emperors conceived it as their civic and religious duty to combat infidelity and heresy; their edicts described Judaism as a *secta nefaria* (nefarious sect) and Jewish religious gatherings as *sacrilegi coetus* (sacrilegious meetings).

In the disordered centuries that followed, the Christian faith became the official religion of the European culture, the Church the central institution of the society and Christian thought the dominant source of ideas on the meaning of human existence. Christendom as a cultural entity, the Catholic Church as an ecclesiastical organization, and the civil community, including the state, all became interpenetrating elements of a single cultural and societal fabric. Under these conditions, unbelievers constituted a challenge to the needed consensus of the society and to the very conception that gave human life its accepted meaning.

Unbelievers who were heretical Christians were exterminated wherever practicable, heresy being seen as an evil to be eradicated, rather than as a mere error that might have been embraced in good faith. The Jews were placed in a different category: "The Church, conscious that Christianity is founded on Judaism, recognized their right to live and to practice their religion without interference. . . . This right, however, was conditioned by the stipulation, which the Fathers of the early Church had often emphasized, that they were to live in a state of misery and degradation. The sons of the bondwoman must be kept in subjection to the sons of the freewoman." [11] Accordingly, Jews were hedged about with restrictions and disabilities. The idea that their "natural rights" were inviolable was a theoretical concession of limited significance; in practice it was frequently transgressed.

Popes, bishops and princes often protected Jews from the fury of popular attacks, but the uncertainty of that protection illustrates the ambiguity and difficulty of the Jews' position. For example, according to Gratian's *Decretum,* the 57th canon of the fourth national Council of Toledo in 633 declared that Jews who had been compelled to become Christians and had received the sacraments should remain Christians; the validity of these compulsory conversions was not to be questioned. In the future, moreover, no one was to be constrained to believe: "The Jews are not to be saved in spite of themselves, but freely, so that all justice be safeguarded. Conversions are to be made by consent, not constraint, by persuasion, not force." Yet only five years later, another council gave thanks to God that the King had ordered the Jews to leave Spain, so that there be none but Christians in the country.[12]

Half a millennium later, in 1120, Pope Calixtus II issued a *Constitutio pro Judaeis* to stop Crusaders from massacring Jews in their own regions; Pope Innocent III reissued it in 1199. The second version of this much-hailed document states: "Although the Jewish perfidy is in every way worthy of condemnation, nevertheless, because through them the truth of our own faith is proved, they are not to be severely oppressed by the faithful." [13] In 1190, moreover, Pope Clement III forbade "anyone to compel the Jews to receive baptism against their will." Thus, St. Thomas Aquinas appears to have spoken for the custom and general mind of the Church when he forbade the baptism of the children of Jews without the consent of their parents.[14] However, no less a thinker than Duns Scotus disagreed with St. Thomas on involuntary conversion; and the very fact that the subject was discussed over such an extended period is suggestive of the psychological atmosphere that surrounded the relations of Christians and Jews throughout the Middle Ages. Moreover, whatever their theological status, in their civil conditions the Jews were considered "serfs of the Church" and "bondsmen of the princes by civil bondage."

Malcolm Hay has said: "The Popes of the Middle Ages often intervened, not always effectively, to defend Jews against personal violence, but seldom wrote a line to condemn the ill-will which made such violence inevitable." [15] At the deeper level of psychological reality, religious imagery filled with hostile sentiments accumulated throughout these centuries, and no institution in the culture attempted to counteract the accumulation. What had begun in the early Christian period continued and deepened: The image of the Jew as perfidious doubter and deicide became ever more fixed. In the sacral society of the Middle Ages, the Jews were sacral outcasts, possessed of what Durkheim would call an impure sacredness.

Simultaneously, the Jew's economic role provided an entire new dimension for animosity. In the classical period, urban minorities had subsisted by commerce and craftmanship, and these had been the Jew's usual pursuits in early Christendom. During the Middle Ages, the Jew was kept out of political life and most other fields. Amid an agrarian society he remained associated with commerce; in Carolingian times the words *Jew* and *merchant* were synonyms. Agrarian societies tend to distrust merchants and, as Tawney and Fanfani have shown, Medieval Europe was particularly prone to do so, because Christian morality viewed commerce with misgivings. Thus, the Jew, already cast as an ethnic and cultural alien, doubter and deicide, was also invested with the suspect role of merchant—in a society where spontaneous dislike of commerce was reinforced by religious sanction.

With the rise of a Christian mercantile class during the twelfth century, the Jews were gradually driven from commerce. They now entered the only activity still open to them: moneylending, an occupation specifically forbidden to Christians (though not with complete success) by the Church. Moneylending, or usury as it was called, was a necessity in the medieval economy, but its role was not the same as in the expanding industrial societies of later ages. Given the conditions of the period, the usurer appeared all too often as one who took advantage of his fellow men's calamity and distress, becoming "one of the most thoroughly despised and hated members of the medieval community." [16] Forced into this despised though necessary function, the Jew became detested for a new reason—one that exhibited, even more than commerce, the negative sacral character with which he was already associated. "Here was a vicious circle from which there was no escape for the Jew. Society conspired to make him a usurer—and usury exposed him to the cupidity of feudal overlords and to the embittered hatred of the people."

Joshua Trachtenberg has shown how the words "Jew" and "usurer" became synonyms at a time when the Church condemned usury much as it did heresy. A new order of imagery arose, in which the Jew was associated with Judas Iscariot and ultimately with the devil. "Thus the Jew was obliged to bear the brunt of popular feeling against the moneylender from the outset, and long after his short-lived prominence in the field had been preëmpted by others, he still remained *the* usurer in the mass memory and had to suffer for the sins of his successors. . . . The Jew-heresy-usury equation became a medieval cliché; not even the terminology suffered change. Christian moneylenders were forced to hear themselves slandered as 'those other Jews, called Christians,' or simply *Kristen-Juden;* in the fifteenth century Christian usury became known in Germany as *Judenspiess,* the 'Jews' spear.' At a time when Jews as such had been unknown in England for several centuries, Sir Francis Bacon recommended in his essay 'Of Usury' (1612) that all usurers 'should have tawny orange bonnets, because they do Judaize.' " In the sixteenth century Luther referred to the Jews as usurers and the "devil's saints." [17]

Thus, the historical experience of more than a millennium created, in what Trachtenberg calls the "mass memory," a complex image which represented the Jew as an ethnic and cultural alien, a mysterious outsider, a doubter and deicide, the repudiator of God and the killer of Christ, a merchant among farmers, a usurer, a Judas in league with the devil. And during all that time, the structural conditions of society were perfectly fitted to preserve these conceptions, indeed to enlarge their psychological depth and emotional impact.

Responding to this experience, Jews became increasingly separate and alien in their self-definition, accepting the institutionalized state of war implicit in their position. They tried to convert Christians on a number of occasions, and were commonly accused of seeking to subvert Christianity.

A passage in Jean de Joinville's *Chronicle of the Crusades* speaks volumes concerning such animosities during the thirteenth century: St. Louis of France, so admirable in most respects, is said to have called for running a sword through a Jew who spoke with disrespect of the Virgin Mary.

The Jews certainly did become, if anything, even more attached to their faith than before; moreover, they organized themselves into separate communities, which were legally recognized in the corporate medieval state. These communities were autonomous, enjoying a considerable degree of self-government, though on a precarious base. The laws they framed were often quite comprehensive, regulating business, religious life, dress, even pleasures and amusements, in such a way as not to arouse the jealousy of gentiles. Institutions of social welfare and education were carefully maintained.

Thus, the Jew and his life became ever more ingrown and alien, providing a more and more plausible basis for charges of clannishness. His visibility —heightened at times by the compulsory wearing of a badge or distinctive dress—further accentuated his otherness. The cultural coexistence under these institutionalized conditions was well suited to deepen the psychological substrate of hostility which Europe was to retain until modern times. Indeed, this discrete yet shared experience of long-lived, institutionalized reciprocal hostility forms the common core of the Jew's and the gentile's histories.

From the time of the First Crusade on, Jewish life was racked by periodic mass onslaughts. The first of the many pogroms that make up this unhappy chronicle occurred in the Rhineland in 1096. Later, mass violence culminated in expulsion, a policy that began in England under Edward I, in 1290, and continued until 1591, when the Jews were driven from the Duchy of Milan, newly occupied by Spain. Western Europe, by and large, gradually became closed to the Jews. There were exceptions: Some were allowed to stay, under ever-tightening restrictions, in parts of northern Italy, certain regions of Germany and the Papal possessions in the south of France; and nominal converts to Christianity, the so-called Marranos, for some time remained in the Iberian Peninsula, practicing their old religion in secret. But the bulk of European Jewry went east during the age of expulsion: to Russia, Poland or the domains of the Turkish Sultan. These events coincided in large part with the period known as the Renaissance, so that what to gentiles is the beginning of enlightened modern times is the start of a new dark age for Jews.

In the imagination of Christians, the Jew had long figured, *inter alia,* as an eternally homeless wanderer—a fate allegedly visited upon him for his rejection of Christ. Before and during the Renaissance, Christian Europe turned this image into reality; and as if to confirm it, massacres in the East about the middle of the seventeenth century set off a new wave of Jewish migration, back to the West.

The Imagery of the Nationalist Era

With the rise of secularism and the modern national states, following the Renaissance, the condition of the Jews became slowly more bearable. From the sixteenth century on, rulers and thinkers showed them growing tolerance. Simultaneously, however, Jews became associated with state finance; and the court Jew of the period, with his international connections and his ability to supply capital to needy monarchs and princes, added new sinister dimensions to the Jewish image.

In a Europe slowly developing national consciousness, the Jew was an international figure; in a society that was mostly poor, a few Jews were rich. Already, the Jew was unfavorably associated in the public's mind with money; now the role of international financier was added to these images. Notions of Jewish solidarity and clannishness, inherited from the earlier periods, were accordingly reinterpreted: The Jew was alleged to possess international power based upon wealth, and later to harbor designs for dominating the world. To the extent that the Jews of the period were not identified with particular nationalities, and that some of them engaged in large financial operations, this new modification of the old stereotype had a basis in reality. Still, it is curious that gentiles should have perceived Jews as plotting for political power. The Jews' mentality was then quite apolitical, and such designs were entirely foreign to them.[18]

Some Jews, usually rich ones, received privileges during this era which in practice amounted to civil rights. Simultaneously, the spread of liberal ideas and natural religion, together with new interpretations of the medieval idea of natural law and natural rights, contributed to a gradual improvement in the condition of Jewry as a whole—an improvement which continued into the Enlightenment. Voltaire, whom we may take as representative of the Age of Reason, disliked Jews but encouraged civil freedom for all men; Montesquieu and Rousseau condemned the traditional treatment and persecution of the Jews; the revolutionist Abbé Gregoire and others advocated their emancipation.

Both in fact and in the minds of gentiles, the Jew and his cause became identified with liberalism. Liberal thought appealed to persons of pro-Jewish sentiment and to the Jews themselves; its profound effect on the Jewish intellectuals of the period is exemplified by the ideas of Moses Mendelssohn. In the imagination of conservatives, activated during periods of reaction, this liberal bent fitted well with traits long attributed to Jews: with the roles of doubter and dissenter. Later, in the nineteenth century, most of Russia's Jews became submerged in the proletariat, because of the restrictions placed upon their mobility and occupational activities; some joined revolutionary movements. One result was that Jews as a group were now seen as radicals, a notion congruent with their earlier representation as liberals. Finally, in the 1920s and 1930s, the notion of the "Jewish Bolshe-vik" was added to the abundant imagery laid up over the centuries.

Political Anti-Semitism and Its Imagery

The pseudo-scientific theories of modern anti-Semitism, from the 1870s until its culmination in the holocaust, pictured the Jew as a political and racial menace—an image which gained wide circulation first through such fantastic propaganda as the forged *Protocols of the Learned Elders of Zion* and later through Hitler's teachings.

Nazi anti-Semitism was more extreme and more horribly thorough than anything that had preceded it (no previous enemy of the Jews in the long history of Europe had advocated or attempted their total annihilation), yet the images Hitler drew were only superficially new. Thus, when he con-demned the Jew as racially inferior, a source of infection for the rest of society, he was offering a biologized version of longstanding religious and cultural distrust. When he named "Jewish finance" and "Jewish Bolshe-vism" as spearheads of a Jewish plot to destroy society and seize world power, he was elaborating on the old image of the Jew as doubter or enemy of the eternal verities.

Modern theologians, such as Paul Tillich and Romano Guardini, have explored the incompatible yet intimate relationship between faith and doubt. The presence of doubters and dissenters tangibly expresses this rela-tionship: The dissenter serves as an objective surrogate for conflicts within the believer's soul, a target for hostile projection. Historians have often pointed to this element in religious fanaticism and intolerance. As we have seen, Christian Europe habitually assigned the subverter's role to the Jew, the supposed challenger of Christian faith. The anti-Semitic nativists of modern times, up to and including Hitler, were doing essentially the same, though in secular terms: They saw the "liberal," "revolutionary" or "ra-cially inferior" Jew as a destroyer of basic values.

The Present Outlook

It has often been said that anti-Semitism is the classic form of religious and ethnic antagonism. But this is true only if a "classic" case is taken to mean one carried to the ultimate extreme, not one that is typical or average. Anti-Semitism possesses a stock of images more deep-seated and protean than does any other form of intergroup hostility known to Western man, because it is the summation of self-confirming experience extending over two millennia. In century after century, hostile sentiments arose from the unhappy relations between gentiles and Jews, fed back into these relation-ships and thus constantly perpetuated and deepened themselves. The ques-tion today is whether this vicious circle is at last being broken.

As we noted at the outset, Stember has shown that expressed anti-Semitism markedly declined in the United States during the last two decades, even though there was no dearth of occasions structurally analogous to those which have given rise to anti-Semitic reactions in the past. Specifically, he has demonstrated that certain unfavorable and pseudo-favorable traits traditionally ascribed to Jews are less widely believed in than formerly or at least less freely referred to. Now, the traits thus noted by Stember are part of the more variegated image whose history we have sketched, and the question thus arises what is happening to this broader image today. Its various aspects probably were never equally accepted or salient among all population groups. Dare we conclude, on the basis of poll findings since 1944, that it is dwindling away altogether?

"It is either impossible, or a task of no mean difficulty, to alter by words what has been of old taken into men's very dispositions," wrote the philosopher, jurist and churchman, Guillaume du Vair (1556–1621). We have assumed that the baneful psychological heritage of anti-Semitic imagery cannot be dissipated unless there is a change in the Jewish-gentile relationships in which it originated and found continual reinforcement; but we have also found reasons to believe that some such alteration has in fact taken place in America. We have seen how the ideology of secularism, the imagery of sectarian Protestantism and the conditions of assimilation to American life combined to make the Catholic (particularly the Irish Catholic) a more salient target of hostility than the Jew. We have observed that, with the progressive secularization of the culture after the Civil War, the Jew became still less salient, gradually losing the characteristic "otherness" that made him a target in the old country. In addition, we note that America's belief in equality, together with her more or less conscious repudiation of certain aspects of European social and political conservatism, subtly helped to make Jewish-gentile relations in this country different from those in Europe. And, finally, we are mindful that assimilation has been the telling, significant long-term process in the history of all ethnic and religious groups in America, notwithstanding nativist (often militantly nativist) episodes.

In short, America has not let ethnic and religious differences remain a solid base for long-term hostility, as has been the case in more homogeneous nations. Today, thanks to structural changes in our society, Jews and gentiles are coming together in a variety of occupational and educational contexts quite unlike traditional forms of confrontation; their relationship does appear to be undergoing a genuine change. We thus might think ourselves safe in accepting the polls at their hopeful face value.

Yet a note of caution is indicated. We have seen how among American Protestants of the 1840s anti-Catholic stereotypes that had been inactive for some time turned quickly into focuses of sentiment and action when immigration brought large numbers of Catholics to these shores. And we know that in later years many onetime Protestants who had become liberal agnostics nevertheless retained the deep-seated anti-Catholic feelings of their sectarian backgrounds, now rationalizing and expressing them in liberal philosophical terms. The same subterranean psychological transfer of energy, the same coalescing of old and new imagery, has so often occurred in the history of anti-Semitism that we dare not jump to overoptimistic conclusions.

Thus our explorations must of necessity close on a tentative note. We do not regard the attitude changes reported in the polls as assured gains in a unitary favorable trend. Rather, they seem to us to stem from two distinct, though related, social processes—the one perhaps ephemeral, the other probably permanent.

From centuries of European history, we know that anti-Semitism may go through periods of quiescence without any diminution in the underlying hostile imagery. In our opinion, part of the reported drop in anti-Jewish feeling during recent decades may well reflect merely such a temporary lull among part of the public. Thus, for all we know, the possibility of renewed anti-Semitism still lurks underground.

But we have also seen that under the particular conditions of American life the basic structure of gentile-Jewish relations has altered to the point where the old hostile imagery evidently is fading at last. Beyond doubt, part of the spectacular opinion change revealed by the polls mirrors this decline of ancient, deep-seated hostility. Obviously, the accumulated hatreds of two thousand years could not have been dissipated altogether in a few decades. Yet, over and above the momentary fluctuations of public opinion, we appear to be witnessing an historic change—a change which opens up new opportunities for studying the deeper socio-psychological reality of intergroup hostility, and for effectively combatting the age-old evil of anti-Semitism.

NOTES

1. Ray Allen Billington, *The Protestant Crusade, 1800–1860* (New York: Rinehart & Co., 1952).

2. Franklin H. Littell, *From State Church to Pluralism* (Garden City, N.Y.: Doubleday Anchor Books, 1962).

3. Will Herberg, *Protestant, Catholic, Jew* (New York: Doubleday & Co., 1955), pp. 270–289.

4. *Ibid.*, pp. 85–104.

5. Seymour M. Lipset, "Religion in America: What Religious Revival?" *Columbia University Forum,* II, No. 1 (Winter 1959), 17–21.

6. Herberg, *op. cit.*

7. Earl Raab, "The Nature of the Conflict: An Introduction," in Earl Raab, editor, *Religious Conflict in America* (Garden City, N.Y.: Doubleday Anchor Books, 1964), pp. 1–28.

8. For a brief presentation of the classical period, see Ralph Marcus, "Antisemitism in the Hellenistic-Roman World," in Koppel S. Pinson, editor, *Essays on Antisemitism* (New York: Conference on Jewish Relations, 1964), pp. 61–78.

9. James Parkes, *Antisemitism* (Chicago: Quadrangle Books, 1964), p. 62.

10. *Ibid.*, p. 64.

11. Malcolm Hay, *The Foot of Pride* (Boston: Beacon Press, 1950), p. 69.

12. Charles Journet, *The Church of the Word Incarnate,* I (New York: Sheed & Ward, 1955), 229.

13. Quoted in Hay, *loc. cit.*

14. See *Summa Theologica,* II–II, q. 10, a. 12; III, q. 68, a. 10. "Jews are bondsmen of the princes by civil bondage which does not exclude the order of natural and divine law" (*Summa,* II–II, q. 10, a. 12, ad. 3). Scotus agrees with the tradition that people cannot generally be baptized against their will, nor children without the consent of their parents; but in the latter case he makes an exception of princes, who can legitimately baptize the children of unbelievers and Jews.

15. Hay, *op. cit.*, p. 68.

16. Joshua Trachtenberg, *The Devil and the Jews: The Medieval Conception of the Jew and Its Relation to Modern Anti-Semitism* (New Haven: Yale University Press, 1943), pp. 188–189.

17. *Ibid.*, pp. 190–194.

18. See Hannah Arendt, *The Origins of Totalitarianism* (Cleveland: World Publishing Co., 1958), p. 24.

The Psychology of Prejudice and

the Future of Anti-Semitism in America

DENNIS H. WRONG

To WHAT EXTENT does the striking decline in the prevalence of anti-Semitic beliefs and attitudes reflect a decline in all forms of ethnic prejudice? Stember writes that "when hostility toward Jews showed an increase in the opinion polls, so did hostility toward other minorities," and goes on to observe that "this finding throws considerable doubt on the theory that ethnic prejudices necessarily displace one another." [1] He does not mention whether the reduction in anti-Semitism has coincided with a general reduction in ethnic prejudice, having confined himself to the formidable task of documenting changes of attitudes toward Jews. There is, however, evidence of a general decline in ethnic and racial prejudice, and any comprehensive effort to interpret Stember's findings regarding anti-Semitism must begin by taking note of it.

Poll questions on attitudes toward Negroes that were repeatedly asked between 1942 and 1964 have been reviewed by Bettelheim and Janowitz and by Hyman and Sheatsley. [2] They reveal a decline in hostility similar to that reported by Stember in the case of the Jews, although the questions asked are fewer and probe less fully the different dimensions of prejudice. The most recent survey, taken in December 1963, shows a continuation of the trend toward greater acceptance of Negroes. It reveals no substantial evidence of increasing resistance by whites to Negro demands, despite signs of such resistance already visible at the time, and despite a growing volume of publicity about "white backlash," which was to make civil rights for Negroes an issue in the 1964 Presidential campaign.

Thus, the easy assumption that the greater salience of the Negro during recent struggles over racial integration accounts for the decline in anti-

323

Semitism finds no support in the polls. If one considers discriminatory behavior rather than expressed attitudes, a stronger, though inferential, case
probably can be made for the view that Negro demands have distracted
attention from the Jews as possible targets of discrimination. But there can
be little doubt that on the level of attitudes—the level explored by the polls
—declining prejudice against Jews has been part of a larger trend embracing
a decline in anti-Negro sentiments as well.

What are the changes in American society which have thus reduced
ethnic prejudice? At least in principle, it is possible that negative images of
Jews, Negroes and Orientals may have been modified by separate and unrelated changes in the relations between each of these minorities and the
majority. But this is highly improbable. First of all, notwithstanding differences in the location of these groups, both regionally and in the social structure, all Americans—majorities and minorities alike—have clearly been
affected by changes that have been nationwide in scope and impact. Moreover, legislatures and public agencies, as well as private organizations striving to improve intergroup relations, have adopted policies and issued
pronouncements bearing on all forms of ethnic prejudice and discrimination. Finally, much research has shown that prejudiced persons rarely confine their hostility to a single ethnic group. While it is unquestionably useful
to know what changes have occurred in the imagery of a particular group,
and what specific historical events have exerted an impact on attitudes toward that group, an interpretation of a general trend toward ethnic acceptance must search for equally general causes.

The Psychodynamic Approach

The most comprehensive generalizations about the forces that promote
and sustain ethnic prejudice in American life have been advanced by the
proponents of a socio-psychoanalytic approach. This school has emphasized the psychic roots and functions of prejudice, viewing them as relatively independent of the target group's real attributes and of the actual
social relationships between prejudiced persons and members of the group
they despise. From the simple "scapegoat" theory, which has lent itself so
readily to popularization through brotherhood dramas in the mass media,
to the elaborate technical conceptions of id and superego projectivity and of
"authoritarian personality," psychological—or, more accurately, psychodynamic—formulations have dominated much of the research and theory
about prejudice and intergroup relations in the postwar years.[3]

At the same time, however, a good deal of trenchant criticism has been
directed against the psychodynamic approach to ethnic relations with its almost exclusive concentration on the subjective dispositions and delusions of
the prejudiced. In general, this criticism has converged on the following
major points:

First, psychodynamic theories are of little or no help in accounting for short-term changes in levels and intensities of prejudice. They cannot answer such questions as: "Why did anti-Semitic sentiment in the United States rise between 1942 and 1946, and abruptly decline thereafter?" Psychic mechanisms that are part of the universal repertory of human responses, motivations rooted in the particular character structure of nations and peoples, the relative frequency of personality types prone to ethnic prejudice—none of these psychological conceptions can answer the question: "Why now and not then?" Indeed, the first one cannot even tell us "why here and not there" when we compare contemporaneous groups or societies. As for national character structures and distributions of personality types, they change too slowly to account for short-run trends in prejudice. The logical canon that one cannot explain a variable by a constant sums up this objection to psychodynamic theories.

Still, as has been noted, the objection applies only to short-run changes in patterns of prejudice. If we wish to account for differences in the general level of prejudice in various societies over long periods of time, we cannot ignore the character of nations. Differences in national character show an impressive degree of pervasiveness and persistence, even though our lack of anything resembling a sophisticated psychodynamic history of nations and peoples makes it difficult to say just how long the long run may be in any given case—whether it is to be reckoned in generations or in centuries. Differences in national character undoubtedly have much to do with the unequal susceptibilities of societies to prejudice. For example, the North European, Protestant, Teutonic peoples' acute sensitivity to racial differences clearly has roots in their common character, as shaped by traditions, family institutions and histories that they do not share with the peoples of Southern and Eastern Europe.[4] It would, of course, be gross psychodynamic or characterological determinism to attribute the North Europeans' treatment of racially distinct subject peoples solely to character structure. Yet character may legitimately be regarded as one factor in the colonial policies of these nations—a factor that is usually ignored.

The changes reported by Stember have obviously occurred within too brief a period of time to be capable of explanation by psychodynamic theories alone. One can only agree with the conclusion of Bettelheim and Janowitz that "changes in underlying psychological mechanisms do not account for the decline in hostile attitudes toward Jews and Negroes"[5] during recent years. Surely, there can have been no sudden decrease in the amount of frustration that prevails in American private lives, generating free-floating aggression which can be mobilized against Jews or Negroes. And surely the proportion of authoritarian personalities in the population cannot have substantially diminished between 1946 and the early 1960s, a period of less than one generation in demographic terms. The same objection, incidentally, applies in slightly less degree to sociological theories that attribute de-

clines in prejudice to changes in the demographic, socio-economic and educational composition of the population; for the trends postulated in such
theories move much too slowly to account for the shifts in prejudice and its
manifestations with which we are here concerned.

A second major objection to psychodynamic theories is that they cannot
explain why a particular ethnic group becomes the object of prejudice—nor
indeed why, out of the infinitude of available social objects, ethnic groups
should be selected for depreciation and victimization.[6] If the choice of Jews
as scapegoats is so arbitrary that the bigots might as well have picked on
bicyclists (as the old anti-Nazi joke had it) or on men with striped ties (as
a character in *Crossfire,* a postwar brotherhood film, put it), then why have
the Jews been chosen so often?

To account for choices of target, the psychodynamic theorists postulate
the existence of derogatory "stereotypes" of ethnic groups. These images
are thought to be transmitted as part of the cultural heritage, and thus become available to canalize the free-floating hostilities and anxieties of people psychically predisposed to project and externalize their inner conflicts.
But to explain the origin of these stereotypes is a task beyond the scope of
psychodynamics. Nor can the theory adequately account for changes in
stereotypes, such as those reported by Stember. In effect, stereotypes serve
the psychodynamic theorist as a social or cultural *deus ex machina:* They
are essential in explaining how prejudice is activated and how it finds its
target, but they themselves are not explained—at least not in psychodynamic terms.

A third objection to psychodynamic theories—essentially a corollary and
extension of the second—is that they ignore the actualities of intergroup
relations. An ethnic minority is not simply a figment of the majority's dis-
eased imagination, but consists of real people with real relations to members of the majority. How these relations bear on the attitudes of both
groups obviously requires investigation. By concentrating on what exists in
the minds of prejudiced members of the majority, the psychodynamic
school neglects the actual characteristics of the minority and its contacts
with the majority.

Sometimes the question whether the target group possesses the qualities
imputed to it is dismissed as irrelevant, prejudice being flatly defined as *any*
negative attitude toward a group.[7] More often, prejudice is defined as a
hostile attitude toward a group, based (or allegedly based) on beliefs that
are demonstrably false.[8] But even the latter, more acceptable definition dis-
courages scrutiny of how actual intergroup relations may be related to particular false beliefs or how social changes may have invalidated beliefs that
once truthfully reflected historical situations.[9]

Attitudes versus Social Realities

The survey researcher or public-opinion analyst builds on an intellectual tradition different from the psychodynamic theorist's; yet he, too, neglects the real qualities of the groups about which his subjects voice opinions and express attitudes. The opinion analyst's emphasis on what is in people's minds stems from his methodological chastity, which restrains him from going beyond the body of survey data he has gathered; but his results curiously resemble the more speculative, less "scientific" psychodynamic insights, in that they stress the subjective sphere at the expense of the real world of events and social relations. Thus, public opinion data, however carefully analyzed, cannot by themselves tell us all we want to know about a topic; they demand further interpretation, drawing upon a wider range of evidence.

Thanks to the current racial upheaval in the United States, the inadequacies of approaching prejudice solely through its possessors are more obvious today than they were a decade ago. As is well known, whites have long cherished irrational fears and fantasies concerning the Negro, many of them with a strong sexual content. But the present crisis clearly arises from conflict between the Negro's political and social aspirations and the white man's resistance to these aspirations, rather than from any increase in sexual anxieties or psychological authoritarianism among the white population. Whites who oppose further collective advance by the Negroes are not necessarily misinformed about the living conditions of Negroes, their crime rates or educational disabilities,[10] whatever their deeper unconscious attitudes toward Negroes may be.

That men can plausibly invoke the very scars of discrimination to justify continued discrimination is, of course, a maddening injustice. But this frequently noted self-fulfilling tendency in racial oppression is irrational only from the standpoint of man considered collectively as the maker of society and history. Individual parents who fear that their children's schooling may suffer if the local public school is integrated, individual homeowners who worry about property values when Negroes try to move into their neighborhoods, may be sustaining the system that has branded the Negro with the mark of oppression, but they have not created it. Nor can their fear be labeled irrational or groundless. They are reacting to a social fact that is truly external to them in the Durkheimian sense—to a real situation not of their individual making. The tragic complexity of the racial crisis lies in the very circumstance that an intolerable evil may breed perfectly well-founded fears, thereby perpetuating itself.

Indeed, emerging conflicts of interest between Negroes and whites, in such areas as school integration and housing, suggest that survey findings of a general decline in anti-Negro sentiment may not be borne out in actual behavior. Increasing proportions of respondents, from only 35 per cent in 1942 to 64 per cent in 1963,[11] have stated they would not object to Negroes living next door; but how these respondents might behave if actually faced with such a situation or how they might vote in a referendum such as those during 1964, in which voters in Detroit, the State of California and elsewhere rejected fair-housing statutes, is another question. We might well be disposed to doubt that professions of tolerance in the polls would be matched by acceptance of racial integration in education and housing. Conversely, we might note that in the recent past individuals and communities have often expressed strong opposition to integration, yet have accepted it peacefully when it was imposed by administrative action.[12]

The Projective Character of Anti-Semitism

What do these contradictions between expressed attitudes and actual behavior imply for Stember's survey data on anti-Semitic sentiment? If growing resistance among whites to the Negroes' demands is not reflected in surveys, may not poll indications of a decrease in anti-Semitism be equally deceptive? Perhaps, as Halpern suggests,[13] the surveys prove merely that anti-Semitic utterances are no longer respectable, not that underlying attitudes relevant (or potentially relevant) to conduct have changed.

The answer would seem to be that anti-Semitism is not entirely comparable with hostility against Negroes, because it stands in a different relation to reality. America's Negro problem (more accurately, its problem of relations between Negroes and whites) is indisputably a thing of objective existence. Discrimination has, after all, long been an established institution in the South and a sanctioned, if unofficial, practice in the North; its elimination is being widely, albeit belatedly, recognized as a real issue requiring real sacrifices. One sociologist, evidently thinking of attitudes toward the Negro, has gone so far as to maintain that the much-studied psychodynamics of prejudice have no bearing at all on the social and historical facts of intergroup relations.[14]

Where Jews are concerned, social reality is quite different. America has never sanctioned anti-Jewish discrimination in the same way as discrimination against Negroes, and has no Jewish problem that is real in the same sense as the so-called Negro problem. Thus, anti-Semitism in this country is much farther removed from actuality, much more subjective, than prejudice against Negroes. It is no accident that psychodynamic theories of prejudice grew primarily out of the study of anti-Semitism and were always at their most tentative and least convincing when applied to anti-Negro attitudes; there is much less reason why ideas hostile to Negroes should be associated with particular personality types than why anti-Semitic stereotypes and ideologies should appeal particularly to certain definable kinds of neurotic personalities.

It is precisely the peculiarly intense, projective character of anti-Semitism in modern Western civilization that has made it appear such an inexplicable "outrage against common sense." [15] Indeed, some interpreters have declared it a mystery forever unfathomable to rational understanding. Their bafflement arises from the enormous disproportion between the actual position of the Jews in modern society and that imputed to them by anti-Semitic ideology. Whoever seeks to understand anti-Semitism must confront this disproportion and is inevitably led to consider psychodynamic processes in trying to account for it—processes that are clearly central to the phenomenon.

Yet, neither psychodynamic constants nor changes in the objective realities of intergroup relations can by themselves explain the waxing and waning of anti-Semitism over short periods. If we are to understand sudden outbursts of previously latent forms of prejudice, we need to combine an understanding of universal psychic mechanisms with a precise historical account of the events and situations, transitory though they may be, that trigger these mechanisms. We must show how crises—collective disasters, disturbances in the routine operations of social structures, temporary physical or social dislocation of large numbers of people—prompt individuals to seek scapegoats, to lust after violence, to assert their group identity at the expense of an out-group. The ways in which we go about explaining the sudden emergence of extremist political movements or moods (for example, McCarthyism) provide a model for inquiries of this sort. Stember briefly suggests such an explanation in attributing the rise of anti-Semitism culminating in 1944 to the tensions and frustrations that resulted from the complete mobilization of the nation in wartime.[16] The suggestion seems persuasive in view of the race riots that occurred during 1943 in Los Angeles, Detroit, New York and several smaller communities—some of them far more destructive than those of 1964.

An approach that deals both with psychic mechanisms and with the specific social situations that activate them can also be applied on a more limited scale to common personal situations and crises affecting single individuals—the scale of "milieu" as opposed to "social structure," in C. Wright Mills' terms.[17] This is the rationale for the many studies attempting to deal with prejudice in relation to the career and social-mobility histories of individuals—studies that "relate degrees of social movement to degrees of prejudice." [18] (Bettelheim and Janowitz argue, incidentally, that changes in aggregate rates of individual mobility since 1950 do not account for the decline in anti-Jewish and other ethnic prejudice since that date.[19])

Thus, by linking the psychodynamics of prejudice to specific social situations breeding mass insecurities, we may overcome some of the limitations of purely psychodynamic theories. But we are still left with the question why one group rather than another becomes the target of prejudice. Unless the Jews possess some saliency and visibility as an ethnic-religious group or have possessed it in the fairly recent past, anti-Semitism cannot survive as a possible response to political and social crisis. Granted that anti-Jewish sentiment has been the "classic prejudice" of the Western world, subjective anti-Semitism still requires at least historical memories of an earlier anti-Semitism related to reality. One reason why hostility against Jews has been weaker in the United States than in most of Europe is that historical memories of conflicts between Christians and Jews have been less vivid here. Moreover, what Christian-Jewish friction has existed here has had relatively little saliency compared to recurrent tensions between immigrants and natives and to the ubiquitous presence of non-white races throughout American history. By the same token, anti-Semitism as a mass ideology has been even more shadowy and projective here than in Europe, and its adherents have been even more unstable and paranoid.

Eva Reichmann has shown that in modern Germany "subjective" or "sham" anti-Semitism, as she calls it,[20] was prominent in precisely those areas and periods which had no significant objective Jewish problem. The Nazis, the final disastrous exploiters of subjective anti-Semitism, made little use of actual tensions between Germans and recent Jewish immigrants from Poland in creating their demoniacal portrait of the symbolic Jew.[21] The very absence of a Jewish group sharply set apart from its neighbors makes it easier for the ideologue and the demagogue to transform anti-Semitism into a sweeping world-historical doctrine—just as the John Birch Society has been able to construct a total, all-encompassing ideology out of anti-Communism more than a decade after American Communists had lost whatever influence they once possessed.

But the world and the Jews are varied and so, therefore, is anti-Semitism, which has existed in many different mixtures of subjective and objective elements. Beyond question, anti-Semitism is the classic case of projective group hatred, and Nazism is the prototype of ideological anti-Semitism with its murderous political potentialities; yet these extreme versions have figured disproportionately large in the psychodynamic interpretations of ethnic prejudice, and the balance needs redressing.

If the Nazis' ideological anti-Semitism and its echoes in this country represent the extreme of subjective anti-Semitism, social discrimination against Jewish *nouveaux riches* by Old American elites, as documented by John Higham,[22] represents the most clear-cut form of objective anti-Semitism in American history (except for earlier anti-immigrant feeling, which did not sharply distinguish Jews from other ethnic newcomers). In contemporary America, both of these extreme types have become inconsequential. Dispositions to subjective anti-Semitism can survive only if the Jews remain salient as possible targets and victims; and Stember's data, as well as much else that has happened since the Second World War, raise doubts about this saliency. At the same time, the basis for objective anti-Semitism has been largely destroyed by the virtually complete acculturation of American Jews.

What we must now ask ourselves is whether some conceivable combination of psychodynamic disposition, prevailing public images of Jews and actual traits of the Jewish population might halt the decline of anti-Semitism described by Stember or even cause anti-Jewish feeling to rise again. Some of the relevant considerations are touched upon in what follows.

The Institutionalization of Judaism

As has often been remarked, anti-Semitism has never possessed even the shadow of official sanction in America, because the country contains so many ethnic and religious minorities, and because both ideology and the pragmatic necessities of democratic politics commit the nation to equality of opportunity. But that is not all. Since the Second World War, Jews actually have been, as it were, institutionalized as part of American society. It was mainly in these years that Judaism was elevated to equal status with Protestantism and Catholicism as a third quasi-official religious division in American society. During the same period, it became standard practice to characterize our civilization as "Judeo-Christian." Growing numbers of Jews have been attaining success as national politicians; in elections Jewish candidates have been increasingly accepted, along with Catholics, as "ticket-balancers." And all this has occurred at a time when the proportion of Jews in the national population was declining, and when large numbers of Jews retained a religious affiliation that was no more than nominal.

This institutionalization of the Jews is clearly a policy followed by powerful elite groups at all levels of government, by the political parties, the churches, professional associations and the mass communications media. Horror at the holocaust and sympathy with the emergence of Israel have influenced the elites, however slight the general public's apparent response to these events may have been.

The new public status accorded Jews promises to assure their continued visibility in American society while reducing pressures on individuals to abandon their Jewish identities through what used to be called assimilation. Still, it may be argued that the recent institutionalization of the Jews as a religious group is no unmixed blessing but carries with it a certain risk. Those who contend, as did Sidney Hook some years ago, that anti-Semitism is a "Christian phenomenon . . . endemic to every Christian culture, whose religions made the Jews the eternal villain in the Christian drama of salvation," [23] will feel that American society has now explicitly underwritten the survival of the ancient, original, objective basis of anti-Semitism (or anti-Judaism, as it should properly be called in this connection).

The view that hostility to Jews is endemic to Christianity is seemingly contradicted by the fact that the recent decline in anti-Semitism has occurred while the importance of religious identities was clearly on the increase.[24] American religious identities obviously do not have the same meaning as in the past, and their new significance is not of a kind to challenge the secular, post-Christian nature of our society. Still, religious conflicts between Christians and Jews over such issues as Christmas pageants in the schools are unlikely to disappear. Judging by the record of one such controversy, in Hamden, Connecticut,[25] they may revive among Christians many of the slumbering stereotypes of anti-Semitism. And one may well doubt whether recent efforts by both Catholics and Protestants to repudiate the belief that the Jews are collectively guilty of deicide will have much effect on the laity.

American Jews are not merely regarded by others as a religious group; they increasingly so regard themselves. In this respect, they appear to have completed a full cycle: With the acculturation of the East European immigrants completed, they are returning to the outlook of the late nineteenth century, when the American Jewish community—largely of German origin and Reform persuasion—saw itself as a marginally differentiated religious group almost completely acculturated to the larger American society. The point of view that was once called "assimilationism" is no longer advanced as such by many American Jews, but perhaps only because it no longer seems necessary to talk about something that is happening to so many persons spontaneously, without external pressure. Intermarriage and the dropping of even nominal affiliation with the Jewish religion are probably increasing, although without the name-changing that was so common before the Second World War.[26] Persons of Jewish origin, with names such as Goldwater, who have married non-Jews and abandoned all affiliations with Judaism or the Jewish community, are likely to become more numerous. The very decline in anti-Semitism makes such complete yet non-defensive assimilation more acceptable by removing the stigma of cowardice from it.

The Upper Middle Class and Anti-Semitism

American Jews today for the most part belong to the metropolitan middle class and in large numbers to the upper middle class. As is well known, their collective socio-economic ascent has been more rapid than that of any other immigrant group. But even before the coming of the East European Jews, the gentile upper and upper middle classes in many communities resisted the efforts of newly wealthy Jews to gain entrance into clubs, summer resorts, private schools, colleges and residential neighborhoods that had long been the exclusive preserves of Old Americans. Such discriminatory behavior, as Max Weber long ago noted, is typical of high-status groups anxious to uphold intangible values against persons who claim social equality on the basis of mere wealth.

The stereotype of the Jew as a flashy and vulgar *arriviste* clearly originated in this context. This explains why it does not loom particularly large in the images of the Jew held by the masses, as reported by Stember, and also why certain anti-Semitic opinions and attitudes are especially common among upper-income and highly educated groups—a finding more fully documented by him in a previous work.[27] Since Jews have for so long penetrated the upper levels of the occupational and income hierarchy and are now heavily concentrated there, the stereotype of the Jewish *parvenu* has not been without objective foundation. Whether to associate with Jews in intimate, informal situations has often been a real issue in circles of insecure would-be patricians.

While such genteel "anti-Semitism from above" [28] has occasionally become an obsession with individual Americans (for example, Henry Adams), it has never been politicized in America as the basis for a right-wing nationalist movement as it has in such countries as pre-Nazi Germany, France and present-day Argentina,[29] although radicals and neo-Marxists, usually misreading the Nazi experience, have often expected it to do so.[30] It has, in fact, had little connection with ideological anti-Semitism in its characteristically American nativist and populist form, which, as Higham has pointed out, has chiefly appealed to rural and small-town dwellers by associating Jews with the hated and feared big city.[31] In recent decades the genteel anti-Semitism of upper-class groups and its manifestation in social discrimination have greatly declined; the Jews are now relatively well established in the upper middle class; and other ethnic minorities—not to speak of Anglo-Saxon Protestants in the West and Southwest—are actually more likely to bear the stigmata of the *nouveau riche*. It is hard to believe that genteel anti-Semitism has much of a future in America.

True, exclusion of Jews from the private clubs of upper-circle white Anglo-Saxon Protestants remains widespread, as E. Digby Baltzell has recently reminded us,[32] and informal residential segregation of Jews from non-Jews is fairly marked in middle-class suburbs such as those of New York. But some of these remaining barriers are upheld by both groups and therefore do not reflect one-sided social discrimination. In any event, growing numbers of Jews are employed by large organizations, especially in technical positions; and Jews increasingly take part in political organizations, civic groups and other types of community-wide voluntary associations. Thus, despite surviving obstacles, the trend by and large is probably toward more intimate contacts between middle-class Jews and non-Jews.

Closer contacts at work and in community life are likely to imbue non-Jews with new attitudes toward Jews, and vice versa. Possibly their relations within the upper middle class will come to resemble those now prevailing in smaller academic, professional and intellectual circles, where Jews and non-Jews are brought into close contact, with high intermarriage rates a frequent result.[33] Relations in such circles are by no means free of frictions and covert group animosities, but these attitudes often coexist with virtual philo-Semitism among some non-Jews and an almost complete abandonment of Jewish identity by some Jews.

The group images formed in such settings reflect the subtle realities of group differences more closely than does the standardized imagery of traditional anti-Semitism or the superficial stereotypes of *parvenu* behavior held by socially insecure snobs. More or less accurately, non-Jews in these circles are apt to attribute to Jews such traits as intellectuality, political liberalism, intense parental solicitude with close bonds between mothers and sons, great concern with the extended family, a liking for food and physical comforts in general, volubility and emotional expressiveness, fear of violence and ironic humor. These traits obviously will be perceived only where there is a degree of intimacy in informal social contexts. They may be evaluated either positively or negatively—either "anti-Semitically" or "philo-Semitically," to use terms that are perhaps too strong in this connection.

Jews living in such environments, for their part, perceive in Anglo-Saxon Protestants certain distinctive traits that also have little to do with formal religious affiliation or with traditional hostile stereotypes. Again more or less accurately, they often see Anglo-Saxons as emotionally reserved, prone to place great value on formally polite manners, inclined to resist contemporary fashions and innovations, loyal to institutional attachments but less so to kin, not specially permissive in child-rearing and touched with asceticism, if not puritanism. These traits, too, may be evaluated positively or negatively.

Thus each group tends to develop new stereotypes of the other as a result of closer contact. The new images, whether favorably or unfavorably evaluated, are far more accurate than the older ones, which are long outdated as well as distorted by projective thinking. New contacts between Jews and Anglo-Saxon Protestants in upper-middle-class circles perhaps do not have much relevance to ethnic prejudice in general and anti-Semitism in particular, as these have been traditionally understood, yet they may well open a new chapter in the relations between Jews and non-Jews in America.

The Occupational Position of the Jews

What about the far more dangerous "anti-Semitism from below"? If some thinkers have viewed anti-Semitism as a permanent ingredient of Christian cultures, others have regarded it as an enduring possibility for as long as Jews remain visibly concentrated in particular occupations and industries.[34] The dominant image of the Jew as "economic man" reported by Stember reflects actual Jewish representation in retailing and certain financial occupations which, unlike manufacturing, involve direct contacts with the public, and in such ostentatiously affluent, publicly visible new industries as the movies. (The same image also pictures the Jew, falsely, as prominent in banking.) Now, the preponderance of Jews in retail trade, commerce, real estate and the communications and entertainment industries still continues;[35] and most of these occupations, as well as the liberal professions which Jews have entered in large numbers, are highly unlikely to be affected by automation. Is it not possible that working-class and white-collar groups threatened by automation with unemployment or occupational demotion might turn on the Jew, as doomed classes have so often done in the past, and provide a mass base for a revival of anti-Semitism?

Several considerations would seem to make this eventuality unlikely, though by no means impossible. In recent years, social discontent has been increasingly directed against large bureaucratic organizations. Noting to what degree the Supreme Court, the State Department, the Federal Government generally, the big foundations and the Ivy League universities have replaced ethnic groups as objects of extremist agitation, Richard Hofstadter has half-facetiously commented that standards of hating appear to have risen along with standards of living.[36] Hofstadter argues that authoritarian personalities now select new targets in place of ethnic groups they formerly maligned. We might suggest an alternative explanation that pays greater attention to the grounds on which scapegoats and objects of prejudice are chosen: The institutions just named may be singled out for punishment because they are deeply involved with social changes that have reduced the power and prestige, if not the wealth, of local and regional interest groups. The resentments of such frustrated groups were strikingly illustrated by many of the followers of Barry M. Goldwater in the 1964 Presidential contest.

In the past, Jews could plausibly be linked to the big city and serve as scapegoats for the disruptive effects of urbanization,[37] but they cannot be similarly associated today with bureaucratization and the expanding powers of the Federal Government. Jews are not especially prominent in the higher ranks of the Federal bureaucracy, the foreign service, the defense establishment or the judiciary, nor, for that matter, in Big Labor, a more traditional target of rightist agitation. To date, they have not typically been "organization men" in business or professional firms; they have usually become independent practitioners, rather than salaried experts or administrators in large organizations like hospitals, big law offices, engineering firms or industrial corporations. Nor have they been directly implicated in the introduction of automation, however immune their occupational distribution may render them to its effects.

In short, although the psychodynamic potentials that formerly found an outlet in ethnic prejudice are still with us, and even though social and technical changes are causing new frustrations for some groups in the population, it seems unlikely that anti-Semitism will return and displace the current targets of radical-right paranoia and conspiracy-mongering—targets conveniently personalized as "creeping socialists," "comsymps" or "effete Eastern intellectuals."

The Anti-Semitism of Other Minorities

Anti-Semitism may arise among groups that are themselves minorities and have been victims of prejudice and discrimination. The Irish and the Italians, who have risen less quickly in American society than the Jews, and who have suffered penalties both as Catholics and as foreigners, have at times been prone to anti-Semitism. But at the present time hostility against Jews is more in evidence among Negroes. James Baldwin some years ago wrote that "Georgia has the Negro and Harlem has the Jew." While that may be an exaggeration, it is a fact that Negro militants today feel a marked antipathy to white liberals, a great many of whom are Jewish, and that the Black Muslims combine the anti-Israel slogans of the Arab countries with appeals to indigenous anti-Semitism.

Manifestations like these suggest that Negro anti-Semitism is not a passing phenomenon. Some writers believe that it derives from the frequent contacts of Negroes with Jewish retailers in the black ghettoes, with Jewish housewives in domestic service, with Jewish employers in low-wage garment factories and with cohesive Jewish communities in residential areas into which Negroes are moving.[38] In all of these situations the Negro confronts the Jew in a subordinate or disadvantaged role. Yet it is unlikely that Negro anti-Semitism is purely objective in character, and its subjective sources and functions need further examination.

Campus Liberalism

In the years of relative prosperity since the Second World War, few durable causes have been available to middle-class, college-educated youth in rebellion against parental standards. Political radicalism has been in abeyance; atheism no longer carries much emotional charge; avant-garde art and literature, having been absorbed by the academy and by conventional cultural entrepreneurs, no longer shock and challenge. Only two causes have remained live issues, offering young people the chance to define themselves as rebels and bearers of new values: greater sexual freedom and ethnic tolerance.

A few years ago, David Riesman complained that his students at the University of Chicago devoted inordinate energy to combating minor and residual forms of racial discrimination on and around the campus. Their time would be better spent, he argued, in exposing the petty tyrannies and irrationalities of the academic institution itself than in concentrating so exclusively on the fight against more remote evils—a fight in which they did not lack powerful allies. Riesman, usually so perceptive on such matters, for once would seem to have missed the point: the symbolic significance of ethnic liberalism to students, in an age when so many other causes have been corrupted or have lost their momentum as a result of partial success. Today, with the Negroes' drive for equality reaching a peak while the economy requires major structural adjustments, Riesman's students no longer seem as quixotic and self-deceived as he found them at the time.

It is true that ethnic liberalism as a fighting posture often draws upon precisely the psychodynamic mechanisms that have in the past sustained ethnic prejudice: on scapegoating, projectivity and compulsive confirmation of identity. As Bettelheim and Janowitz acutely remark: "Fighting against prejudice as a means to buttress one's own threatened identity is an ineffective way to eliminate it in others, because those who are prejudiced feel the self-seeking nature of this pressure." [39] Yet the same psychodynamic causes in this instance produce opposite social and political effects, for the rigid or authoritarian liberal at least helps create the minimal consensus needed for effective action on behalf of equality and freedom.

It is often held that young people today show more ethnic tolerance than their elders because, with parental authority undermined by outside forces, they are particularly receptive to the mass media's pleas for ethnic harmony. Even if this is so, however, another factor probably plays a larger role: the need of young people in a rapidly changing, complex society to identify themselves with distinctive values (at times with values which they may consider far newer and more radical than they are). True, only a minority among the college students of recent years have defined themselves as fighting ethnic liberals, and even fewer have taken part in picketing, freedom rides or Mississippi voter-registration campaigns. But this minority has set the dominant tone on the campuses—witness the dismal failure of counterefforts by the Young Americans for Freedom and other *soi-disant* conservative student organizations. As for attitudes toward Jews, a kind of philo-Semitism prevails; many non-Jewish liberals who would hesitate to solve the Negro problem in marriage choose Jews for spouses, as the rates of intermarriage in university communities attest.[40] Whatever its causes, it is hard to believe that the ethnic liberalism of the campus is anything but an irreversible development in American life.

Conclusion

These random observations, it is hoped, will cast some light on the trend shown by Stember's poll tabulations. They also suggest that anti-Semitism in America will remain in a state of decline, though it will not totally disappear. A word of caution, however, is in order, for sociologists have too often found themselves in the position of the owl of Minerva, which, in Hegel's words, "spreads its wings only with the falling of the dusk": They have put forward comprehensive explanations of a social trend just at the moment when it ceased to exist or was reversed by unforeseen historical mutations.

Sociological explanations are biased in favor of long-term, gradual social change, of slow structural drifts that insensibly modify the shape of institutions and values, and gently edge people away from their previous moorings —processes slow enough to be measurable by sociology's ponderous methods of collecting and assessing evidence. After the fact, the historian, who does not have to estimate future possibilities and probabilities, may chide the sociologist for having given insufficient weight to the unforeseeable, unique events that set these slowly developing processes in motion, and for mistakenly treating the slow processes themselves as prime movers. And to the extent that the sociologist may have presumed to "predict" the future simply by projecting an imperfectly understood trend, this censure is justified.

Yet the future is a dimension of time that we already inhabit in the present, and we cannot do without guidelines to it. As it happens, it is not easy to foresee what future historical events might significantly raise the temperature of anti-Semitism in America. At present the most likely cause would seem to be intensified resistance to racial desegregation, by both white Southerners and white Northern city dwellers, giving rise to an ideology that would throw the blame on "Jew Communists"; but Stember's data indicate that so far this has not come to pass. Cold War defeats, frustrations in international relations, economic tensions resulting from automation and, of course, the ultimate threat of nuclear war could also create mass insecurities sufficient to unleash all the psychodynamic reactions to panic that have generated anti-Semitism in the past. But we have already experienced most of these things (in relatively mild form, it is true), and anti-Semitism has not figured importantly in the public response. Furthermore, for reasons indicated earlier, we may doubt that Jews—in contrast to certain other groups and institutions—will become objects of what Hofstadter has called "projective politics" in the future. Perhaps the study of the psychodynamics of ethnic prejudice should be redirected and reformulated as the study of collective irrationality in general.

NOTES

1. See pp. 214–215.

2. Bruno Bettelheim and Morris Janowitz, *Social Change and Prejudice* (New York: The Free Press of Glencoe, 1964), pp. 11–14; Herbert H. Hyman and Paul B. Sheatsley, "Attitudes Toward Desegregation," *Scientific American,* CCXI, No. 1 (July 1964), 16–23.

3. Most of this research and the theories underlying it has been summarized in Gordon W. Allport, *The Nature of Prejudice* (Cambridge, Mass.: Addison-Wesley Publishing Co., 1954).

4. See the suggestions of Philip Mason, *An Essay on Racial Tension* (London and New York: Royal Institute of International Affairs, 1954), pp. 37–42.

5. Bettelheim and Janowitz, *op. cit.*, p. 80.

6. One of the best criticisms of the scapegoat theory may be found in Hannah Arendt, *The Origins of Totalitarianism* (New York: Harcourt, Brace & Co., 1951), pp. 3–10.

7. See the criticism of this definition by William Petersen, *The Politics of Population* (Garden City, N.Y.: Doubleday & Co., 1964), pp. 238–246.

8. This essentially is Allport's definiton, *op. cit.*, p. 10.

9. See Paul Kecskemeti, "The Psychological Theory of Prejudice," *Commentary*, XVIII:359–366 (1954).

10. See William Lee Miller, "Analysis of the 'White Backlash,'" *The New York Times Magazine*, August 23, 1964, pp. 26, 87–88.

11. Hyman and Sheatsley, *op. cit.*, p. 19.

12. Earl Raab and Seymour Martin Lipset, "The Prejudiced Society," in Earl Raab, editor, *American Race Relations Today* (Garden City, N.Y.: Doubleday Anchor Books, 1962), pp. 29–55.

13. See p. 285.

14. Arnold M. Rose, "Intergroup Relations vs. Prejudice," *Social Problems*, IV:173–176 (1956).

15. The phrase is Hannah Arendt's, *loc. cit.*

16. See p. 133.

17. C. Wright Mills, *The Sociological Imagination* (New York: Oxford University Press, 1959), pp. 8–13.

18. Bettelheim and Janowitz, *op. cit.*, p. 68.

19. *Ibid.*, pp. 25–48.

20. Eva G. Reichmann, *Hostages of Civilization* (Boston: The Beacon Press, 1951), pp. 37–39.

21. *Ibid.*, pp. 227–235.

22. John Higham, "Social Discrimination Against Jews in America, 1830–1930," *Publication of The American Jewish Historical Society*, XLVII:1–33 (1957).

23. Sidney Hook, "Reflections on the Jewish Question," *Partisan Review*, XVI:471–472 (1949).

24. Gerhard Lenski, *The Religious Factor* (rev. ed.; Garden City, N.Y.: Doubleday Anchor Books, 1963).

25. "Community Conflict: Christmas Observance in the Public Schools," in Earl Raab, editor, *Religious Conflict in America* (Garden City, N.Y.: Doubleday Anchor Books, 1964), pp. 198–208.

26. Marshall Sklare, "Intermarriage and the Jewish Future," *Commentary*, XXXVII, No. 4 (April 1964), 46–52.

27. Charles Herbert Stember, *Education and Attitude Change* (New York: Institute of Human Relations Press, 1961).

28. I have borrowed the terms "from above" and "from below" from Kecskemeti, *op. cit.*

29. For Argentina, see Irving Louis Horowitz, "The Jewish Community of Buenos Aires," *Jewish Social Studies,* XXIV:214–220 (1962).

30. See Paul Kecskemeti, "Prejudice in the Catastrophic Perspective," *Commentary,* XI:286–292 (1951).

31. Higham, *op. cit.;* also, "Anti-Semitism in the Gilded Age: A Reinterpretation," *The Mississippi Valley Historical Review,* XLIII:559–578 (1957).

32. E. Digby Baltzell, *The Protestant Establishment: Aristocracy and Caste in America* (New York: Random House, 1964).

33. Sklare, *op. cit.,* pp. 49–51.

34. For example, Werner J. Cahnman, "Socio-economic Causes of Antisemitism," *Social Problems,* V:21–29 (1957).

35. Nathan Glazer and Daniel Patrick Moynihan, *Beyond the Melting Pot* (Cambridge, Mass.: The M.I.T. Press and Harvard University Press, 1963), pp. 143–155.

36. Richard Hofstadter, "The Pseudo-Conservative Revolt—1955," in Daniel Bell, editor, *The Radical Right* (Garden City, N.Y.: Doubleday & Co., 1963), p. 76.

37. Arnold Rose, "Anti-Semitism's Root in City Hatred," *Commentary,* VI:374–378 (1948).

38. Glazer and Moynihan, *op. cit.,* pp. 71–73.

39. Bettelheim and Janowitz, *op. cit.,* p. 60.

40. Sklare, *op. cit.*

Changes in Value Orientation

ROBIN M. WILLIAMS, JR.

THE QUESTIONS POSED for consideration in this paper constitute an impressive, almost an intimidating, list. We are asked to examine the following issues:

What American value orientations shape the attitude toward the Jew?

What changes in American value orientations are suggested by the data?

Do the differences between the earlier and later findings suggest thoroughgoing value changes or do they suggest the presence of different social conditions which inhibit or encourage the expression of the value system?

To what extent is the present position of the Jew expressive of value orientations of the American public so fundamental that a change in the Jewish position is conceivable only if social changes of the most drastic kind occur?

Under what conditions are present trends reversible?

Clearly, changes of American value orientations in relation to attitudes toward Jews and Judaism are too large a subject to be fully explored in a brief paper. We will accordingly assume that it is not our task to offer anything like a comprehensive "explanation" of anti-Semitism or its trends in terms of values, but only to examine what an analysis of value orientations, as one component among several, conceivably might contribute to an understanding of the situation. Only when all other relevant components— economic, political, religious, demographic and so on—have been considered can the role of values be seen in proper perspective. In short, we aspire to no imperialistic claims, as it were, for the causal hegemony of values, but we do hope that analysis of values can make a modest contribution toward an explanatory synthesis.

Our discussion will briefly sketch some of the major value orientations or themes in American society. Under these various heads, we will appraise recent changes in the particular value, examine the interaction between value and social structure (a topic sometimes neglected by value theorists) and identify conditions that either impede or facilitate the expression of the values in behavior relevant to Jewish-gentile relationships.

Assumptions and Definitions

We accept Charles Herbert Stember's analysis as a demonstration that anti-Semitism in the United States has undergone a genuine and marked decline since the end of the Second World War. The evidence seems to us to show that non-Jews have grown less and less likely to be aware of Jews as a distinct segment or grouping, or to find Jews salient in events that attract public attention and concern. We agree that the declining frequency of various stereotyped anti-Jewish opinions, as registered in nationwide public-opinion surveys, reflects a substantial decline in the actual prevalence and intensity of generalized anti-Semitism. We also agree that it is necessary to explain why the American public has not resorted to anti-Semitism as an easy response to the numerous frustrations of national purpose or the pervasive anxieties and fears attendant on recent international tensions and nuclear threats. For the moment, we leave open the question how widely remaining latent anti-Jewish attitudes or beliefs might be reactivated under some future hypothetical circumstances.

Not only do the nationwide survey data show an impressive degree of internal consistency; they also make sense in terms of other, external evidence. For example, there can be little doubt that overt discrimination against Jews has greatly declined during the last twenty years or so. Even so long ago as the New Deal era, ethnic, racial, religious and class elements that hitherto had occupied the margins of acceptance or "respectability" began to be welcomed into responsible political life. At the same time, the central Executive, the Congress, and especially the Supreme Court began to extend the equal protection of the law to guard the civil liberties and civil rights of various minority groups and dissenting individuals.[1] Thus, the attitude trends reported by Stember find persuasive support in the course of actual events, and we see no reason to question his findings.

In the discussions that follow, we will use the terms "values" or "value orientations" interchangeably to refer to the standards of desirability by which men make and justify their choices or selections of objects, events and modes of behavior. In essence, values are simply important notions of what is good or bad in various senses. However, as we examine major value orientations, we shall also have to consider knowledge and beliefs; for in any appraisal of reality, evaluations are connected with cognitive aspects. Our judgments of what is are always relevant to our assessments of what should be.

For a case in point, we may turn to a recent change in belief that is partly documented by opinion polls. The idea that distinguishable segments of the population—particularly Negroes and whites—differ innately in intelligence is fading; and the decline of racist beliefs like this one probably has begun to cast doubt on the whole habit of imputing inherent traits to whole "races" or other categories of the population. The change is one of knowledge, not, *per se,* of values; but such progressive revision of knowledge and belief, if widespread and long-continued, is almost bound to lead to some alteration in standards of good and proper conduct. Most of the value orientations to which we refer later will turn out to be similarly complex mixtures of knowledge, belief and evaluation.

Any generalizations we may make about values in American society will be limited by the quality of available data, which are scanty, unsystematic and often difficult to interpret. Generalizations concerning changes in values are even harder to come by than are descriptions of current value patterns, because comparable information for the past and present is rarely available. Even when certain values can be identified and located, we usually lack reliable information concerning their salience, intensity and exact relation to specified kinds of overt behavior. Besides, when we analyze something as complicated as a highly differentiated society of more than 190 million people, we are sure to find great diversity of values.

Finally, we must bear in mind that in a given group or society any one identifiable value theme will be present simultaneously with all other current values. Almost always the opposite, or at least various kinds of modifying values, will be simultaneously held by at least some people in the society. Take, for example, the ideas of freedom (in the sense of the British tradition) and of equality (in the sense of the French Revolution). As shown by George H. Sabine in a classic essay some years ago, the two ideas are demonstrably in conflict with one another; yet both are omnipresent, inescapable components of democracy, and it is impossible to imagine a genuine democratic philosophy without either.[2]

This kind of complex interpenetration, or tension and opposition, is characteristic of large-scale and complex societies. Therefore, we must remember that one cannot attach any neat over-all summary or label to an entire nation without misleading simplification. We would hold, for example, that the Southern states have a value system too distinctive to be a mere variant of a unitary national system, and would generally tend to stress the diversity or "pluralism," meaning the marked differences in values, among different segments, sections, strata and other divisions within America's social structure. Still, when all the necessary qualifications have been taken into account, we believe that some fairly important general conclusions can be drawn.

What, then, can we say about American value orientations that would be relevant to understanding the attitudes of non-Jews toward Jews? The following list of main value themes, adapted from an earlier analysis,[3] may serve as the framework of our explorations:

1. *Achievement values:* activity, work, accomplishment, success.

2. *Material and rational values:* material comfort and progress; efficiency and practicality; science and secular rationality.

3. *Humane values:* humanitarianism, freedom, equality; ethical universalism; moral orientation.

4. *Miscellaneous values:* conformity; nationalism; democracy; racial or group superiority; value of the individual.

Between them, these complex orientations imbue the culture as a whole with a tendency to emphasize active mastery rather than passive acceptance of events; an external rather than an inward view of the world; an outlook that perceives society and history as open-ended, not static; a faith in rationalism, as opposed to traditionalism; an interest in orderliness; a universalistic rather than a particularistic social ethic; horizontal or equalitarian rather than hierarchical social relationships; and unique individual personality rather than collective identity and responsibility.[4]

Achievement Values

One whole complex of American values centers around a high regard for *acitivity, work, accomplishment and success.* This theme, called "instrumental activism" by Talcott Parsons, is illustrated by the habit of saying, "Well, don't just stand there, do something!"—even at times when it might be better to do nothing and just stand for a while. The interrelated emphases on being active in the world, making things happen, mastering the environment and attaining competitive success against some standard of excellence certainly would seem to be important components, if anything is, of a distinctly American ethos.

Social scientists have discussed at length what has been happening to values in this general area. Some observers say the nation is losing its concern with achievement, whereas others claim that Americans have simply changed modes of expression and are actually just as much oriented toward achievement as ever.

A recent study shows that emphasis on achievement has declined in the content of children's textbooks between the early years of this century and the present. An analysis of certain literature used by 4-H clubs finds a similar decline, and there are other fragments of data in the same vein. But elsewhere, evidence is cited of continuing emphasis on occupational competition and, at least since Sputnik, of a new stress on intellectual achievement. It is also pointed out that Americans tend to make use of their new leisure almost in a spirit of obligation: Having as much fun as possible has become virtually a duty, the argument goes, and people work very hard indeed at this new challenge to achievement.

The evidence seems to demonstrate no change so decisive that we would be led to expect any dramatic difference in the public's orientation toward Jews. In this connection we must also recall that, all along, historic "Jewish" values have fitted relatively well with non-Jewish "American" ones. In this country, Jews and gentiles alike have prized personal achievement and success, active striving and ambition, religious freedom and cultural pluralism, humanitarianism, voluntarism, material prosperity, democracy, individual freedom and responsibility. Those similarities have not always been apparent; but if one looks at the historic stereotypes of the Yankee and the Jew and removes the labels, it is hard to know which is being talked about.[5] When people are asked to describe "Americans," they often use almost the same adjectives as for the stereotype Jew: ambitious, active, industrious, aggressive and so on.

That these alleged traits always seem laudable when seen in the context of "us," and threatening when seen in the context of "them," proves no radical opposition between sets of Jewish and of American non-Jewish values. On the contrary, there has been a great deal of congruity, and it is difficult to imagine Jewish history in the United States without it. Although other, sometimes opposing, values also have existed and sometimes have been dominant, we believe any careful and systematic appraisal will show the main value patterns of American Jewish culture unmistakably converging with those of the American Protestant culture—the "core" culture, as some students call it.

We have to be careful in assessing this point, because similarity of values obviously does not by itself guarantee mutual acceptance or freedom from prejudice and discrimination. Since Jews in the United States have been primarily an urban, upwardly mobile population, with a cultural tradition to match, a congruity of values was present early; but, for a time, behavior reflecting this very congruity often became a stimulus to anti-Semitism. Given the historical background and the group definitions that were at work, shared standards of active achievement meant effective competition and could well cause gentiles to feel threatened by, or hostile toward, Jews. Still, as achievement values gradually permeate the whole society, it becomes increasingly difficult to deny anyone the right to participate on these terms. Today, all the pressures are toward recognizing and respecting position based on accomplishment, regardless of person.

Many students suggest that Americans have been shifting from a stress on "achievement," that is, the accomplishment of valued purposes, to "success," that is, the material reward for accomplishment. To put it crudely, it is thought that the individual was once valued for whatever great things he did, but now is admired for the expensive things he gets: a high income, a big home with a swimming pool and so forth. Much has been made of this interpretation by some recent social commentators; but as one looks back into history, it is not at all obvious that we of today overvalue success more than did the denizens of the Gilded Age. On the contrary, sheer success seems to have enjoyed particularly garish display in the last twenty years of the nineteenth century and the first quarter of the twentieth.

Material Progress, Practicality and Rationality

Material comfort and progress are the themes of another salient set of American values and beliefs. They are aspects of a pragmatic cult of "the good life." The ready acceptance of material comfort as a good thing runs counter to a strain of asceticism which has come down to us through several major religious traditions, but it probably has increased in recent years. There seems to be a more relaxed attitude about enjoying the comforts and luxuries of life without feeling that something sinful is thereby being perpetrated. In this respect, the general culture would seem to have moved toward greater congruence with at least certain aspects of contemporary American-Jewish life. The situation is very complicated, however, since in both Jewish and Christian culture ascetic traditions have always coexisted with other emphases.

In any event, it seems likely that many of the outstanding changes in this sphere during the last twenty years have tended to make Jews less distinctive and less conspicuous in the eyes of non-Jews. Since 1945, the entire nation has become more urbanized, better educated, more prosperous, more middle-class in style of life. In all these respects, therefore, gentiles and Jews have become more similar. When nearly everyone is becoming a city dweller or at least adopting city ways, it no longer makes sense to condemn Jews for being city folk. When affluence is widespread and levels of material welfare are generally rising, the middle-class position of most Jews becomes less salient and less likely to elicit envy. When educational achievement is stressed as practically a patriotic duty, it is absurd to resent the Jews' high educational aspirations and attainments. When four-fifths of the population enjoys relatively abundant consumption of the fruits of mass production, the stereotype of the "wealthy Jew" loses much of its sharpness.

There are no satisfactory data linking possible value changes directly to these developments. It is quite likely, however, that the majority of the population has moved away from asceticism or self-denial toward an appreciation of material abundance and the enjoyment of creature comforts. If so, envy and moralistic condemnation of the relatively prosperous Jewish minority may be expected to diminish.

Efficiency and practicality are points of American national pride—perhaps sometimes of self-deceiving or misplaced pride. Our culture has always prized quick, pragmatic adaptation to immediate problems, rather than adherence to time-honored, traditional ways of doing things. In keeping with the increasingly task-centered and innovative character of the modern urban world, American society as a whole has tended more and more to rate individuals on the strength of their contribution to efficiency, material comfort, "progress" and the like, rather than on the basis of traditional group membership or group characteristics—Jewish or otherwise.

In the American culture, regard for *science and secular rationality* are closely related both to instrumental activism and to efficiency or practicality; that is, the technological products of science have usually been valued more than its theoretical aspects. True, so eminent a scientist as J. Robert Oppenheimer holds that in recent years this country has been placing greater emphasis on basic science and theoretical development, but the trend is as yet far from clear. In any case, during the period under review here, the general public has accorded increased prestige to what it understands by science and probably to intellectual work generally. Many of us can remember the days when the term "intellectual" was used, if at all, as a damaging epithet; today, fewer people take this attitude.

To the extent that non-Jews accept the values of education and science, they commit themselves to a position consistent with the Jews' traditional high regard for learning. Of course, Jews may still represent a competitive threat to non-Jews; but when competitors are widely scattered throughout most segments of the society, it becomes difficult to isolate them or any one group as salient. Besides, the commitment to the value of universalism (of which more later) reinforces acceptance of the standards of personal achievement.

Humanitarian Values

Since the 1930s, American society as a whole has increasingly acknowledged a public obligation to guard, nurture and care for various types of disadvantaged or unfortunate persons: women, children, Negroes, the unemployed, the destitute, the handicapped, the physically or emotionally ill, the victims of disaster. This deepening concern reflects the values of *humanitarianism* or regard for the individual personality, of *freedom,* and of *equality*. At the same time, it is an expression of the instrumental activism of which we have spoken; for by providing support to check misfortune short of complete disaster, society also protects the individual's capacity to achieve. In accepting new collective obligations to care for its less fortunate members, the general culture again appears to have moved toward a position consistent with a strongly marked Jewish tradition.

With some exceptions and some strong countermovements, the total configuration of interpersonal values and beliefs most widely shared in the United States probably has moved away from harshly punitive moralism. The nation seems to be headed toward greater openness and permissiveness concerning emotional expression and psychological "problems"; toward less rigidity and dogmatism in personal rules of conduct; toward more understanding and empathy among individuals. Whatever the extent of these hypothetical changes, they are bound to foster mutual acceptance and co-operation between different groups, and to reduce discrimination and conflict.

In the guiding conceptions of human nature, the trend evidently has been from an emphasis upon sin and evil toward the view that people are either "naturally" good or neither good nor evil. In terms of time perspective, emphasis has tended to shift from the future to be attained toward the present to be enjoyed. Probably there is a correlated tendency toward less concern with "doing" and more with "being"—toward expressive rather than instrumental emphases. The preferred basic mode of relationships between the individual and other persons appears to be less often competitive than formerly, and more often cooperative. Freedom and achievement remain basic values, but they have been modified by an increasing concern with, and realization of, equality—expecially as regards the task of equalizing certain kinds of opportunity.

By picking and choosing one-sided evidence, one possibly could make a superficially persuasive case for the contention that America had undergone increased pressures toward conformity to nationalistic demands for "loyalty" since 1900. But it would be extremely difficult to draw an even momentarily plausible picture of a decrease in the value placed upon equality of rights since then. The present century began, after all, with white-supremacy doctrines firmly dominant in law and social practice, with anti-Semitic attitudes widespread and anti-Jewish discrimination prevalent in every sector of life. By the time of the First World War with its suppressive chauvinism, the "tide of legal lawlessness" [6] had all but overwhelmed the freedom and equality of anyone who opposed the dominant mood.

In subsequent years, these conditions were superseded by a gradual institutionalization of procedural equality—a process which, in our political democracy with its nominally universal suffrage, may be regarded as an expression of *ethical universalism*. One by one, various segments of the population (women, the propertyless, aliens, Negroes, Indians, unpopular religious sects) began to receive equal rights; and these successive equalitarian moves established the principle that individuals should be treated by universal standards, rather than on the basis of particular social relations or group ties.

Since the end of the Second World War, events in the domestic political and administrative arena have served mainly to extend and reinforce this institutionalized universalism—notwithstanding contrary tendencies, sometimes evident even in decisions of the Supreme Court. The task of elaborating and extending ethical universalism undoubtedly was made easier by the end of large-scale immigration and by the increasing cultural similarity of "majority" and "minority" Americans.

In the realm of political ideology, both equality and freedom have long been American ideals. Taking a broad common-sense notion, we might describe freedom as minimum interference with the individual in carrying out what he prefers to do. By a similarly common-sense standard, we may conceive of equality as the treatment of everyone according to the same rules (procedural equality) plus life opportunities that are, as nearly as practicable, the same for all (substantive equality). In this sense, public actions undertaken during the past generation to remove disabilities due to racial or religious discrimination have brought the previously disadvantaged nearer to both equality and freedom—with the chief stress upon the former. The equalitarian movement has usually sought to extend universalistic principles to more and more groups and sectors of national life, rather than to establish substantive equality of condition (for example, of income). It has thus become progressively more difficult to continue gross public discrimination against members of ethnic, racial or religious minorities.

As the themes of equality and universalism have gained a more central place in public policy and in many private relationships, values have come to be stated more explicitly, and with this greater articulateness, value conflicts have also become more evident. Increased pressure toward consistency in values and in their fulfillment probably has been one result; the new explicit emphasis on universal equality of rights has made it more difficult to compartmentalize racial, ethnic or religious discrimination.

At this point, we must call attention to a whole complex of values centering around a *moral orientation* to the world—particularly to the idea that there are obligatory moral principles in human life which transcend considerations of expediency. Our culture is fundamentally committed to this idea; but nobody has any clear evidence showing whether and how much the commitment may have increased or decreased over any particular period of the nation's life. By picking and choosing among historical anecdotes—from the Grant Administration, for example, or from any other corrupt era—one can support almost any case one might wish to make. The particular trait of humanitarianism, of a moral concern for helping others, certainly is prominent in the American self-image, even though, as Stember's analysis shows, it often is restricted in scope. In our judgment—admittedly an impressionistic one—humanitarian values over the long run have found increased practical realization. All other things being equal, this tendency would seem calculated to reduce anti-Jewish prejudice.

Other Values

Group conformity is a standard of conduct only insofar as it is considered in relation to a specific content. Changes in pressure toward certain particular kinds of conformity are likely to be linked with changes in anti-Semitism. Thus, as has often been noted, heightened demands for political conformity tend to coincide with increases in anti-Jewish feeling.

Social scientists' appraisals of conformity in American life have been unstable, subject to fashions and fads. Not very long ago, certain scholars in the field feared that our society might disintegrate for lack of conformity to a set of common values. A few years later, some of the same experts were warning against the hazards of an alleged new, excessive conventionality. In our opinion, much of the latter concern was misplaced. As regards conformity regardless of content (that is, the mere fact of group pressure to abide by some generally accepted norm), a reading of earlier American history suggests that our rural areas and small towns were never notable havens for drastic dissent.

American life has long put a premium on being a good member of one's group and, above all, on the shibboleth of teamwork. Since any right-thinking person is supposed to go along with the team, someone who does not fit in is suspected of having something wrong with him, and dissident persons or groups often come to be regarded as strange. However, this insistence on conformity has to be viewed in relation to the particulars of the social structure, because in some degree it is simply a necessity dictated by existing conditions. Modern life inevitably demands many kinds of conformity that were not required in nineteenth-century America; you can permit yourself only a very limited degree of eccentricity in driving an automobile through the streets of New York today.

In other contexts, present-day reactions to group differences seem to represent not conformism but rather a kind of generalized indifference. Of course, people still expect others to conform to certain norms in direct personal relations; but for many the expectation evidently ends there. Apparently, large numbers of Americans think of all the people outside their own small circles as a great gray mass, with whose behavior they are not concerned. To put it briefly and no doubt too simply, these persons say, in effect: "There is just too much of the rest of the world to bother about, and we'll let them go their way as long as they don't step on our toes."

The values of *nationalism* and patriotism, or Americanism, have always been of at least two kinds. One is uncritical and self-contained ("My country, right or wrong"). The other is more discriminating and focuses more on other value themes such as *democracy,* freedom or ethical universalism. To the extent that these latter values are thought to be characteristic of this country, they serve the more discriminating type of patriot as the core of his national identification and loyalty.

Changes in nationalistic values and sentiments always bear watching with regard to minority relations, because extreme upsurges of nationalism typically result in pressures on the ethnic minorities found within a given country. This effect is being demonstrated daily around the world right now.

Popular allegiance to the idea of the American nation certainly does not seem to have diminished in recent years, but it probably has become more complex and differentiated, at least more so than it was in the era of Joseph

R. McCarthy. Still, it is clear that a kind of simplistic "right-or-wrong" nationalism remains present, and is once more being strongly activated among some groups. Given favorable circumstances, it could perhaps become the dominant national mood and in that case, failing countermeasures, it might result in an increase of anti-Semitism; but no such trend is now in evidence.

Ideas about *racial or group superiority* are an unpalatable theme; but we must contend that they are not mere aberrations or deviations. Racism has been a persistent major component of the nation's culture for a long time; a strong current of group-superiority doctrine has run through American life almost from the beginning. By the time of the Spanish-American War, various forces in our national life had fused together a complex of such beliefs and values that was coherent and almost organic. It is clear, however, that during recent years these notions have rapidly receded. Although Stember does not find hostility against Jews closely related to racist ideas now, the general weakening of racism would seem bound in the long run to help undercut ideas of group superiority based on ethnic or religious as well as racial differences. We may suspect that much of this undercutting has already been accomplished, thanks to intellectual developments and sheer increase in knowledge. Racist ideology is not likely to disappear; but it may conceivably be reduced to a fairly low level within the next twenty-five years or so.

Finally, an enduring central faith in the *value of the individual* runs like a leitmotif through many of the themes we have sketched. The uniqueness and dignity of every human being rank high in the traditions of the American creed. Often disregarded in the rough-and-tumble of economic and political life, often submerged in times of war or internal crisis, this conviction yet persists in our day. Indeed, it may have been strengthened by revulsion against the horror and dehumanization at large in the modern world, especially in the Nazi era.

The General Perspective

The period here under review is so short that really drastic changes in values are perhaps not to be expected. No completely new value orientations have become evident since the Second World War, nor have any major ones disappeared. As we indicated, important shifts have occurred in emphasis and arrangement; but it would have been surprising to uncover any revolutionary discontinuities.

Perhaps there has been less change in basic values than in information, in social structure, in occupational distribution and style of life. As we observed earlier, the whole country has become more middle-class, more urban and more educated. In several important characteristics, the society has moved toward positions already occupied by the majority of Jews in the

United States. Therefore, talk about Jews today means, to a growing number of middle-class gentiles, talk about people much like themselves.

Furthermore, the public's attention has undergone important shifts, in part because the main agencies that define issues and objects of attention for the public—specifically, government policy and the mass media—play other roles than formerly. What does today's average subway rider hear and read about in the course of a week? Issues like the struggle in Vietnam, the future of Africa, Communism, Chinese atomic power, threats of major war, poverty, racial tension North and South, controversy over the welfare state or over the state of affairs in Washington. No matter how often he wishes all these things would go away, they are what commands his attention—not the Jews. Current national or international concerns and abstract issues tend to monopolize much of the attention and energy that went into anti-Semitism during the 1930s.

Finally, basic attitudes toward religious differences appear to be in a process of transformation. We do not think about religious differences the way we did thirty years ago. Strictly theological disagreements, differences in the specific content of particular faiths, are not as salient now. This is one reason for the new ecumenical spirit. Another is the rediscovery of common ground among the major faiths. Popular assumptions about the meaning of religious differences have subtly changed; more and more Americans feel that everybody need not hold the same beliefs in order to live in the same society.

What changes in America's culture and social system, aside from changes in values, may have contributed to the reduction in anti-Jewish attitudes and behavior? As other contributors to this book have indicated, the list of possible factors is long. Thus, the flow of immigration has been stemmed and assimilation has progressed. Prosperity is greater and more widely diffused than formerly, while occupational and economic competition among lower- and middle-income strata is less intense. More and more persons are able, in one way or another, to attain valued goals. Christian teachings are being improved. Social and economic problems are being defined in ideological and institutional rather than in ethnic or religious terms. Most of these factors, I believe, have in some measure helped directly to lower the prevalence or intensity of anti-Semitism. But these so-called "objective" social conditions also must have affected attitudes toward Jews via the values we have discussed. For instance, respect for the value of the individual personality always is put under strain when people are severely frustrated, deprived or brutalized; when gratification is more available and tension less acute, they find it much easier to treat the other person with some consideration for his humanity and individuality.

Beliefs and values seemingly calculated to foster anti-Semitism, even if widely held, are not necessarily sufficient to evoke an appreciable amount of overt anti-Semitic opinion or action.[7] Many anti-Jewish stereotypes are still current among a substantial part of the nation; but they have lost their intensity and respectability. Besides, institutionalized forms of social organization have become modified so that they now bar overt manifestations of "prejudice" from important fields. In this area of life, as in others, organizational structure may change quite decisively without immediately setting off a corresponding radical shift in popular attitudes; yet once the new structural forms become established, they create new vested interests and new ideas of normality and "taken-for-grantedness." Thus, with each passing year, it is becoming more difficult to reactivate classical anti-Semitism in the United States—even though to date our society has rearranged itself structurally rather than in terms of basic values.

NOTES

1. Even before Franklin D. Roosevelt had appointed any new Justices, the Supreme Court had acted to make ". . . due process of law in the area of *human* rights . . . an active ingredient of American constitutionalism." John P. Roche, *The Quest for the Dream* (New York: The Macmillan Co., 1963), p. 151.

2. George H. Sabine, "The Two Democratic Traditions," *The Philosophical Review,* LXI:451–474 (1952).

3. See Robin M. Williams, Jr., *American Society* (2d ed.; New York: Alfred A. Knopf, 1963), pp. 415–468, where these themes are examined at some length.

4. *Ibid.,* pp. 468–470.

5. Simeon Strunsky, *No Mean City* (New York: E. P. Dutton & Co., 1944), pp. 86–91.

6. For a vivid portrait of these periods, see Roche, *op. cit.,* pp. 1–75.

7. "A generalized belief may have lain dormant for a long time before any movement bearing its name arises; in order for this belief to become a determinant in such a movement it must be activated by conditions of conduciveness and strain." Neil J. Smelser, *Theory of Collective Behavior* (New York: The Free Press of Glencoe, 1963), p. 278.

Demographic Trends and
the Decline of Anti-Semitism

ROBERT GUTMAN

THERE ARE APPROXIMATELY five and one-half million Jews living in the United States at present—more than at any other time in the country's history. Yet Jews today constitute only about 3.0 per cent of the nation, the lowest ratio in roughly half a century (Table A). In 1907,

Table A Total, Gentile and Jewish Populations. United States, 1877–1961

Year	Total Population	Gentile Population	Jewish Population	Ratio of Jewish to Total Population
1877	46,353,000	46,123,913	229,087	0.52
1888	59,974,000	59,574,000	400,000	0.67
1897	71,592,000	70,654,200	937,800	1.31
1907	85,817,239	84,040,054	1,777,185	2.00
1917	103,266,000	98,877,049	3,388,951	3.27
1927	119,038,000	114,809,971	4,228,029	3.58
1937	128,961,000	124,190,353	4,770,647	3.69
1947	144,126,000	139,126,000	5,000,000	3.66
1957	171,198,000	165,943,000	5,255,000	3.09
1961	184,000,000	178,490,000	5,510,000	3.01

SOURCES: Total population figures from *Statistical Abstract of the United States;* Jewish population estimates from *American Jewish Year Book,* XXX (1928–29), XLI (1939–40), IL (1947–48), LIX (1958), LXIII (1962). Gentile population equals total minus estimated Jewish population.

the proportion of Jews in the total population stood at a mere 2.0 per cent, but at some time between this date and America's entrance into the First

World War it rose above the 3.0 per cent mark, and by the 1930s it had increased to an estimated 3.7 per cent. The decline since then is a sign that the rate of population growth among Jews has not kept pace with that among gentiles.

The differences in the two groups' growth rates over the last century are a fascinating subject for demographic analysis (Table B). From 1818[1] until

Table B Annual Rates of Population Increase among Total, Gentile and Jewish Populations in Different Periods. United States, 1877–1961

	Annual Rates of Increase		
Period	Total Population	Gentile Population	Jewish Population
1877–1887	2.7	2.7	6.8
1888–1896	2.2	2.1	14.9
1897–1906	2.0	1.9	9.0
1907–1916	2.0	1.8	9.1
1917–1926	1.5	1.6	2.5
1927–1936	0.8	0.8	1.3
1937–1946	1.2	1.2	0.5
1947–1956	1.9	1.9	0.5
1957–1961	1.9	1.9	1.0

SOURCE: Table A.

1936, the Jews' annual rate constantly exceeded that of the gentiles; at times it was six or seven times as great. But in the decade of the Great Depression, the relationship between the two was dramatically reversed. During the last full ten-year period covered by the available data, 1947–56, the rate of increase among Jews was only one-quarter of that among gentiles.

A population can change its size and rate of growth in only three ways: through alterations in fertility, mortality or the rate of net migration (that is, of immigration minus emigration or vice versa). In varying degrees, all three processes have played a part in the curious demographic history of American Jews.

Mortality of Jews

In the late nineteenth century, mortality apparently was lower among Jews than among other religious groups. One reason, it is believed, was that their welfare and communal organizations operated more efficiently than those of other ethnic enclaves within cities.[2] Besides, Jews probably were more careful in their eating habits and domestic sanitation; they were concentrated in the larger Eastern cities, where public health controls were more advanced; and from the beginning they were readier to make use of physicians' services, as well as to recognize the importance of public-health measures like pasteurization and antisepsis. Studies of the comparative death rates of religious groups conducted in the last thirty-five years still reflect a lower mortality rate among Jews.[3]

Even so, greater longevity has been only a minor factor in the Jews' unique growth rates, both in the late nineteenth century and in recent years. Comparative death rates have not differed enough to account for more than a small portion of the excess of Jewish over gentile growth rates before the 1930s.[4] Furthermore, the expectation of life at birth among Jews has remained remarkably constant over the last hundred years; their mortality rate was lower than the gentiles' after as well as before their growth rate fell below the gentiles' rate.

Trends in Jewish Immigration

In the upward and downward gyrations of the Jewish population growth rate, immigration has figured far larger than mortality (Tables C and D). The period when the Jewish population grew at four or more times the rate of the gentile coincided roughly with the years of the heaviest Jewish influx. Between 1888 and 1916, almost two million Jews immigrated to this country permanently—nearly five times as many as had lived here previously. In the period from 1888 to 1896 alone, the number of Jewish newcomers amounted to 83 per cent of the number of older Jewish settlers; in the decade from 1907 to 1916, it still came to 44 per cent. It was this massive movement that contributed the major share of Jewish population growth in the decades before and after the turn of the century; in the three periods from 1888 to 1916, net immigration accounted respectively for 62, 81 and 49 per cent of increases in the number of Jews.

Gentile immigration, too, reached a peak about the turn of the century, but its effect on the over-all statistics of gentiles was necessarily small by comparison. Thus, between 1907 and 1916, a net of roughly five million non-Jewish newcomers, more than in any earlier or later decade, came here to stay, but this huge number amounts to only 6 per cent of the gentile population of 1907 and accounts for only 32 per cent of gentile population growth during the decade.

The quota laws of the 1920s reserved their severest restrictions for immigration from Southern and Eastern Europe—the regions from which Jews had been migrating in the largest numbers. The change was immediately reflected in the Jewish growth rate.[5] Having profited more than the gentiles from a liberal immigration policy, the Jews suffered more when this policy was reversed. Previously 9 per cent or more, the Jewish annual growth rate between 1917 and 1926 dropped to 2.5 per cent. In this decade and the

Table C Increase and Net Migration of Jewish and Gentile Populations in Different Periods. United States, 1888–1956

Period	Population Increase		Net Migration		Ratio of Net Migration to Population Increase	
	Gentile	Jewish	Gentile	Jewish	Gentile	Jewish
1888–1896	11,080,200	537,800	2,372,625	334,338	21.4	62.2
1897–1906	13,385,854	839,385	3,618,190	679,598	27.0	81.0
1907–1916	15,836,995	1,611,766	5,003,973	787,971	31.6	48.9
1917–1926	14,932,562	839,078	2,246,689	326,778	16.4	38.9
1927–1936	9,380,382	542,618	717,897	70,092	7.6	12.9
1937–1946	14,935,647	229,353	253,210	168,613	1.7	73.5
1947–1956	26,817,000	255,000	2,015,134	146,225	7.5	57.3

SOURCES: Figures for population increases are derived from Table A. Net Jewish migration between 1888 and 1943 was estimated by approximately the procedure described in *American Jewish Year Book*, IL (1947–48), 745–747. A comparable procedure was followed in estimating the net migration of the total population, from which figures for the gentile population were then obtained. From 1944 on, net migration was assumed to equal the number of Jewish immigrants admitted, as given in *American Jewish Year Book*, LXII (1961), 64.

This calculation does not take into account the changing contribution of natural increase (the excess of births over deaths) to population growth in successive decades. In general, fertility exceeded mortality among both gentiles and Jews throughout the period covered. The ratios given in the last two columns therefore consistently overestimate the true contribution of migration to population growth. However, since natural increase was higher among gentiles than among Jews, the difference between the proportional contribution of net migration to Jewish and to gentile growth probably is even greater than the values suggest.

Table D Initial Size and Net Migration of Jewish and Gentile Populations in Different Periods. United States, 1888–1956

Period	Initial Population		Net Migration		Ratio of Net Migration to Initial Population	
	Gentile	Jewish	Gentile	Jewish	Gentile	Jewish
1888–1896	59,574,000	400,000	2,372,625	334,338	4.0	83.0
1897–1906	70,654,200	937,800	3,618,190	679,598	5.1	72.5
1907–1916	84,040,054	1,777,185	5,003,973	787,971	6.0	44.4
1917–1926	99,877,049	3,388,951	2,246,689	326,778	2.3	9.5
1927–1936	114,089,971	4,228,029	717,897	70,092	0.6	1.7
1937–1946	124,190,353	4,770,647	253,210	168,613	0.2	3.5
1947–1956	139,126,000	5,000,000	2,015,134	146,225	1.4	2.9

SOURCES: Same as Table C.

next, it was less than twice the gentile rate; by the decade from 1937 to 1946, it had dropped below the latter, and it has stayed there ever since.

It should be noted that even today's Jewish population growth, low as it is, depends on immigration to a truly amazing degree. The ratio of immigrants to prior residents is more than twice as high among Jews as among gentiles. Even more striking is the substantial proportion of Jewish population growth from 1937 to 1946, and again from 1947 to 1956, that was still attributable to net immigration.[6] However, these high proportions are less significant than those of earlier decades, since the absolute volume of immigration as well as of population increase has been small. Fewer than 150,000 Jewish immigrants were admitted to the United States between 1947 and 1956, as against almost 800,000 between 1907 and 1916.

Nativity Composition and Attitudes toward Jews

What light, if any, do these demographic findings shed on the recent decrease in anti-Semitism observed by Stember? During the past three decades, Jewish immigration has become almost invisible compared to its saliency in earlier decades, and the rate of Jewish population growth has slipped below that of the nation as a whole. If we were to hold, with some of the contributors to this volume, that anti-Semitism in the United States has been largely a product of the great influx of Jews from Eastern Europe which began in the 1880s, we might argue that the recent decline in anti-Semitic feeling stems partly from the reduction of immigration in the last few decades. At least we might assert that the lessening of the stream of newcomers gave more room to democratic attitudes and pluralistic ideologies calculated to foster cordial relations between Jews and gentiles.

How greatly the end of large-scale immigration has altered the complexion of American Jewry during recent decades is illustrated by a large array of data on the changing nativity composition of various cities (Table E). Any national statistics must be estimated from community population surveys like these, and therefore lack a certain precision; yet the trend is unmistakable.

The surveys, extending from 1936 to 1964, suggest first of all that today only about 15 per cent of the Jewish population is foreign-born; in cities and metropolitan regions with long-established, sizable Jewish communities, such as San Francisco, the proportion is somewhat larger.

Second, it appears that foreign-born persons still are two to three times as numerous among Jews as in the total population, judging by census data for the latter. The gap seems to be widest in Midwestern cities, where Jews probably constitute an unusually large segment of the foreign-born; it is narrowest in Northeastern cities, where many ethnic groups besides Jews reside.

Finally, the proportion of foreign-born persons among the Jews appears

Table E Percentages of Foreign-Born Persons in Jewish and Total Populations. Selected U. S. Cities and Metropolitan Areas, 1936–1954

City or Metropolitan Area	Jewish Population		Total Population	
	Survey Date	Per Cent Foreign-Born	Census Date	Per Cent Foreign-Born
Minneapolis, Minn.	1936	38.9	1940	13.1
Passaic, N. J.	1937	40.0	1940	28.9
Trenton, N. J.	1937	34.2	1940	17.6
Buffalo, N. Y.	1938	35.9	1940	16.0
New London, Conn.	1938	37.4	1940	16.6
Norwich, Conn.	1938	35.8	1940	18.3
Pittsburgh, Pa.	1938	37.4	1940	12.6
San Francisco, Calif.	1938	31.8	1940	22.1
Newark, N. J. (city only)	1948	31.2	1950	16.1
Newark, N. J. (including suburbs)	1948	22.2	1950	14.9
Passaic, N. J.	1949	31.1	1950	24.2
Los Angeles, Calif.	1950	32.1	1950	12.5
New Orleans, La.	1950	16.9	1950	2.6
Port Chester, N. Y.	1950	25.4	1950	18.0
Washington, D. C.	1956	17.0	1960	4.2
San Francisco, Calif.	1958	22.8	1960	19.3
Los Angeles, Calif.	1959	24.8	1960	12.6
Rochester, N. Y.	1961	21.0	1960	10.0
South Bend, Ind.	1961	20.3	1960	5.9
Trenton, N. J.	1961	15.0	1960	11.5
Providence, R. I.	1963	17.2	1960	10.4
Camden, N. J.	1964	9.0	1960	6.8

SOURCES: Information on nativity of total population from U. S. Department of Commerce, Bureau of the Census, *Sixteenth Census of the United States: 1940*, vol. II, parts 1, 2, 4, 5, 6; *U. S. Census of the Population: 1950*, vol. II, parts 5, 9, 18, 30, 32; *U. S. Census of the Population: 1960*, vol. I, parts 6, 10, 16, 32, 34, 40, 41. Information on Jewish nativity in the 1930s from Sophia M. Robison, editor, *Jewish Population Studies* (New York: Conference on Jewish Relations, 1943); in the late 1940s and 1950 from Ben B. Seligman, "Some Aspects of Jewish Demography," in Marshall Sklare, editor, *The Jews* (Glencoe, Ill.: The Free Press, 1958), pp. 45–93; in 1956 and later from Jewish population surveys in cities listed.

to be going down rapidly. In the surveys of the 1930s, 30 and 40 per cent were common figures; in those of the 1940s, the proportions were reduced by approximately one-third, and in the most recent studies by another third. The downward trend is clearly shown in cities whose Jewish populations have been surveyed more than once during the last 30 years. Of the Jews in

Trenton, New Jersey, for example, more than 34 per cent were foreign-born in 1937, but only 15 per cent in 1961. Similar decreases occurred in Passaic, New Jersey, as well as in San Francisco and Los Angeles. Since the foreign-born today include a disproportionate number of aged persons, it should not be long before the nativity composition of the Jews will resemble that of the nation as a whole.

Unfortunately, none of these statistics by themselves tell us whether the increasingly native-born complexion of American Jewry has anything to do with the trends reported by Stember—whether the hostile imagery of anti-Semites has come to appear irrelevant as Jews become more and more similar to Americans generally. If Stember's findings were classified by metropolitan areas, we might examine these possibilities more closely; we could then see whether the incidence of anti-Semitism varied with the percentage of foreign-born Jews in particular localities, and whether anti-Jewish feeling declined at rates parallel to the shrinking of the foreign-born Jewish population. As it is, the data permit no such analysis.

Trends in Jewish Fertility

If the marked dependence of Jewish population growth on immigration is the obverse of the coin, the characteristic low fertility of American Jews is the reverse. The Jews' small families, their failure to reproduce at the same rate as gentiles, are often held to be a pattern of the recent past, associated with the decline of religious orthodoxy. The fact of the matter appears to be, however, that Jews have been less fertile than gentiles throughout the years for which we have information, that is, at least since the late nineteenth century. True, the available data are sparse, and they deal with different samples of Jews, some of which probably are unrepresentative in the statistical sense; but they point plainly in this direction.

Thus, a famous special investigation conducted in 1889 by John Shaw Billings, Director of the United States Census, found the average birth rate of Jews to be 21 per 1,000, that of the United States population as a whole 31 per 1,000.[7] According to population data of the period, the native-born were generally less fertile than immigrants, so that the earlier a family had come to this country, the fewer children it was likely to have; but Billings found the decline in fertility over the generations especially marked among the Jews, even during these early years.

That American Jews have long been reproducing at a lower rate than gentiles is also indicated by Sidney Goldstein's community study of Providence (1963), by far the most thorough of the various population surveys conducted by Jewish community organizations. Goldstein found that married or formerly married Jewish women in Providence who were between 70 and 74 years old in 1963, and who thus had borne children around the time of the First World War, had an average of 3.2 children. Women who were aged 75 or more in 1963 had borne an average of 3.0 children. In the national population, women of the same age groups then had about four children on the average.[8]

Fertility data for Jews after the First World War are equal in quality to those for any other subgroup in the United States and for the nation as a whole. They again show that Jews reproduced at a lower rate than gentiles. For example, a special survey by the United States Census Bureau in 1957 indicated that married Jewish women who were born in 1912 or earlier, and had borne their children in the late 1920s and 1930s, had an average of 2.2 children. In the population as a whole, the comparable figure was 2.8, among Catholics 3.1 and among Protestants 2.7. Of the latter, only Presbyterians matched the low fertility level of the Jews, with 2.1 children per couple.[9] These data are consistent with Goldstein's detailed tabulations: In Providence during 1963, married or formerly married Jewish women of the age groups 45–49, 50–54, 55–59 and 60–64 averaged 2.0, 1.8, 1.6 and 2.0 children respectively.[10]

The general birth rate reached its lowest point in the depths of the Great Depression: 17 per 1,000 in 1934. By 1950, thanks to the postwar "baby boom," it had risen to a figure more than half as high again. The Jewish population participated in this reversal, perhaps to an even more marked degree than Protestants and Catholics, but still not enough to reduce the traditional gap between gentile and Jewish fertility. Recent studies of the numbers of children desired and expected among various religious groups in the United States suggest that the discrepancy will remain for some time. A nationwide survey of women in the childbearing years, conducted in 1955, notes that "the Jewish couples . . . expect significantly fewer children (2.4) than either Catholics (3.4) or Protestants (2.9)." [11] In 1960, a comparable group in the population was again interviewed; the Jewish women's expectations had now risen slightly, to 2.5, but those of the gentiles had increased as much or more: the Protestants' to 3.0, and the Catholics' to 3.7.[12]

The lower fertility levels of the Jews are, of course, not a consequence of lower reproductive capacity. Indeed, there is some evidence that Jewish women suffer a little less than gentile from impaired fecundity.[13] They reproduce at a lower rate because they marry later, use contraception earlier in marriage, rely on more effective contraceptive techniques (for example, the diaphragm-jelly method), and employ them more conscientiously.[14] Not all students of Jewish demography consider this reproductive pattern intrinsically Jewish; some point out that fertility expectations, contraceptive practices and actual fertility are similar among other religious groups (notably Episcopalians and Presbyterians), who share the Jews' distinctive social, educational and occupational characteristics.[15]

Is the decline of the Jewish growth rate in the United States likely to come to a halt? May we at least expect that the proportion of Jews in the national population will stop shrinking? The prospects are not good. Erich Rosenthal has considered the problem in great detail, taking into account not only mortality, fertility and net migration but also the loss due to inter-marriage with gentiles. He concludes: "While other population groups in the United States are experiencing considerable growth of population, the Jewish community is faced with the prospect of remaining at or declining from its present strength of about five million people." [16]

Rosenthal's forecast will prove overly pessimistic only if the current rate of intermarriage drops or if the birth rate of gentiles resumes its downward trend while that of the Jews does not. But such a change in fertility patterns is unlikely, considering the demographic history of the Jewish people; it is more reasonable to expect that any decline in the birth rate of gentiles would be accompanied by a greater decline in that of Jews.

Jewish Fertility Patterns and Anti-Semitism

The Jewish community's low reproduction rate probably has nothing to do with the improvement of attitudes toward Jews during recent decades. Neither Stember's data nor other sources contain any indication that Jews are pictured in anti-Semitic imagery as especially or threateningly prolific— in contrast to the Irish and Negroes, who still are frequently stereotyped in such terms. Indeed, this stereotype may well be an unconscious source of anti-Negro and anti-Irish feeling among Jews themselves.

If trends in reproduction among Jews are related to anti-Semitism at all, the causal connection probably runs the other way, hostility being the cause and low fertility the effect. That the fertility pattern of Jews is identical with those of certain gentiles when matched according to social, educational and residential criteria does not, in our opinion, exclude the possibility that the Jews' pattern may derive in part from their distinctive situation in society. We do not know that Jews and Episcopolians or Presbyterians acquire their similar middle-class characteristics and their preference for small families through the same motivations and psychodynamic processes. Nathan Goldberg suggests that, on the contrary, a special process probably is at work among Jews:

The attitude of the outside world accounts to a certain extent for the lower Jewish birth rate. Discrimination means insecurity. Persons who face discrimination therefore tend to work harder, try to excel others, and are more likely to think in terms of the future than members of less insecure groups.[17]

This interpretation is consistent not only with the lower reproduction rate of the Jews and their pattern of contraceptive practice, but also with their tendency—reported in Jewish community studies and national fertility surveys—to marry later than gentiles.

Trends in Population Distribution

In analyzing a given population, demographers usually examine not only the fundamental processes of fertility, mortality and migration, but also the group's internal structure—specifically, its geographic distribution and occupational composition. So far we have considered whether the growth patterns of the American Jewish community might be related to the decline in anti-Semitism. We must now ask the same questions about the structural patterns of the Jewish population in comparison to those of the nation.

The geographical distribution of Jews in the United States was first estimated as of 1877. For many years following that date, trends in the movement of Jews ran counter to those in the nation as a whole (Table F). Between 1877 and 1937, each decade showed smaller proportions of the total population residing in the North, and larger ones in the South and West; but the Jewish population concentrated more and more in the North, particularly in the Northeastern states. At the beginning of the period, about three-quarters of the Jews in the country lived in the North, just under 15 per cent in the South and not quite 10 per cent in the West; at the end, all but 10 per cent lived in the North, with the South and West evenly sharing the remainder.

Since 1937, Jewish population shifts have followed the same direction as gentile ones, so that the distribution of Jews has gradually become more like that of the nation as a whole. By 1957, the West's share of the Jewish population was almost double what it had been during the Depression, the South's share had also increased and the North's had declined from 90 to 81 per cent.

Besides redistributing themselves over the different regions of the country, America's Jews have also shared in the nation's growing suburbanization. Once more, the evidence is somewhat less compelling than might be expected by a demographer familiar with American population phenomena other than the behavior of religious groups; yet the conclusion is convincingly suggested by various community population surveys, as well as by the *American Jewish Year Book*'s periodic reports of the number of Jews in different cities and suburbs.

Indeed, there is reason to believe that Jews may have shifted to the suburbs at a faster rate than gentiles. A public-opinion study conducted during the 1950s examined the distribution of Protestants, Catholics and Jews by county of residence. As a rough measure of industrialization, the counties were ranked according to the proportion of their labor force employed in manufacturing and mining. It was found that the Catholic, not the Jewish, population was most concentrated in the industrial counties, that is, in those containing central cities.[18]

If Jews did in fact move to the suburbs earlier and in larger proportions

Table F Total and Jewish Population, by Regions. United States, 1877–1957

	Population of Region		Percentage of National Population in Region		Ratio of Jewish to Total Population within Region
	Total	Jewish	Total	Jewish	
North					
1877	30,428,480	174,930	69.7	76.4	0.6
1887	—	—	—	—	—
1897	46,945,468	748,000	65.1	76.8	1.6
1907	55,761,703	1,622,000	62.6	91.3	2.9
1917	63,835,562	3,126,394	61.6	92.3	4.9
1927	72,710,620	3,821,045	61.5	90.4	5.3
1937	78,870,989	4,325,273	59.9	90.6	5.5
1947	—	—	—	—	—
1957*	66,089,000	3,131,000	55.4	81.0	4.7
South					
1877	11,894,780	32,692	27.2	14.3	0.3
1887	—	—	—	—	—
1897	21,113,735	127,500	29.3	13.6	0.6
1907	27,180,855	90,185	30.6	5.1	0.3
1917	30,983,045	155,281	29.9	4.6	0.5
1927	34,531,618	225,940	29.2	5.4	0.7
1937	38,915,511	229,049	29.6	4.8	0.6
1947	—	—	—	—	—
1957*	36,551,000	299,000	30.6	7.7	0.8
West					
1877	1,338,708	21,465	3.1	9.4	1.6
1887	—	—	—	—	—
1897	4,046,917	62,300	5.6	6.6	1.4
1907	5,844,500	64,700	6.6	3.6	1.1
1917	8,821,866	107,306	8.5	3.2	1.2
1927	10,898,407	181,044	9.2	4.3	1.7
1937	13,883,265	219,322	10.6	4.6	1.6
1947	—	—	—	—	—
1957*	16,693,000	438,000	14.0	11.3	2.6

SOURCES: Figures through 1927 from Harry S. Linfield, "The Jewish Population of the United States, 1927," *American Jewish Year Book*, XXX (1928–29), 101–198. Estimates for 1937 calculated from data given *ibid.*, XLVII (1945–46), 645. The data for 1957 are probably the most accurate; they are from a Current Population survey by the Census Bureau. For the data and a discussion of them, see Donald J. Bogue, *The Population of the United States* (Glencoe, Ill.: The Free Press, 1959), pp. 688–709.

* 1957 figures include only persons aged 14 or older.

than gentiles, their exodus probably reflects their greater affluence—though, as in the case of fertility patterns, specifically Jewish values and attitudes may also have played a role. There is some evidence from housing market studies that Jews are more willing than gentiles to sell their dwellings and move, provided the new neighborhood has other Jews among its residents and offers proper educational, community and recreation facilities for the various stages of the family cycle.[19]

Geographic Distribution and Gentile-Jewish Contact

The history of Jewish population distribution might seem to offer certain intriguing explanations of trends in anti-Semitism. Before the Civil War, Jews probably were scattered throughout the nation in much the same pattern as gentiles.[20] Their subsequent concentration in the North and East coincided with the emergence of anti-Semitism as a force on the American scene; and their recent return to a more nearly even distribution has taken place concurrently with a diminution in anti-Semitism. Now, as Stember reported in an earlier study, broadened opportunities for social contact often help reduce prejudice between members of majority and minority groups.[21] Is it possible that the recent redistribution of Jews away from the North and East has improved the opportunities for contact elsewhere and thereby has contributed substantially to recent declines in hostility?

We believe any such explanation is too simplistic to account for the crests and troughs in the cycle of anti-Semitic sentiment over the last century. Certainly between 1939 and 1962—the period for which poll data broken by region are available—shifts in the geographical distribution of Jews were not great enough to account for the vast reported reduction in anti-Semitism. Besides, the data in Stembers' Appendix I leave us far from certain whether anti-Semitism has been least prevalent in regions where Jews (and opportunities for social contact with Jews) are few or in regions where they are many. On the contrary, perhaps the most striking aspect of the findings is how much anti-Semitism has declined in *all* regions, independently of the changing residence of Jews.

We cannot take it for granted, moreover, that the ratio of Jews to gentiles in a given region is always positively correlated with the number of opportunities for contact. Above a certain point, the correlation may be inverse. It is known, for example, that many Jews in New York never meet non-Jews socially—precisely because the city's Jewish population is so enormously large.

Trends in Occupational Composition

The extension of the boundaries of Jewish settlement, both in the nation as a whole and within metropolitan areas, has been paralleled by changes in occupational composition.

Occupations can be described from various perspectives—for example, in terms of earnings, of prestige, of required education and training, of the organizational setting in which work is done, of mobility from job to job or of emphasis on personality traits. Demographic studies, beginning with Billings' survey of 1889, suggest that Jews in the United States have long concentrated in the better-paid occupations and in those with a degree of prestige.

Billings' sample consisted of about 15 per cent of the nation's Jews. Of 18,000 working males in the sample, over 14,000, or approximately three-quarters, conducted their own businesses. About 1,000 were in the professions: 285 were lawyers, 173 physicians or surgeons and the rest mostly teachers or accountants. Some 2,000 were skilled workers; only 84 were ordinary laborers or servants. Gentiles at the time were concentrated in most of the very occupations in which the Jews were underrepresented. Only in the professions did the two groups appear with similar frequencies; Billings found about 5 per cent of the Jews in this category, and estimates made in 1890 suggest the same figure for the nation as a whole.[22]

As Jewish immigrants from Eastern Europe arrived in growing numbers and found jobs as skilled or semiskilled laborers in urban industries, the contrast between the gentiles' and the Jews' occupational profiles became less marked—though even then Jews tended toward the better-paid occupations and those with prestige. The Jews' participation in the industrial work force is mirrored in statistics as late as the 1930s and 1940s. In Detroit during 1935, and in Buffalo during 1938, about one-fourth of Jewish males were skilled or semiskilled workers (Table G)—a startling increase from the one-ninth thus employed in 1889. On the other hand, only one-third were now conducting businesses of their own or holding executive and managerial posts, as against three-fourths at the time of Billings' survey. Still, certain peculiarities in occupational distribution remained unchanged. In the 1930s as in the 1890s, Jews were thinly represented at either extreme of the status hierarchy; during both periods, they were virtually absent from unskilled or service jobs, and in the professions they were not much more numerous proportionately than were gentiles.

The distinctive, in some ways unique, occupational history of American Jews until the 1930s is only imperfectly reflected in broad measurements and categories like these. Within a given classification, Jews often pursued activities quite different from those of gentiles. Thus, their businesses were typically small enterprises; even garment-making, the one major industry in which they predominated, differed from other lines of manufacture in consisting mostly of small factories, often run by one boss with a few assistants and 25 or fewer employees.[23] In the professional field, Jews tended toward careers which permitted the individual to succeed without the support of an organization—notably one-man practices in law, medicine and dentistry.

The Jewish small businessman, lawyer, doctor or dentist was independent in the sense that he required only limited cooperation from fellow businessmen or colleagues. But he had virtually no mobility, because he depended on a clientele that could only be built up over a long period of time—usually a neighborhood clientele of the same ethnic and personal background as his own. This circumstance no doubt was a factor in the geographical distribution of Jews. Their businesses or professions made it extremely difficult for them to pull up stakes and to abandon established communities for new settlements, unless their Jewish clients moved along with them.

According to the conventional wisdom of the time, occupational choices like these stemmed purely from preference—a palatable explanation, which found a degree of acceptance even in Jewish circles. Jews, so the argument went, did not like to work in large bureaucratic organizations, to be moved from job to job or to be judged by impersonal standards of performance. They supposedly were happiest and worked most effectively when firmly established among their own kind, with room for their personal ways and the freedom of "being their own bosses." In reality, however, the choices undoubtedly were often dictated by the prejudices of the outside world: the refusal of corporations and large professional firms to hire Jews or the restrictive quota systems maintained by colleges and graduate schools.

Since the days between the two World Wars, the occupational composition of the Jewish population has altered again. In terms of income and prestige alone, a good case can be made for the generalization that the Jews once more enjoy a uniquely favorable occupational profile. As in Billings' time, few Jews are industrial workers: Of eight cities and metropolitan areas surveyed between 1955 and 1964, only one (Rochester) showed more than 15 per cent of Jews in skilled or semiskilled occupations, and in most of the others the proportion was less than 10 per cent. Some of the former manual laborers and factory workers or their children have returned to the pattern of the 1880s and gone into business;[24] in four of the eight communities, approximately one-half of the Jewish males were recorded as "proprietors, managers or officials." Jews also have for the first time entered the professions in significant numbers: In four of the eight areas (Rochester, Trenton, Camden and Washington), over one-fourth of the Jewish males were employed in professional work, and in another (Providence), over one-fifth was so engaged.

These ratios are substantially higher than they were in comparable cities thirty years ago, and they far exceed the proportions reported by Billings in 1889. The change may be even greater than the above data show. Today Washington, with the Federal civil service, and the Camden area, with its numerous electronics companies and other defense industries, actually have more Jewish professionals than Jewish businessmen; and when we cross-tabulate the occupational data for these cities by age, we discover that the proportions of Jews who are professionals are higher in the youngest age

Table G Occupational Distribution of Persons Aged 14 and Over, among Jewish and Total Populations. Selected U. S. Cities and Metropolitan Areas, 1935–1964

	Detroit		Buffalo		Passaic	
	Jews 1935	Total 1940	Jews 1938	Total 1940	Jews 1949	Total 1950
MALES						
Professional	6.8	6.1	14.3	6.7	11.9	7.7
Proprietors and Managers	33.1	8.7	32.2	10.9	43.6	13.7
Clerical and Sales	31.5	16.4	24.0	17.2	18.8	12.9
Skilled and Semiskilled	26.0	52.4	23.7	46.3	14.1	50.0
Service and Unskilled	2.6	15.6	4.6	18.0	5.5	15.0
Others, Not Reported	—	0.6	1.2	0.8	6.1	0.7
FEMALES						
Professional	10.3	11.3	14.1	15.0	12.3	9.2
Proprietors and Managers	4.8	3.2	2.9	4.0	13.5	3.9
Clerical and Sales	66.2	38.1	77.9	35.8	55.4	26.8
Skilled and Semiskilled	15.2	18.4	3.2	17.7	7.5	47.8
Service and Unskilled	3.5	28.1	0.9	26.4	2.0	11.4
Others, Not Reported	—	0.8	1.0	1.2	9.3	1.0

	Des Moines		Washington		Rochester	
	Jews 1956	Total 1960	Jews 1956	Total 1960	Jews 1961	Total 1960
MALES						
Professional	13.7	11.3	37.9	21.4	26.7	14.7
Proprietors and Managers	52.8	13.5	24.5	12.2	29.5	9.5
Clerical and Sales	23.6	20.3	20.8	18.6	24.2	15.8
Skilled and Semiskilled	5.1	37.4	8.4	26.1	16.6	43.6
Service and Unskilled	2.3	13.0	1.2	14.2	2.9	10.5
Others, Not Reported	2.5	4.4	7.2	7.4	—	5.9
FEMALES						
Professional	9.7	13.0	15.1	15.6	17.8	13.9
Proprietors and Managers	23.6	4.0	7.8	3.8	7.1	2.5
Clerical and Sales	55.6	50.9	59.8	49.3	55.5	40.0
Skilled and Semiskilled	1.4	8.5	2.3	4.6	16.6	23.3
Service and Unskilled	2.8	19.2	6.4	19.2	3.0	14.6
Others, Not Reported	6.9	4.4	8.6	7.5	—	5.7

SOURCES: Figures for total population from U. S. Department of Commerce, Bureau of the Census, *Sixteenth Census of the United States: 1940*, vol. II, parts 3, 5; *U. S. Census of the Population: 1950*, vol. II, parts 5, 18, 30, 32; *U. S. Census of the Population: 1960*, vol. I, parts 10, 16, 17, 32, 34, 37, 40, 41. Information on Jewish population in Buffalo and Detroit from Robison, *op. cit.*; in Los Angeles, Passaic, New Orleans and Port Chester from Seligman, *op. cit.*; in Providence, Rochester, Trenton, South Bend, Des Moines and Canton from

Los Angeles		New Orleans		Port Chester		Canton	
Jews 1950	Total 1950	Jews 1950	Total 1950	Jews 1950	Total 1950	Jews 1955	Total 1960
17.5	12.4	23.5	8.9	14.9	7.7	14.0	7.6
36.9	15.1	46.0	13.7	56.3	14.8	54.8	7.4
24.9	18.0	22.0	18.8	16.1	13.0	14.4	13.4
17.2	36.6	4.0	33.7	5.9	46.5	8.8	50.3
3.5	16.6	2.8	23.9	4.1	17.1	2.7	16.7
—	1.3	1.6	1.1	2.7	1.0	5.3	4.6
14.6	13.1	14.5	12.1	17.1	11.0	14.1	13.1
13.0	6.2	25.1	4.6	20.3	3.7	30.6	2.9
50.3	41.2	53.4	38.0	47.8	32.9	44.7	38.7
13.5	18.2	2.7	13.8	11.0	36.1	4.7	12.7
8.6	20.1	3.3	30.5	1.3	15.2	1.2	26.6
—	1.2	1.0	1.0	2.5	1.1	4.7	6.0

South Bend		Trenton		Providence		Camden	
Jews 1961	Total 1960	Jews 1961	Total 1960	Jews 1963	Total 1960	Jews 1964	Total 1960
17.6	12.5	27.4	13.8	20.7	9.0	34.0	11.9
56.5	9.3	54.0	10.2	40.7	10.0	31.0	10.3
15.3	14.5	13.4	13.8	25.4	14.4	22.0	16.7
8.0	46.8	} 5.2 { 41.8		11.0	47.1	11.0	42.3
2.6	11.6	15.4		1.1	12.4	2.0	13.2
—	5.3	—	5.0	1.1	7.1	—	5.6
17.2	13.3	17.0	14.2	17.9	10.5	25.0	11.9
24.1	3.2	29.3	3.1	12.7	2.3	18.0	2.7
51.1	40.7	46.3	38.6	59.8	32.1	47.0	39.9
4.7	16.4	} 7.4 { 20.1		5.6	35.4	4.0	20.2
3.0	21.6	19.0		1.5	12.4	6.0	19.1
—	4.8	—	5.0	2.5	7.3	—	6.3

Sidney Goldstein, *The Greater Providence Jewish Community: A Population Survey* (Providence: The General Jewish Committee of Providence, Inc., 1964), Table 42; in Camden from Charles F. Westoff, *Population and Social Characteristics of the Jewish Community of the Camden Area: 1964* (Camden: Jewish Federation of Camden County, 1965); in Washington from Stanley K. Bigman, *The Jewish Population of Greater Washington, 1956* (Washington: Jewish Committee of Greater Washington, 1957).

group than in any other (Table H). In Camden, no fewer than 55 per cent
of Jewish males under 35 are doing professional work! This figure is doubly
astounding because a man's ultimate social rank is usually expected to be
higher than his status below age 35 indicates. Many men in that age bracket

Table H Occupational Distribution, by Age Groups, among Jewish and
Total Population. Washington, Providence and Camden Metropolitan
Areas, 1956–1964

		Washington		Providence		Camden	
		Jews	Total	Jews	Total	Jews	Total
Professional and Technical							
MALES:	14 to 34	45.2	20.0	22.0	10.3	55.0	14.0
	35 to 44	38.8	24.4	23.0	9.6	36.0	12.8
	45 to 54	32.4	22.0	21.0	7.6	28.0	9.9
	55 and over	27.5	19.0	18.0	7.5	19.0	9.1
FEMALES:	14 to 34	15.9	14.5	31.0	11.3	43.0	13.7
	35 to 44	28.8	15.4	24.0	8.2	27.0	9.9
	45 to 54	8.5	17.6	15.0	10.1	19.0	11.4
	55 and over	—	15.8	6.0	2.6	17.0	11.3
Managers, Officials and Proprietors							
MALES:	14 to 34	21.5	7.1	32.0	5.9	22.0	6.0
	35 to 44	24.8	14.1	41.0	10.9	29.0	11.4
	45 to 54	23.3	16.6	42.0	13.2	36.0	12.9
	55 and over	32.3	15.8	44.0	12.4	40.0	13.4
FEMALES:	14 to 34	1.1	1.8	9.0	1.1	6.0	1.1
	35 to 44	7.1	4.2	9.0	2.2	15.0	3.0
	45 to 54	12.5	5.4	10.0	2.9	25.0	3.7
	55 and over	—	5.8	21.0	3.9	26.0	4.2
Clerical and Sales							
MALES:	14 to 34	17.8	22.3	34.0	17.6	18.0	19.7
	35 to 44	15.4	16.8	26.0	13.7	24.0	15.0
	45 to 54	30.6	15.7	23.0	11.8	20.0	14.8
	55 and over	25.9	16.8	22.0	13.0	25.0	16.0
FEMALES:	14 to 34	61.9	54.2	54.0	42.5	43.0	49.0
	35 to 44	55.5	49.2	58.0	29.3	47.0	36.9
	45 to 54	68.7	45.6	66.0	25.7	42.0	35.3
	55 and over	—	42.7	59.0	24.6	46.0	31.3
Manual							
MALES:	14 to 34	11.4	42.3	10.0	58.3	5.0	54.0
	35 to 44	9.7	38.1	9.0	59.8	11.0	56.0
	45 to 54	5.9	39.1	12.0	60.4	16.0	57.3
	55 and over	12.1	40.7	14.0	59.6	16.0	55.6

		Washington		Providence		Camden	
		Jews	Total	Jews	Total	Jews	Total
FEMALES:	14 to 34	14.9	21.7	5.0	37.5	8.0	29.6
	35 to 44	1.3	24.5	7.0	54.1	11.0	44.3
	45 to 54	7.6	24.1	7.0	54.1	14.0	44.0
	55 and over	—	27.1	10.0	50.4	11.0	46.0
Others, Not Reported							
MALES:	14 to 34	4.1	8.3	2.0	7.9	—	6.3
	35 to 44	11.3	6.6	1.0	6.0	—	4.8
	45 to 54	7.8	6.6	2.0	7.0	—	5.1
	55 and over	2.2	7.6	2.0	7.5	—	5.9
FEMALES:	14 to 34	6.2	7.8	1.0	7.6	—	6.6
	35 to 44	8.1	6.7	2.0	6.2	—	5.9
	45 to 54	2.7	7.3	2.0	7.2	—	5.6
	55 and over	—	8.6	4.0	8.5	—	7.2

SOURCES: Figures for total populations from U. S. Department of Commerce, Bureau of the Census, *U. S. Census of the Population: 1960,* vol. I, parts 10, 40, 41. Figures for Jewish population in Washington from Bigman, *op. cit.;* in Camden from Westoff, *op. cit.;* in Providence estimated from data in Goldstein, *op. cit.*

still attend school part time, receive in-plant training or occupy the lowest rungs of a career ladder that will afford them considerable occupational mobility when they reach middle age.

The Jews' phenomenal involvement with professional work cannot be attributed exclusively, or even mainly, to the economy's ever-growing need for educated and professionally trained personnel. It is evidently a fact special to this group—or so we are led to infer when we compare the occupational distribution of Jews in different age brackets with the corresponding figures for the total population (Table H). In each of the three cities thus analyzed (Washington, Providence and Camden), we see the proportion of Jews in the professions increasing at a rapid pace as we proceed from the older to the younger groups; among the population as a whole, the increases are far smaller.

One major reason for the rapid influx of Jews into the professions is, of course, that fields formerly more or less closed to them are now open. This circumstance is not reflected in our tables, which deal only with gross occupational categories, but it is plainly documented in other studies based on more refined job information. Among the newly opened careers are university teaching, engineering, the natural sciences, city planning and public administration. We may note in passing that these occupations, now eagerly pursued by Jews, have certain characteristics diametrically opposed to those which once were thought necessary to attract and hold Jews: They are set in large bureaucratic organizations; they address themselves to a clientele which is not predominantly Jewish; and they often demand mobility from job to job and from region to region.

As noted, Jews are once more strongly represented in the category of "proprietor, manager or official"; but recent studies suggest that this may mean something else than formerly. In the past, the Jews in this category were nearly all operators of independent small businesses or managerial employees of manufacturing and wholesaling industries catering to Jewish distributors and retailers; today, a number of them are executives in large national corporations. Though to date Jews have found less acceptance in managerial roles than in technical occupations, some of them are beginning to assume important responsibilities in the administration of big business.

Occupational Trends and the Decline of Anti-Semitism

When we seek to relate the changing occupational composition of the American Jewish population to Stember's findings on the decline of anti-Semitism, we again run into the difficulties we encountered while considering the possible influence of geographical redistribution. For example, we ought to investigate whether anti-Semitism has declined most sharply in cities where the professionalization of the Jewish population has advanced most rapidly; but again the two sets of information cannot be correlated, because the poll findings are presented in categories that do not correspond to the classification of the demographic data.

However, one can pay too high a price for methodological purity. When we ignore the fact that occupational composition varies from city to city, and focus instead on the probable occupational profiles of Jews and gentiles in the nation as a whole, we do find what looks like an association between the occupational mobility of the Jews and the reported decline in anti-Semitism. It is the younger and wealthier gentiles who have been in the best position to observe the new American Jew or to become acquainted with him; and the data in Stember's Appendix I suggest that anti-Jewish feeling has decreased most profoundly among this segment of the population.

Apart from these data, it seems reasonable to assume that the reported increases in the gentiles' acceptance of Jewish marriage partners, college classmates and neighbors grow from the manifold working or professional contacts now occurring between the two groups. Even the most prejudiced of anti-Semites (other than an outright psychopath) would seem likely to modify his stereotypes as he meets with various Jews in settings unlike those which form the backdrop for the classical anti-Jewish image.

Alternatively, it might be argued that Jews could not have entered the salaried professions and achieved their present occupational status if gentiles had not been capable of overcoming traditional anti-Jewish ideas and subduing long-standing anti-Jewish feelings. After all, the admissions offices which have allowed Jews to enter colleges or graduate schools for professional preparation are usually in gentile hands; and the same is true of personnel departments in the scientific institutions, government departments and corporations in which increasing numbers of Jewish salaried professionals are finding employment. But whether we assume that the new occupational status of the Jews is causing the diminution in anti-Semitism, or vice versa, the two phenomena are inextricably linked together.

The Future of Anti-Semitism

Having come this far, the reader—certainly the Jewish reader—will ask what Stember's findings in conjunction with demographic data can tell us about the future of anti-Semitism in the United States. At this point, unfortunately, the evidence begins to resemble the ink blots or pictures used in projective tests. As we have seen, the demographic statistics are not especially refined and do not lend themselves well to analysis in conjunction with the available public-opinion data. Besides, any individual's interpretation is almost sure to be colored by his personal experience of, or beliefs about, anti-Semitism. Thus, it is only too easy for the reader to see in these facts and figures whatever his ideas about the Jews' role in American society lead him to see.

No one really knows what the future holds for the Jews in America. But the data we have reviewed would seem to prompt at least one prediction: If anti-Semitism is revived as a political and social force, it will have to express itself in images with a new social content. For example, the anti-Semite of the future may well resurrect the idea that the Jew is "shrewd" and "tricky"; but he will not find this shrewdness at the market or in the store as formerly. Rather, with Jews firmly established in the professional class, he will inveigh against the "conniving" Jewish organization man, professor or public servant. In the Soviet Union, anti-Semitism has already acquired a content of this sort, and brutally severe measures have been taken against functionaries thus accused.[25] If a similar variety of anti-Jewish hostility came into being in this country, presumably no individuals would be shot; but Jews might well be deprived once more of the opportunity to enter and remain in professional careers.

Two sociologists who have studied an American Jewish community believe that this new variety of anti-Semitism is not so unlikely a prospect as might be thought. Judith R. Kramer and Seymour Leventman argue that the relative absence of anti-Semitism in the professions today is merely a reflection of a desperate need for personnel. Gentiles in these professions have not had time, they say, to establish restrictive practices.[26] By the same reasoning, it might be argued that the new suburban communities in which many Jews now live are too new and unstable to have developed customs of exclusion, but may yet do so.

These are challenging notions which should be tested. Is anti-Semitism indeed greater in established suburbs, as Kramer and Leventman seem to imply? Is hostility against Jews increasing in professions where personnel needs are gradually being met (as is reportedly the case in certain areas of physics) or where job opportunities are becoming scarce because of reductions in defense spending or for other reasons? These and similar questions cannot be answered with the poll data presented by Stember; but they should be amenable to investigation through future opinion polls, and through inquiries by demographers and sociologists concerned with the future of the Jews in the United States.

NOTES

1. Estimates of the number of Jews in the United States go back to 1818, although the present study focuses on the more reliable statistics kept since the 1880s. For a general discussion of Jewish population statistics, see Robert Gutman, "Non-Conventional Methods of Obtaining Data on the Religious Composition of the United States Population: The Case of Jewish Population Statistics," in United Nations, *Proceedings of the United Nations World Population Conference,* Belgrade, Yugoslavia, August 30–September 10, 1965.

2. John Shaw Billings, *Vital Statistics of the Jews in the United States* (United States Bureau of the Census, Census Bulletin No. 19, December 1890).

3. Mortimer Speigelman, "The Longevity of Jews in Canada, 1940–1942," *Population Studies,* II:292–304 (1948); Herbert Seidman and Others, "Death Rates in New York City by Socio-Economic Class and Religious Group and by Country of Birth, 1949–51," *Jewish Journal of Sociology,* IV:254–273 (1962); Kurt Gorwitz, "Jewish Mortality in St. Louis and St. Louis County, 1955–1957," *Jewish Social Studies,* XXIV:248–254 (1962); A. J. Jaffe, "A Study of Chicago Jewry (1930) Based on Death Certificates," in Sophia M. Robison, editor, *Jewish Population Studies* (New York: Conference on Jewish Relations, 1943), pp. 131–151; Charles Bolduan and Louis Weiner, "Causes of Death among Jews in New York City," *New England Journal of Medicine,* CCVIII:407–416 (1933).

4. Ansley J. Coale, "The Effect of Declines in Mortality on Age Distribution," in *Trends and Differentials in Mortality* (New York: Milbank Memorial Fund, 1956), pp. 125–132.

5. William Petersen, *The Politics of Population* (Garden City, N.Y.: Doubleday & Co., 1964), pp. 195–215.

6. It should be noted that the contribution of net migration to population growth, though substantial, was undoubtedly less than the values shown in Table C (74 per cent between 1937 and 1946, and 57 per cent between 1947 and 1956). These values do not compensate for the contribution of natural increase to population growth, a factor of some importance during the postwar period, when Jewish fertility was rising. See footnote to Table C for a fuller discussion of this point.

7. Billings, *op. cit.*, pp. 9–10.

8. Sidney Goldstein, *The Greater Providence Jewish Community: A Population Survey* (Providence: The General Jewish Committee of Providence, Inc., 1964), p. 68. See also William Petersen, *Population* (New York: The Macmillan Co., 1961), p. 213.

9. U. S. Department of Commerce, Bureau of the Census, *Current Population Reports,* Series P–20, No. 79 (February 2, 1958).

10. Goldstein, *loc. cit.*

11. Ronald Freedman, Pascal K. Whelpton and Arthur A. Campbell, *Family Planning, Sterility and Population Growth* (New York: McGraw-Hill Book Co., 1959), pp. 287–288.

12. Pascal K. Whelpton, Arthur A. Campbell and John Patterson, *Fertility and Family Planning in the United States* (Princeton: Princeton University Press, 1965), Chapter III.

13. *Ibid.,* Chapter II.

14. Charles F. Westoff and Others, *Family Growth in Metropolitan America* (Princeton: Princeton University Press, 1961).

15. Erich Rosenthal, "Jewish Fertility in the United States," *American Jewish Year Book,* LXII (1961), 3–27. See also Ronald Freedman, Pascal K. Whelpton and John W. Smit, "Socio-Economic Factors in Religious Differentials in Fertility," *American Sociological Review,* XXVI:608–614 (1961).

16. Erich Rosenthal, "Socio-Economic Factors" (mimeographed paper; Department of Sociology and Anthropology, Queens College, Flushing, N. Y.). I wish to thank Professor Rosenthal for making this paper available to me.

17. Nathan Goldberg, "The Jewish Population in the United States," in *The Jewish People: Past and Present,* II (New York: Central Yiddish Culture Organization, 1948), 28.

18. Donald J. Bogue, *The Population of the United States* (Glencoe, Ill.: The Free Press, 1959), pp. 688–708.

19. Morton Hoffman, "The Outlook for Downtown Housing," *Journal of the American Institute of Planners,* XXVII: 43–55 (1961); Donald M. Fenmore, "Comment on Hoffman's 'Outlook for Downtown Housing,' " *Ibid.,* XXVII:334.

20. A rough idea of the Jews' geographical distribution immediately before and after the Civil War can be obtained from the information on Jewish congregations collected in successive censuses of population, beginning in 1850. These sources are discussed in Gutman, *op. cit.* Some of the data are summarized in Harry S. Linfield, *Statistics of Jews and Jewish Organizations: Historical Review of Ten Censuses, 1850–1937* (New York: American Jewish Committee, 1939), Tables A and B.

21. Charles Herbert Stember, *Education and Attitude Change* (New York: Institute of Human Relations Press, 1961), pp. 10–11, 175.

22. Billings, *op. cit.;* Alba M. Edwards, *Comparative Occupation Statistics for the United States, 1870–1940* (Washington: U. S. Government Printing Office, 1943), Tables XXI and XXII.

23. Max Hall, editor, *Made in New York* (Cambridge, Mass.: Harvard University Press, 1959), pp. 21–46.

24. For an interesting analysis of intergenerational mobility, see Joseph S. Fauman, "Occupational Selection Among Detroit Jews," in Marshall Sklare, editor, *The Jews* (Glencoe, Ill.: The Free Press, 1958), pp. 119–137.

25. In the Soviet trials for "economic crimes," conducted since 1961, more than 50 per cent of the accused were Jews. For a summary of the events and statistics indicating the proportion of Jews among the defendants, see *Near East Report,* VIII: 15 (1964).

26. Judith R. Kramer and Seymour Leventman, *Children of the Gilded Ghetto* (New Haven: Yale University Press, 1961), Chapter VI, especially p. 134.

I am grateful for the support of the Rutgers University Urban
Studies Center and the assistance of Ethel C. Fowler.

Parallel and Distinctive Changes in Anti-Semitic and Anti-Negro Attitudes

THOMAS F. PETTIGREW

A REVEALING INCIDENT occurred in Little Rock, Arkansas, during the city's hectic days in the late 1950s. The vociferous local chapter of the segregationist White Citizens' Council suddenly and summarily expelled one of its principal leaders on the grounds that he was an anti-Semite. "You see," explained a Council official candidly, "we had to throw him out, because we can't afford to be seen as an anti-Jewish organization. Why, we are having trouble enough just being anti-Negro!"

Even for the White Citizens' Council in Little Rock, then, it has become inadvisable to be too explicitly bigoted. Indeed, "prejudice" is now a derogatory term in the United States. Obviously, this is not to say that the nation is free from prejudice. Many bigoted groups and individuals are extremely active on the current scene, but they generally take pains to maintain that they are not prejudiced.[1] Thus, the White Citizens' Councils stoutly insist that they work, not to keep the Negro down, but only to prevent racial strife. Similarly, in Northern cities, segregationist groups of white parents claim not to resist desegregation but only to support neighborhood schools.

This phenomenon signals a significant change in American minority relations. The new situation has, perhaps, been captured best in Peter Viereck's concept of "transtolerance":

Transtolerance is ready to give all minorities their glorious democratic freedom —provided they accept McCarthyism or some other mob conformism of Right or Left. . . . Transtolerance is also a sublimated Jim Crow: against "wrong" thinkers, not "wrong" races. . . . It is . . . a strictly kosher anti-Semitism.[2]

There is considerable evidence that transtolerance has its uses. Thus, Robert Welch, the leader of the far-right John Birch Society, boasts of his

377

group's Jewish and Roman Catholic members. According to Alan Westin, the Society even has two segregated Negro chapters in the South.[3] Though well-known anti-Semitic and anti-Negro figures are prominent in the organization, Welch insists that it is a "Communist tactic to stir up distrust and hatred between Jews and Gentiles, Catholics and Protestants, Negroes and Whites." [4] In the same vein, the Reverend Billy James Hargis, a far-right Fundamentalist minister who leads a self-styled crusade against Communism, tells his followers: "We cannot tolerate anti-Semitic statements [or] anti-Negro statements . . ." [5]

Transtolerance was widely apparent in the campaigns of the Republican Presidential and Vice-Presidential candidates in 1964—the candidates overwhelmingly supported by far-right organizations. The triple religious nature of the team of Barry M. Goldwater and William E. Miller had a special appeal. "Barry's a Protestant and a Jew, and I'm a Catholic," Miller was quoted as remarking during the campaign. "Anybody who's against that ticket is a damn bigot." [6] The lyrics are different, but the tune is somehow the same.

From data such as these, Seymour Martin Lipset concludes:

. . . The object of intolerance in America has never been as important as the style, the emotion, the antagonism and envy toward some specified other who is seen as wealthier, more powerful, or particularly, as a corrupter of basic values. . . . Anti-elitism oriented toward groups that cannot be regarded as oppressed minorities or victims of bigotry, or anti-Communism directed against the agents or dupes of an evil foreign power, can serve as much more palatable outlets for those who require a scapegoat than "un-American" attacks on minorities. . . . The current crop of radical rightists seems to understand this difference.[7]

Obviously, this shift on the part of the far right reflects a sharp change of public norms concerning minorities in the United States during recent years. Charles Herbert Stember's useful compilation of opinion-poll data demonstrates conclusively that the alteration is reflected in attitudes toward Jews. The present paper explores further aspects of this critical change in norms. Have the attitudes of white Americans toward Negro Americans also undergone major change? How do anti-Semitic and anti-Negro attitudes today resemble each other, and how do they differ?

Parallel Changes in Anti-Semitic and Anti-Negro Poll Responses

In many ways, attitudes toward Negroes provide the acid test of American tolerance of minorities. From the first landing of Africans at Jamestown in 1619 to the racial crisis of the 1960s, the relations between Negroes and Caucasians have been inseparably intertwined with the nation's roots and development. Anti-Semitism is not nearly as deeply embedded in American life as anti-Negro sentiment; explicit discrimination against Jews did not begin here until late in the nineteenth century, two centuries after slavery had received legal sanction. Therefore, if we want to learn whether the striking reduction in anti-Semitism between 1937 and 1962 represents a more general trend in intergroup relations, we must see if poll responses hostile to Negroes show a similar reduction over the same years.

Herbert H. Hyman and Paul B. Sheatsley present the relevant data in an analysis of replies to certain questions concerning Negroes, which were asked periodically from 1942 to 1963 by the National Opinion Research Center.[8] A look at their results reveals marked parallels with Stember's, both where stereotypes and where discriminatory practices were concerned. Thus, while the percentage of Americans who did not think Jews less honest than others rose from 56 to 82 between 1938 and 1962, the percentage who believed Negroes to be as intelligent as whites rose from 42 to 74 between 1942 and 1963. While the percentage who did not think colleges should limit enrollment of Jews increased from 74 to 96, the percentage favoring racially desegregated schools increased from 30 to 63. Analogous shifts also occurred in attitudes toward heterogeneous neighborhoods: Over the same years, the proportions voicing no objections to a Jewish neighbor went up from 75 to 97 per cent, and those with no objections to a Negro neighbor from 35 to 63 per cent.[9]

A further parallel may be found in the high points of animosity against the two groups. Stember shows that during the closing years of the Second World War American anti-Semitism reached its highest point within the last generation; Hyman and Sheatsley note a peak in anti-Negro opinions about the same time. Indeed, Stember presents evidence of this parallel intensity as of 1944. Four groups—Protestants, Catholics, Jews and Negroes—were named, and respondents were asked: "Against which *one* of these groups, *if any,* do you think prejudice or feeling has increased the most?" Thirty-seven per cent named Jews, while another 31 per cent chose Negroes.[10] Anti-Semitic and anti-Negro attitudes, then, have both declined over the past two decades from peaks of intensity reached simultaneously during the tense war years.

Such striking parallels raise two questions. Do the changes in poll responses reflect actual reductions in prejudice? And are these reductions endangered by the so-called "white backlash"—the widely reported reaction of threatened whites in Northern cities against the Negroes' civil-rights revolution? Each of these issues deserves discussion, for each might well limit severely the conclusions which can be safely drawn from the poll data so carefully compiled by Stember and by Hyman and Sheatsley.

With some justification, certain observers doubt whether polling can fathom the full depth of most respondents' anti-Semitic or anti-Negro prejudices. Ben Halpern submits his reasons for skepticism in a provocative paper in this volume. What has decreased from the late 1930s to today, he and others argue, is not prejudice, but the respectability of prejudice—in this case, readiness to admit blatant bigotry to a poll taker. Yet, as Stember notes, even if only standards of respectability had changed, this alteration would be noteworthy. For what is "real" prejudice? A change in verbal behavior is certainly "real" in a most important sense.

In any case, need we be so limiting? No doubt the open espousal of anti-Jewish and anti-Negro attitudes became markedly less respectable during the past generation. But this change would seem to be only one among many symptoms of a deeper, more meaningful lessening of prejudice. Indeed, there are a number of reasons for accepting the major shifts reported by the opinion polls as genuine, at least in large part.

First, rapport in the polling situation is generally far closer than those unfamiliar with the technique realize. A pleasant, attentive stranger who has gone to some trouble to record your opinion on vital issues, and who does not provide any cues of disagreement, is often a much safer confidant than acquaintances.

Second, the remarkable consistency of the trends in attitudes toward Jews and Negroes extends to a wide variety of questions, asked by different polling agencies. Presumably, the questions vary considerably in "respectability bias" (or, to use the parlance of modern testing theory, in "social desirability"); thus, if the results were largely a reflection of "respectability bias," we would not expect the consistency noted both by Stember and by Hyman and Sheatsley.

Third, certain questions concerning Jews and Negroes which appear to involve a built-in "respectability bias" as great as any of Stember's items have *not* changed over the past few decades. For example, the National Opinion Research Center has repeatedly asked representative nationwide samples if they "think most Negroes in the United States are being treated fairly or unfairly." The responses have remained quite stable over the years; in both 1946 and 1956, 63 per cent answered, "Fairly." [11]

Fourth, election results have borne out public-opinion poll evidence on intergroup attitudes. Ithiel de Sola Pool and his associates attempted to simulate the 1960 Presidential election using only opinion-poll data gathered before 1959.[12] To predict the crucial anti-Catholic vote against the late John F. Kennedy, Pool used the simple and straightforward poll question, "Would you be willing to vote for a qualified Catholic for President?" —surely as frontal a measure of prejudice as any employed to explore attitudes toward Jews and Negroes. Yet, for all its obviousness, the question produced a response that proved remarkably accurate and useful in simulating the actual 1960 election. As the authors state in their intriguing volume:

Millions of Protestants and other non-Catholics who would otherwise have voted Democratic could not bring themselves to vote for a Catholic. In total—so our model says—roughly one out of five Protestant Democrats or Protestant Independents who would otherwise have voted Democratic bolted because of the religious issue. The actual number of bolters varied with the voter-type and was determined in the model by the proportion of that voter-type who had replied on surveys that they would not want to vote for a Catholic for President. What our model tends to show is that the poll question was a good one. The model suggests that the number of people who overcame the social inhibitions to admitting prejudice to a polltaker was about the same as the number who overcame the politcal inhibitions to bolting their party for reasons of bias.[13]

The final reason for accepting poll data as an adequate measure of prejudice is the most compelling of all. The sharp diminution of anti-minority responses in the polls is completely consistent with the changes in the treatment of minorities over the same years. Discrimination in a wide range of American institutions has lessened at least as much as verbalized prejudice. This process is a two-way street: On the one hand, reductions of prejudice speed the erosion of discrimination; on the other hand, and probably more important, the decline of discrimination permits increasing contact between groups on a basis of equality, and thus makes for decreased prejudice.[14]

Of course, none of these arguments imply that discriminatory practices against minorities have ceased in the United States. Roughly two-thirds of the nation's private clubs retain religious restrictions; housing patterns based on religious discrimination continue; and some major law firms as well as the executive corps of the automotive and utility industries still discriminate against Jews in their recruitment.[15] Moreover, the most elaborate and debilitating barriers of all—those maintained for three centuries against the Negro—are only now slowly beginning to be dismantled. The polls clearly reflect these remaining barriers, indicating that prejudice is still intense in certain sectors of the society. The actual treatment of Jews and Negroes, then, substantiates poll findings concerning attitudes toward these groups in two separate respects: It confirms that hostility has markedly diminished during recent years, but also that it remains concentrated in particular sectors.

What about the "white backlash"? Does this much-publicized phenomenon not indicate a rise in anti-Negro prejudice? Relevant data strongly suggest that it does not. The concept of a backlash was fashioned by journalists for its sensational flavor, not by social scientists for its heuristic value; the evidence that purports to demonstrate its existence lacks the most rudimentary research controls and safeguards. A more detached view, free from the pressure of mass-media deadlines and relying upon controlled data, leads one to doubt that a significant anti-Negro reaction is sweeping the nation.

The term "backlash" implies that many whites in the North, once mildly sympathetic to Negro aspirations, suddenly have changed their minds and hardened their resistance to racial change. The term first gained favor in the mass media during 1964, when the segregationist Governor of Alabama, George C. Wallace, made a number of relatively successful political sorties into the North. He entered the Democratic Presidential primaries in Wisconsin, Indiana and Maryland and, to the surprise of many, polled sizable minorities—from roughly 25 per cent in Wisconsin to 43 per cent in border-state Maryland. Many observers inferred from these results that an anti-Negro "backlash" was in full swing. Soon every reasonably large vote for a reactionary candidate anywhere in the North and West was cited as a symptom of the supposed "backlash," and even the President of the United States freely used the term in his conversations with reporters.

Overlooked throughout this period, however, were national public-opinion polls, conducted by Louis Harris, which revealed a steadily mounting majority in favor of pending civil-rights legislation. In November 1963, an estimated 63 per cent of adult Americans favored the Federal Civil Rights Bill; by February 1964 the figure had risen to 68 per cent, and by May it stood at 70 per cent—a steady gain of 7 per cent in six months and a strange phenomenon to be occurring in the midst of an alleged anti-Negro reaction.

Why, then, did Wallace do so well in the primaries in three Northern and border states? An array of well-established principles of social science suggests a number of answers. The mass media emphasized the percentage of the votes won by Wallace without thoroughly considering the size of the total vote. Especially in Indiana and Maryland, where the Alabamian did best, the number of votes cast was considerably above the usual turnouts for Democratic Presidential primaries. The so-called "backlash," then, was apparently caused by large numbers of people who do not normally vote in these primaries, people attracted to the polls by the protest implied in Wallace's candidacy but not necessarily by his position on race questions.

Furthermore, the Alabama Governor's candidacy did not have to be regarded seriously, a factor of major importance in protest voting. Hadley Cantril has shown, for instance, that many French and Italian voters find their support of the Communist ticket a satisfying expression of protest, though they are not members of the Communist Party and would not want the Communists to gain control of their governments.[16] "Voting Communist can't hurt me," reasons one Frenchman. "It may help me. Nothing like putting a big scare into the *patron*." [17] By the same token, Wallace made an ideal magnet for protest voters of all varieties, precisely because there was so little chance of his actually becoming President. His relative success in the primaries, then, did not necessarily require or reflect any large-scale changing of minds. The many journalists who reasoned that it did were guilty of a blatant form of the ecological fallacy.[18]

The mass-media analysis also assumed, without the benefit of before-and-after comparisons, that the racial attitudes of many white Americans were changing, notably in Northern metropolitan areas. To be certain that people were generally more anti-Negro in July 1964 than they had been in 1963, we obviously need to know their attitudes in both years. Yet the media did not provide such necessary evidence.

The nearest attempt to obtain before-and-after data was a city-wide poll administered by reporters for *The New York Times* in September 1964.[19] This survey employed the risky procedure of asking the respondent in retrospect whether he had changed his mind. In addition, the wording of the questions asked was strongly biased: "Have you been affected in any way by a 'white backlash'? Have you changed your thinking during the last couple of months? Which category [of those detailed below] describes your feelings?" To mention the supposed phenomenon by its familiar name and then to suggest forcefully which alternative the respondent is expected to select is, of course, contrary to all standards of competent polling. Indeed, it is virtually equivalent to asking a sample of ladies: "Do you like the chic new Parisian fashions which simply everyone is raving about?"

As it happens, New Yorkers are a relatively hardy, independent lot. Only 27 per cent of a roughly random selection of the city's whites agreed they were now "more opposed to what Negroes want"; 62 per cent insisted they still felt "pretty much the same"; and 6 per cent maintained that they actually were "more strongly in favor of what Negroes want" than earlier. Abandoning its usual caution, the *Times* captioned the story, "Results Indicate 'Backlash' Exists"; but, once again, the evidence is hardly conclusive. Many of the persons included in the critical 27 per cent may actually have been as hostile to Negroes in 1963 as in 1964, and an undetermined number were undoubtedly swayed by the "loaded" questions.

Fortunately, before-and-after data derived from both elections and polls do exist. In Boston's School Committee elections, for example, a ticket of candidates ran for five positions in 1961, before the explosive *de facto* school segregation issue had erupted in the city, and a similar group ran again in 1963, after the issue had become focal. One of the candidates on both occasions was a militant Negro; another was a white woman who between the two elections had distinguished herself as an outspoken defender of school segregation. In both contests the Negro candidate ran a strong, though losing, seventh, while the segregationist won a seat each time. The mass media emphasized that the segregationist had received a sharply higher percentage of the vote in 1963 than in 1961, presenting this fact as evidence of a powerful "white backlash." Actually, in this case as in the Wallace primaries, great numbers of voters seem to "have come out from under the rocks." About twice as many voters went to the polls in 1963 as in 1961, an increase large enough to account for the segregationist's improved showing. The Negro candidate, too, held or bettered his record in total votes in virtually every precinct; moreover, an outspoken white integrationist won re-election, doing better in total votes than he had in 1961.

Relevant public-opinion poll data have been compiled by the National

Opinion Research Center.[20] An intensive study of racial attitudes through-out the United States was conducted in December 1963. In a follow-up the next summer, re-interviews using the same unbiased questions were held with those white members of the original sample who lived in large North-ern industrial areas, where the "backlash" was allegedly occurring. Prelimi-nary analyses of the results are instructive. Basic attitudes toward the goals of racial change had not shifted: Those whites who had previously favored the desegregation of schools, public facilities and neighborhoods still pre-dominantly favored it; those who had previously opposed it still opposed it.[21] Nor had Presidential voting intentions shifted because of the race issue, except among a minute fraction.[22] The latter finding was to be amply borne out in the November election, when the heralded "white backlash" for Goldwater failed to materialize.

What *was* apparent was opposition to the current form and pace of the civil-rights movement.[23] "The Negroes are pushing too hard too fast," went the familiar phrase. But this charge was not new, either; polls had consis-tently turned it up throughout the 1960s, with each new militant technique initially provoking a comparable degree of white resistance.[24] Thus, in 1961, a nationwide Gallup poll found that 64 per cent of the public disap-proved of "freedom rides" and 57 per cent believed the rides would "hurt the Negroes' chance of being integrated in the South." [25] In 1963, 65 per cent of white Northerners and 73 per cent of white Southerners thought mass demonstrations by Negroes were "likely to hurt the Negro's cause for racial equality." [26] It is noteworthy that in each case the resistance of white Americans focused upon means, not ends; throughout all the racial turbu-lence—in part perhaps because of it—attitudes toward the Negroes' ulti-mate aspirations have continued to improve.

Finally, a comparison of nationwide Gallup polls taken in 1963 and 1965 affords significant evidence. During these years, when the "backlash" was presumed to be raging, increasing percentages of white parents in the South and North said they would not object to sending their children to a school with Negro children. The most dramatic shifts occurred in the South; the proportion of Southern white parents who stated that they would not object to having their children attend classes with "a few" Negro children rose from only 38 per cent in 1963 to 62 per cent by 1965.[27] Yet consis-tently favorable shifts also characterized white opinion in the North. Here, a school with "a few" Negro children was declared unobjectionable by 87 per cent of white parents in 1963, by 91 per cent in 1965; a school where the student body was one-half Negro was acceptable to 56 per cent in 1963, to 65 per cent in 1965; and a school with a majority of Negro students found no objection among 31 per cent in 1963, among 37 per cent in 1965. Once again, specific data directly refute the notion of a widespread growth in anti-Negro sentiment among white Americans during the period from 1963 to 1965.

The developments popularly described as a "white backlash," then, turn out to have been something quite different when placed in full scientific perspective. Anti-Negro candidates for political office in the North, conspicuous under the glare of television klieg lights, focused on the race issue and made it more salient; they drew upon pre-existing bigotry and alienation, and they often succeeded, at least for a time, in attracting to the polls many apathetic, alienated, authoritarian or uninformed citizens who usually do not vote.[28] What followed was the familiar phenomenon of activation in a crisis: Persons who favored racial change in the first place became more active, and so did persons who opposed it.

The mass media, interpreting this process as a "backlash," went wrong in ignoring the size of the total vote in elections involving anti-Negro candidates; in disregarding the rising support for the Civil Rights Act of 1964 among whites; in misunderstanding the "out-from-under-the-rocks" quality of protest voting; in neglecting to seek before-and-after evidence of change; in relying upon questions with highly biased wording; in failing to differentiate clearly between attitudes toward the means and toward the goals of the civil-rights movement; and, because of all these errors, in mistaking activation for opinion change. What really happened in the course of the so-called white backlash does not contradict the steady and dramatic reduction in anti-Negro prejudice throughout the nation over the past two decades.

Basically, the expectation of a simple negative reaction among whites against the Negroes' recent demands failed because the attitudes of white Americans toward Negro Americans are anything but simple. And here we come to a final parallel between attitudes toward Jews and toward Negroes in the United States: In both cases, a fundamental ambivalence between bigotry and tolerance is at work. Elsewhere in this book, Halpern traces the deeply ambiguous orientation of gentiles toward Jews through the years, and Stember presents poll data that document it for the past generation. A similar ambivalence is to be found in the white American's orientation toward the Negro. But here the parallel falters, for the ambivalences stem from markedly contrasting images; and this is only one among many distinctions between hostility against Jews and against Negroes.

Distinctions between Anti-Semitic and Anti-Negro Attitudes

Bettelheim and Janowitz, among others, have observed that Americans' attitudes toward the Jew are rooted in superego concerns, and their attitudes toward the Negro in id concerns.[29] Witness the adjectives typically applied to Jews by anti-Semites: ambitious, striving, crafty, clannish, shrewd, hyperintelligent, sly and dishonest. And compare these with the qualities typically ascribed to Negroes by Negrophobes: unambitious, lazy, happy-go-lucky, irresponsible, stupid, dirty, smelly, uninhibited and oversexed. The psychoanalytic interpretation of these distinctive, though strangely reciprocal, stereotypes is straightforward: Intergroup animosity is explained as a projecton of the bigot's unacceptable inner impulses. Jews and Negroes serve in part as *alter egos* for the bigot. The superego sins of the bigot himself, such as ambition, deceit and egotism, are personified in the Jew, while his id sins of the flesh are seen in the Negro.[30]

The psychoanalytic distinction between superego and id stereotypes is useful in a wide range of cross-cultural situations, because many groups besides Jews and Negroes have evoked these contrasting images. Out-groups that are assigned a superego image are typically alien merchants or middlemen caught between the landed and laboring classes. This, of course, was the typical position of European Jews during the Middle Ages, and the similarity is not lost on people who project superego stereotypes upon other groups: The Chinese merchants of Malaysia and Indonesia are often called the "Jews of Asia," and the Muslim Indian merchants of East and South Africa the "Jews of Africa." The id image is attributed, in many parts of the world, to groups that rank at the bottom of the social structure; in Europe, Gypsies and Southern Italians often play this role.[31] Occasionally, the two types of images are fused into a single, contradictory stereotype; in Germany before the Second World War, for instance, the lack of a significant id-type out-group made it necessary for the anti-Semitic image of the Jew to do double duty as the personification of both id and superego concerns, with the result that Jews were seen as both lazy and overambitious, both oversexed and anemic. In America, however, bigots enjoy the luxury of having a variety of out-groups to choose from, and more specific, differentiated stereotypes have evolved.

These cross-cultural examples suggest some further reasons why the images of Jews and Negroes in the United States are so distinctively different. The two stereotypes are, of course, more than just projections of the bigot's impulses; they also reflect, if only in distorted ways, the two groups' contrasting social positions and values, and particularly their radically different histories both in and outside America. As detailed elsewhere in this volume, anti-Semitism in the United States is derived in large part from the image of the Jew as middleman or "economic man," a stigma originally developed in Europe. Anti-Negro prejudice stems from the far more serious stigma left upon Negroes by the uniquely destructive form of slavery sanctioned in the South, and by the subsequent century of segregation and poverty.[32]

A crucial element in these historically implanted stigmata is the concept of "race." In its distorted popular meaning, the term "race" often carries connotations of innate inferiority, of unalterable distinctiveness, of a biological threat. It is thus not surprising that, as Stember shows, persons who think of Jews as a race are somewhat more anti-Semitic than others; and it is significant that this mode of thinking has sharply declined since 1946, with Jews more often viewed now as either a nationality or a religious group.[33] In attitudes toward Negroes, no such shift is discernible. Though an estimated 25 per cent of the genes in the total gene pool of Negro Americans is Caucasian in origin,[34] Negroes will probably be viewed as a markedly separate "race" for some time to come.

The greatly different positions of Jews and Negroes in the American social structure are another determinant of their contrasting stereotypes. Jewish Americans are overwhelmingly middle-class. Disproportionately large numbers of them engage in the professions and other white-collar occupations; their median family income easily surpasses the national median, rivaling those of such wealthy religious groups as the Presbyterians and the Episcopalians. Negro Americans, on the other hand, are overwhelmingly lower-class workers. They are found disproportionately often in the service and blue-collar occupations; their median family income is low, barely exceeding one-half of the national median, and reflecting a degree of poverty unequaled among whites save for such destitute groups as the Appalachian mountain folk. There are, of course, poor Jews of lower-class status and prosperous Negroes of middle-class status, but they represent only small segments of their respective groups.

Finally, there are differences in the values held by Jews and by Negroes —a natural outcome of their different histories and social positions. As documented in the papers by Morton Keller and John Higham in this volume, the close similarity of the Jews' values and those of the dominant Anglo-Saxon Protestants has been a striking and important aspect of the Jewish experience in America. To use Florence Kluckhohn's convenient scheme, Jewish and Protestant Americans both tend to hold "man-over-nature," "doing," "individualistic" and "future-time" value orientations.[35] Indeed, research on the so-called Protestant ethic often finds Jewish subjects far surpassing Protestants in their devotion to such central components of the ethic as achievement values.[36]

The picture is less clear in the case of Negro Americans. The crushing impact of slavery stripped Negroes of any uniquely African values, so that their value models from the beginning were entirely Protestant American. Yet their experience in this country did little to encourage a "man-over-nature," "doing," "individualistic," "future-time" view of life. To be sure, the first moderately prosperous classes of Negroes did evince the Protestant ethic in its purest form.[37] But continued denial of opportunity and increasing racial separation have fostered countervalues among many of the younger, lower-status, less religious Negroes in today's enormous urban ghettos.

The consequences of these historical, social and value differences between Jewish and Negro Americans are vast. To begin with, attitudes toward intermarriage with members of the two groups are markedly different. Stember shows that in 1962 only 37 per cent of a nationwide sample stated they "definitely would not marry a Jew," a diminution of 20 percentage points since 1950.[38] In contrast, attitudes toward intermarriage between Negroes and Caucasians have changed very little over the past decades. On the basis of distorted notions of "race," over 80 per cent of white Americans opposed interracial marriage in 1963, and twenty states still outlawed it.[39]

A second consequence, highlighted by Higham in this volume, is that "old Americans," by and large, have responded to Jews and immigrants generally in one way, to Negroes in quite another. In the case of immigrants, including Jews, assimilation was expected; the problem, it was felt, was how to bring them into the mainstream of American life—though, as Higham wryly points out, "not too fast." In the case of Negroes, assimilation was opposed; the problem, until recently, was defined as how to keep them out of the mainstream. The two contrasting patterns naturally have affected the personalities of individuals in quite different ways. Immigrants and their children have undergone cultural conflicts, painful adjustments in the second generation and special strains while striving to become "all-American." Negroes, on the other hand, have suffered unique identity conflicts, agonizing threats to their survival and dignity and a crushing sense of rejection and defeat.[40] Significantly, mental illness among Jewish Americans is marked by relatively high neurosis and low psychosis rates, while among Negro Americans the opposite is true.[41]

Because of the many differences between Jews and Negroes, prejudices against the two groups relate differently to social class. Stember shows, for example, that anti-Semitism is relatively widespread among individuals of higher status, especially when measured by questions which paint Jews as a "race," "more radical than others" or having "objectionable qualities." [42] By contrast, anti-Negro responses in polls come most frequently from lower-status whites. Thus, as Hyman and Sheatsley have shown, the poorly educated respondents in nationwide surveys favor desegregation of public schools and buses much less often than do the better educated. Apparently, prejudice against Jews and Negroes is most commonly found where a competitive threat is most acutely perceived: Anti-Semitism tends to be particularly intense among Christians of social status similar to that of most Jews; and anti-Negro sentiment is likely to be strongest among Caucasians of social status similar to that of most Negroes. A revealing exception, however, is to be found in the residential field: According to Hyman and Sheatsley, the more educated are just as resistant to racially desegregated housing as the less educated.[43]

More surprising are the relationships between group prejudice and political viewpoints as revealed in attitudes toward the late Joseph R. McCarthy. A survey conducted in 1954 by the National Opinion Research Center found that persons who favored the controversial Senator, especially the better educated, were slightly less willing than others to accept Jewish neighbors;[44] on the other hand, a study carried out in the same year by International Research Associates demonstrated that supporters of McCarthy were actually more willing than others to vote for a hypothetical Jewish candidate for Congress.[45] There was, in short, no strong and consistent association between anti-Semitism and McCarthyism. A clearer relationship was evident where attitudes toward Negroes were concerned: A Gallup survey in 1954 noted that opponents of the Wisconsin Senator approved the recent Supreme Court ruling outlawing segregated schools far more often than did his supporters,[46] though the same poll did not find a consistent relationship between attitudes toward McCarthy and objections to sending children to predominantly Negro schools.[47]

The general tendency of right-wing movements to evince anti-Negro rather than anti-Jewish prejudice again became evident ten years later in the Presidential race of Barry Goldwater. Though the candidate, in the new style of "transtolerance," insisted throughout that he was not anti-Negro, he and his spokesmen openly rejected the Civil Rights Act of 1964 and attacked racially integrated housing as well as other objectives of the Negro's drive for first-class citizenship. In contrast, no anti-Semitic appeals were broached.

The Jew, then, is no longer a safe target for public attack, while the Negro still is—in line with the differences between the two types of prejudice which we have noted. Though both types have sharply declined in recent years, anti-Negro prejudice is still far more prevalent in modern America than anti-Semitism, as is shown in the responses to poll questions which apply equally to each group. During 1958, roughly two-thirds of whites in a nationwide Gallup poll said they would vote for a well-qualified man nominated by their party if he were Jewish; only two-fifths said they would if he were a Negro.[48]

Even sharper differences are found when social-distance questions are asked. For instance, surveys of four communities by Cornell University in the early 1950s asked respondents if they would find it "a little distasteful to eat at the same table" with a Negro or a Jew. The percentages of white Christians who said it would be distasteful with a Negro ranged from 50 in Elmira, New York, to 92 in Savannah, Georgia; the percentages saying it would be distasteful with a Jew varied only from 8 in Steubenville, Ohio, to 13 in Savannah.[49] Similar responses were obtained by an additional question about going to a party and finding that most of the people there were Negroes or were Jews. The percentages who disliked the idea of a party attended by Negroes ranged from 80 in Bakersfield, California, to 89 in Steubenville, the percentages for a party attended by Jews from 25 in Steubenville to 34 in Savannah.[50]

More intensive investigations have led to the same conclusion. Bettelheim and Janowitz interviewed in depth 150 white Christians from Chicago, all of them Second World War veterans of enlisted rank. Using the same criteria for prejudice against both groups, they rated 65 per cent of their subjects as either intensely or outspokenly anti-Negro, another 27 per cent as harboring stereotyped anti-Negro attitudes and a mere 8 per cent as truly tolerant of Negroes.[51] When it came to attitudes toward Jews, only about half as many were rated intensely or outspokenly prejudiced (31 per cent), a similar percentage as holding stereotyped beliefs (28 per cent) and five times as many as tolerant (41 per cent).[52]

Not only are attitudes toward Negroes more negative than attitudes toward Jews, but they are also far more salient to most Americans. A fairly accurate measure of saliency is provided in polls by the percentages of persons who are uncertain, say they don't know or otherwise fail to choose one of the offered alternatives. In surveys dealing with prejudice against Negroes, these percentages are generally small; thus, Hyman and Sheatsley report that in four polls from 1942 to 1963, questions on racial desegregation consistently obtained noncommittal responses of only about 4 per cent.[53] With anti-Semitic items, the proportions are generally higher; thus, the 137 percentages of noncommittal replies recorded by Stember range from 1 to 42, with a median of 11.

Anti-Negro and anti-Jewish attitudes, being shaped by somewhat different social forces, do not necessarily rise or fall together. True, both have declined sharply over the past two decades in the nation as a whole; but, as is often the case, the South shows a deviant pattern and thereby provides special clues. Anti-Negro sentiments have notably lessened in the South since 1942, actually changing faster in many ways than was true elsewhere; meanwhile, anti-Semitism seems to have declined at a markedly slower pace in the South than in other regions.

The Hyman and Sheatsley analysis of nationwide surveys from 1942 to 1963 conclusively demonstrates massive shifts in whites' opinions about the Negro in the South.[54] With more room for improvement, the South shows generally higher relative and absolute rates of modification than the North. Thus, the white public's belief in the equal intelligence of Negroes rose from 21 to 59 per cent in the South, from 50 to 80 per cent in the North; white support of desegregated public transportation climbed from 4 to 51 per cent in the South, from 57 to 88 per cent in the North; and white approval of desegregated neighborhoods increased from 12 to 51 per cent in the South, from 42 to 70 per cent in the North. In short, the white South, for all its ugly signs of resistance to racial change, is rapidly altering its most basic sentiments toward the Negro.

Anti-Semitism in the South presents a contrasting situation. The South has traditionally been one of the least anti-Semitic regions in the nation, and a considerable body of data suggests that it remained so until the 1940s. Stember shows, for example, that in 1939–46 Southerners ranked lowest in anti-Semitic responses to six of nine questions.[55] In polls conducted during 1946 and 1947, Roper found the South, together with the Far West, to be among the least anti-Semitic areas of the United States.[56] A study of over 1,000 wartime rumors from all parts of the nation, conducted by R. H. Knapp in 1942, lends further weight to this conclusion.[57] He noted that anti-Semitic stories constituted 9 per cent of the nation's rumors but only 3 per cent of the South's; in contrast, anti-Negro rumors made up over 8 per cent of the South's total but only 3 per cent of the nation's. Consistent with these data, other inquiries have found large numbers of white Southerners intensely anti-Negro and highly favorable to Jews at the same time.[58]

The last twenty years have witnessed a diminution of anti-Semitism in the South as elsewhere, but a minimal one compared to other regions. Some institutional indications of the South's earlier relative standing still exist; thus, the Anti-Defamation League of B'nai B'rith, in its exhaustive study of religious barriers in social clubs, found discrimination less prevalent in the South, Southwest and Far West than in other areas.[59] But Stember's broader data present another picture: In seven of his nine comparisons over time, percentage declines in anti-Semitism between 1939 and 1962 were smaller in the South than in any other region; by the latter year, the South ranked slightly above all other areas in anti-Semitic responses to four of the nine questions.[60]

Stember offers a methodological explanation for this regional change. The 1939 survey drew its sample from voters, limiting the participation of Negro respondents, whereas the 1962 survey included Negroes in approximately their true proportion of the adult Southern population. Consequently, Stember suggests, a possible greater degree of anti-Semitism among Negroes might have distorted the results in the South.

Additional data, however, cast doubt upon this explanation. The Cornell survey of Savannah, conducted in the early 1950s, found approximately the same percentages of Negroes and whites responding to stereotype questions about Jews in an anti-Semitic fashion.[61] For instance, 44 per cent of whites and 48 per cent of Negroes agreed that "Jews are dishonest in their business dealings." [62] Social-distance questions, such as the one about eating at the same table with a Jew, uncovered somewhat larger differences between races, but the Negroes' greater preference for distance is probably more a function of racial taboos than of religious bigotry. In any event, only two of Stember's nine comparisons deal with social distance, and one of these can be tested for racial differences by combining three national surveys which asked the same question during the early 1950s.[63] When asked, "How would you feel if a Jewish family were going to move next door to you?" 8.7 per cent of whites and 8.0 per cent of Negroes in the South stated they "wouldn't like it at all"; 15.5 per cent of whites and 12.9 per cent of Negroes said it "wouldn't matter too much." [64] In other words, roughly one of every four whites but only one of every five Negroes in the South had some qualms about a Jewish neighbor.

The inclusion of more Negro Southerners in the 1962 survey, then, apparently does not explain away the relatively slow decline of anti-Semitism in the South between the soundings in 1939 and 1962. The deviant pattern of the South—faster diminution of anti-Negro attitudes but slower diminution of anti-Semitism than elsewhere—provides suggestive clues about the differential social forces underlying the two types of prejudice. As the region's cities grow into major metropolitan centers, and its expanding industries erode the older agricultural economy, traditional institutions and attitudes are inevitably undergoing drastic alteration. Basically, the South is fast becoming more American and less Confederate. The deviant pattern described here is part of this process of deregionalization: The white South, formerly unique in its rejection of the Negro and its acceptance of the Jew, is becoming more and more like the rest of the nation.

Numerous studies have revealed that urbanization and industrialization are significantly associated with marked reductions in racial animosity.[65] As white Southerners rise into the middle class, receive more and better education and develop into acclimated urbanites, the fears and threats traditionally associated with the Negro lose some of their force. But these same changes in the face of the South often perpetuate or even heighten anti-Semitism.

To see the full importance of this point, we must consider the traditional position of Jews in Southern life. Though few in number, they have long occupied prominent roles in the region—from cabinet posts in the Confederate Government to current ownership of the major department stores in virtually every large city. Acceptance of Jews was facilitated by the special emphasis which Fundamentalist Protestants placed on the Old Testament. Moreover, the superego stereotype, elsewhere reserved for the Jew, was largely projected onto the Yankee, who was caricatured by the poor, defeated and defensive South as crafty, pushy, materialistic, too successful and not to be trusted. Most significant of all, the German Jews who constituted the bulk of the earlier Jewish population in the South were an integral part of antebellum and Civil War folklore. The writer remembers well the respect which the leading Jewish family enjoyed in his Southern home town. Though this family included the foremost bankers and jewelers of the city, the usual anti-Semitic stereotypes were never applied; for, after all, the family's social postition was solidly grounded on the fame of its brave Civil War ancestor, Colonel Kahn.[66]

The rapid social changes in today's South are weakening much of this tradition-linked protection against anti-Semitism. An increasing percentage of Southern Jewry is not of pre-Civil War German stock and thus is not draped in the Confederate battle flag. In addition, typical forms of anti-Semitism are being fostered by many of the very processes which reduce anti-Negro animosities—for example, the growth of the middle class, immigration of Northerners and competitive urban life. The inference is clear:

Anti-Semitism and anti-Negro attitudes are by no means shaped by identical social forces; hence, they do not necessarily rise and diminish together.

Do Prejudices Necessarily Replace One Another?

The many distinctions between anti-Jewish and anti-Negro attitudes raise the question of how hostile sentiments toward various minorities are related to one another. Conventional wisdom holds that a reduction in one type invariably leads to an increase in another. But is this true? If prejudice against one minority drops, does prejudice against another necessarily rise?

To tackle this central question, a choice must be made between two contrasting conceptions of aggression. Sigmund Freud and later psychoanalytic writers have generally postulated a closed system on the order of a steam boiler, containing a fixed amount of instinctive aggression which, if not released through one outlet, will seek and find another. According to this view, society's problem is how to channel aggression through appropriate safety valves. Indeed, creative, constructive work is seen as an important means of sublimating fundamentally aggressive instincts.

Gordon W. Allport objects to this finite-quantity conception.[67] He argues that no single closed-system model can account for the vast range of phenomena which Freudians classify under the single instinct of aggression (from individual rage to war) and under sublimation (from counting up to ten to painting the *Mona Lisa*). The model he proposes is of an open-system, feedback type. Rather than a finite, instinctual force that demands release, aggression in Allport's view is a variable capacity whose expression is governed by both inner and outer conditions; once it is released, further aggression is more, not less, likely to occur. Creative, constructive endeavors, he maintains, are ends in themselves, meeting specific needs, rather than mere reflections of aggression.

How we answer our question depends on which of these rival models we choose. If we accept the Freudian model, we will expect a reduction of prejudice against one minority to cause an increase of prejudice against another, unless the inevitable flow of aggression finds a substitute outlet. Prejudice, goes the old saying, will always be with us. Allport's model opens up markedly different expectations. From his theoretical vantage point, there is nothing inevitable about prejudice. In fact, his feedback model suggests that greater tolerance of one minority would improve the chances for greater tolerance of others. Hence, prejudice need not always be with us; both personal and social conditions can be achieved which essentially eliminate this societal liability.

The available evidence tends to support Allport's more optimistic open-system view. Social psychological studies of prejudice have repeatedly found hostility toward one out-group to be highly and positively correlated with hostility toward other out-groups; that is, individuals who are prejudiced against Jews also tend to be prejudiced against Negroes, Catholics and out-groups in general.[68] One ingenious experiment tested attitudes of students toward the peoples of 32 nations and races plus three non-existent groups ("Daniereans," "Pirireneans" and "Wallonians"),[69] and found, as the open-system model would predict, that persons who rejected the real groups tended to reject the imaginary ones as well. Unless we assume that the quantities of instinctual aggression, while finite, vary vastly among individuals, it is difficult to see how a fixed-quantity, closed-system model of aggression could easily account for this well-established finding.

The principal data in the present volume provide further evidence. Anti-Jewish responses to poll questions were most intense during the later stages of the Second World War—presumably the high point in the nation's release of aggression. More important, Stember's data, together with those of Hyman and Sheatsley described above, prove that anti-Semitic and anti-Negro attitudes have since then undergone a sharp simultaneous decline. A similar conclusion is reached by G. M. Gilbert, who compared the stereotypes of ten groups as held by Princeton undergraduates of similar backgrounds in 1932 and in 1950:[70] Across the board, stereotypes had "faded" and lost their saliency. Data like these are what we would expect with the open-system model of aggression.

Closed-system theorists might challenge such results on the grounds that the studies did not properly allow for substitute channels of aggression. Thus, some individuals might use prejudice against out-groups as their principal outlet for aggression, while others might channel all of their aggressive energies in other directions. But research by Ross Stagner casts doubt upon this method of explaining away the findings of Stember and others.[71] Stagner found that students who channeled aggression in one direction were especially likely to channel it in others as well.

Finally, cross-cultural research further confirms the Allportian position. S. T. Boggs found positive relationships between individual, group and ideological aggression within societies; in war-oriented societies, individuals were inclined to behave aggressively toward one another, and myths and legends tended to be aggressive in content.[72]

Though such evidence is not conclusive, it weighs heavily in favor of Allport's open-system, feedback conception of aggression. We may therefore answer our basic question in the negative: Available evidence suggests that a reduction in prejudice against one minority does *not* necessarily lead to any increase in prejudice against another. On the contrary, prejudices against different groups, even when shaped by somewhat different social forces, are likely to decline together.

Note that this expectation rejects only the Freudian closed-system or "drainage" theory, not the more limited displacement theory; it still allows for possible substitution of scapegoats. Just as in the South the Yankee long replaced the Jew as the object of superego stereotyping and hostility, so today the political establishment is perhaps substituting for the Jews as a target of animosity on the national scene. The phenomenon of transtolerance and other aspects of the Radical Right strongly suggest this possibility.[73] Incidentally, any such anti-elite bias would be noteworthy as counterevidence to the widely held dogma that scapegoats must be weak and vulnerable. In any event, such substitutions are possible, but not, according to the open-system view, inevitable.

The Future of Anti-Minority Prejudice in the United States

The open-system model, together with recent social psychological research advances in the study of attitude change, suggests possible future trends of ethnic and religious prejudice in the United States. In brief, long-term alterations in American society are slowly institutionalizing acceptance of minorities and non-discrimination. These evolving institutional safeguards provide the necessary "outer" conditions for the reduction of group prejudice specified by Allport; many of them also provide the setting for consequent changes in the behavior of individuals. These behavior changes in turn produce the "inner" conditions for reducing group prejudice. Increasingly, Americans accept the *fait accompli* of their new institutions and behavior as "the American way." As noted throughout this volume, this process has been under way since 1945, and there are good reasons for expecting it to continue.

Slowly evolving institutional safeguards against bigotry are well illustrated in Herbert Hyman's analysis of the toleration of political nonconformists in England.[74] Hyman was intrigued by the fact that since the Second World War England had seen fewer overt acts against such persons than the United States. There was no obvious reason for this difference, he felt. America's political traditions were originally modeled after English ones of an earlier time; England herself had a long history of ugly overt acts against noncomformists, extending until recent times; and the public's attitudes on the subject did not seem vastly different in the two countries. His persuasive answer to the riddle was that England over the past centuries had slowly evolved distinctive political institutions and mechanisms which restrained latent public intolerance. For example, the English public allows its elite far more privacy and deference than the American—save for an occasional affair as sensational as the Profumo case of 1963. However, this example also points up a vital qualification to the process outlined above: Some institutional safeguards against bigotry merely restrain intolerance without requiring new, positive forms of behavior, and consequently do not by themselves initiate a reduction in prejudice.

In the United States, institutional protections for minorities have so far evolved in various ways. Sometimes they emerge dramatically, as did the Civil Rights Act of 1964; more often they come quietly, without national attention, like the acceptance of minorities in such previously discriminatory sectors as the engineering profession and college social fraternities. But generally the new safeguards have been won, at least in large part, by pressure exerted by the minorities themselves. Witness the desegregation of lunch counters that was achieved by sit-in protests. The process has been aided by the circumstance that groups of Americans, though usually minorities by themselves, can often be combined into a majority. Thus, the nation's largest political party is a delicately balanced coalition of minorities, including the major share of the country's Negroes, Jews and Roman Catholics. And this party has managed to win seven of the last nine Presidential elections, in part because of what it has done to establish institutional protections of the type under discussion. The momentum of this trend, together with the growing militancy among practically all of the nation's minorities, who feel entitled to full citizens' rights and mean to obtain them, afford good reason to expect that the evolution of institutional protections will continue.

Institutional safeguards which go beyond mere restraint and prompt new intergroup behavior act to reduce group prejudice directly.[75] Once again, the actual process contradicts conventional wisdom. It is commonly held that attitudes must change *before* behavior does; therefore, goes the argument, intergroup problems can be solved only through what is vaguely described as "education." Yet recent advances in social psychology point conclusively to the opposite order of events. Behavior changes first, because of new laws or other institutional interventions; after the fact, individuals modify their ideas to fit their new acts, often proving amazingly adaptable in doing so. Indeed, considerable research suggests that this behavior-to-attitude cycle of change is generally easier and more effective than the attitude-to-behavior cycle.

A number of psychological mechanisms are at work in this process. Commitment is one such mechanism. An individual who has publicly behaved in a new manner and been rewarded for doing so is likely to become committed to the change. Acceptance of the *fait accompli* is another. When a person first encounters Negro sales clerks in a department store, busily at work and accepted naturally by others, he is likely to accept the innovation even though he may previously have opposed the idea. If he objected vocally, he would create a scene, and risk being isolated as a bigot without social support. This process is buttressed by the sanction of the "American creed" of equality for all; measures to attain "fair play" for minorities today command a widespread ideological and moral support, such as Prohibition in the 1920s, for example, never enjoyed.

The new behavior occasioned by institutional changes does most to reduce prejudice when it involves intergroup contact of special dimensions. In his review of the relevant research, Allport notes that the positive effects are greatest when the interacting groups (1) possess approximately equal status, (2) seek common goals, (3) are cooperatively dependent upon one another and (4) engage in contact which has the positive support of authorities, law or custom.[76] Thus, not all forms of intergroup contact reduce hostility; some may actually exacerbate it. The optimal form is rarely achieved without extensive institutional modifications, such as abolition of college quotas against Jewish students or the racial desegregation of public schools.

Lest this discussion appear too optimistic about the future, two strong caveats must be emphasized. First, American life retains many deeply rooted institutional supports for group prejudice and many barriers to beneficial intergroup contact, especially with respect to Negroes. As long as some Governors and an occasional candidate for the Presidency openly or implicitly sanction racial oppression, as long as the great majority of Negroes remain tightly sealed off in sprawling urban ghettos, as long as most young Negroes in both the North and the South remain permanently handicapped by separate and inferior education, as long as the typical Negro family has an annual income barely half that of the typical white family, anti-Negro prejudice will continue to thrive. It will be a long time before the animosity of whites against Negroes sinks to the low level which gentile animosity against Jews has reached. Those who would hasten that day would be best advised to help demolish the institutional barriers that still hinder racial progress—such as housing discrimination fostered by real-estate interests with the acquiescence of government, or *de facto* segregated education upheld by citizens who have suddenly become attached to neighborhood schools.

A second caveat concerns the current activities of the Radical Right, a movement that has proved powerful enough to seize, at least for a time, the machinery of a major political party. True, the examples of transtolerance which we noted at the outset suggest that explicit anti-minority attitudes are not an essential ingredient of the far right today. In modern parlance, the movement is primarily status-oriented, not class-oriented.[77] Moreover, as Talcott Parsons has stressed, its ideology differs from those of extremists in the 1930s: Whereas the Nazis needed the Jew as an ideological link between capitalism and Communism, today's Radical Right supports its own version of capitalism and has no need of anti-Semitism in this sense.[78] However, the movement is vehemently opposed to the nation's elite and to the Federal Government, the sponsors of the trend toward institutional protection of minorities; and it attracts elements known for their previous activities in anti-Semitic and anti-Negro organizations.

The rightists' anti-elite ideology is not likely to abate soon—not because of any instinctual need for a perpetual scapegoat, but because of the times in which we live. As Alan Westin observes, the world scene will almost certainly become increasingly complex; America will suffer unavoidable reverses; real threats will continue to plague international affairs. These are the conditions upon which the simple jingoist ideology of the Radical Right feeds.[79] In addition, as Hyman has noted, the United States—unlike England—lacks the developed political structure needed to restrain such a movement. All told, it would appear that today's virulent far right could well deter the optimistic process of institutional change outlined above.

Recapitulation

We have compared anti-Jewish with anti-Negro sentiments, against the background of our age of "transtolerance," when prejudice is a derogatory term. According to extensive national survey data, both prejudices reached a peak near the close of the Second World War, and have markedly and steadily declined since that time. There are convincing reasons for accepting these survey results as reasonably accurate reflections of the level of prejudice in American society. And there are equally good reasons for discounting the much-publicized "white backlash" against the Negro, which was presumed by the mass media to have begun in 1964.

Apart from these similarities, the two types of prejudice differ in many important ways. Though anti-Semites and Negrophobes both reveal a strong ambivalence toward their targets, the two stereotypes show sharp differences. The image of the Jew is related to superego concerns (for example, ambition, intelligence, dishonesty), while that of the Negro is related to id concerns (for example, sexuality, uncleanliness, laziness). These contrasting stereotypes can be traced directly to the two groups' histories; to the significance imputed to racial, as against religious, differences; to the very different positions which Jews and Negroes typically occupy in the American social and economic structure; and to the similarity of the values held by "old Americans" and Jewish Americans.

The consequences of these distinctions are manifold. Jews and others of immigrant stock have been traditionally criticized for failing to enter the mainstream of American culture; Negroes have been traditionally rebuked for wishing to enter it. Anti-Semitism is often most widespread among upper-status individuals; Negrophobia is frequently most common among persons of lower status. Not surprisingly, then, far higher levels of anti-Negro prejudice than of anti-Jewish prejudice remain in the United States—especially where intermarriage is at issue. Survey results also suggest that attitudes toward Negroes are generally more salient to most Americans than attitudes toward Jews. Finally, the special case of the South—where anti-Negro sentiment has declined faster and anti-Semitism slower than in the rest of the nation—highlights the fact that somewhat different social forces underlie the two forms of bigotry, with the result that they do not necessarily rise and decline together.

It also seems clear that reductions in prejudice against one minority do not necessarily lead to increases in prejudice against another. The available evidence suggests a feedback, open-system conception of aggression, rather than a steam-boiler, closed-system model. According to this open-system view, it is more likely that lessened prejudice against one group will occasion lessened prejudice against other groups.

When the trends of the past two decades are projected into the future, it appears that institutional protection of minorities in the United States will continue to advance slowly. Many barriers to progress, especially to improved race relations, remain in our society, and the current Radical Right political movement presents a serious threat to this progress. Nevertheless, institutional safeguards are increasingly creating both the societal and the individual conditions necessary for harmonious intergroup relations in the America of the future.

NOTES

1. A blatant exception is, of course, the still openly anti-Negro, anti-Jewish and anti-Catholic Ku Klux Klan. But, significantly, today's Klan is a mere ghost of its namesake of the 1920s; it is isolated in numbers and locale, shunned even by the vast majority of Southern segregationists.

2. Daniel Bell, editor, *The Radical Right* (Garden City, N.Y.: Doubleday Anchor Books, 1963), p. 168.

3. *Ibid.*, p. 250.

4. *Ibid.*, p. 256. Similarly, Welch was "pleased" to reprint *Color, Communism and Common Sense* by Manning Johnson, a Negro and former member of the Communist Party.

5. *Ibid.*, p. 445.

6. Fletcher Knebel, "Race Riots: Goldwater Boon," *Look*, September 22, 1964, p. 41.

7. Bell, *op. cit.*, pp. 442, 444.

8. Herbert H. Hyman and Paul B. Sheatsley, "Attitudes Toward Desegregation," *Scientific American*, CCXI, No. 1 (July 1964), 16–23.

9. Data on anti-Semitic responses from pp. 69, 104, 96.

10. See p. 81.

11. Hazel Gaudet Erskine, "The Polls: Race Relations," *Public Opinion Quarterly*, XXVI:139 (1962). It should be noted that the failure of this item to provoke different response patterns in 1946 and 1956 does not conflict with the earlier finding of a sharp reduction in anti-Negro prejudice. The item does not correlate well with known measures of prejudice.

12. Ithiel de Sola Pool, Robert P. Abelson and Samuel L. Popkin, *Candidates, Issues, and Strategies: A Computer Simulation of the 1960 Presidential Election* (Cambridge, Mass.: M.I.T. Press, 1964).

13. *Ibid.*, p. 115.

14. Gordon W. Allport, *The Nature of Prejudice* (Cambridge, Mass.: Addison-Wesley Publishing Co., 1954), pp. 261–282.

15. See Anti-Defamation League of B'nai B'rith, "A Study of Religious Discrimination by Social Clubs," *Rights,* IV, No. 3 (1962); "The Jewish Law Student and New York Jobs," *ibid.,* V, No. 4 (1964); "Employment of Jewish Personnel in the Automobile Industry," *ibid.,* V, No. 2 (1963); American Jewish Committee, *Patterns of Exclusion From the Executive Suite: The Public Utilities Industry,* December 1963.

16. Hadley Cantril, *The Politics of Despair* (New York: Basic Books, 1958).

17. *Ibid.*, p. 71.

18. The "ecological fallacy" is committed when the characteristics or behavior of individuals (in this case, shifts of their opinion in an anti-Negro direction) are inferred from group data only (in this case, statewide voting for an anti-Negro candidate). The fallacy is easily recognizable in some instances. For example, when we sample by city block units, say in Chicago, we will find a high positive correlation between the percentages on each block of adult illiterates and of adult readers of comic books, though these group percentages obviously cannot represent the characteristics of the same individuals. For a thorough discussion of this common fallacy, see W. S. Robinson, "Ecological Correlations and the Behavior of Individuals," *American Sociological Review,* XV:351–357 (1950); Herbert Menzel, "Comment on Robinson's 'Ecological Correlations and the Behavior of Individuals,' " *ibid.,* p. 674; Hanan C. Selvin, "Durkheim's *Suicide* and Problems of Empirical Research," *American Journal of Sociology,* LXIII:607–619 (1958). All three papers may be found in Seymour M. Lipset and Neil J. Smelser, editors, *Sociology: The Progress of a Decade* (Englewood Cliffs, N.J.: Prentice-Hall, 1961), pp. 132–152.

19. Fred Powledge, "Poll Shows Whites in City Resent Civil Rights Drive," *The New York Times,* September 21, 1964, pp. 1, 26.

20. Information kindly supplied by the Director of N.O.R.C., Professor Peter Rossi of the University of Chicago, and used with his permission.

21. This was also suggested in the *New York Times* results, which showed large majorities of white New Yorkers supporting the employment title of the 1964 Civil Rights Act and stating that they would not be uncomfortable if some "nice" Negro families lived near them. Powledge, *op. cit.*

22. In this particular, too, the *New York Times* poll agreed as far as it went; indeed, a slightly larger majority favored Johnson over Goldwater than had chosen Kennedy over Nixon in 1960.

23. Once again, the findings of the *New York Times* poll agree with those of the more definitive N.O.R.C. study. Fifty-four per cent of the New Yorkers interviewed felt the civil-rights movement "should slow down," and 49 per cent felt non-violent demonstrations "hurt the Negro's cause." See also James W. Carey, "An Ethnic Backlash?" *The Commonweal,* October 16, 1964, pp. 91–93.

24. For examples of these earlier polls, see Stewart Alsop and Oliver Quayle, "What Northerners Really Think of Negroes," *The Saturday Evening Post,*

September 7, 1963, pp. 17–21; "How Whites Feel About Negroes: A Painful American Dilemma," *Newsweek,* October 21, 1963, pp. 44–57.

25. Erskine, *op. cit.*

26. American Institute of Public Opinion, press release, July 18, 1963.

27. American Institute of Public Opinion, press release, May 22, 1965.

28. A large body of literature supports the proposition that people who generally do not vote are more apathetic, alienated, authoritarian and uninformed than those who do. Relevant studies include Gordon M. Connelly and Harry H. Field, "The Non-Voter—Who He Is, What He Thinks," *Public Opinion Quarterly,* VIII:175–187 (1944); Philip K. Hastings, "The Non-Voter in 1952: A Study of Pittsfield, Mass.," *Journal of Psychology,* XXXVIII:301–312 (1954); *idem,* "The Voter and the Non-Voter," *American Journal of Sociology,* LXII: 302–307 (1956); Herbert H. Hyman and Paul B. Sheatsley, "Some Reasons Why Information Campaigns Fail," *Public Opinion Quarterly,* XI: 412–423 (1947); Morris Janowitz and Dwaine Marvick, "Authoritarianism and Political Behavior," *Public Opinion Quarterly,* XVII: 185–201 (1953); Seymour M. Lipset, *Political Man* (Garden City, N.Y.: Doubleday & Co., 1960), pp. 79–103; Fillmore H. Sanford, *Authoritarianism and Leadership* (Philadelphia: Institute for Research in Human Relations, 1950), p. 168; Samuel A. Stouffer, *Communism, Conformity, and Civil Liberties* (Garden City, N.Y.: Doubleday & Co., 1955).

29. Bruno Bettelheim and Morris Janowitz, *Social Change and Prejudice* (New York: The Free Press of Glencoe, 1964).

30. *Ibid.;* Theodor W. Adorno, Else Frenkel-Brunswik, Daniel J. Levinson and R. Nevitt Sanford, *The Authoritarian Personality* (New York: Harper & Bros., 1950). Each of these studies provides impressive case and quantitative data in support of this psychoanalytic interpretation of prejudice.

31. Direct evidence on the parallels between the American stereotype of the Negro and the Northern Italian stereotype of the Southern Italian is provided in Marco Walter Battacchi, *Meridionali e settentrionali nella struttura del pregiudizio etnico in Italia* [Southerners and Northerners in the Structure of Ethnic Prejudice in Italy], (Bologna: Società Editrice Il Mulino, 1959).

32. Stanley M. Elkins, *Slavery* (New York: Grosset & Dunlap, 1963).

33. See pp. 53, 50.

34. B. Glass, "On the Unlikelihood of Significant Admixture of Genes from the North American Indians in the Crescent Composition of the Negroes of the United States," *American Journal of Human Genetics,* VII:368–385 (1955).

35. Florence R. Kluckhohn, "Dominant and Variant Cultural Value Orientations," in Hugh Cabot and Joseph A. Kahl, *Human Relations,* I (Cambridge, Mass.: Harvard University Press, 1953), 88–98.

36. Bernard C. Rosen, "Race, Ethnicity, and the Achievement Syndrome," *American Sociological Review,* XXIV:47–60 (1959).

37. E. Franklin Frazier, *Black Bourgeoisie* (New York: Collier Books, 1962).

38. See p. 106.

39. In the Harris poll of whites in 1963, 84 per cent objected to a "close friend or relative marrying a Negro," and 90 per cent objected to their "own teen-age daughter dating a Negro." William Brink and Louis Harris, *The Negro Revolution in America* (New York: Simon & Schuster, 1964), p. 148.

40. Thomas F. Pettigrew, *A Profile of the Negro American* (Princeton, N.J.: D. Van Nostrand Co., 1964), Chapters I and II.

41. *Ibid.*, Chapter IV.

42. See p. 227.

43. Herbert H. Hyman and Paul B. Sheatsley, "Attitudes Toward Desegregation," *Scientific American*, CXCV, No. 6 (December 1956), 35–39.

44. Bell, *op. cit.*, p. 416; Charles Herbert Stember, *Education and Attitude Change* (New York: Institute of Human Relations Press, 1961), p. 118.

45. Bell, *op. cit.*, p. 415.

46. Stember, *op. cit.*, p. 95. This relationship manifested itself strongly among persons with a high-school or college education; it was, however, reversed among those with only a grammar-school education.

47. *Ibid.*, p. 143.

48. *Ibid.*, pp. 62, 76.

49. Robin M. Williams, Jr., *Strangers Next Door* (Englewood Cliffs, N.J.: Prentice-Hall, 1964), p. 52.

50. *Ibid.*

51. Bettelheim and Janowitz, *op. cit.*

52. *Ibid.*

53. Hyman and Sheatsley (1964), *op. cit.*

54. *Ibid.*

55. See p. 224.

56. "The Fortune Survey," *Fortune*, February 1946, pp. 257–260; October 1947, pp. 5–10.

57. Robert H. Knapp, "A Psychology of Rumor," *Public Opinion Quarterly*, VIII:22–37 (1944).

58. See, for example, E. Terry Prothro, "Ethnocentrism and Anti-Negro Attitudes in the Deep South," *Journal of Abnormal and Social Psychology*, XLVII:105–108 (1952).

59. Anti-Defamation League, "A Study of Religious Discrimination by Social Clubs," *op. cit.*

60. See p. 224.

61. Williams, *op. cit.*

62. *Ibid.*, p. 50.

63. These data are based on a secondary analysis by the writer of three national surveys by the National Opinion Research Center: Studies No. 294 (November 8, 1950), 342 (June 30, 1953), and 365 (November 26, 1954). The writer wishes to thank the Roper Public Opinion Research Center at Williams

College and its director, Professor Philip K. Hastings, for making these studies available.

64. With the three surveys combined, these percentages involve 854 white Southerners and 201 Negro Southerners.

65. Thomas F. Pettigrew and M. Richard Cramer, "The Demography of Desegregation," *Journal of Social Issues*, XV, No. 4 (1959), 61–71.

66. Not the actual name. Incidentally, this special role of the Jew provides an additional explanation for Ringer's finding that in the South Jews are generally perceived as being far less in favor of racial desegregation than they actually are. See pp. 201–202.

67. Allport, *op. cit.*, pp. 354–366.

68. *Ibid.*, pp. 68–81; Adorno, *op. cit.*

69. Eugene L. Hartley, *Problems in Prejudice* (New York: Kings Crown Press, 1946).

70. G. M. Gilbert, "Stereotype Persistence and Change Among College Students," *Journal of Abnormal and Social Psychology*, XLVI:245–254 (1951).

71. Ross Stagner, "Studies of Aggressive Social Attitudes: I. Measurement and Inter-relation of Selected Attitudes," *Journal of Social Psychology*, XX: 109–120 (1944).

72. S. T. Boggs, *A Comparative Cultural Study of Aggression* (unpublished honors thesis, Social Relations Library, Harvard University, 1947).

73. Bell, *op. cit.*

74. *Ibid.*

75. Thomas F. Pettigrew, "Prejudice and the Situation," in John P. Davis, editor, *The American Negro Reference Book* (Englewood Cliffs, N.J.: Prentice-Hall, 1966), pp. 714–723.

76. Allport, *op. cit.*, pp. 261–282.

77. Bell, *op. cit.*

78. *Ibid.*

79. *Ibid.*

Index